Learning PostgreSQL 10

Second Edition

A beginner's guide to building high-performance PostgreSQL database solutions

Salahaldin Juba
Andrey Volkov

BIRMINGHAM - MUMBAI

Learning PostgreSQL 10

Second Edition

First published: November 2015

Second Edition: November 2017

Production reference: 1231117

Published by Packt Publishing Ltd.
Livery Place
35 Livery Street
Birmingham
B3 2PB, UK.
ISBN 978-1-78839-201-3

www.packtpub.com

Credits

Author
Salahaldin Juba
Andrey Volkov

Reviewers
Dr. Isabel M.D. Rosa
Sheldon E. Strauch

Commissioning Editor
Amey Varangaonkar

Acquisition Editor
Varsha Shetty

Content Development Editor
Aaryaman Singh

Technical Editor
Dinesh Chaudhary

Copy Editors
Tasneem Fatehi
Safis Editing

Project Coordinator
Manthan Patel

Proofreader
Safis Editing

Indexer
Rekha Nair

Graphics
Tania Dutta

Production Coordinator
Melwyn Dsa

About the Authors

Salahaldin Juba has over than a decade of experience in the industry and academia, with a focus on database development for large-scale and enterprise applications. He holds a master's degree of science in environmental management with a distinction, and a bachelor's degree of engineering in computer systems. He is also a **Microsoft Certified Solution Developer (MCSD)**.

He has worked mainly with SQL server, PostgreSQL, and Greenplum databases. He has developed applications for scientific communities to process GIS information in a distributed manner, and he has participated in many international projects and standards for image processing during his work in the academic sector.

As a software engineer, he works mainly with defining ETL processes with external parties, defining software solution, promoting SQL best practices, designing OLTP and OLAP application, scouting and evaluating new technologies, and providing training and consultation services.

I would like to express my deepest gratitude to my colleague Andrey Volkov for making this work possible. Also, I would like to thank all the people who provided support, especially the team at Packt for their great support and feedback with proofreading, design, comments, and remarks. I would also like to thank my family for their support despite all of the time that I had to devote to this book over them. Finally, very warm and deep thanks to my late father, Ikrayem Juba, for his utmost support, help, and guidance.

Andrey Volkov has studied information systems in banking. He started his career as a financial analyst in a commercial bank. Using databases as a main tool in his work, he realized that querying the database directly and mastering SQL is much more efficient for ad hoc analysis than using any visual reporting software. He joined the data warehouse team, and after some time, he lead the team by taking the position of the data warehouse architect.

He has worked mainly with Oracle and used to develop logical and physical models of financial and accounting data, implement them in the database, develop ETL processes, and perform analytical tasks. He was also responsible for teaching the users how to use the data warehouse and BI tools. SQL training was also a part of that work.

After 10 years in the financial sector, he changed his field and now works as a senior database developer in a telecommunications company. Here, he works mainly with PostgreSQL databases, being responsible for data modeling and implementing physical data structures, developing stored procedures, integrating databases with other software components, and developing a data warehouse.

Having a lot of experience with both Oracle and PostgreSQL--the leading commercial and one of the most advanced open source RDBMSes--he is able to compare them and recognize and evaluate the key advantages of both of them. Working as a software developer and implementing different kinds of database applications, as well as working as a business analyst and using databases as a tool for analysis, let him learn and understand different database features in different use cases. This experience made him able and willing to work on this book.

I would like to thank my wife and son for their support and for letting me work on weekends and evenings. Big thanks to the editors team for their support, guidance, and organization. And most of all, I would like to thank the main author of the book, Salahaldin Juba, who invited me to work on the book, introduced me to the team, and, in fact, has done most of the work.

About the Reviewers

Dr. Isabel M.D. Rosa has been a Marie Skłodowska-Curie Research Fellow since May 2016 at the German Centre for Integrative Biodiversity Research (iDiv). Born in Lisbon, Portugal, in 1986 she holds a BSc in forestry engineering (2007), an MSc in natural resources management (2009) from the University of Lisbon, and a PhD in computational ecology (2013) from Imperial College London in the United Kingdom. She is the PI of the research project *Using Land Cover Change Models to Address Important Conservation Issues* funded by H2020-MSCA-IF-2015. She also has contributed to two international projects as a team member since 2013, including one European-funded project supported with 1.5 M € budget (Terragenesis, ERC-2011-StG_20101109). She is the author of 15 peer-reviewed publications in scientific journals such as *Nature Ecology and Evolution, Current Biology and Global Change Biology,* accumulating 252 citations (Google citations, October 2017), H index = 8. During her academic career, she has acquired several skills, such as statistical analysis, programming (R, C++, and Python), working with geographic information systems (ArcGIS and QGIS), and creating databases (PostgreSQL/PostGIS and SQLServer). She also reviewed the book *Learning PostgreSQL*, also by Packt.

Sheldon Strauch is a 23-year veteran of software consulting at companies such as IBM, Sears, Ernst & Young, and Kraft Foods. He has a bachelor's degree in business administration and leverages his technical skills to improve business' self-awareness. His interests include data gathering, management, and mining; maps and mapping; business intelligence; and application of data analysis for continuous improvement. He is currently focused on development of end-to-end data management and mining at Enova International, a financial services company located in Chicago. In his spare time, he enjoys the performing arts, particularly music, and traveling with his wife, Marilyn.

www.PacktPub.com

For support files and downloads related to your book, please visit www.PacktPub.com. Did you know that Packt offers eBook versions of every book published, with PDF and ePub files available? You can upgrade to the eBook version at www.PacktPub.com and as a print book customer, you are entitled to a discount on the eBook copy. Get in touch with us at service@packtpub.com for more details. At www.PacktPub.com, you can also read a collection of free technical articles, sign up for a range of free newsletters and receive exclusive discounts and offers on Packt books and eBooks.

https://www.packtpub.com/mapt

Get the most in-demand software skills with Mapt. Mapt gives you full access to all Packt books and video courses, as well as industry-leading tools to help you plan your personal development and advance your career.

Why subscribe?

- Fully searchable across every book published by Packt
- Copy and paste, print, and bookmark content
- On demand and accessible via a web browser

Customer Feedback

Thanks for purchasing this Packt book. At Packt, quality is at the heart of our editorial process. To help us improve, please leave us an honest review on this book's Amazon page at https://www.amazon.com/dp/1788392019. If you'd like to join our team of regular reviewers, you can email us at customerreviews@packtpub.com. We award our regular reviewers with free eBooks and videos in exchange for their valuable feedback. Help us be relentless in improving our products!

Table of Contents

Preface

Picking the right database management system is a difficult task due to the vast number of options on the market. Depending on the business model, one can pick a commercial database or an open source database with commercial support. In addition to this, there are several technical and non-technical factors to assess. When it comes to a relational database management system, PostgreSQL stands at the top for several reasons. The PostgreSQL slogan, *The world's most advanced open source database*, shows the sophistication of its features and community confidence.

PostgreSQL is an open source object relational database management system. It emphasizes extensibility and competes with major relational database vendors such as Oracle, SQL Server, and MySQL. Due to its rich extensions and open source license, it is often used for research purposes, but PostgreSQL code is also the base for many open source and commercial database management systems such as Greenplum and Vertica. Furthermore, start-ups often favor PostgreSQL due to its licensing costs and because there are a lot of companies that provide commercial support.

PostgreSQL runs on most modern operating systems, including Windows, Mac, and Linux flavors. Also, there are several extensions to access, manage, and monitor PostgreSQL clusters, such as pgAdmin, OmniDB, and psql. PostgreSQL installation and configuration is moderately easy as it is supported by most packaging tools, such as yum and apt. Database developers can easily learn and use PostgreSQL because it complies with **ANSI SQL** standards. Other than this, there are a lot of resources to help developers learn PostgreSQL; it has a very good documentation manual and a very active and organized community.

PostgreSQL can be used for both **OLTP** and **OLAP** applications. As it is **ACID** compliant, it can be used out of the box for **OLTP** applications. For OLAP applications, PostgreSQL supports Window functions, **FDW**, and table inheritance; there are many external extensions for this purpose as well.

Even though PostgreSQL is ACID compliant, it has very good performance as it utilizes state-of-the-art algorithms and techniques. For example, PostgreSQL utilizes **MVCC** architecture to allow concurrent access to data. In addition to that, PostgreSQL supports both pessimistic and optimistic concurrency control, and the locking behavior can be altered based on the use case. Also, PostgreSQL provides a very good analyzer and advanced features, such as data partitioning using table inheritance and constraint exclusion, to speed up the handling of very large amounts of data. PostgreSQL supports several types of indexes, such as **B-Tree**, **GiN**, and **GiST**, and **BRIN** indexes. Also, parallel query execution has been supported since PostgreSQL 9.6. Finally, one can use replication to load balance the load to different database clusters.

PostgreSQL is scalable thanks to the many replication solutions in the market, such as Slony and pgpool-II. Additionally, PostgreSQL supports out-of-the-box synchronous and asynchronous streaming replication, as well as logical replication. This makes PostgreSQL very attractive because it can be used to set up highly available and performant systems.

What this book covers

Chapter 01, *Relational Databases*, introduces relational database system concepts, including relational database properties, relational algebra, and database modeling. Also, it describes different database management systems such as graph, document, key value, and columnar databases.

Chapter 02, *PostgreSQL in Action*, provides first-hand experience of installing the PostgreSQL server and client tools on different platforms. This chapter also introduces PostgreSQL capabilities, such as out-of-the-box replication support and its very rich data types.

Chapter 03, *PostgreSQL Basic Building Blocks*, provides some coding best practices, such as coding conventions of PostgreSQL and identifier names. This chapter describes the basic building blocks and the interaction between these blocks, mainly template databases, user databases, tablespaces, roles, and settings. Also, it describes basic data types and tables.

Chapter 04, *PostgreSQL Advanced Building Blocks*, introduces several building blocks, including views, indexes, functions, user-defined data types, triggers, and rules. This chapter provides use cases of these building blocks and compares building blocks that can be used for the same case, such as rules and triggers.

Chapter 05, *SQL Language*, introduces **structured query language (SQL)**, which is used to interact with a database, create and maintain data structures, and enter data into databases as well as, change it, retrieve it, and delete it. SQL has commands related to **data definition language (DDL)**, **data manipulation language (DML)**, and **data control language (DCL)**. Four SQL statements form the basis of DML and are described in this chapter. The SELECT statement is examined in detail to explain SQL concepts such as grouping and filtering to show what SQL expressions and conditions are and how to use subqueries. Some relational algebra topics are also covered in application to joining tables.

Chapter 06, *Advanced Query Writing*, describes advanced SQL concepts and features such as common table expressions and window functions. This helps you implement a logic that would not be possible without them, such as recursive queries. Other techniques explained here, such as the DISTINCT ON clause, the FILTER clause, and lateral subqueries, are not irreplaceable. However, they can help make a query smaller, easier, and faster.

Chapter 07, *Server-Side Programming with PL/pgSQL*, covers function parameters, such as the number of returned rows and function cost, which is mainly used by the query planner. Also, it presents control statements such as conditionals and iteration. Finally, it explains the concept of dynamic SQL and some recommended practices when using dynamic SQL.

Chapter 08, *OLAP and Data Warehousing*, introduces several concepts regarding the usage of recreational databases in the realm of analytical processing. It discusses the deference between OLTP load and OLAP loads; furthermore, it discusses the modeling aspect of OLAP applications. In addition to that, it discusses some technical methods to perform **ETL** (extract, transform, and load) operations such as the COPY command. Also, it discusses some features of PostgreSQL which increasing data retrieval performance such as index-only scans and table partitioning.

Chapter 09, *Beyond Conventional Data types*, discusses several rich data types, including arrays, hash stores, JSON documents, and full-text search. It presents operations and functions for each data type to initialize, insert, update, access, and delete these data types. Finally, it shows how PostgreSQL can be combined with Nginx to serve read-only restful requests.

Chapter 10, *Transactions and Concurrency Control*, discusses in detail the ACID properties and the relation between these properties and concurrency controls. This chapter also discusses concepts such as isolation levels and their side-effects and it shows these side-effects using SQL examples. Finally, the chapter discusses different locking methods, including pessimistic locking strategies such as row locking and advisory locks.

Chapter 11, *PostgreSQL Security*, covers concepts of authentication and authorization. It describes PostgreSQL authentication methods and explains the structure of a PostgreSQL host-based authentication configuration file. It also discusses the permissions that can be granted to database building objects such as schemas, tables, views, indexes, and columns. Finally, it shows how sensitive data, such as passwords, can be protected using different techniques, including one-way and two-way encryption.

Chapter 12, *The PostgreSQL Catalog*, provides several recipes to maintain a database cluster, including cleaning up data, maintaining user processes, cleaning up indexes and unused databases objects, discovering and adding indexes to foreign keys, and so on.

Chapter 13, *Optimizing Database Performance*, discusses several approaches to optimize performance. It presents PostgreSQL cluster configuration settings, which are used in tuning the whole cluster's performance. Also, it presents common mistakes in writing queries and discusses several approaches to increase performance, such as using indexes or table partitioning and constraint exclusion.

Chapter 14, *Testing*, covers some aspects of the software testing process and how it can be applied to databases. Unit tests for databases can be written as SQL scripts or stored functions in a database. There are several frameworks that help us write unit tests and process the results of testing.

Chapter 15, *Using PostgreSQL in Python Applications*, discusses several advanced concepts, such as connection pooling, asynchronous access, and **object relational mappers (ORMs)**. The chapter shows by example how to connect to database, query it, and perform updates using Python. Finally, it introduces different technologies that interact with PostgreSQL, and this gives the developer a broad overview of the state-of-the-art technologies.

Chapter 16, *Scalability*, discusses the problem of scalability and the **CAP** theorem in detail. Also, it covers data replication in PostgreSQL, including physical replication and logical replication. Finally, it shows different scaling scenarios and their implementation in PostgreSQL.

What you need for this book

In general, PostgreSQL server and client tools do not need exceptional hardware. PostgreSQL can be installed on almost all modern platforms, including Linux, Windows, and Mac. Also, in the book, when a certain library is needed, the installation instructions are given.

You need PostgreSQL version 10; however, most of the examples can be executed on earlier versions as well. In order to execute the sample code, scripts, and examples provided in the book, you need to have at least a PostgreSQL client tool installed on your machine—preferably psql—and access to a remote server running the PostgreSQL server.

In a Windows environment, the cmd.exe command prompt is not very convenient; thus, the user might consider using Cygwin (http://www.cygwin.com/) or another alternative, such as PowerShell.

Some chapters might requires additional software. For example, in Chapter 15, *Using PostgreSQL in Python application,* you need to install Python and the required Python libraries to interact with PostgreSQL. In Chapter 16, *Scalability,* Docker is used to give the reader a better user experience.

For other chapters, such as Chapter 09, *Beyond Conventional Data types, and* Chapter 11, *PostgreSQL Security,* it is better to use Linux because some of the software used is not very convenient on Windows such as Nginx and GnuPG. To run a Linux distribution on your Windows machine, you can use Virtual Box (https://www.virtualbox.org/).

Who this book is for

If you're interested in learning more about PostgreSQL--one of the most popular relational databases in the world--then this book is for you. Those looking to build solid database or data warehousing applications with PostgreSQL 10 will also find this book a useful resource. No prior knowledge of database programming or administration is required to get started with this book.

Conventions

In this book, you will find a number of text styles that distinguish between different kinds of information. Here are some examples of these styles and an explanation of their meaning.

Code words in text, database table names, folder names, filenames, file extensions, pathnames, dummy URLs, user input, and Twitter handles are shown as follows: "The next lines of code read the link and assign it to the open function."

A block of code is set as follows:

```
fin = open('data/fake_weather_data.csv','r',newline='')
reader = csv.reader(fin)
for row in reader:
    myData.append(row)
```

Any command-line input or output is written as follows:

```
$ mongoimport --file fake_weather_data.csv
```

New terms and **important words** are shown in bold.

Words that you see on the screen, for example, in menus or dialog boxes, appear in the text like this: "In order to download new modules, we will go to **Files** | **Settings** | **Project Name** | **Project Interpreter**."

 Warnings or important notes appear like this.

 Tips and tricks appear like this.

Reader feedback

Feedback from our readers is always welcome. Let us know what you think about this book-what you liked or disliked. Reader feedback is important for us as it helps us develop titles that you will really get the most out of. To send us general feedback, simply email feedback@packtpub.com, and mention the book's title in the subject of your message. If there is a topic that you have expertise in and you are interested in either writing or contributing to a book, see our author guide at www.packtpub.com/authors.

Customer support

Now that you are the proud owner of a Packt book, we have a number of things to help you to get the most from your purchase.

Downloading the example code

You can download the example code files for this book from your account at `http://www.packtpub.com`. If you purchased this book elsewhere, you can visit `http://www.packtpub.com/support` and register to have the files emailed directly to you. You can download the code files by following these steps:

1. Log in or register to our website using your email address and password.
2. Hover the mouse pointer on the **SUPPORT** tab at the top.
3. Click on **Code Downloads & Errata**.
4. Enter the name of the book in the **Search** box.
5. Select the book for which you're looking to download the code files.
6. Choose from the drop-down menu where you purchased this book from.
7. Click on **Code Download**.

Once the file is downloaded, please make sure that you unzip or extract the folder using the latest version of:

- WinRAR / 7-Zip for Windows
- Zipeg / iZip / UnRarX for Mac
- 7-Zip / PeaZip for Linux

The code bundle for the book is also hosted on GitHub at `https://github.com/PacktPublishing/Learning-PostgreSQL-10-Second-Edition`. We also have other code bundles from our rich catalog of books and videos available at `https://github.com/PacktPublishing/`. Check them out!

Downloading the color images of this book

We also provide you with a PDF file that has color images of the screenshots/diagrams used in this book. The color images will help you better understand the changes in the output. You can download this file from `https://www.packtpub.com/sites/default/files/downloads/LearningPostgreSQL10SecondEdition_ColorImages.pdf`.

Errata

Although we have taken every care to ensure the accuracy of our content, mistakes do happen. If you find a mistake in one of our books-maybe a mistake in the text or the code-we would be grateful if you could report this to us. By doing so, you can save other readers from frustration and help us improve subsequent versions of this book. If you find any errata, please report them by visiting http://www.packtpub.com/submit-errata, selecting your book, clicking on the **Errata Submission Form** link, and entering the details of your errata. Once your errata are verified, your submission will be accepted and the errata will be uploaded to our website or added to any list of existing errata under the Errata section of that title. To view the previously submitted errata, go to https://www.packtpub.com/books/content/support and enter the name of the book in the search field. The required information will appear under the **Errata** section.

Piracy

Piracy of copyrighted material on the internet is an ongoing problem across all media. At Packt, we take the protection of our copyright and licenses very seriously. If you come across any illegal copies of our works in any form on the internet, please provide us with the location address or website name immediately so that we can pursue a remedy. Please contact us at copyright@packtpub.com with a link to the suspected pirated material. We appreciate your help in protecting our authors and our ability to bring you valuable content.

Questions

If you have a problem with any aspect of this book, you can contact us at questions@packtpub.com, and we will do our best to address the problem.

1
Relational Databases

This chapter, and the next chapters, will provide a high-level overview of topics related to database development. These topics will cover the theoretical aspect of relational databases. The first two chapters try to summarize theoretical topics that are seen on a daily basis. Understanding these theoretical concepts will enable the developers to not only come up with clean designs, but also to master relational databases.

This chapter is not restricted to learning PostgreSQL, but covers all relational databases. The topics covered in this chapter include the following:

- **Database management systems**: Understanding the different database categories enables the developer to utilize the best in each world
- **Relational algebra**: Understanding relational algebra enables the developers to master the SQL language, especially SQL code rewriting
- **Data modeling**: Using data modeling techniques leads to better communication

Database management systems

Different database management systems support diverse application scenarios, use cases, and requirements. Database management systems have a long history. First, we will quickly take a look at the recent history, and then explore the market-dominant database management system categories.

A brief history

Broadly, the term database can be used to present a collection of things. Moreover, this term brings to mind many other terms including data, information, data structure, and management. A database can be defined as a collection or repository of data, which has a certain structure, managed by a **database management system (DBMS)**. Data can be structured as tabular data, semi-structured as XML documents, or unstructured data that does not fit a predefined data model.

In the early days, databases were mainly aimed at supporting business applications; this led us to the well-defined relational algebra and relational database systems. With the introduction of object-oriented languages, new paradigms of database management systems appeared such as object-relational databases and object-oriented databases. Also, many businesses as well as scientific applications use arrays, images, and spatial data; thus, new models such as raster, map, and array algebra are supported. Graph databases are used to support graph queries such as the shortest path from one node to another, along with supporting traversal queries easily.

With the advent of web applications such as social portals, it is now necessary to support a huge number of requests in a distributed manner. This has led to another new paradigm of databases called **NoSQL (Not Only SQL)**, which has different requirements such as performance over fault tolerance and horizontal scaling capabilities. In general, the timeline of database evolution was greatly affected by many factors such as the following:

- **Functional requirements**: The nature of the applications using a DBMS has led to the development of extensions on top of relational databases such as PostGIS (for spatial data) or even dedicated DBMS such as SciDB (for scientific data analytics).
- **Nonfunctional requirements**: The success of object-oriented programming languages has created new trends such as object-oriented databases. Object relational database management systems have appeared to bridge the gap between relational databases and the object-oriented programming languages. Data explosion and the necessity to handle terabytes of data on commodity hardware have led to columnar databases, which can easily scale up horizontally.

Database categories

Many database models have appeared and vanished such as the network model and hierarchical model. The predominant categories now in the market are relational, object-relational databases, and NoSQL databases. One should not think of NoSQL and SQL databases as rivals--they are complementary to each other. By utilizing different database systems, one can overcome many limitations and get the best of different technologies.

The NoSQL databases

The NoSQL databases are affected by the CAP theorem, also known as Brewer's theorem. In 2002, S. Gilbert and N. Lynch published a formal proof of the CAP theorem in their article, *Brewer's conjecture and the feasibility of consistent, available, partition-tolerant web services*. In 2009, the NoSQL movement began. Currently, there are over 150 NoSQL databases (`nosql-database.org`).

The CAP theorem

The CAP theorem states that it is impossible for a distributed computing system to simultaneously provide all three of the following guarantees:

- **Consistency**: All clients see (immediately) the latest data even in the case of updates.
- **Availability**: All clients can find a replica of some data even in the case of a node failure. This means that even if some part of the system goes down, the clients can still access the data.
- **Partition tolerance**: The system continues to work regardless of arbitrary message loss or failure of part of the system.

The choice of which feature to discard determines the nature of the system. For example, one could sacrifice consistency to get a scalable, simple, and high performance database management system. Often, the main difference between a relational database and a NoSQL database is consistency. A relational database enforces **ACID** (**atomicity, consistency, isolation, durability**) properties. In contrast, many NoSQL databases adopt the **basically available soft-state, eventual consistency (base)** model.

NoSQL motivation

A NoSQL database provides a means for data storage, manipulation, and retrieval for non-relational data. The NoSQL databases are distributed, open source, and horizontally scalable. NoSQL often adopts the base model, which prizes availability over consistency, and informally guarantees that if no new updates are made on a data item, eventually all access to that data item will return the latest version of that data item. The advantages of this approach include the following:

- Simplicity of design
- Horizontal scaling and easy replication

- Schema free
- Huge amount of data support

We will now explore a few types of NoSQL databases.

Key-value databases

The key-value store is the simplest database store. In this database model, the storage, as its name suggests, is based on maps or hash tables. Some key-value databases allow complex values to be stored as lists and hash tables. Key-value pairs are extremely fast for certain scenarios, but lack the support for complex queries and aggregation. Some of the existing open source key-value databases are Riak, Redis, Memebase, and MemcacheDB.

Columnar databases

Columnar or column-oriented databases are based on columns. Data in a certain column in a two-dimensional relation is stored together.

Unlike relational databases, adding columns is inexpensive and is done on a row-by-row basis. Rows can have a different set of columns. Tables can benefit from this structure by eliminating the storage cost of the null values. This model is best suited for distributed databases.

HBase is one of the most famous columnar databases. It is based on the Google Bigtable storage system. Column-oriented databases are designed for huge data scenarios, so they scale up easily. For small datasets, HBase is not a suitable architecture. First, the recommended hardware topology for HBase is a five-node or server deployment. Also, it needs a lot of administration and is difficult to master and learn.

Document databases

A document-oriented database is suitable for documents and semi-structured data. The central concept of a document-oriented database is the notion of a document. Documents encapsulate and encode data (or information) in some standard formats or encodings such as XML, JSON, and BSON. Documents do not adhere to a standard schema or have the same structure, so they provide a high degree of flexibility. Unlike relational databases, changing the structure of the document is simple and does not lock the clients from accessing the data.

Document databases merge the power of relational databases and column-oriented databases. They provide support for ad hoc queries and can be scaled up easily. Depending on the design of the document database, MongoDB is designed to handle a huge amount of data efficiently. On the other hand, CouchDB provides high availability even in the case of hardware failure.

Graph databases

Graph databases are based on the graph theory, where a database consists of nodes and edges. The nodes as well as the edges can be assigned data. Graph databases allow traversing between the nodes using edges. As a graph is a generic data structure, graph databases are capable of representing different data. A famous implementation of an open source commercially supported graph database is Neo4j.

Relational and object relational databases

Relational database management systems are one of the most widely-used DBMSs in the world. It is highly unlikely that any organization, institution, or personal computer today does not have or use a piece of software that rely on RBDMS.

Software applications can use relational databases via dedicated database servers or via lightweight RDBMS engines, embedded in the software applications as shared libraries. The capabilities of a relational database management system vary from one vendor to another, but most of them adhere to the ANSI SQL standards. A relational database is formally described by relational algebra, and is based on the relational model. **Object-relational database (ORD)** are similar to relational databases. They support the following object-oriented model concepts:

- User-defined and complex data types
- Inheritance

ACID properties

In a relational database, a single logical operation is called a **transaction**. The technical translation of a transaction is a set of database operations, which are **create**, **read**, **update**, and **delete** (**CRUD**). An example of explaining a transaction is budget assignment to several projects in the company assuming we have a fixed amount of money. If we increase a certain project budget, we need to deduct this amount of increase from another project. The ACID properties in this context could be described as follows:

- **Atomicity**: All or nothing, which means that if a part of a transaction fails, then the transaction fails as a whole.
- **Consistency**: Any transaction gets the database from one valid state to another valid state. Database consistency is governed normally by data constraints and the relation between data and any combination thereof. For example, imagine if one would like to completely purge his account on a shopping service. In order to purge his account, his account details, such as a list of addresses, will also need to be purged. This is governed by foreign key constraints, which will be explained in detail in the coming chapter.
- **Isolation**: Concurrent execution of transactions results in a system state that would be obtained if the transactions were executed serially.
- **Durability**: The transactions that are committed--that is, executed successfully-- are persistent even with power loss or some server crashes. In PostgreSQL, this is done normally by a technique called **write-ahead log** (**WAL**). Other database refers to this as a transaction log such as in Oracle.

The SQL language

Relational databases are often linked to the **structured query language** (**SQL**). SQL is a declarative programming language and is the standard relational database language. The **American National Standard Institute** (**ANSI**) and the **International Standard Organization** (**ISO**) published the SQL standard for the first time in 1986, followed by many versions such as SQL:1999, SQL:2003, SQL:2006, SQL:2008, SQL:2011, and SQL:2016. The SQL language has several parts:

- **Data definition language** (**DDL**): It defines and amends the relational structure
- **Data manipulation language** (**DML**): It retrieves and extracts information from the relations
- **Data control language** (**DCL**): It controls the access rights to relations

Relational model concepts

A relational model is a first-order predicate logic, which was first introduced by Edgar F. Codd in 1970 in his paper A relational model of data for large shared data banks. A database is represented as a collection of relations. The state of the whole database is defined by the state of all the relations in the database. Different information can be extracted from the relations by joining and aggregating data from different relations and by applying filters on the data. In this section, the basic concepts of the relational model are introduced using the top-down approach by first describing the relation, tuple, attribute, and domain.

The terms relation, tuple, attribute, and unknown, which are used in the formal relational model, are equivalent to table, row, column, and null in the SQL language.

Relation

Think of a relation as a table with a header, columns, and rows. The table name and the header help in interpreting the data in the rows. Each row represents a group of related data, which points to a certain object.

A relation is represented by a set of tuples. Tuples should have the same set of ordered attributes. Attributes have a domain, that is, a type and a name:

	customer_id	first_name	last_name	email
Tuple →	1		thomas	sieh	thomas@example.com
Tuple →	2		wang	kim	kim@example.com
	Attribute ↑	Attribute ↑	Attribute ↑	Attribute ↑

The relation schema is denoted by the relation name and the relation attributes. For example, customer (customer_id, first_name, last_name, and email) is the relation schema for the customer relation. **Relation state** is defined by the set of relation tuples; thus, adding, deleting, and amending a tuple will change the relation to another state.

Tuple order or position in the relation is not important, and the relation is not sensitive to tuple order. The tuples in the relation could be ordered by a single attribute or a set of attributes. Also, a relation cannot have duplicate tuples.

A relation can represent entities in the real world, such as a customer, or can be used to represent an association between relations. For example, the customer could have several services and a service can be offered to several customers. This could be modeled by three relations: `customer`, `service`, and `customer_service`. The `customer_service` relation associates the customer and the service relations. Separating the data in different relations is a key concept in relational database modeling, which is called normalization. Normalization is the process of organizing relation columns and relations to reduce data redundancy. For example, assume that a collection of services is stored in the customer relation. If a service is assigned to multiple customers, this would result in data redundancy. Also, updating a certain service would require updating all its copies in the customer table.

Tuple

A tuple is a set of ordered attributes. They are written by listing the elements within parentheses () and separated by commas, such as (john, smith, 1971). Tuple elements are identified via the attribute name. Tuples have the following properties:

- $(a_1, a_2, a_3,...,a_n) = (b_1, b_2, b_3,...,b_n)$ *if and only if* $a_1 = b_1$, $a_2 = b_2$, ...,$a_n = b_n$
- A tuple is not a set; the order of attributes matters as well as duplicate members
  - $(a_1, a_2) \neq (a_2, a_1)$
  - $(a_1, a_1) \neq (a_1)$
- A tuple has a finite set of attributes

In the formal relational model, multi-valued attributes as well as composite attributes are not allowed. This is important to reduce data redundancy and increase data consistency. This isn't strictly true in modern relational database systems because of the utilization of complex data types such as JSON and key-value stores.

There is a lot of debate regarding the application of normalization; the rule of thumb is to apply normalization unless there is a good reason not to do so.

NULL value

Predicates in relational databases use **three-valued logic** (**3VL**), where there are three truth values: true, false, and unknown aka NULL. In a relational database, the third value, NULL, can be interpreted in many ways, such as unknown data, missing data, not applicable, or will be loaded later. The three-valued logic is used to remove ambiguity. For example, no two NULL values are equal.

The following table shows logical OR / AND truth operator; note that these operators are commutative, that is, *A AND B = B AND A*:

A	B	A AND B	A OR B
TRUE	TRUE	TRUE	TRUE
FALSE	TRUE	FALSE	TRUE
NULL	TRUE	NULL	TRUE
FALSE	FALSE	FALSE	FALSE
NULL	FALSE	FALSE	NULL
NULL	NULL	NULL	NULL

The following table shows the NOT truth operator:

A	NOT A
TRUE	FALSE
FALSE	TRUE
NULL	NULL

Attribute

Each attribute has a name and a domain, and the name should be distinct within the relation. The domain defines the possible set of values that the attribute can have. One way to define the domain is to define the data type and a constraint on this data type. For example, hourly wage should be a positive real number and bigger than five if we assume that the minimum hourly wage is five dollars. The domain could be continuous, such as salary, which is any positive real number, or discrete, such as gender.

The formal relational model puts a constraint on the domain: the value should be atomic. Atomic means that each value in the domain is indivisible. For instance, the name attribute domain is not atomic because it can be divided into first name and last name. Some examples of domains are as follows:

- **Phone number**: Numeric text with a certain length.
- **Country code**: Defined by ISO 3166 as a list of two letter codes (ISO alpha-2) and three letter codes (ISO alpha-3). The country codes for Germany are DE and DEU for alpha-2 and alpha-3 respectively.

In real-life applications, it is better to use ISO and international standards for lookup tables such as country and currency. This enables you to expose your data much easily for third-party software and increases your data quality.

Constraint

The relational model defines many constraints in order to control data integrity, redundancy, and validity:

- **Redundancy**: Duplicate tuples are not allowed in the relation.
- **Validity**: Domain constraints control data validity.
- **Integrity**: The relations within a single database are linked to each other. An action on a relation such as updating or deleting a tuple might leave the other relations in an invalid state.

We could classify the constraints in a relational database roughly into two categories:

- Inherited constraints from the relational model: Domain integrity, entity integrity, and referential integrity constraints.
- Semantic constraint, business rules, and application specific constraints: These constraints cannot be expressed explicitly by the relational model. However, with the introduction of procedural SQL languages such as PL/pgsql for PostgreSQL, relational databases can also be used to model these constraints.

Domain integrity constraint

The domain integrity constraint ensures data validity. The first step in defining the domain integrity constraint is to determine the appropriate data type. The domain data types could be integer, real, boolean, character, text, inet, and so on. For example, the data type of first name and email address is text. After specifying the data type, check constraints, such as the mail address pattern, need to be defined.

- **Check constraint**: A check constraint can be applied to a single attribute or a combination of many attributes in a tuple. Let's assume that the `customer_service` schema is defined as `customer_id`, `service_id`, `start_date`, `end_date`, `order_date`. For this relation, we can have a check constraint to make sure that `start_date` and `end_date` are entered correctly by applying the following check `start_date<end_date`.

- **Default constraint**: The attribute can have a default value. The default value could be a fixed value such as the default hourly wage of the employees, for example, $10. It may also have a dynamic value based on a function such as random, current time, and date. For example, in the `customer_service` relation, `order_date` can have a default value, which is the current date.
- **Unique constraint**: A unique constraint guarantees that the attribute has a distinct value in each tuple. It allows null values. For example, let's assume that we have a relation player defined as player (`player_id`, `player_nickname`). The player uses his ID to play with others; he can also pick up a nickname which is also unique to identify himself.
- **Not null constraint**: By default, the attribute value can be null. The not null constraint restricts an attribute from having a null value. For example, each person in the birth registry record should have a name.

Entity integrity constraint

In the relational model, a relation is defined as a set of tuples. This means that all the tuples in a relation must be distinct. The entity integrity constraint is enforced by having a primary key which is an attribute/set of attributes having the following characteristics:

- The attribute should be unique
- The attributes should be not null

Each relation must have only one primary key, but can have many unique keys. A candidate key is a minimal set of attributes that can identify a tuple. All unique, not null attributes can be candidate keys. The set of all attributes form a super key. In practice, we often pick up a single attribute to be a primary key instead of a compound key (a key that consists of two or more attributes that uniquely identify a tuple) to ease the joining of the relations with each other.

If the primary key is generated by the DBMS, then it is called a **surrogate key** or **synthetic key** . Otherwise, it is called a **natural key**. The surrogate key candidates can be sequences and **universal unique identifiers** (**UUID**). A surrogate key has many advantages such as performance, requirement change tolerance, agility, and compatibility with object relational mappers. The chief disadvantage of surrogate keys is that , it makes redundant tuples possible.

Referential integrity constraints

Relations are associated with each other via common attributes. Referential integrity constraints govern the association between two relations and ensure data consistency between tuples. If a tuple in one relation references a tuple in another relation, then the referenced tuple must exist. In the customer service example, if a service is assigned to a customer, then the service and the customer must exist, as shown in the following example. For instance, in the `customer_service` relation, we cannot have a tuple with values (5, 1,01-01-2014, NULL), because we do not have a customer with `customer_id` equal to 5.

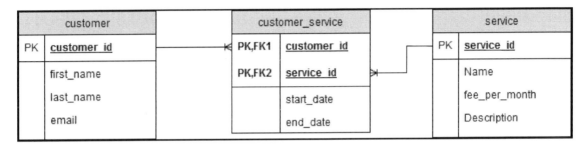

The lack of referential integrity constraints can lead to many problems:

- Invalid data in the common attributes
- Invalid information during joining of data from different relations
- Performance degradation either due to bad execution plans generated by the PostgreSQL planner or by a third-party tool.

Foreign keys can increase performance in reading data from multiple tables. The query execution planner will have a better estimation of the number of rows that need to be processed. Disabling foreign keys when doing a bulk insert will lead to a performance boost.

Referential integrity constraints are achieved via foreign keys. A **foreign key** is an attribute or a set of attributes that can identify a tuple in the referenced relation. As the purpose of a foreign key is to identify a tuple in the referenced relation, foreign keys are generally primary keys in the referenced relation. Unlike a primary key, a foreign key can have a null value. It can also reference a unique attribute in the referenced relation. Allowing a foreign key to have a null value enables us to model different cardinality constraints. Cardinality constraints define the participation between two different relations. For example, a parent can have more than one child; this relation is called one-to-many relationship, because one tuple in the referenced relation is associated with many tuples in the referencing relation. Also, a relation could reference itself. This foreign key is called a **self-referencing** or **recursive foreign key**.

For example, a company acquired by another company:

company				company_id	name	acquisitioned_by
PK	company_id			1	Facebook	
	name			2	WhatsApp	1
FK	acquisitioned_by					

To ensure data integrity, foreign keys can be used to define several behaviors when a tuple in the referenced relation is updated or deleted. The following behaviors are called referential actions:

- **Cascade**: When a tuple is deleted or updated in the referenced relation, the tuples in the referencing relation are also updated or deleted
- **Restrict**: The tuple cannot be deleted or the referenced attribute cannot be updated if it is referenced by another relation
- **No action**: Similar to restrict, but it is deferred to the end of the transaction
- **Set default**: When a tuple in the referenced relation is deleted or the referenced attribute is updated, then the foreign key value is assigned the default value
- **Set null**: The foreign key attribute value is set to null when the referenced tuple is deleted

Semantic constraints

Integrity constraints or business logic constraints describe the database application constraints in general. These constraints are either enforced by the business logic tier of the application program or by SQL procedural languages. Trigger and rule systems can also be used for this purpose. For example, the customer should have at most one active service at a time. Based on the nature of the application, one could favor using an SQL procedural language or a high-level programming language to meet the semantic constraints, or mix the two approaches.

The advantages of using the SQL programming language are as follows:

- **Performance**: RDBMSs often have complex analyzers to generate efficient execution plans. Also, in some cases such as data mining, the amount of data that needs to be manipulated is very large. Manipulating the data using procedural SQL language eliminates the network data transfer. Finally, some procedural SQL languages utilize clever caching algorithms.

- **Last minute change**: For the SQL procedural languages, one could deploy bug fixes without service disruption.

Implementing business logic in database tier has a lot of pros and cons and it is a highly arguable topic. For example, some disadvantages of implementing business logic in the database is visibility, developers efficiency in writing code due to a lack of proper tools and IDEs, and code reuse.

Relational algebra

Relational algebra is the formal language of the relational model. It defines a set of closed operations over relations, that is, the result of each operation is a new relation. Relational algebra inherits many operators from set algebra. Relational algebra operations can be categorized into two groups:

- The first one is a group of operations that are inherited from a set theory such as `union`, `intersection`, `set difference`, and `cartesian product`, also known as `cross product`.

- The second is a group of operations that are specific to the relational model such as `select` and `project`. Relational algebra operations could also be classified as binary and unary operations.

The primitive operators are as follows:

- `select` (σ): A unary operation written as $\sigma\phi_R$ where ϕ is a predicate. The selection retrieves the tuples in R, where ϕ holds.
- `project` (π): A unary operation used to slice the relation in a vertical dimension, that is, attributes. This operation is written as $\pi_{a1,a2,...,an} R()$, where *a1, a2, ..., an* are a set of attribute names.
- `cartesian product` ($\times$): A binary operation used to generate a more complex relation by joining each tuple of its operands together. Let's assume that R and S are two relations, then $R \times S = (r_1, r_2, ..., r_n, s_1, s_2, ..., s_n)$ where $(r_1, r_2,...,r_n) \in R$ and $(s_1, s_2, ..., s_n) \in S$.
- `union` ($\cup$): Appends two relations together; note that the relations should be union compatible, that is, they should have the same set of ordered attributes. Formally, $R \cup S = (r_1,r_2...r_n) \cup (s_1,s_2...,s_n)$ where $(r_1, r_2,...,r_n) \in R$ and $(s_1, s_2, ..., s_n) \in S$.

- difference (-): A binary operation in which the operands should be union compatible. Difference creates a new relation from the tuples, which exist in one relation but not in the other. The set difference for the relation R and S can be given as R-S = $(r_1, r_2, ...r_n)$ where $(r_1, r_2, ...r_n) \in R$ *and* $(r_1, r_2, ...r_n) \notin S$.
- rename (ρ): A unary operation that works on attributes. This operator is mainly used to distinguish the attributes with the same names but in different relation when joined together, or it is used to give more user friendly name for the attribute for presentation purposes. Rename is expressed as $\rho_{a/b}R$, where a and b are attribute names and b is an attribute of R.

In addition to the primitive operators, there are aggregation functions such as sum, count, min, max, and avg aggregates. Primitive operators can be used to define other relation operators such as left-join, right-join, equi-join, and intersection. Relational algebra is very important due to its expressive power in optimizing and rewriting queries. For example, the selection is commutative, so $\sigma_a \sigma_b R = \sigma_b \sigma_a R$. A cascaded selection may also be replaced by a single selection with a conjunction of all the predicates, that is, $\sigma_a \sigma_b R = \sigma_{a \, AND \, b} R$.

The select and project operations

SELECT is used to restrict tuples from the relation. SELECT always returns a unique set of tuples this is inherited form entity integrity constraint. For example, the query *give me the customer information where the customer_id equals to 2* is written as follows:

$$\sigma_{customer\_id = 2} \; customer$$

The selection, as mentioned earlier, is commutative; the query *give me all customers where the customer mail is known, and the customer first name is kim* is written in three different ways, as follows:

$$\sigma_{email \; is \; not \; null}(\sigma_{first\_name = kim} \; customer)$$

$$\sigma_{first\_name = kim}(\sigma_{email \; is \; not \; null} \; customer)$$

$$\sigma_{first\_name = kim \; and \; email \; is \; not \; null} \; (customer)$$

The selection predicates are certainly determined by the data types. For numeric data types, the comparison operator might be $\neq$, $=$, $<$, $>$, $\geq$, or $\leq$. The predicate expression can also contain complex expressions and functions. The equivalent SQL statement for the SELECT operator is the SELECT * statement, and the predicate is defined in the WHERE clause.

The symbol ⋆ means all the relation attributes; note that in the production environment, it is not recommended to use ⋆. Instead, one should list all the relation attributes explicitly.

The following SELECT statement is equivalent for the relational algebra expression σ</span>_{customer_id =2} customer:

```
SELECT * FROM customer WHERE customer_id = 2;
```

The project operation could be visualized as vertical slicing of the table. The query, *give me the customer names*, is written in relational algebra as follows:

$$\pi_{first\_name, last\_name} \text{ customer}$$

The following is the result of projection expression:

first_name	last_name
thomas	sieh
wang	kim

Duplicate tuples are not allowed in the formal relational model; the number of returned tuples from the PROJECT operator is always equal to or less than the number of total tuples in the relation. If a PROJECT operator's attribute list contains a primary key, then the resulting relation has the same number of tuples as the projected relation.

The projection operator also can be optimized, for example, cascading projections could be optimized as the following expression:

$$\pi_a(\pi_{a,}\pi_b(R)) = \pi_a(R)$$

The SQL equivalent for the PROJECT operator is SELECT DISTINCT. The DISTINCT keyword is used to eliminate duplicates. To get the result shown in the preceding expression, one could execute the following SQL statement:

```
SELECT DISTINCT first_name, last_name FROM customers;
```

The sequence of the execution of the PROJECT and SELECT operations can be interchangeable in some cases. The query *give me the name of the customer with customer_id equal to 2* could be written as follows:

$$\sigma_{customer\_id\,=2} \left(\pi_{first\_name,\,last\_name}\ customer \right)$$

$$\pi_{first\_name,\,last\_name} \left(\sigma_{customer\_id\,=2}\ customer \right)$$

In other cases, the PROJECT and SELECT operators must have an explicit order as shown in the following example; otherwise, it will lead to an incorrect expression. The query, *give me the last name of the customers where the first name is kim*, could be written in the following way:

$$\pi_{last\_name} \left(\sigma_{first\_name=kim}\ customer \right)$$

The rename operation

The rename operation is used to alter the attribute name of the resultant relation or to give a specific name to the resultant relation. The rename operation is used to perform the following:

- Remove confusion if two or more relations have attributes with the same name
- Provide user-friendly names for attributes, especially when interfacing with reporting engines
- Provide a convenient way to change the relation definition and still be backward compatible

The AS keyword in SQL is the equivalent of the rename operator in relational algebra. The following SQL example creates a relation with one tuple and one attribute, which is renamed PI:

```
SELECT 3.14::real AS PI;
```

The set theory operations

The set theory operations are `union`, `intersection`, and `minus` (difference). `Intersection` is not a primitive relational algebra operator, because it can be written using the union and difference operators:

$$A \cap B = ((A \cup B)-(A-B))-(B-A)$$

The intersection and union are commutative:

$$A \cap B = B \cap A$$

$$A \cup B = B \cup A$$

For example, the query, *give me all the customer IDs where the customer does not have a service assigned to him*, could be written as follows:

$$\pi_{customer\_id} \, \text{customer-} \pi_{customer\_id} \, \text{customer\_service}$$

The cartesian product operation

The `cartesian product` operation is used to combine tuples from two relations into a single one. The number of attributes in single relation equals the sum of the number of attributes of the two relations. The number of tuples in the single relation equals the product of the number of tuples in the two relations. Let's assume that A and B are two relations, and $C = A \times B$:

The number of attribute of C = the number of attribute in A + the number of attribute of B

*The number of tuples of C = the number of tuples of A * The number of tuples of B*

The following image shows the cross join of customer and customer service:

customer_id	first_name	las_name
1	thomas	sieh
2	wang	kim

X

customer_service_id	customer_id	start_date	end_date
1	1	2017-11-01	2018-11-01
2	1	2017-11-01	2018-11-01

=

customer_id	first_name	las_name	customer_service_id	customer_id	start_date	end_date
1	thomas	sieh	1	1	2017-11-01	2018-11-01
2	wang	kim	1	1	2017-11-01	2018-11-01
1	thomas	sieh	2	1	2017-11-01	2018-11-01
2	wang	kim	2	1	2017-11-01	2018-11-01

The equivalent SQL join for `Cartesian product` is `CROSS JOIN`, the query *for the customer with customer_id equal to 1, retrieve the customer id, name and the customer service IDs* can be written in SQL as follows:

```
SELECT DISTINCT customer_id, first_name, last_name, service_id FROM
customer AS c CROSS JOIN customer_service AS cs WHERE
c.customer_id=cs.customer_id AND c.customer_id = 1;
```

In the preceding example, one can see the relationship between relational algebra and the SQL language. For example, we have used `select`, `rename`, `project`, and `Cartesian product`. The preceding example shows how relational algebra could be used to optimize query execution. This example could be executed in several ways:

Execution plan 1:

1. Select the customer where `customer_id = 1`.
2. Select the customer service where `customer_id = 1`.
3. `Cross JOIN` the relations resulting from steps 1 and 2.
4. Project `customer_id`, `first_name`, `last_name`, and `service_id` from the relation resulting from step 3.

Execution plan 2:

1. `Cross JOIN` customer and `customer_service`.
2. Select all the tuples where
   `Customer_service.customer_id=customer.customer_id` and
   `customer.customer_id = 1`.
3. Project `customer_id`, `first_name`, `last_name`, and `service_id` from the relation resulting from step 2.

The SELECT query is written in this way to show how to translate relational algebra to SQL. In modern SQL code, we can project attributes without using DISTINCT. In addition to that, one should use a proper join instead of cross join.

Each execution plan has a cost in terms of CPU, **random access memory (RAM)**, and hard disk operations. The RDBMS picks the one with the lowest cost. In the preceding execution plans, the rename as well as distinct operator were ignored for simplicity.

Data modeling

Data models describe real-world entities such as customer, service, products, and the relation between these entities. Data models provide an abstraction for the relations in the database. Data models aid the developers in modeling business requirements, and translating business requirements to relations. They are also used for the exchange of information between the developers and business owners.

In the enterprise, data models play a very important role in achieving data consistency across interacting systems. For example, if an entity is not defined, or is poorly defined, then this will lead to inconsistent and misinterpreted data across the enterprise. For instance, if the semantics of the customer entity not defined clearly, and different business departments use different names for the same entity such as customer and client, this may lead to confusion in the operational departments.

Data model perspectives

Data model perspectives are defined by ANSI as follows:

- **Conceptual data model**: Describes the domain semantics, and is used to communicate the main business rules, actors, and concepts. It describes the business requirements at a high level and is often called a high-level data model.
- **Logical data model**: Describes the semantics for a certain technology, for example, the UML class diagram for object-oriented languages.
- **Physical data model**: Describes how data is actually stored and manipulated at the hardware level such as storage area network, table space, CPUs, and so on.

According to ANSI, this abstraction allows changing one part of the three perspectives without amending the other parts. One could change both the logical and the physical data models without changing the conceptual model. To explain, sorting data using bubble or quick sort is not of interest for the conceptual data model. Also, changing the structure of the relations could be transparent to the conceptual model. One could split one relation into many relations after applying normalization rules, or by using `enum` data types in order to model the lookup tables.

The entity-relation model

The **entity-relation** (ER) model falls in the conceptual data model category. It captures and represents the data model for both business users and developers. The ER model can be transformed into the relational model by following certain techniques.

Conceptual modeling is a part of the **software development life cycle (SDLC)**. It is normally done after the functional and data requirements-gathering stage. At this point, the developer is able to make the first draft of the ER diagram as well as describe functional requirements using data flow diagrams, sequence diagrams, user stories, and many other techniques.

During the design phase, the database developer should give great attention to the design, run a benchmark stack to ensure performance, and validate user requirements. Developers modeling simple systems could start coding directly. However, care should be taken when making the design, since data modeling involves not only algorithms in modeling the application but also data. The change in design might lead to a lot of complexities in the future such as data migration from one data structure to another.

While designing a database schema, avoiding design pitfalls is not enough. There are alternative designs, where one could be chosen. The following pitfalls should be avoided:

- **Data redundancy**: Bad database designs elicit redundant data. Redundant data can cause several other problems including data inconsistency and performance degradation. When updating a tuple which contains redundant data, the changes on the redundant data should be reflected in all the tuples that contain this data.
- **Null saturation**: By nature, some applications have sparse data, such as medical applications. Imagine a relation called diagnostics which has hundreds of attributes for symptoms like fever, headache, sneezing, and so on. Most of them are not valid for certain diagnostics, but they are valid in general. This could be modeled by utilizing complex data types like JSON.

- **Tight coupling**: In some cases, tight coupling leads to complex and difficult to change data structures. Since business requirements change with time, some requirements might become obsolete. Modeling generalization and specialization (for example, a part-time student is a student) in a tightly coupled way may cause problems.

Sample application

In order to explain the basics of the ER model, an online web portal to buy and sell cars will be modeled. The requirements of this sample application are listed as follows, and an ER model will be developed step by step:

1. The portal provides the facility to register the users online and provides different services for the users based on their categories.
2. The users might be sellers or normal users. The sellers can create new car advertisements; other users can explore and search for cars.
3. All users should provide there full name and a valid email address during registration. The email address will be used for logging in.
4. The seller should also provide an address.
5. The user can rate the advertisement and the seller's service quality.
6. All users' search history should be maintained for later use.
7. The sellers have ranks and this affects the advertisement search; the rank is determined by the number of posted advertisements and the user's rank.
8. The car advertisement has a date and the car can have many attributes such as color, number of doors, number of previous owners, registration number, pictures, and so on.

Entities, attributes, and keys

The ER diagram represents entities, attributes, and relationships. An entity is a representation of a real-world object such as car or a user. An attribute is a property of an object and describes it. A relationship represents an association between two or more entities.

The attributes might be composite or simple (atomic). Composite attributes can be divided into smaller subparts. A subpart of a composite attribute provides incomplete information that is semantically not useful by itself. For example, the address is composed of street name, building number, and postal code. Any one of them isn't useful alone without its counterparts.

Attributes could also be single-valued or multi-valued. The color of a bird is an example of a multi-valued attribute. It can be red and black, or a combination of any other colors. A multi-valued attribute can have a lower and upper bound to constrain the number of values allowed. In addition, some attributes can be derived from other attributes. Age can be derived from the birth date. In our example, the final rank of a seller is derived from the number of advertisements and the user ratings.

Finally, key attributes can identify an entity in the real world. A key attribute should be marked as a unique attribute, but not necessarily as a primary key, when physically modeling the relation. Finally, several attribute types could be grouped together to form a complex attribute.

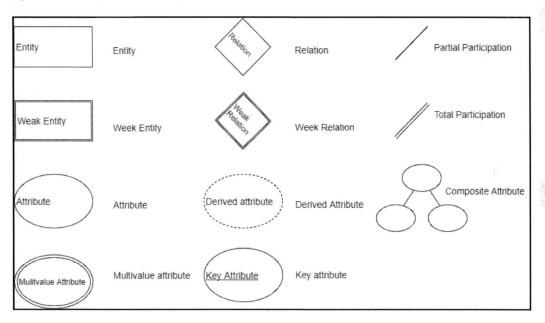

Entities should have a name and a set of attributes. They are classified into the following:

- **Weak entity**: Does not have key attributes of its own
- **Strong entity** or **regular entity**: Has a key attribute

A weak entity is usually related to another strong entity. This strong entity is called the **identifying entity**. Weak entities have a partial key, aka discriminator, which is an attribute that can uniquely identify the weak entity, and it is related to the identifying entity. In our example, if we assume that the search key is distinct each time the user searches for cars, then the search key is the partial key. The weak entity symbol is distinguished by surrounding the entity box with a double line.

The next image shows the preliminary design of car portal application. The user entity has several attributes. The name attribute is a composite attribute, and email is a key attribute. The seller entity is a specialization of the user entity. The total rank is a derived attribute calculated by aggregating the user ratings and the number of advertisements. The color attribute of the car is multi-valued. The seller can be rated by the users for certain advertisements; this relation is a ternary relation, because the rating involves three entities which are car, seller, and user. The car picture is a subpart attribute of the advertisement. The following diagram shows that the car can be advertised more than once by different sellers. In the real world, this makes sense, because one could ask more than one seller to sell his car.

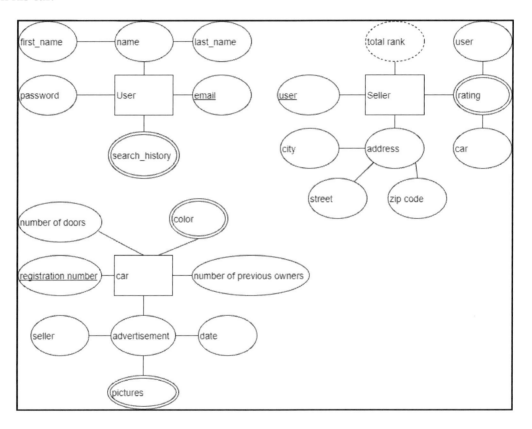

When an attribute of one entity refers to another entity, some relationships exist. In the ER model, these references should not be modeled as attributes but as relationships or weak entities. Similar to entities, there are two classes of relationships: weak and strong. Weak relationships associate the weak entities with other entities. Relationships can have attributes as entities. In our example, the car is advertised by the seller; the advertisement date is a property of the relationship.

Relationships have cardinality constraints to limit the possible combinations of entities that participate in a relationship. The cardinality constraint of car and seller is 1:N; the car is advertised by one seller, and the seller can advertise many cars. The participation between seller and user is called total participation, and is denoted by a double line. This means that a seller cannot exist alone, and he must be a user.

The many-to-many relationship cardinality constraint is denoted by N:M to emphasize different participation from the entities.

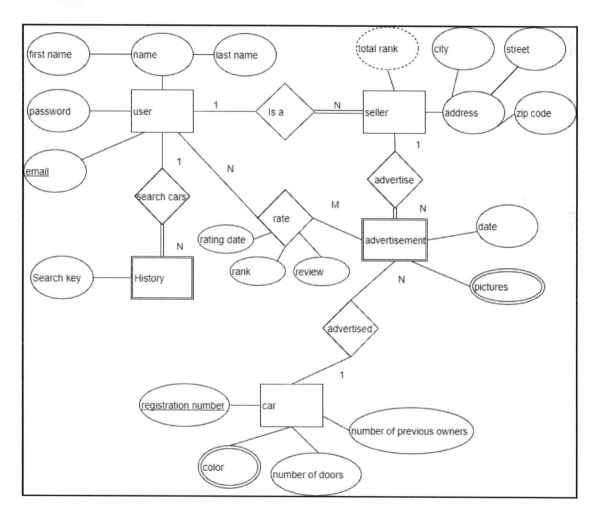

Up until now, only the basic concepts of ER diagrams have been covered. Some concepts such as (min, max) cardinality notation, ternary/n-ary relationships, generalization, specialization, and **enhanced entity relation diagrams** (**EER**) have not been discussed.

Mapping ER to relations

The rules to map an ER diagram to a set of relations (that is, the database schema) are almost straightforward but not rigid. One could model an entity as an attribute, and then refine it to a relationship. An attribute which belongs to several entities can be promoted to be an independent entity. The most common rules are listed as follows (note that only basic rules have been covered, and the list is not exhaustive):

- Map regular entities to relations, If entities have composite attributes, then include all the subparts of the attributes. Pick one of the key attributes as a primary key.
- Map weak entities to relations, include simple attributes and the subparts of the composite attributes. Add a foreign key to reference the identifying entity. The primary key is normally the combination of the partial key and the foreign key.
- If a relationship has an attribute and the relation cardinality is 1:1, then the relation attribute can be assigned to one of the participating entities.
- If a relationship has an attribute and the relation cardinality is 1:N, then the relation attribute can be assigned to the participating entity on the N side.
- Map many-to-many relationships, also known as N:M, to a new relation. Add foreign keys to reference the participating entities. The primary key is the composition of foreign keys.
- Map a multi-valued attribute to a relation. Add a foreign key to reference the entity that owns the multi-valued attribute. The primary key is the composition of the foreign key and the multi-valued attribute.

UML class diagrams

Unified modeling language (**UML**) is a standard developed by the **Object Management Group** (**OMG**). UML diagrams are widely used in modeling software solutions, and there are several types of UML diagrams for different modeling purposes including class, use case, activity, and implementation diagrams.

A class diagram can represent several types of associations, that is, the relationship between classes. They can depict attributes as well as methods. An ER diagram can be easily translated into a UML class diagram. UML class diagrams also have the following advantages:

- **Code reverse engineering**: The database schema can be easily reversed to generate a UML class diagram
- **Modeling extended relational database objects**: Modern relational databases have several object types such as sequences, views, indexes, functions, and stored procedures. UML class diagrams have the capability to represent these objects types

Summary

The design of a database management system is affected by the CAP theorem. Relational databases and NoSQL databases are not rivals but complementary. One can utilize different database categories in a single software application. In certain scenarios, one can use the key-value store as a cache engine on top of the relational database to gain performance.

Relational and object-relational databases are the market-dominant databases. Relational databases are based on the concept of relation and have a very robust mathematical model. Object-relational databases such as PostgreSQL overcome the limitations of relational databases by introducing complex data types, inheritance, and rich extensions.

Relational databases are based on the relation, tuple, and attribute concepts. They ensure data validity and consistency by employing several techniques such as entity integrity, constraints, referential integrity, and data normalization.

The next chapter, provides first-hand experience in installing the PostgreSQL server and client tools on different platforms. The next chapter also introduces PostgreSQL capabilities, such as out-of-the-box replication support and its very rich data types.

2
PostgreSQL in Action

PostgreSQL (pronounced Post-Gres-Q-L) or **postgres** for short is an open source object relational database management system. It emphasizes extensibility and creativity as well as compatibility. It competes with the major relational database vendors such as Oracle, MySQL, SQL servers, and others. It is used by different sectors including government agencies and the public and private sectors. It is a cross-platform DBMS, and runs on most modern operating systems including Windows, macOS, and Linux flavors. It conforms to SQL and is ACID-compliant.

In this chapter, we will explore several topics including:

- PostgreSQL history.
- Selected PostgreSQL forks.
- Companies utilizing PostgreSQL and success stories
- PostgreSQL usage pattern.
- PostgreSQL architecture, capabilities and features.
- PostgreSQL installation on Linux as well as windows.
- PostgreSQL client tools with emphases on `psql` because it is often used on a daily basis.

An overview of PostgreSQL

PostgreSQL (`http://www.PostgreSQL.org/`) has many rich features. It provides enterprise-level services including performance, unique features, and scalability. It has a very supportive community and very good documentation.

PostgreSQL history

PostgreSQL has started as a research project in the **University of California at Berkeley (UCB)**, then it has been developed by the community in 1996, up till now PostgreSQL is actively developed by the PostgreSQL community as well as universities. The following time frames shows the history of PostgreSQL development:

- **1977-1985, the Ingres projec**t: Michael Stonebraker created an RDBMS based on the formal relational model
- **1986-1994, postgres**: Michael Stonebraker created postgres in order to support complex data types and the object relational model
- **1995, Postgres95**: Andrew Yu and Jolly Chen changed the postgres PostQUEL query language with an extended subset of SQL
- **1996, PostgreSQL**: Several developers dedicated a lot of labor and time to stabilize postgres95. The first open source version was released on January 29, 1997. With the introduction of new features, enhancements, and due to it being an open source project, the postgres95 name was changed to PostgreSQL.
- PostgreSQL began at version 6, with a very strong starting point due to the advantage of several years of research and development. Being an open source project with a very good reputation, PostgreSQL attracted hundreds of developers. Currently, PostgreSQL has an uncountable number of extensions and a very active community.

The advantages of PostgreSQL

PostgreSQL provides many features that attract developers, administrators, architects, and companies.

Business advantages of PostgreSQL

PostgreSQL is a free **open source software** (**OSS**). It is released under the PostgreSQL license. The PostgreSQL license is highly permissive, and PostgreSQL is not subject to monopoly and acquisition--due to which, companies have the following advantages:

- No associated licensing cost to PostgreSQL.
- Unlimited number of deployments of PostgreSQL.
- More profitable business model.

- PostgreSQL is SQL standards compliant; thus, finding professional developers is not very difficult. PostgreSQL is easy to learn, and porting code from one database vendor to PostgreSQL is cost-efficient. Also, the PostgreSQL administrative tasks are easy to automate, thus reducing the staffing cost significantly.
- PostgreSQL is cross-platform, and it has drivers for all modern programming languages, so there is no need to change the company policy regarding the software stack in order to use PostgreSQL.
- PostgreSQL is scalable and gives high performance.
- PostgreSQL is very reliable; it rarely crashes. Also, PostgreSQL is ACID compliant, which means that it can tolerate some hardware failure. In addition to that, it can be configured and installed as a cluster to ensure **high availability (HA)**.

PostgreSQL user advantages

PostgreSQL is very attractive for developers, administrators, and architects. It has rich features that enable developers to perform tasks in an agile way. The following are some of the features that are attractive to developers:

- A new release almost every year; there have been 24 major releases until now, starting from postgres 6.0.
- Very good documentation and an active community enables developers to find and solve problems quickly. The PostgreSQL manual is over 2,500 pages.
- A rich extension repository enables developers to focus on business logic. Also, it enables developers to meet requirement changes easily.
- The source code is available free of charge. It can be customized and extended without huge effort.
- Rich clients and administrative tools enable developers to perform routine tasks such as describing database objects, exporting and importing data, and dumping and restoring databases very quickly.
- Database administration tasks do not require a lot of time and can be automated.
- PostgreSQL can be integrated easily with other database management systems giving the software architecture a good flexibility for implementing software designs.

PostgreSQL applications

PostgreSQL can be used with a variety of applications. The main PostgreSQL application domains can be classified into two categories:

- **Online transactional processing (OLTP)**: **OLTP** is characterized by a large amount of insert , update, and delete operations, very fast processing of operations, and the maintaining of data integrity in a multi-access environment. Performance is measured in the number of transactions per second.
- **Online analytical processing (OLAP)**: **OLAP** is characterized by a small amount of requests, complex queries which involve data aggregation, huge amounts of data from different sources and with different formats, data mining, and historical data analysis.

OLTP is used to model business operations such as **customer relationship management (CRM)**. For example, the car web portal example in `Chapter 01`, *Relational Databases*, is an example of an OLTP application. OLAP applications are used for business intelligence, decision support, reporting, and planning. An OLTP database size is relatively small as compared to an OLAP database. OLTP normally follows relational model concepts, such as normalization, when designing the database, while OLAP has less relation; the schema often has the shape of a star or a snowflake. Finally, the data is denormalized.

In the car web portal example, we could have another database to store and maintain all the *sellers* and *users* historical data to analyze user preferences and seller activities. This database is an example of an OLAP application.

Unlike OLTP, OLAP's main operation is data analysis and retrieval. OLAP data is often generated by a process called **ETL (extract, transform, and load)** processes. ETL is used to load data in to the OLAP database from different data sources and different formats. PostgreSQL can be used out of the box for OLTP applications. For OLAP, there are many extensions and tools to support it such as **foreign data wrappers (FDW)**, table partitioning, and recently, parallel query execution.

Success stories

PostgreSQL is used in many application domains including communication, medical, geographical, and e-commerce applications. Many companies provide consultation as well as commercial services, such as migrating proprietary RDBMS to PostgreSQL in order to cut off the licensing costs. These companies often influence and enhance PostgreSQL by developing and submitting new features. The following are a few companies that have used PostgreSQL:

- Skype uses PostgreSQL to store user chats and activities. Skype has also affected PostgreSQL by developing many tools called **SkyTools.**
- Instagram is a social networking service that enables its user to share pictures and photos.
- The **American Chemical Society (ACS)** uses PostgreSQL to store more than one terabyte of data for the journal archive.

In addition to the companies mentioned in the preceding list, PostgreSQL is used by HP, VMware, and Heroku. PostgreSQL is used by many scientific communities and organizations, such as NASA, due to its extensibility and rich data types.

Forks

A fork is an independent development of a software project based on another project. there are more than 20 PostgreSQL forks; PostgreSQL extensible APIs make PostgreSQL a great candidate for forking. Over the years, many groups forked PostgreSQL and contributed their findings to PostgreSQL.

HadoopDB is a hybrid between the PostgreSQL RDBMS and MapReduce technologies to target analytical workload. The following is a list of the popular PostgreSQL forks:

- **Greenplum** is built on the foundation of PostgreSQL. It utilizes the shared-nothing and **massively parallel processing (MPP)** architectures. It is used as a data warehouse and for analytical workloads. Greenplum started as proprietary software and open sourced in 2015.
- The **EnterpriseDB Advanced Server** is a proprietary DBMS that provides Oracle with the capability to cap the oracle fees.
- **Postgres-XC (eXtensible Cluster)** is a multi-master PostgreSQL cluster based on the shared-nothing architecture. It emphasis write-scalability, and provides the same APIs to applications as PostgreSQL.

- **Vertica** is a column-oriented database system that was started by Michael Stonebraker in 2005, and was acquisitioned by HP in 2011. Vertica reused the SQL parser, semantic analyzer, and standard SQL rewrites from the PostgreSQL implementation.
- **Netzza**, a popular data warehouse appliances solution, was started as a PostgreSQL fork.
- **Amazon Redshift** is a popular data warehouse management system based on PostgreSQL 8.0.2. It is mainly designed for OLAP applications.

PostgreSQL architecture

PostgreSQL uses the client/server model, where the client and server programs can be on different hosts. The communication between the client and server is normally done via TCP/IP protocols or via Linux sockets. PostgreSQL can handle multiple connections from a client. A common PostgreSQL program consists of the following operating system processes:

- **Client process or program (frontend)**: The database frontend application performs a database action. The frontend can be a web server that wants to display a web page or a command-line tool to do maintenance tasks. PostgreSQL provides frontend tools such as `psql`, `createdb`, `dropdb`, and `createuser`.
- **Server process (backend)**: The server process manages database files, accepts connections from client applications, and performs actions on behalf of the client. The server process name is postgres. PostgreSQL forks a new process for each new connection; thus, client and server processes communicate with each other without the intervention of the server main process (postgres), and they have a certain lifetime that is determined by accepting and terminating a client connection.

The aforementioned abstract conceptual PostgreSQL architecture gives an overview of the PostgreSQL capabilities and its interaction with the client, and the operating system. The PostgreSQL server could be divided roughly into four subsystems, as follows:

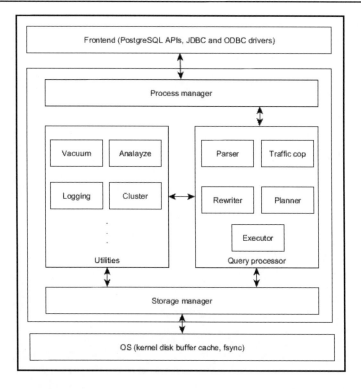

- **Process manager**: The process manager manages client connections such as forking and the terminating process.
- **Query processor**: When a client sends a query to PostgreSQL, the query is parsed by the parser, and then the traffic cop subsystem determines the query type. A utility query is passed to the utilities subsystem. Select, insert, update, and delete queries are rewritten by the rewriter following which an execution plan is generated by the planner. Finally, the query is executed and the result is returned to the client.
- **Utilities**: The utilities subsystem provides a means to maintain the database such as claiming storage, updating statistics, exporting and importing data with a certain format, and logging.
- **Storage manager**: The storage manager handles the memory cache, disk buffers, and storage allocation.

Almost all PostgreSQL components can be configured, including a logger, planner, statistical analyzer, and storage manager. PostgreSQL configuration is governed by the nature of the application, such as OLAP and OLTP.

The PostgreSQL community

PostgreSQL has a very cooperative, active, and organized community. In the last 8 years, the PostgreSQL community has published eight major releases. Announcements are brought to the developers via the PostgreSQL weekly newsletter.

There are dozens of mailing lists organized into categories such as user, developer, and associations. Examples of user mailing lists are pgsql-general, psql-doc, and psql-bugs. pgsql-general is a very important mailing list for beginners. All non bugs related questions regarding PostgreSQL installation, tuning, basic administration, PostgreSQL features, and general discussions are submitted to this list.

The PostgreSQL community runs a blog aggregation service called **Planet PostgreSQL** (`planet.PostgreSQL.org`). Several PostgreSQL developers and companies use this service to share their experience and knowledge.

PostgreSQL capabilities

PostgreSQL provides enterprise-level services that guarantee the continuation of the business. For example, PostgreSQL supports replication, this enables the developers to provide high availability **(HA)** solutions. PostgreSQL can integrate data form different data sources , this makes it easy for developer to use it for extract , transform, and load **(ETL)** jobs .In addition to that PostgreSQL security is treated as a first class citizen and not as a good to have feature, security updates are shipped in minor releases. Finally, the features of PostgreSQL is uncountable, PostgreSQL provides advanced SQL statements, very rich extensions, and interactive tools.

Replication

Replication allows data from one database server to be replicated to another server. Replication is used mainly to achieve the following:

- **High availability**: A second server can take over if the primary server fails
- **Load balancing**: Several servers can serve the same requests
- **Faster execution**: A query is executed on several machines at once to gain performance

PostgreSQL supports replication out of the box via streaming replication. **Streaming replication** is a master-slave replication that uses file-based log shipping. Streaming replication is a binary replication technique, because SQL statements are not analyzed. It is based on taking a snapshot of the master node, and then shipping the changes—the WAL files—from the master node to the slave node and replaying them on the slave. The master can be used for read/write operations, and the slave can be used to serve read requests. Streaming replication is relatively easy to set up and configure; it can support synchronous and asynchronous replications as well as cascading replication. In synchronous replication, a data modifying operation must be committed on all servers in order to be considered successful. In cascading replication, one could add a replica to a slave. This allows PostgreSQL to scale horizontally for read operations.

In PostgreSQL 10, additional replication technique is added, which is logical replication; unlike streaming replication, which replicates the binary data bit by bit, logical replication translate the WAL files back to logical changes. This gives us the freedom to have more control over the replication such as applying filters. For example, in logical replication, parts of data can be replicated, while in streaming replication the slave is a clone of the master. Another important aspect of logical replication is being able to write on the replicated server such as extra indexes, as well as temporary tables. Finally, one can replicate data from several servers and combine it on a single server.

In addition to PostgreSQL replication techniques, there are several other open source solutions to target different workloads:

- **Slony-1**: This is a master to multiple slave replication systems. Unlike PostgreSQL, it can be used with different server versions. So, one could replicate the 9.6 server data to the 10 server. Slony is very useful for upgrading servers without downtime.
- **pgpool-II**: This is middleware between PostgreSQL and the client. In addition to replication, it can be used for connection pooling, load balancing, and parallel query execution.
- **Distributed Replicated Block Device (DRBD)**: A general solution for HA. It can be understood as a network RAID-1.

Security

PostgreSQL supports several authentication methods including trust, password, LDAB, GSSAPI, SSPI, Kerberos, ident-based, RADUIS, certificate, and PAM authentication. All database vulnerabilities are listed in the PostgreSQL security information web page—http://www.PostgreSQL.org/support/security/—with information about the affected version, vulnerability class, and the affected component.

The PostgreSQL security updates are made available as minor updates. Also, known security issues are always fixed with the next major releases. Publishing security updates in minor updates makes it easy for a PostgreSQL administrator to keep PostgreSQL secure and up to date with minimal downtime.

PostgreSQL can control the database object access at several levels including database, table, view, function, sequence, and column. This enables PostgreSQL to have a great authorization control.

PostgreSQL can use encryption to protect data by hardware encryption. Also, one can encrypt certain information by utilizing the pgcrypto extension.

Extension

PostgreSQL can be extended to support new data types. PostgreSQL provides the CREATE EXTENSION command to load extensions to the current database. Also, PostgreSQL has a central distribution network (**PGXN**)—www.pgxn.org—which allows users to explore and download extensions. When installing the PostgreSQL binaries, the postgresql-contib package contains many useful extensions such as tablefunc, which allows table pivoting and pgcrypto extension; the README file in the installation directory contains the summary information.

The ability of PostgreSQL to support extensions is a result of the following features:

- **PostgreSQL data types**: PostgreSQL has very rich data types. It supports primitive data types as well as some primitive data structures, such as arrays, out of the box. In addition to that, it supports the following complex data types:
    - **Geometric data types**: Including point, line segment (lseg), path, polygon, and box
    - **Network address types**: Including cidr, inet, and macaddr
    - **tsvector and tsquery**: This is a sorted list of lexemes that enables postgres to perform full text search

- **Universal unique identifiers (UUID)**: UUID solves many problems related to databases, such as offline data generation
- **NoSQL**: It supports several NoSQL data types including XML, Hstore, and JSONB.Enum, range and domain are user-defined data types with specific constraints, such as a set of allowed values, data range constraint, and check constraints
- Composite data type is a user-defined data type, where an attribute is composed of several attributes

- **Supported languages**: PostgreSQL allows functions to be written in several languages. The PostgreSQL community supports the following languages: SQL, C, Python, PL/pgSQL, Perl, and Tcl. In addition to these, there are many externally maintained procedural languages, including Java, R, PHP, Ruby, and UNIX shell.

The following example shows you how to create a new composite type called phone_number. An equality operator is also created to check whether two phone numbers are equal by comparing the area code and the line number:

```
--This example shows how to create a composite data type.
CREATE TYPE phone_number AS (
    area_code varchar(3),
    line_number varchar(7)
);
CREATE OR REPLACE FUNCTION phone_number_equal (phone_
number,phone_number) RETURNS boolean AS $$
BEGIN
    IF $1.area_code=$2.area_code AND $1.line_number=$2.line_number THEN
        RETURN TRUE ;
    ELSE
        RETURN FALSE;
    END IF;
END; $$ LANGUAGE plpgsql;
CREATE OPERATOR = (
LEFTARG = phone_number,
RIGHTARG = phone_number,
PROCEDURE = phone_number_equal
);
--For test purpose
SELECT row('123','222244')::phone_number = row('1','222244')::phone_number;
```

The above examples show how one can create new data types. a Data type called `phone_number` is created. The `phone_number` datatype is composed of two atomic datatypes which are `area_code` and `line_number`. The operator = is overloaded to handle also the equality of the new datatype. To define the behavior of = operator , one need to define the operator arguments and the function that handles the arguments, and in this case the function is `phone_number_equal` and the arguments are of type `phone_number`.

NoSQL capabilities

PostgreSQL is more than a relational database and an SQL language. PostgreSQL is now home to different NoSQL data types. The power of PostgreSQL and schemaless data stores enable the developers to build reliable and flexible applications in an agile way.

PostgreSQL supports the **JavaScript Simple Object Notation (JSON)** data type, which is often used to share data across different systems in modern RESTful web applications. In PostgreSQL release 9.4, PostgreSQL introduced another structured binary format to save JSON documents instead of using the JSON format in the prior versions. The new data type is called JSONB. This data type eliminates the need to parse a JSON document before it is committed to the database. In other words, PostgreSQL can ingest a JSON document at a speed comparable with document databases, while still maintaining compliance with ACID. In PostgreSQL version 9.5 several functions are added to make handling JSON documents much easier. In version 10, full text search is supported for JSON and JSONB documents.

Key/value pairs are also supported by the PostgreSQL hstore extension. The Hstore is used to store semi-structured data, and it can be used in several scenarios to decrease the number of attributes that are rarely used and often contain null values.

Finally, PostgreSQL supports the Extensible Markup Language (XML) data type. XML is very flexible and it is often used to define document formats. XML is used in RSS, Atom, SOAP, and XHTML. PostgreSQL supports several XML functions to generate and create XML documents. Also, it supports xpath to find information in an XML document.

Foreign data wrappers

In 2011, PostgreSQL 9.1 was released with a read-only support for SQL / Management of External Data (MED) ISO/IEC 9075-9:2003 standard. SQL/MED defines foreign data wrappers (FDW) to allow the relational database to manage external data. Foreign data wrappers can be used to achieve data integration in a federated database system environment. PostgreSQL supports RDBMS, NoSQL, and file foreign data wrappers including Oracle, Redis, Mongodb, and delimited files.

A simple use case for FDW is to have one database server for analytical purposes, and then ship the result of this server to another server that works as a caching layer.

Also, FDW can be used to test data changes. Imagine you have two databases, one with different data due to applying a certain development patch. One could use FDW to assess the effect of this patch by comparing the data from the two databases.

PostgreSQL supports `postgres_fdw` starting from release 9.3. `postgres_fdw` is used to enable data sharing and access between different PostgreSQL databases. It supports the `SELECT`, `INSERT`, `UPDATE`, and `DELETE` operations on foreign tables.

The following example shows you how to read **comma-separated value (CSV)** files using FDW; one can read CSV files to parse logs. Let's assume that we would like to read the database logs generated by PostgreSQL. This is quite useful in production environment as one can have statistics about executed queries; the table structure can be found in the documentation at `https://www.PostgreSQL.org/docs/current/static/runtime-config-logging.html`. To enable CSV logging, one needs to change the following values in `PostgreSQL.conf`. For simplicity, all statements will be logged but this is not recommended in a production environment:

```
log_destination = 'csvlog'
logging_collector = on
log_filename = 'PostgreSQL.log'
log_statement = 'all'
```

For the changes to take effect, one needs to restart PostgreSQL:

```
$sudo service PostgreSQL restart
```

To install the file Foreign data wrapper, we need to run the following command:

```
postgres=# CREATE EXTENSION file_fdw ;
CREATE EXTENSION
```

To access the file, we need to create FDW server as follows:

```
postgres=# CREATE SERVER fileserver FOREIGN DATA WRAPPER file_fdw;
CREATE SERVER
```

Also, we need to create an FDW table and link it to the log file; in our case, it is located in the log folder in PostgreSQL cluster directory:

```
postgres=# CREATE FOREIGN TABLE postgres_log
(
  log_time timestamp(3) with time zone,
  user_name text,
  database_name text,
  process_id integer,
  connection_from text,
  session_id text,
  session_line_num bigint,
  command_tag text,
  session_start_time timestamp with time zone,
  virtual_transaction_id text,
  transaction_id bigint,
  error_severity text,
  sql_state_code text,
  message text,
  detail text,
  hint text,
  internal_query text,
  internal_query_pos integer,
  context text,
  query text,
  query_pos integer,
  location text,
  application_name text
) SERVER fileserver OPTIONS ( filename
'/var/lib/PostgreSQL/10/main/log/PostgreSQL.csv', header 'true', format
'csv' );
CREATE FOREIGN TABLE
```

To test our example, let us count how many log lines are logged:

```
postgres=# SELECT count(*) FROM postgres_log;
 count
-------
    62
(1 row)
```

Performance

PostgreSQL has a proven performance. It employs several techniques to improve concurrency and scalability, including the following:

- **PostgreSQL locking system**: PostgreSQL provides several types of locks at the table and row levels. PostgreSQL is able to use more granular locks that prevent locking/blocking more than necessary; this increases concurrency and decreases the blocking time.

- **Indexes**: PostgreSQL provides six types of indexes: B-Tree, hash, **generalized inverted index (GIN)**, and the **Generalized Search Tree (GiST)** index, SP-GiST, and **Block Range Indexes (BRIN)**. Each index type can be used for a certain scenario. For example, B-tree can be used for equality and range queries efficiently. GIST can be used for text search and for geospatial data. PostgreSQL supports partial, unique, and multicolumn indexes. It also supports indexes on expressions and operator classes.

- **Explain, analyze, vacuum, and cluster**: PostgreSQL provides several commands to boost performance and provide transparency. The `explain` command shows the execution plan of an SQL statement. One can change some parameter settings such as memory settings, and then compare the execution plan before and after the change. The `analyze` command is used to collect the statistics on tables and columns. The `vacuum` command is used for garbage collection to reclaim unused hard disk space. The `cluster` command is used to arrange data physically on the hard disk. All these commands can be configured based on the database workload.

- **Table inheritance and constraint exclusion**: Table inheritance allows the creation of tables with the same structure easily. Those tables are used to store subsets of data based on a certain criteria. This allows a very fast retrieval of information in certain scenarios, because only a subset of data is accessed when answering a query,

- **Very rich SQL constructs**: PostgreSQL supports very rich SQL constructs. It supports correlated and uncorrelated subqueries. It supports **common table expression (CTE)**, window functions, and recursive queries. Once developers have learned these SQL constructs, they will be able to write a crisp SQL code very quickly. Moreover, they will be able to write complex queries with minimal effort. The PostgreSQL community keeps adding new SQL features in each release; in release 9.6, three SQL clauses were added: `GROUPING SETS`, `CUBE`, and `ROLLUP`.

Installing PostgreSQL

PostgreSQL can be installed on almost all modern operating systems. It can be installed on all recent Linux distributions, Windows 2000 SP4 and later, FreeBSD, OpenBSD, macOS, AIX, and Solaris. Also, PostgreSQL can work on various CPU architectures including x86, x86_64, IA64, and others. One can check whether a platform (operating system and CPU architecture combination) is supported by exploring the PostgreSQL Build farm (`http://buildfarm.PostgreSQL.org/`). One can compile and install PostgreSQL from the source code or download its binary and install it.

In order to automate PostgreSQL installation and to reduce server administrative tasks, it is recommended to use PostgreSQL binaries, which come with the operating system packaging system. This approach normally has one drawback: not up-to-date binaries. However, the PostgreSQL official website maintains the binaries for the most common platforms, including BSD, Linux, macOS, Solaris and Windows.

The instructions as well as the binaries to install PostgreSQL can be found on the official web page `https://www.PostgreSQL.org/download/`. The following image shows the instruction to add **APT** repository to Ubuntu Zesty release. Note that, the installation instructions are generated based on the release name.

To use the apt repository, follow these steps:

- Zesty (17.04) ▼
- Create the file */etc/apt/sources.list.d/pgdg.list*, and add a line for the repository

  ```
  deb http://apt.postgresql.org/pub/repos/apt/ zesty-pgdg main
  ```

- Import the repository signing key, and update the package lists

  ```
  wget --quiet -O - https://www.postgresql.org/media/keys/ACCC4CF8.asc | \
    sudo apt-key add -
  sudo apt-get update
  ```

Installing PostgreSQL using Advanced Package Tool

Advanced Package Tool (**APT**) is used to handle the installation and removal of software on Debian and Debian-based distributions such as Ubuntu operating system.

As has been stated earlier, recent PostgreSQL binaries might not yet be integrated with the official Debian and Ubuntu repositories. To setup PostgreSQL `apt` repository on Debian or Ubuntu one can execute the following:

```
$sudo sh -c 'echo "deb http://apt.PostgreSQL.org/pub/repos/apt/
$(lsb_release -cs)-pgdg main" > /etc/apt/sources.list.d/pgdg.list'
$wget --quiet -O - https://www.PostgreSQL.org/media/keys/ACCC4CF8.asc |
sudo apt-key add -
$sudo apt-get update
```

After adding a new `apt` repository, it is good to upgrade your system as follows:

```
$sudo apt-get upgrade
```

Client installation

If you have a PostgreSQL server already installed and you need to interact with it, then you need to install the `posttgresql-client` software package. In order to do so, open a terminal and execute the following command:

```
sudo apt-get install PostgreSQL-client-10
```

With the installation of `postgrsql-client-10`, several tools are installed including the PostgreSQL interactive terminal (`psql`), which is a very powerful interactive frontend tool for PostgreSQL. To see the full list of installed programs, one can browse the installation directory. Note that the installation path might vary depending on the installed PostgreSQL version and also depending on the operating system:

```
ls /usr/lib/PostgreSQL/10/bin/
clusterdb createdb createuser dropdb dropuser pg_basebackup pg_dump
pg_dumpall pg_isready pg_receiveWAL pg_recvlogical pg_restore psql
reindexdb vacuumdb
```

In order to connect to an existing PostgreSQL server using `psql`, one needs to specify the connection string, which might include the host, the database, the port, and the username.

Another powerful frontend **graphical user interface (GUI)** tool is pgadmin4, which is used for PostgreSQL administration and development. pgAdmin is favored by beginners, while psql can be used for shell scripting.

pgadmin4 has many features, such as cross-platform, web-based, server and desktop modes, and so on. In order to install pgAdmin in desktop mode, one should run the following command:

```
# get virtual environment and pip
sudo apt-get install pip
sudo pip install --upgrade pip
sudo pip install virtualenvwrapper

# create a virtual environment and activate it
virtualenv pgadmin && cd pgadmin && source bin/activate

# get recent version f pgadmin and install it.
wget
https://ftp.PostgreSQL.org/pub/pgadmin/pgadmin4/v2.0/pip/pgadmin4-2.0-py2.p
y3-none-any.whl
pip install pgadmin4-2.0-py2.py3-none-any.whl

# create a configuration based on config.py and run it
cp ./lib/python2.7/site-packages/pgadmin4/config.py ./lib/python2.7/site-
packages/pgadmin4/config-local.py
python ./lib/python2.7/site-packages/pgadmin4/pgAdmin4.py
```

Another GUI tool to interact with PostgreSQL is DBeaver https://dbeaver.jkiss.org/. This tool provides a universal SQL client for many databases including PostgreSQL.

Server installation

In order to install the server, one should run the following command:

```
$sudo apt-get install PostgreSQL-10
```

The installation will give you information about the location of the PostgreSQL configuration files, data location, locale, port, and PostgreSQL status, as shown in the following output:

```
Creating config file /etc/PostgreSQL-common/createcluster.conf with new
version
Setting up PostgreSQL-10 (10.0-1.pgdg80+1) ...
Creating new PostgreSQL cluster 10/main ...
/usr/lib/PostgreSQL/10/bin/initdb -D /var/lib/PostgreSQL/10/main --auth-
local peer --auth-host md5
```

```
The files belonging to this database system will be owned by user
"postgres".
This user must also own the server process.

The database cluster will be initialized with locale "en_US.UTF-8".
The default database encoding has accordingly been set to "UTF8".
The default text search configuration will be set to "english".

Data page checksums are disabled.

fixing permissions on existing directory /var/lib/PostgreSQL/10/main ... ok
creating subdirectories ... ok
selecting default max_connections ... 100
selecting default shared_buffers ... 128MB
selecting dynamic shared memory implementation ... posix
creating configuration files ... ok
running bootstrap script ... ok
performing post-bootstrap initialization ... ok
syncing data to disk ... ok

Success. You can now start the database server using:

    /usr/lib/PostgreSQL/10/bin/pg_ctl -D /var/lib/PostgreSQL/10/main -l
logfile start

Ver Cluster Port Status Owner Data directory Log file
10 main 5432 down postgres /var/lib/PostgreSQL/10/main
/var/log/PostgreSQL/PostgreSQL-10-main.log
update-alternatives: using
/usr/share/PostgreSQL/10/man/man1/postmaster.1.gz to provide
/usr/share/man/man1/postmaster.1.gz (postmaster.1.gz) in auto mode
Processing triggers for libc-bin (2.19-18+deb8u10) ...
Processing triggers for systemd (215-17+deb8u7) ...
```

PostgreSQL initializes a storage area on the hard disk called a database cluster. A database cluster is a collection of databases managed by a single instance of a running database server. This means that one can have more than one instance of PostgreSQL running on the same server by initializing several database clusters. These instances can be of different PostgreSQL server versions or the same version.

The database cluster locale is en_US.UTF-8 by default; when a database cluster is created, the database cluster will be initialized with the locale setting of its execution environment. This can be controlled by specifying the locale when creating a database cluster.

Another important package is `postgresql-contrib`, which contains community-approved extensions. Often, this package is provided separately. However, in PostgreSQL 10 APT repository, it has been integrated with the server package.

To check the installation, one can grep the `postgres` processes, as follows:

```
$pgrep -a postgres
3807 /usr/lib/PostgreSQL/10/bin/postgres -D /var/lib/PostgreSQL/10/main -c
config_file=/etc/PostgreSQL/10/main/PostgreSQL.conf
3809 postgres: 10/main: checkpointer process
3810 postgres: 10/main: writer process
3811 postgres: 10/main: WAL writer process
3812 postgres: 10/main: autovacuum launcher process
3813 postgres: 10/main: stats collector process
3814 postgres: 10/main: bgworker: logical replication launcher
```

The preceding query shows the server main process with two options: the -D option specifies the database cluster, and the -c option specifies the configuration file. Also, it shows many utility processes, such as `autovacuum`, and statistics collector processes.

Finally, one could also install the server and the `client` in one command, as follows:

```
sudo apt-get install PostgreSQL-10 PostgreSQL-client-10
```

Basic server configuration

In order to access the server, we need to understand the PostgreSQL authentication mechanism. On Linux systems, one can connect to PostgreSQL using a unix-socket or TCP/IP protocol. Also, PostgreSQL supports many types of authentication methods.

When a PostgreSQL server is installed, a new operating system user, as well as a database user, with the name `postgres` is created. This user can connect to the database server using peer authentication. The peer authentication gets the client's operating system username and uses it to access the databases that can be accessed. Peer authentication is supported only by local connections—connections that use Unix sockets. Peer authentication is supported by Linux distribution but not by Windows.

Client authentication is controlled by a configuration file named `pg_hba.conf`, where **pg** stands for PostgreSQL and **hba** stands for **host-based authentication**. To take a look at peer authentication, one should execute the following command:

```
grep -v '^#' /etc/PostgreSQL/10/main/pg_hba.conf|grep 'peer'
local all postgres peer
local replication all peer
```

The interpretation of the first line of the result is shown here: The postgres user can connect to all the databases using Unix-socket and the peer authentication method.

To connect to the database servers using the `postgres` user, first we need to switch the operating system's current user to `postgres` and then invoke `psql`. This is done via the Linux command as follows:

```
$sudo -u postgres psql
psql (10.0)
Type "help" for help.

postgres=# SELECT version();
                                                             version
-----------------------------------------------------------------------------------
-------------------------------------------------
 PostgreSQL 10.0 on x86_64-pc-linux-gnu, compiled by gcc (Ubuntu
5.4.0-6ubuntu1~16.04.4) 5.4.0 20160609, 64-bit
(1 row)
```

The preceding query shows the `psql` interactive terminal. The select statement SELECT version (); was executed, and the PostgreSQL version information was displayed. As shown in the preceding result, the installed version is PostgreSQL 10.0.

Prior to PostgreSQL 10, the PostgreSQL version number has three digits. Major releases occur roughly on an annual basis and usually change the internal format of the data. This means that the stored data's backward compatibility between major releases is not maintained. A major release is numbered by incrementing either the first or the second digit such as 9.5 and 9.6. Minor releases are numbered by increasing the third digit of the release number, for example 9.6.1 to 9.6.2. Minor releases are only bug fixes.

In PostgreSQL 10, the versioning policy has changed, major releases are numbered by incrementing the first number that is from 10 to 11. Minor releases are numbered by incrementing the second part of the number, for example, 10.0 to 10.1.

Installing PostgreSQL on Windows

The installation of PostgreSQL on Windows is easier than Linux for beginners. One can download the PostgreSQL binaries from EnterpriseDB (https://www.enterprisedb.com/downloads/postgres-PostgreSQL-downloads#windows). The installer wizard will guide the user through the installation process. The installation wizard gives the user the ability to specify the binaries location, the database cluster location, port, the postgres user password, and the locale:

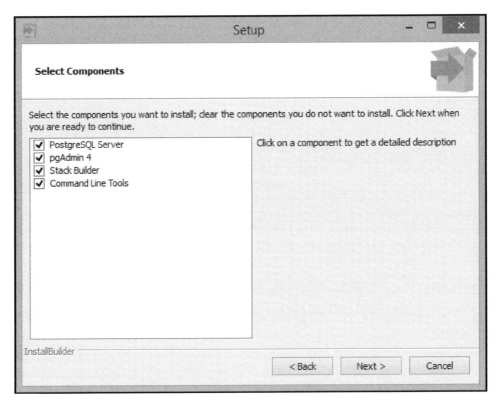

The installer will also launch the stack builder wizard, which is used to install the PostgreSQL drivers and many other utilities, as shown in the following figure:

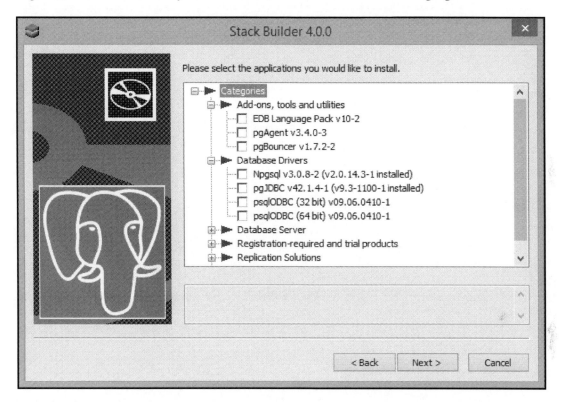

Using the `psql` client is not very convenient in the latest version of Windows due to the lack of some capabilities such as copy, paste, and resizing in the Windows command prompt (`CMD.exe`). pgAdmin is often used in the Windows operating system. Another option is to use a command prompt alternative such as `PowerShell` or a Linux emulator such as `Cygwin` and `MobaXterm`.

PostgreSQL in Windows is installed as a service; in order to validate the installation, one can view the service tab in the task manager utility.

The PostgreSQL clients

In addition to PgAdmin III and the `psql` client tools, there are a lot of vendors producing tools for PostgreSQL that cover different areas, such as database administration, modeling, development, reporting, ETL, and reverse engineering. In addition to the `psql` tool, PostgreSQL is shipped with several client tools, including the following:

- **Wrappers**: The wrappers are built around SQL commands such as CREATE USER. These wrappers facilitate the interaction between the database server and the developer, and automate the daily routine tasks.
- **Backup and replication**: PostgreSQL supports physical and logical backups. The physical backup is performed by taking a snapshot of the database files. The physical backup can be combined with WAL in order to achieve streaming replication or a hot standby solution. Logical backup is used to dump the database in the form of SQL statements. Unlike physical backup, one can dump and restore a single database.
- **Utilities**: PostgreSQL comes with several utilities to ease extraction of information and to help in diagnosing the problems.

The PostgreSQL community unifies the look and feel of the client tools as much as possible; this makes it easy to use and learn. For example, the connection options are unified across all client tools. The following list shows the connection options for `psql`, which are common for other PostgreSQL clients as well:

- `-d`: The database name
- `-h`: The host name or IP address
- `-u`: The username
- `-p`: The port

Also, most PostgreSQL clients can use the environment variables supported by `libpq`, such as PGHOST, PGDATABASE, and PGUSER. The `libpq` environment variables can be used to determine the default connection parameter values.

The psql client

The `psql` client is maintained by the PostgreSQL community, and it is a part of the PostgreSQL binary distribution. `psql` has many overwhelming features such as the following:

- **psql is configurable**: `psql` can be configured easily. The configuration might be applied to user session behavior such as `commit` and `rollback`, `psql` prompt, history files, and even shortcuts for predefined SQL statements.
- **Integration with editor and pager tools**: The `psql` query result can be directed to one's favorite pager such as less or more. Also, `psql` does not come with an editor, but it can utilize several editors. The following example shows how to use `nano` editor in editing a function as follows:

```
postgres=# \setenv PSQL_EDITOR /bin/nano
postgres=# \ef
```

- **Auto completion and SQL syntax help**: `psql` supports auto completion for database object names and SQL constructs query result format control: `psql` supports different formats such as HTML and latex. For example, when using the `\ef` meta command, a template is generated as follows:

```
CREATE FUNCTION ( )
 RETURNS
 LANGUAGE
 -- common options: IMMUTABLE STABLE STRICT SECURITY DEFINER
AS $function$

$function$
```

- The `psql` client tool is very handy in shell scripting, information retrieval, and learning the PostgreSQL internals. The following are some of the `psql` meta commands that are often used daily:
  - `\d+ [pattern]`: This describes all the relevant information for a relation. In PostgreSQL, the term relation is used for a table, view, sequence, or index.
  - `\df+ [pattern]`: This describes a function.
  - `\z [pattern]`: This shows the relation access privileges.

For shell scripting, there are several options that make `psql` very convenient:

- `-A`: The output is not aligned; by default, the output is aligned.
- `-q` (`quiet`): This option forces `psql` not to write a welcome message or any other informational output.
- `-t`: This option tells `psql` to write the tuples only, without any header information.
- `-X`: This option informs `psql` to ignore the `psql` configuration that is stored in `~/.psqlrc` file.
- `-o`: This option specifies `psql` to output the query result to a certain location.
- `-F`: This option determines the field separator between columns. This option can be used to generate CSV, which is useful to import data to Excel files.
- `PGOPTIONS`: `psql` can use `PGOPTIONS` to add command-line options to send to the server at runtime. This can be used to control statement behavior such as to allow index scan only or to specify the statement timeout.

Let's assume that we would like to write a `bash` script to check the number of opened connection systems:

```
#!/bin/bash
connection_number=`PGOPTIONS='--statement_timeout=0' psql -AqXt -c"SELECT
count(*) FROM pg_stat_activity"`
```

The result of the command `psql -AqXt -d postgres -c "SELECT count(*) FROM pg_stat_activity"` is assigned to a bash variable. The options `-AqXt`, as discussed previously, cause `psql` to return only the result without any decoration, as follows:

```
$psql -AqXt -c "SELECT count(*) FROM pg_stat_activity"
1
```

psql advanced settings

The `psql` client can be personalized. The `.psqlrc` file is used to store the user preference for later use. There are several aspects of `psql` personalization, including the following:

- Look and feel
- Behavior
- Shortcuts

One can change the `psql` prompt to show the connection string information including the server name, database name, username, and port. The `psql` variables PROMPT1, PROMPT2, and PROMPT3 can be used to customize the user preference. PROMPT1 and PROMPT2 are issued when creating a new command and a command expecting more input respectively. The following example shows some of the prompt options; by default, when one connects to the database, only the name of the database is shown.

The `\set` meta command is used to assign a `psql` variable to a value. In this case, it assigns PROMPT1 to (%n@%M:%>) [%/]%R%#%x >. The percent sign (%) is used as a placeholder for substitution. The substitutions in the example will be as follows:

```
postgres=# \set PROMPT1 '(%n@%M:%>) [%/]%R%#%x > '
(postgres@[local]:5432) [postgres]=# > BEGIN;
BEGIN
(postgres@[local]:5432) [postgres]=#* > SELECT 1;
 ?column?
----------
        1
(1 row)

(postgres@[local]:5432) [postgres]=#* > SELECT 1/0;
ERROR: division by zero
(postgres@[local]:5432) [postgres]=#! > ROLLBACK;
ROLLBACK
(postgres@[local]:5432) [postgres]=# > SELECT
postgres-# 1;
```

The following list of signs are used in the previous example; the meanings of the signs are as follows:

- %M: The full host name. In the example, [local] is displayed, because we use the Linux socket.
- %>: The PostgreSQL port number.
- %n: The database session username.
- %/: The current database name.
- %R: Normally substituted by =; ; if the session is disconnected for a certain reason, then it is substituted with (!).
- %#: Used to distinguish super users from normal users. The (#) hash sign indicates that the user is a super user. For a normal user, the sign is (>).
- %x: The transaction status. The * sign is used to indicate the transaction block, and the (!) sign to indicate a failed transaction block.

Notice how PROMPT2 was issued when the SQL statement SELECT 1 was written over two lines. Finally, notice the * sign, which indicates a transaction block.

In the psql tool, one can create shortcuts that can be used for a common query such as showing the current database activities using variables assignment \set meta command. Again, the : symbol is used for substitution. The following example shows how one can add a shortcut for a query:

```
postgres=# \set activity 'SELECT pid, query, backend_type, state FROM
pg_stat_activity';
postgres=# :activity;
  pid | query | backend_type | state
-------+-------------------------------------------------------------------+---
-----------------+--------
 3814 | | background worker |
 3812 | | autovacuum launcher |
 22827 | SELECT pid, query, backend_type, state FROM pg_stat_activity; |
client backend | active
 3810 | | background writer |
 3809 | | checkpointer |
 3811 | | WALwriter |
(6 rows)
```

In psql, one can configure the transaction execution behavior. psql provides three variables, which are ON_ERROR_ROLLBACK , ON_ERROR_STOP, and AUTOCOMMIT:

- ON_ERROR_STOP: By default, psql continues executing commands even after encountering an error. This is useful for some operations, such as dumping and restoring the whole database, where some errors can be ignored, such as missing extensions. However, in developing applications, such as deploying new application, errors cannot be ignored, and it is good to set this variable to ON. This variable is useful with the -f, \i, \ir options.

```
$ echo -e 'SELECT 1/0;\nSELECT 1;'>/tmp/test_rollback.sql
$ psql
psql (10.0)
Type "help" for help.

postgres=# \i /tmp/test_rollback.sql
psql:/tmp/test_rollback.sql:1: ERROR: division by zero
 ?column?
----------
        1
(1 row)

postgres=# \set ON_ERROR_STOP true
```

```
postgres=# \i /tmp/test_rollback.sql
psql:/tmp/test_rollback.sql:1: ERROR: division by zero
```

- ON_ERROR_ROLLBACK: When an error occurs in a transaction block, one of three actions is performed depending on the value of this variable. When the variable value is off, then the whole transaction is rolled back—this is the default behavior. When the variable value is on, then the error is ignored, and the transaction is continued. The interactive mode ignores the errors in the interactive sessions, but not when reading files.
- AUTOCOMMIT: This option causes SQL statements outside an explicit transaction block to be committed implicitly. To reduce human error, one can turn this option off.

Disabling the AUTOCOMMIT setting is quite useful because it allows the developer to rollback the unwanted changes. Note that when deploying or amending the database on life systems, it is recommended to make the changes within a transaction block and also prepare a rollback script.

Finally, the \timing meta command in psql shows the query execution time and is often used to quickly assess performance issues. The \pset meta command can also be used to control the output formatting.

PostgreSQL utility tools

Several PostgreSQL utility tools are wrappers around SQL constructs. These tools are used to create and drop databases, users and languages. For example, dropdb and createdb commands are wrappers around DROP DATABASE [IF EXISTS] and CREATE DATABASE respectively.

Also PostgreSQL provide tools to maintain the system objects, mainly clusterdb and reindexdb. The clusterdb is a wrapper around the CLUSTER statement, which is used to physically reorder the table based on a certain index information. This can increase database performance read operation due to the locality of reference principles, mainly spatial locality. Clustering the table helps in retrieving data from adjacent storage blocks and thus reduces hard disk access cost.

reindexdb tool is a wrapper a round around reindex SQL statement. There are several reasons to reindex an index, for example, the index might get corrupted--which rarely happens in practice--or bloated.

In addition to the previous ones, postgreSQL provides tools for the following:

- **Physical backup**: This is used to back up the PostgreSQL database files by taking a hard disk snapshot. This method is a very fast way to create a backup, but the backup can only be restored on compatible PostgreSQL versions. The tool pg_basebackup is used for this purpose. The pg_basebackup is often used for setting up streaming replication as the slave is a clone of a master.
- **Logical backup**: This is used to back up the database objects in the form of SQL statements such as CREATE TABLE, CREATE VIEW, COPY, and so on. The generated backup can be restored on different PostgreSQL cluster versions, but it is slow. The tools pg_dump, pg_dumpall are used to dump a single database or a database cluster respectively. pg_dump also can be used to dump a specific relation or set of relation and schema. Also it has a lot of features such as dumping schema only or data only. pg_dumpall internally uses pg_dump to dump all databases on the cluster. Finally, the pg_restore tool is used to restore the dumps generated by pg_dump or pg_dumpall.

pg_dump does not dump the CREATE DATABASE statement command. For example, one can dump a database called customer to another database called client. Due to this, if you have a special privileges assigned to the database such as CONNECT, you need to assign these privileges to the new database.

Summary

PostgreSQL is an open source, object-oriented relational database system. It supports many advanced features and complies with the ANSI-SQL standard. It has won industry recognition and user appreciation. The PostgreSQL slogan *The world's most advanced open source database* reflects the sophistication of the PostgreSQL features. It is a result of many years of research and collaboration between academia and industry. Start-up companies often favor PostgreSQL due to licensing costs and it can aid profitable business models. PostgreSQL is also favored by many developers because of its capabilities and advantages.

PostgreSQL can be used for OLTP and OLAP applications. It is ACID compliant; thus, it can be used out of the box for OLTP applications. For OLAP applications, PostgreSQL supports the Windows functions, FDW, and table inheritance. Also, there are many external extensions. Several proprietary DBMSs are based on PostgreSQL. In addition to that, there are several open source forks that add new features and technologies to PostgreSQL such as MPP and MapReduce.

PostgreSQL has a very organized active community including users, developers, companies, and associations. The community contributes to PostgreSQL on a daily basis; many companies have contributed to PostgreSQL by publishing best practices or articles, submitting feature requests to the development group, submitting new features, and developing new tools and software.

The first interaction with PostgreSQL is quick and easy, and one requires a few minutes to install it. PostgreSQL is shipped with many client tools to help user interactions. PostgreSQL is user-friendly the `psql` meta command `\h, \?, \timing</kbd>, \pset, auto-completion, and so on make it easy for the developer to complete his tasks quickly.`

In the next chapter, the PostgreSQL building components will be introduced. Also, the user will be able to create his first database and use some **DDL** statements such as `CREATE TABLE` and `CREATE VIEW`. The next chapter will provide some advice regarding coding and coding style for SQL and will provide an overview of high-level component interactions.

3
PostgreSQL Basic Building Blocks

In this chapter, we will build a PostgreSQL database, and explore the basic building blocks of PostgreSQL. The conceptual model of a car web portal, which was presented in `Chapter 01`, *Relational Databases*, will be translated to a physical model. Also, some data modeling techniques, such as surrogate keys, will be discussed briefly and some coding best practices will be presented.

We will also take a look at the hierarchy of the database objects in PostgreSQL. This will help you to understand how to configure the database cluster and tune its settings. More detailed information will be presented to show the usage of template databases, user databases, roles, tablespaces, schemas, configuration settings, and tables. The topics that we will be covering in this chapter are:

- Database coding
- PostgreSQL objects hierarchy
- PostgreSQL database components
- The car web portal database

Database coding

The software engineering principles should be applied on database coding. This is important to keep the code clean and to speed development cycles. This section will address several issues such as naming convention, documentation, and version control.

If you are familiar with these concepts, feel free to skip the section. Some of these principles are:

Database naming conventions

A naming convention describes how names are to be formulated. Naming conventions allow some information to be derived based on patterns, which helps the developer to easily search for and predict the database object names. Database naming conventions should be standardized across the organization. There is a lot of debate on how to name database objects. For example, some developers prefer to have prefixes or suffixes to distinguish the database object type from the names. For example, one could suffix a table or a view with tbl and vw respectively.

With regard to database object names, one should try to use descriptive names, and avoid acronyms and abbreviations if possible. Also, singular names are preferred, because a table is often mapped to an entity in a high-level programming language; thus, singular names lead to unified naming across the database tier and the business logic tier. Furthermore, specifying the cardinality and participation between tables is straightforward when the table names are singular.

In the database world, compound object names often use underscore but not camel case due to the ANSI SQL standard specifications regarding identifiers quotation and case sensitivity. In the ANSI SQL standard, non-quoted identifiers are case-insensitive.

In general, it is up to the developer to come up with a naming convention that suits with the needs at hand; in existing projects, do not invent any new naming conventions, unless the new naming conventions are communicated to the team members. In this book, we use the following conventions:

- The names of tables and views are not suffixed
- The database object names are unique across the database
- The identifiers are singulars including table, view, and column names
- Underscore is used for compound names
- The primary key is composed of the table name and the suffix id
- A foreign key has the same name of the referenced primary key in the linked table
- The internal naming conventions of PostgreSQL are used to rename the primary keys, foreign keys, and sequences

Do not use keywords to rename your database objects. The list of SQL keywords can be found at `https://www.postgresql.org/docs/current/static/sql-keywords-appendix.html`.

PostgreSQL identifiers

The length of PostgreSQL object names is 63 characters; PostgreSQL also follows ANSI SQL regarding case sensitivity. If you wanted to use camel case for naming database objects, you could achieve that by putting the identifier name in double quotes. PostgreSQL identifier names have the following constraints:

1. The identifier name should start with an underscore or a letter. Letters can be Latin or non-Latin letters.
2. The identifier name can be composed of letters, digits, underscore, and the dollar sign. For compatibility reasons, the use of the dollar sign is not recommended.
3. The minimum length of the identifier is typically one character, and the maximum length is 63.

In addition to the preceding points, it is not recommended to use keywords as table names.

Documentation

Documentation is essential for developers as well as business owners to understand the full picture. Documentation for database schema, objects, and code should be maintained. ER and class diagrams are very useful in understanding the full picture. There are tons of programs that support UML and ER diagrams. One can generate ER and UML diagrams by using graph editing tools such as yEd or the online tool `draw.io`. Also, there are many commercial UML modeling tools that support code reverse engineering.

Code documentation provides an insight into complex SQL statements. PostgreSQL uses `--` and `/**/` for single line and multiline comments respectively. The single line comment `--` works on the rest of the line after the comment marker. Therefore, it can be used on the same line as the actual statement. Finally, PostgreSQL allows the developer to store the database object description via the COMMENT ON command.

Version control system

It is a good idea to maintain your code using a revision control system such as Git or SVN. When writing an SQL code, it is better to create an installation script and execute it in one transaction. This approach makes it easy to clean up if an error occurs.

Database objects have different properties: some are a part of the physical schema, and some control database access. The following is a proposal for organizing the database code in order to increase the **separation of concern (SoC)**.

For each database in a PostgreSQL cluster, one should maintain the DDL script for objects that are part of the physical schema, and the DML script, which populates the tables with static data together. The state of an object in the physical schema is defined by the object structure and the data that is contained by this object; thus, the object cannot be recreated without being dropped first. Also, the structure of the physical schema object does not change often. In addition to that, the refactoring of some of the physical schema objects, such as tables, might require data migration. In other words, changing the definition of a physical schema object requires some planning.

Store the DDL scripts for objects that are not part of the physical schema, such as views and functions, separately. Keeping the definitions of views and functions together allows the developer to refactor them easily. Also, the developer will be able to extract the dependency trees between these objects.

Maintain the DCL script separately. This allows the developer to separate the security aspect from the functional requirements of the database. It allows the database developers and administrators to work closely without interfering with each other's work.

Database migration tool

One can integrate a database migration tool such as Flywaydb `https://flywaydb.org/` with Git. This gives the developer the ability to perform continuous integration. In addition to that, it gives the administrators a great overview of the database activities.

PostgreSQL objects hierarchy

Understanding the organization of PostgreSQL database logical objects helps with the understanding of object relations and interactions. PostgreSQL databases, roles, tablespaces, settings, and template languages have the same level of hierarchy, as shown in the following diagram:

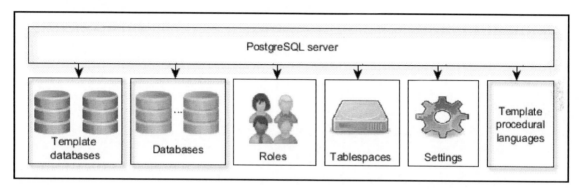

All objects in the hierarchy are explained in detail as follows.

Template databases

By default, when a database is created, it is cloned from a template database called `template1`. The template database contains a set of tables, views, and functions, which is used to model the relation between the user-defined database objects. These tables, views, and functions are a part of the system catalog schema called `pg_catalog`.

> The schema is very close to the namespace concept in object-oriented languages. It is often used to organize the database objects, functionality, security access, or to eliminate name collision.

The PostgreSQL server has two template databases:

- `template1`: The default database to be cloned. It can be modified to allow global modification to all the newly created databases. For example, if someone intends to use a certain extension in all the databases, then they can install this extension in the `template1` database. Certainly, installing an extension in `template1` will not be cascaded to the already existing databases, but it will affect the databases that will be created after this installation.

- template0: A safeguard or version database that has several purposes:
  - If template1 is corrupted by a user, then it can be used to fix template1.
  - It is handy in restoring a database dump. When a developer dumps a database, all the extensions are also dumped. If the extension is already installed in template1, this will lead to a collision, because the newly created database already contains the extensions. Unlike template1, template0 does not contain encoding-specific or locale-specific data.

One can create a database using a user database as a template. This is very handy for testing, database refactoring purposes, deployment plans, and more.

User databases

One can have as many databases as one wants in a database cluster. A client connection to the PostgreSQL server can access only the data in a single database that is specified in the connection string. That means that data is not shared between the databases, unless the PostgreSQL foreign data wrapper or dblink extensions are used.

Every database in the database cluster has an owner and a set of associated permissions to control the actions allowed for a particular role. The privileges on PostgreSQL objects, which include databases, views, tables, and sequences, are represented in the psql client as follows:

```
<user>=<privileges>/granted by
```

If the user part of the privileges is not present, it means that the privileges are applied to the PostgreSQL special PUBLIC role.

The psql client tool \l meta-command is used to list all the databases in the database cluster with the associated attributes:

```
postgres=# \l
                                   List of databases
      Name | Owner | Encoding | Collate | Ctype | Access privileges
-----------------+----------------+----------+------------+------------+-
----------------------
  car_portal | car_portal_app | UTF8 | en_US.UTF-8 | en_US.UTF-8 |
  postgres | postgres | UTF8 | en_US.UTF-8 | en_US.UTF-8 |
```

```
template0 | postgres | UTF8 | en_US.UTF-8 | en_US.UTF-8 | =c/postgres +
                | | | | | postgres=CTc/postgres
template1 | postgres | UTF8 | en_US.UTF-8 | en_US.UTF-8 | =c/postgres +
                | | | | | postgres=CTc/postgres
```

The database access privileges are the following:

- Create (-C): The create access privilege allows the specified role to create new schemas in the database.
- Connect (-c): When a role tries to connect to a database, the connect permissions are checked.
- Temporary (-T): The temporary access privilege allows the specified role to create temporary tables. Temporary tables are very similar to tables, but they are not persistent, and they are destroyed after the user session is terminated.

In the preceding example, the Postgres database has no explicit privileges assigned. Also notice that the PUBLIC role is allowed to connect to the template1 database by default.

Encoding allows you to store text in a variety of character sets, including one byte character sets such as SQL_ASCII or multiple byte character sets such as UTF-8. PostgreSQL supports a rich set of character encodings. For the full list of character encodings, please visit http://www.postgresql.org/docs/current/static/multibyte.html.

In addition to these attributes, PostgreSQL has several other attributes for various purposes, including the following:

- Maintenance: The attribute datfrozenxid is used to determine if a database vacuum is required.
- Storage management: The dattablespace attribute is used to determine the database tablespace.
- Concurrency: The datconnlimit attribute is used to determine the number of allowed connections (-1 means no limits).
- Protection: The datallowconn attribute disables the connection to a database. This is used mainly to protect template0 from being altered.

The psql \c meta-command establishes a new connection to a database and closes the current one. It also accepts a connection string such as username and password.

```
postgres=# \c template0
FATAL: database "template0" is not currently accepting connections Previous
connection kept
```

pg_catalog tables are regular tables, thus one can use the SELECT, UPDATE, and DELETE operations to manipulate them. Doing so is not recommended, and needs the utmost attention.

The catalog tables are very useful for automating some tasks; Chapter 12, *The PostgreSQL Catalog*, is dedicated to pg_catalog. The following example shows how one can alter the connection limit database property by using the ALTER database command. The following example changes the datconnlimit value from −1 to 1:

```
postgres=# SELECT datconnlimit FROM pg_database WHERE datname='postgres';
 datconnlimit
--------------
           -1
(1 row)

postgres=# ALTER DATABASE postgres CONNECTION LIMIT 1;
ALTER DATABASE
postgres=# SELECT datconnlimit FROM pg_database WHERE datname='postgres';
 datconnlimit
--------------
 1
(1 row)
```

Roles

Roles belong to the PostgreSQL server cluster and not to a certain database. A role can either be a database user or a database group. The role concept subsumes the concepts of users and groups in the old PostgreSQL versions. For compatibility reasons, with PostgreSQL version 8.1 and later, the CREATE USER and CREATE GROUP SQL commands are still supported.

The roles have several attributes, which are as follows:

- **Superuser**: A superuser role can bypass all permission checks except the login attribute.
- **Login**: A role with the login attribute can be used by a client to connect to a database.
- **Createdb**: A role with the create database attribute can create databases.
- **Createrole**: A role with this feature enabled can create, delete, and later other roles.
- **Replication**: A role with this attribute can be used for streaming replication.

- **Password**: The role password can be used with the md5 authentication method. Also, it can be encrypted. The password expiration can be controlled by specifying the validity period. Note that this password differs from the OS password.
- **Connection limit**: Connection limit specifies the number of concurrent connections that the user can initiate. Connection creation consumes hardware resources; thus, it is recommended to use connection pooling tools such as **pgpool-II** or **PgBouncer**, or some APIs such as Apache **DBCP** or **c3p0**.
- **Inherit**: If specified, the role will inherit the privileges assigned to the roles that it is a member of. If not specified, Inherit is the default.
- **Bypassrls**: if specified, the role can bypass row level security (**RLS**).

During the installation of PostgreSQL, the postgres superuser role is created. CREATE USER is equivalent to CREATE ROLE with the LOGIN option, and CREATE GROUP is equivalent to CREATE ROLE with the NOLOGIN option.

A role can be a member of another role to simplify accessing and managing the database permissions; for example, one can create a role with no login, also known as group, and grant its permissions to access the database objects. If a new role needs to access the same database objects with the same permissions as the group, the new role could be assigned a membership to this group. This is achieved by the GRANT and REVOKE SQL commands, which are discussed in detail in Chapter 11, *PostgreSQL Security*.

The roles of a cluster do not necessarily have the privilege to access every database in the cluster.

Tablespace

A **tablespace** is a defined storage location for a database or database objects. Tablespaces are used by administrators to achieve the following:

- **Maintenance**: If the hard disk partition runs out of space where the database cluster is created and cannot be extended, a tablespace on another partition can be created to solve this problem by moving the data to another location.
- **Optimization**: Heavily accessed data could be stored in fast media such as a **solid-state drive (SSD)**. At the same time, tables that are not performance critical could be stored on a slow disk.

The SQL statement to create a tablespace is CREATE TABLESPACE.

Template procedural languages

Template procedural languages are used to register a new language in a convenient way. There are two ways to create a programming language; the first way is by specifying only the name of the programming language. In this method, PostgreSQL consults the programming language template and determines the parameters. The second way is to specify the name as well as the parameters. The SQL command to create a language is CREATE LANGUAGE.

In PostgreSQL versions 9.1 and later, CREATE EXTENSION can be used to install a programming language. The template procedural languages are maintained in the table pg_pltemplate. This table might be decommissioned in favor of keeping the procedural language information in their installation scripts.

Settings

The PostgreSQL settings control different aspects of the PostgreSQL server, including replication, write-ahead logs, resource consumption, query planning, logging, authentication, statistic collection, garbage collection, client connections, lock management, error handling, and debug options.

The following SQL command shows the number of PostgreSQL settings. Note that this number might differ slightly between different installations as well as customized settings:

```
postgres=# SELECT count(*) FROM pg_settings;
 count
-------
   269
(1 row)
```

The parameters can be as follows:

- **Boolean**: 0, 1, true, false, on, off, or any case-insensitive form of the previous values. The ENABLE_SEQSCAN setting falls into this category.
- **Integer**: An integer might specify a memory or time value; there is an implicit unit for each setting such as second or minute. In order to avoid confusion, PostgreSQL allows units to be specified. For example, one could specify 128 MB as a shared_buffers setting value.

- **Enum**: These are predefined values such as ERROR and WARNING.
- **Floating point**: cpu_operator_cost has a floating point domain. cpu_operator_cost is used to optimize the PostgreSQL execution plans.
- **String**: A string might be used to specify the file location on a hard disk, such as the location of the authentication file.

The setting context determines how to change a setting's value and when the change can take effect. The setting contexts are as follows:

- **Internal**: The setting cannot be changed directly. One might need to recompile the server source code or initialize the database cluster to change this. For example, the length of PostgreSQL identifiers is 63 characters.
- **Postmaster**: Changing a setting value requires restarting the server. Values for these settings are typically stored in the PostgreSQL postgresql.conf file.
- **Sighup**: No server restart is required. The setting change can be made by amending the postgresql.conf file, followed by sending a SIGHUP signal to the PostgreSQL server process.
- **Backend**: No server restart is required. They can also be set for a particular session.
- **Superuser**: Only a superuser can change this setting. This setting can be set in postgresql.conf or via the SET command.
- **User**: This is similar to superuser, and is typically used to change the session-local values.

PostgreSQL provides the SET and SHOW commands to change and inspect the value of a setting parameter respectively. These commands are used to change the setting parameters in the superuser and user context. Typically, changing the value of a setting parameter in the postgresql.conf file makes the effect global.

The settings can also have a local effect, and can be applied to different contexts, such as sessions and tables. For example, let's assume that you would like some clients to be able to perform the read-only operation; this is useful for configuring tools such as Confluence (Atlassian). In this case, you can achieve that by setting the default_transaction_read_only **parameter**:

```
postgres=# SET default_transaction_read_only to on;
SET
postgres=# CREATE TABLE test_readonly AS SELECT 1;
ERROR: cannot execute CREATE TABLE AS in a read-only transaction
```

In the preceding example, the creation of a table has failed within the opened session; however, if one opens a new session and tries to execute the CREATE TABLE command, it will be executed successfully because the default value of the default_transaction_read_only setting is off. Setting the default_transaction_read_only parameter in the postgresql.conf file will have a global effect, as mentioned earlier.

PostgreSQL also provides the pg_reload_conf() function, which is equivalent to sending the SIGHUP signal to the PostgreSQL process.

In general, it is preferable to use pg_reload_conf() or reload the configuration settings via the init script because it is safer than the SIGHUP kill signal due to human error.

In order to set the database in the read-only mode in a Debian Linux distribution, one can do the following:

1. Edit postgresql.conf and alter the value of default_transaction_read_only. This can be done in Ubuntu with the following commands:

```
$sudo su postgres
$CONF=/etc/postgresql/10/main/postgresql.conf
$sed -i "s/#default_transaction_read_only =
off/default_transaction_read_only = on/" $CONF
```

2. Reload the configuration by executing the pg_reload_conf() function:

```
$psql -U postgres -c "SELECT pg_reload_conf()"
```

One needs to plan carefully for changing the setting parameter values that require server down time. For non-critical changes, one can change the postgresql.conf file in order to make sure that the change will take effect when the server is restarted due to security updates. For urgent changes, one should follow certain processes, such as scheduling downtime and informing the user of this downtime. Developers, in general, are concerned with two settings categories, which are as follows:

- **Client connection defaults**: These settings control the statement behaviors, locale, and formatting
- **Query planning**: These settings control the planner configuration, and give hints to the developer on how to rewrite SQL queries

PostgreSQL high-level object interaction

To sum up, a PostgreSQL server can contain many databases, programming languages, roles, and tablespaces. Each database has an owner and a default tablespace; a role can be granted permission to access or can own several databases. The settings can be used to control the behavior of the PostgreSQL server on several levels, such as database and session. Finally, a database can use several programming languages:

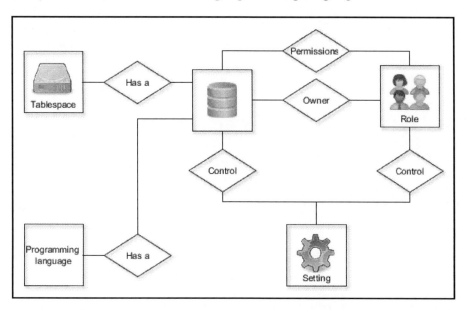

In order to create a database, one needs to specify the owner and the encoding of the database; if the encoding of `template1` does not match the required encoding, `template0` should be used explicitly.

For the car web high-level objects interaction portal database, let's assume that the database owner is the `car_portal_role` role and the encoding is `UTF-8`. In order to create this database, one can execute the following commands:

```
CREATE ROLE car_portal_app LOGIN;
CREATE DATABASE car_portal ENCODING 'UTF-8' LC_COLLATE 'en_US.UTF-8'
LC_CTYPE 'en_US.UTF-8' TEMPLATE template0 OWNER car_portal_app;
```

PostgreSQL database components

A PostgreSQL database could be considered as a container for database schema; the database must contain at least one schema. A database schema is used to organize the database objects in a manner similar to namespaces in high-level programming languages.

Schema

Object names can be reused in different schema without conflict. The schema contains all the database named objects, including tables, views, functions, aggregates, indexes, sequences, triggers, data types, domains, and ranges:

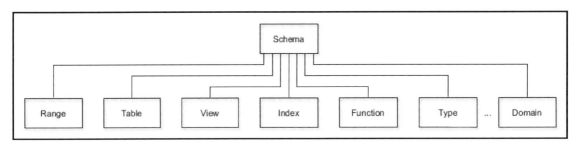

By default, there is a schema called *public* in the template databases. That means all the newly created databases also contain this schema. All users, by default, can access this schema implicitly. Again, this is inherited from the template databases. Allowing this access pattern simulates the situation where the server is not schema-aware. This is useful in small companies where there is no need to have complex security. Also, this enables smooth transition from non-schema-aware databases.

> In a multiuser and multidatabase environment setup, remember to revoke the ability for all users to create objects in the public schema. This is done by the following command in the newly created database, or in the `template1` **database:** `REVOKE CREATE ON SCHEMA public FROM PUBLIC;`

When a user wants to access a certain object, he needs to specify the schema name and the object name separated by a period . If the `search_path` database setting does not contain this name, or if the developer likes to use fully qualified names (for example, to select all the entries in `pg_database` in the `pg_catalog` schema), one needs to write the following command:

```
SELECT * FROM pg_catalog.pg_database;
--Alternatively you can also use the following command:
TABLE pg_catalog.pg_database;
```

Qualified database object names are sometimes tedious to write, so many developers prefer to use the unqualified object name, which is composed of the object name without the schema. PostgreSQL provides a `search_path` setting that is similar to the using directive in the C++ language. The search path is composed of schemas that are used by the server to search for the object. The default search path, as shown in the following code, is `$user`, `public`. If there is a schema with the same name as the user, then it will be used first to search for objects or to create new objects. If the object is not found in the schemas specified in the `search_path`, then an error will be thrown:

```
postgres=# SHOW search_path;
   search_path
-----------------
 "$user", public
(1 row)
```

Schema usages

Schemas are used for the following reasons:

- **Control authorization**: In a multiuser database environment, one can use schemas to group objects based on roles.
- **Organize database objects**: One can organize the database objects in groups based on the business logic. For example, historical and auditing data could be logically grouped and organized in a specific schema.
- **Maintain third-party SQL code**: The extensions available in the contribution package can be used with several applications. Maintaining these extensions in separate schemas enables the developer to reuse these extensions and to update them easily.

In the car web portal, let's assume that we would like to create a schema named `car_portal_app`, owned by `car_portal_app` role. This can be done as follows:

```
CREATE SCHEMA car_portal_app AUTHORIZATION car_portal_app;
 --The schema owner is the same as the schema name if not given
CREATE SCHEMA AUTHORIZATION car_portal_app;
```

For more information about the syntax of the `CREATE SCHEMA` command, one can use the `psql \h` meta-command, which displays the `psql` client tool inline help, or take a look at the PostgreSQL manual at `http://www.postgresql.org/docs/current/static/sql-createschema.html`.

Table

The `CREATE TABLE` statement is very rich. It can be used for several purposes such as cloning a table, which is handy for database refactoring to create the uninstallation script to rollback changes. Also, it can be used to materialize the result of the `SELECT` statement to boost performance, or for temporarily storing the data for later use.

The PostgreSQL tables are used internally to model views and sequences. In PostgreSQL, tables can be of different types:

- **Permanent table**: The table life span starts with table creation and ends with table dropping.
- **Temporary table**: The table life span is the user session. This is used often with procedural languages to model business logic.
- **Unlogged table**: Operations on unlogged tables are much faster than on permanent tables, because data is not written into the WAL files. Unlogged tables are not crash-safe. Also, since streaming replication is based on shipping the log files, unlogged tables cannot be replicated to the slave node.
- **Child table**: A child table is a table that inherits one or more tables. The inheritance is often used with constraint exclusion to physically partition the data on the hard disk and to improve performance by retrieving a subset of data that has a certain value.

The create table syntax is quite long; the full syntax of create table can be found at `http://www.postgresql.org/docs/current/static/sql-createtable.html`. The create table SQL command normally requires the following input:

- Table name of the created table.
- The table type.
- The table storage parameters. These parameters are used to control the table storage allocation and several other administrative tasks.
- The table columns, including the data type, default values, and constraint.
- The cloned table name and the options to clone the table.

PostgreSQL native data types

When designing a database table, one should take care in picking the appropriate data type. When the database goes to production, changing the data type of a column might become a very costly operation, especially for heavily loaded tables. The cost often comes from locking the table, and in some cases, rewriting it. When picking a data type, consider a balance between the following factors:

- **Extensibility**: Can the maximum length of a type be increased or decreased without a full table rewrite and a full table scan?
- **Data type size**: Going for a safe option, such as choosing big integers instead of integers, will cause more storage consumption.

PostgreSQL provides a very extensive set of data types. Some of the native data type categories are as follows:

- Numeric type
- Character type
- Date and time types

These data types are common for most relational databases. Moreover, they are often sufficient for modeling traditional applications.

Numeric types

The following table shows the various numeric types:

Name	Comments	Size	Range
smallint	SQL equivalent: `Int2`	2 bytes	-32,768 to +32,767
Int	SQL equivalent: `Int4` Integer is an alias for int	4 bytes	-2,147,483,648 to +2,147,483,647
Bigint	SQL equivalent: Int8 8 bytes	8 bytes	-9,223,372,036,854,775,808 to +9,223,372,036,854,775,807
Numeric or decimal	No difference in PostgreSQL	Variable	Up to 131,072 digits before the decimal point; up to 16,383 digits after the decimal point
real	Special values: -Infinity, Infinity, NaN	4 bytes	Platform-dependent, at least six-digit precision. Often, the range is 1E-37 to 1E+37.
Double precision	Special values: -Infinity, Infinity, NaN	8 bytes	Platform dependent, at least 15-digit precision. Often, the range is 1E-307 to 1E+308.

PostgreSQL supports various mathematical operators and functions, such as geometric functions and bitwise operations. The `smallint` data type can be used to save disk space, while `bigint` can be used if the integer range is not sufficient.

Serial types, namely `smallserial`, `serial`, and `bigserial` are wrappers on top of `smallint`, `int`, and `biginteger` respectively. Serial types are often used as surrogate keys, and by default, they are not allowed to have a null value. The serial type utilizes the sequences behind the scene. A sequence is a database object that is used to generate sequences by specifying the minimum, maximum, and increment values. For example, the following code creates a table customer with a `customer_id` column:

```
CREATE TABLE customer (
  customer_id SERIAL
);
```

This will generate the following code behind the scenes:

```
CREATE SEQUENCE custome_customer_id_seq;
CREATE TABLE customer (
  customer_id integer NOT NULL DEFAULT nextval('customer_customer_id_seq')
);
ALTER SEQUENCE customer_customer_id_seq OWNED BY customer.Customer_id;
```

When creating a column with type serial, remember the following things:

- A sequence will be created with the name `tableName_columnName_seq`. In the preceding example, the sequence name is `customer_customer_id_seq`.
- The column will have a `Not Null` constraint.
- The column will have a default value generated by the `nextval()` function.
- The sequence will be owned by the column, which means that the sequence will be dropped automatically if the column is dropped.

The preceding example shows how PostgreSQL names an object if the object name is not specified explicitly. PostgreSQL names objects using the `{tablename}_{columnname(s)}_{suffix}` pattern, where the `pkey`, `key`, `excl`, `idx`, `fkey`, and check suffixes stand for a primary key constraint, a unique constraint, an exclusion constraint, an index, a foreign key constraint, and a check constraint respectively. A common mistake when using the serial type is forgetting to grant proper permissions to the generated sequence.

Similar to the C language, the result of an integer expression is also an integer. So, the results of the mathematical operations $3/2$ and $1/3$ is 1 and 0 respectively. Thus, the fractional part is always truncated. Unlike in C, PostgreSQL uses round half to even algorithm when casting a `double` value to `int`:

```
postgres=# SELECT CAST (5.9 AS INT) AS rounded_up, CAST(5.1 AS INTEGER) AS
rounded_down, CAST (-23.5 AS INT) as round_negative , 5.5::INT AS
another_syntax;
 rounded_up | rounded_down | round_negative | another_syntax
------------+--------------+----------------+----------------
          6 | 5 | -24 | 6
(1 row)
postgres=# SELECT 2/3 AS "2/3", 1/3 AS "1/3", 3/2 AS "3/2";
 2/3 | 1/3 | 3/2
-----+-----+-----
   0 | 0 | 1
(1 row)
```

The numeric and decimal types are recommended for storing monetary and other amounts where precision is required. There are three forms for defining a numeric or a decimal value:

- Numeric (precision, scale)
- Numeric (precision)
- Numeric

Precision is the total number of digits, while scale is the number of digits of the fraction part. For example, the number 12.344 has a precision of five and a scale of three. If a numeric type is used to define a column type without precision or scale, then the column can store any number with any precision and scale.

If precision is not required, do not use the numeric and decimal types. Operations on numeric types are slower than floats and double precision.

Floating point and double precision are inexact; that means that the values in some cases cannot be represented in the internal binary format, and are stored as approximation. The full documentation about numeric data types can be found at https://www.postgresql.org/docs/10/static/datatype-numeric.htm

Character types

The following table shows the various character types:

Name	Comments	Trailing spaces	Maximum length
char	Equivalent to char(1), it must be quoted as shown in the name.	Semantically insignificant	1
name	Equivalent to varchar(64). Used by postgres for object names.	Semantically significant	64
char(n)	Alias: character(n) Fixed length character where the length is n. Internally called bpchar (blank padded character).	Semantically insignificant	1 to 10485760
Varchar(n)	Alias: character varying(n). Variable length character where the maximum length is n.	Semantically significant	1 to 10485760
Text	Variable length character.	Semantically significant	Unlimited

PostgreSQL provides two general text types, which are the char(n) and varchar(n) data types, where n is the number of characters allowed. In the char data type, if a value is less than the specified length, then trailing spaces are padded at the end of the value. Operations on the char data types ignore the trailing spaces. Take a look at the following example:

```
postgres=# SELECT 'a'::CHAR(2) = 'a '::CHAR(2) ,length('a '::CHAR(10));
 ?column? | length
----------+--------
 t | 1
(1 row)
```

It is not recommended to perform binary operations on varchar or text and char strings due to trailing spaces.

For both char and varchar data types, if the string is longer than the maximum allowed length, then an error will be raised in the case of insert or update unless the extra characters are all spaces. In the latter case, the string will be truncated. In the case of casting, extra characters will be truncated automatically without raising an error. The following example shows how mixing different data types might cause problems:

```
postgres=# SELECT 'a '::VARCHAR(2)='a '::text, 'a '::CHAR(2)='a '::text, 'a
'::CHAR(2)='a '::VARCHAR(2);
 ?column? | ?column? | ?column?
----------+----------+----------
 t | f | t
(1 row)

postgres=# SELECT length ('a '::CHAR(2)), length ('a '::VARCHAR(2));
 length | length
--------+--------
      1 | 2
(1 row)
```

The preceding example shows that `'a '::CHAR(2)` equals `'a '::VARCHAR(2)`, but both have different lengths, which is not logical. Also, it shows that `'a'::CHAR(2)` is not equal to `'a '::text`. Finally, `'a '::VARCHAR(2)` equals `'a'::text`. The preceding example causes confusion because if a variable a is equal to b and b is equal to c, then a should be equal to c according to mathematics.

The PostgreSQL text storage size depends on several factors, namely, the length of the text value and the text decoding and compression. The text data type can be considered as an unlimited `varchar()` type. The maximum text size that can be stored is 1 GB, which is the maximum column size.

For fixed length strings, the character data type and the character varying data type consume the same amount of hard disk space. For variable length strings, the character varying data type consumes less space, because character type appends the string with space. The following code shows the storage consumption for fixed and variable length texts for the character and character varying data types. It simply creates two tables, populates the tables with fictional data using fixed and variable length strings, and finally gets the table size in a human-readable form:

```
CREATE TABLE char_size_test (
  size CHAR(10)
);
CREATE TABLE varchar_size_test(
  size varchar(10)
);
WITH test_data AS (
  SELECT substring(md5(random()::text), 1, 5) FROM generate_series (1,
1000000)
),char_data_insert AS (
  INSERT INTO char_size_test SELECT * FROM test_data
)INSERT INTO varchar_size_test SELECT * FROM test_data;
```

Use this code to get the table size:

```
postgres=# \dt+ varchar_size_test
                    List of relations
 Schema | Name | Type | Owner | Size | Description
--------+------------------+-------+----------+-------+-------------
 public | varchar_size_test | table | postgres | 35 MB |
(1 row)

postgres=# \dt+ char_size_test
                    List of relations
 Schema | Name | Type | Owner | Size | Description
--------+----------------+-------+----------+-------+-------------
 public | char_size_test | table | postgres | 42 MB |
(1 row)
```

The varchar data type can be emulated by the text data type and a check constraint to check the text length. For example, the following code snippets are semantically equivalent:

```
CREATE TABLE emulate_varchar(
    test VARCHAR(4)
);
--semantically equivalent to
CREATE TABLE emulate_varchar (
    test TEXT,
    CONSTRAINT test_length CHECK (length(test) <= 4)
);
```

In PostgreSQL, there is no difference in performance between the different character types, so it is recommended to use the `text` data type. It allows the developer to react quickly to the changes in business requirements. For example, one common business case is changing the text length, such as changing the length of a customer ticket number from six to eight characters due to length limitation, or changing how certain information is stored in the database. In such a scenario, if the data type is `text`, this could be done by amending the check constraint without altering the table structure. The full documentation of character datatypes can be found at `https://www.postgresql.org/docs/10/static/datatype-character.html`

Date and time types

The date and time data types are commonly used to describe the occurrence of events such as birth date. PostgreSQL supports the following date and time types:

Name	Size in bytes	Description	Low value	High value
Timestamp without time zone	8	Date and time without time zone, equivalent to timestamp	4713 BC	294276 AD
Timestamp with time zone	8	Date and time with timezone, equivalent to timestamptz	4713 BC	294276 AD
Date	4	Date only	4713 BC	294276 AD
Time without time zone	8	Time of day	00:00:00	24:00:00

Time with time zone	12	Time of day with time zone	00:00:00+1459	24:00:00-1459
Interval	16	Time interval	-178,000,000 years	+178,000,000 years

PostgreSQL stores the timestamp with and without the time zone in the **universal coordinated time** (UTC) format, and only the time is stored without the time zone. This explains the identical storage size for both the timestamp with time zone and the timestamp without the time zone.

There are two approaches for handling the timestamp correctly. The first approach is to use the timestamp without the time zone, and let the client side handle the time zone differences. This is useful for in-house development, applications with only one time zone, and when the clients know the time zone differences.

The other approach is to use the timestamp with the time zone. The following are some of the best practices to avoid the common pitfalls when using timestamptz:

- Make sure to set the default time zone for all connections. This is done by setting the time zone configuration in the postgresql.conf file. Since PostgreSQL stores the timestamp with the time zone in UTC format internally, it is a good practice to set the default connection to UTC as well. Also, UTC helps in overcoming the potential problems due to **Daylight Saving Time** (DST).
- The time zone should be specified in each CRUD operation.
- Do not perform operations on the timestamp without time zone and the timestamp with time zone, this will normally lead to the wrong results due to implicit conversion.
- Do not invent your own conversion; instead, use the database server to convert between the different time zones.
- Investigate the data types of high-level languages to determine which type could be used with PostgreSQL without extra handling.

PostgreSQL has two important settings: time zone and datestyle. The datestyle has two purposes:

- **Setting the display format**: The datestyle specifies the timestamp and timestamptz rendering style
- **Interpreting ambiguous data**: The datestyle specifies how to interpret timestamp and timestamptz

The `pg_timezone_names` and `pg_timezone_abbrevs` views provide a list of the time zone names and abbreviations respectively. They also provide information regarding the time offset from UTC, and if the time zone is a DST. For example, the following code snippet sets the `timezone` setting to Jerusalem, and then retrieves the local date and time in Jerusalem:

```
postgres=# SET timezone TO 'Asia/jerusalem';
SET
postgres=# SELECT now();
              now
-------------------------------
 2017-11-02 18:06:29.336462+02
(1 row)
```

The PostgreSQL `AT TIME ZONE` statement converts the timestamp with or without the `timezone` to a specified time zone; its behavior depends on the converted type. The following example clarifies this construct:

```
postgres=# SHOW timezone;
    TimeZone
----------------
 Asia/Jerusalem
(1 row)

postgres=# SELECT now(), now()::timestamp, now() AT TIME ZONE 'CST',
now()::timestamp AT TIME ZONE 'CST';
             now | now | timezone | timezone
-----------------------------+-------------------------+------------------
--------+---------------------------
 2017-11-02 18:07:33.8087+02 | 2017-11-02 18:07:33.8087 | 2017-11-02
10:07:33.8087 | 2017-11-03 02:07:33.8087+02
(1 row)
```

The `now()` function returns the current timestamp with the time zone in the Asia/Jerusalem time zone. Notice that the time zone offset is +02. When casting the timestamp with the time zone to timestamp as in `now()::timestamp`, the time zone offset is truncated.

The `now() AT TIME ZONE 'CST'` expression converts the timestamp with the Jerusalem `timezone` to the timestamp in the specified time zone, CST. Since the central standard time offset is −6 from UTC, then 8 hours are deducted, since Jerusalem is offset 2 hours from UTC.

The last expression `now()::timestamp AT TIME ZONE 'CST'` is reinterpreted as a timestamp as being in that time zone, CST, for the purposes of converting it to the connection default time zone, `Asia/jerusalem`. So, the last expression is equivalent to the following:

```
postgres=# SELECT ('2017-11-02 18:07:33.8087'::timestamp AT time zone 'CST'
AT TIME ZONE 'Asia/jerusalem')::timestamptz;
 timezone
------------------------------
 2017-11-03 02:07:33.8087+02
(1 row)
```

One can summarize the conversion between the timestamp with and without the time zone as follows:

- The expression `'y'::TIMESTAMP WITHOUT TIMEZONE AT TIME ZONE 'x'` is interpreted as follows: the value y of type `TIMESTAMP` will be converted from the time zone x to the session time zone.
- The expression `'y'::TIMESTAMP WITH TIMEZONE AT TIME ZONE 'x'` converts the value `'y'` of type `TIMESTAMP` to a value of type `TIMESTAMP` at the specified time zone x.

PostgreSQL is intelligent in handling timestamp with time zone. The following example shows how PostgreSQL handles **Daylight Saving Time (DST)**:

```
postgres=# SET timezone TO 'Europe/Berlin';
SET
postgres=# SELECT '2017-03-26 2:00:00'::timestamptz;
      timestamptz
------------------------
 2017-03-26 03:00:00+02
(1 row)
```

The date is recommended when there is no need to specify the time, such as birth date, holidays, and absence days. Time with time zone storage is 12 bytes: 8 bytes are used to store the time, and 4 bytes are used to store the time zone. The time without time zone consumes only 8 bytes. Conversions between time zones can be made using the AT TIME ZONE construct.

Finally, the interval data type is very important in handling the timestamp operations as well as describing some business cases. From the point of view of functional requirements, the interval data type can represent a period of time such as estimation time for the completion of a certain task.

The result type of the basic arithmetic operations such as + and - on timestamp, timestamptz, time, and time with time zone is of the type interval. The result of the same operations on date type is an integer. The following example shows timestamptz and date subtraction. Notice the format of the specifying intervals:

```
postgres=# SELECT '2014-10-11'::date -'2014-10-10'::date = 1, '2014-09-01
23:30:00'::timestamptz -'2014-09-01 22:00:00'::timestamptz= Interval '1
hour, 30 minutes';
 ?column? | ?column?
----------+----------
 t | t
(1 row)
```

The car web portal database

At this stage, one can convert the logical model of the car web portal presented in `Chapter 01`, *Relational Databases*, to a physical model. To help the developer to create a table, one can follow this minimal checklist:

- What is the primary key?
- What is the default value for each column?
- What is the type of each column?
- What are the constraints on each column or set of columns?
- Are permissions set correctly on tables, sequences, and schemas?
- Are foreign keys specified with the proper actions?
- What is the data life cycle?
- What are the operations allowed on the data?

To create the car web portal schema, the formal relational model will not be applied strictly. Also, surrogate keys will be used instead of natural keys. The advantages for using surrogate keys is as follows:

- Natural keys can change; one can change the current email address to another one. On one hand, one could argue that, if a *natural key* can change, what has been identified is, in point of fact, NOT an actual natural key. On the other hand, this argument is valid, but then on can argue what is the natural key to identify a person. Using a surrogate key guarantees that if a row is referenced by another row, then this reference is not lost, because the surrogate key has not changed.

- Incorrect assumptions about natural keys. Let's take an email address as an example. The general assumption about an email address is that it identifies a person uniquely. This is not true; some email service providers set policies such as email expiration based on activity. Private companies might have general email addresses such as `contact@...`, `support@...`, and so on. The same is applicable to phone and mobile numbers.
- Surrogate keys can be used to support a temporal database design within the relational database world. For example, some companies have a very strict security requirement, and data should be versioned for each operation.
- Surrogate keys often use compact data types such as integers. This enables better performance than composite natural keys.
- Surrogate keys can be used in PostgreSQL to eliminate the effects of cross column statistic limitation. PostgreSQL collects statistics per single column by default. In some cases, this is not convenient because columns might be correlated. In this case, PostgreSQL gives a wrong estimation to the planner, and thus, imperfect execution plans are generated. To overcome this limitation, the developer can educate PostgreSQL about cross column statistics.
- Surrogate keys are better supported than the natural keys by object relational mappers such as hibernate.

Despite all these advantages of surrogate keys, they also have a few disadvantages:

- A surrogate key is auto-generated, and the generation of the value might give different results. For example, one inserts a data in a test database and a staging database, and after the comparison of data, the data was not identical.
- A surrogate key is not descriptive. From a communication point of view, it is easier to refer to a person by a name instead of an auto-generated number.
- Surrogate keys can lead to data redundancy and it can generate duplicate tuples if not handled carefully.

In the web car portal ER diagram, there is an entity with the name user. Since `user` is a reserved keyword, the name `account` will be used for creating the table. Note that to create a database object using a PostgreSQL keyword, the name should be quoted. The following example shows how to create a table user:

```
postgres=# \set VERBOSITY 'verbose'
postgres=# CREATE TABLE user AS SELECT 1;
ERROR: 42601: syntax error at or near "user"
LINE 1: CREATE TABLE user AS SELECT 1;
                     ^
LOCATION: scanner_yyerror, scan.l:1086
```

```
postgres=# CREATE TABLE "user" AS SELECT 1;
SELECT 1
```

In the preceding example, the VERBOSITY setting for psql can be used to show error codes. Error codes are useful in detecting errors and trapping exceptions.

To create a table account, one can execute the following command:

```
CREATE TABLE account (
    account_id SERIAL PRIMARY KEY,
    first_name TEXT NOT NULL,
    last_name TEXT NOT NULL,
    email TEXT NOT NULL UNIQUE,
    password TEXT NOT NULL,
    CHECK (email ~* '^\w+@\w+[.]\w+$'),
    CHECK (char_length(password)>=8)
);
```

To summarize the user table:

- The account_id is defined as the primary key with type serial. The account_id is naturally unique and not null.
- The first_name, last_name, email, and password attributes are not allowed to have null values.
- The password should be at least eight characters in length. In reality, the password length is handled in business logic, since passwords should not be stored in a plain text format in the database. For more information about securing data, have a look at Chapter 11, *PostgreSQL Security*.
- The email should match a certain regex expression. Note that the email regular expression is really simplistic.

Behind the scencs, the following objects are created:

- A sequence to emulate the serial type.
- Two indices, both unique. The first one is used to validate the primary key, account_id. The second is used to validate the email address.

To create the seller_account, one can execute the following statement:

```
CREATE TABLE seller_account (
    seller_account_id SERIAL PRIMARY KEY,
    account_id INT UNIQUE NOT NULL REFERENCES
    account(account_id),
    number_of_advertizement INT DEFAULT 0,
    user_ranking float,
```

```
      total_rank float
    );
```

As we can see, the seller account has a one-to-one relationship with the account. This is enforced by the `account_id` that consists of `NOT NULL` and `UNIQUE` constraints. Also, in this case, one can model the seller account as follows by marking the `account_id` as the `PRIMARY KEY`:

```
CREATE TABLE seller_account (
  account_id INT PRIMARY KEY REFERENCES account(account_id)
  ...
);
```

The first design is more flexible and less ambiguous. First of all, the requirement might change, and the user account and the seller account relation might change from one-to-one to one-to-many. For example, the user concept might be generalized to handle companies where the company has several seller accounts.

To model the car table, we need first to create the car model. This is quite important because it will help the application user mainly the seller to pick up a model instead of entering the model information. In addition to that, the seller might not have a full information about the car model. Finally, allowing the seller to enter the model information might lead to data inconsistency due to human errors. In real applications, lookup information such as currency, countries, car model can be downloaded from certain providers. For example, country information is provided by ISO `https://www.iso.org/iso-3166-country-codes.html`.

Summary

In this chapter, we explored the basic building blocks of PostgreSQL. There are several shared objects across the database cluster. These shared objects are roles, tablespaces, databases including template databases, template procedural languages, and some setting parameters. The tablespace is a defined storage used normally by the databases administrator for optimization or maintenance purposes.

The `template1` database is cloned each time a database is created. It can be loaded with extensions that should be available for all new databases. The `template0` database provides a fallback strategy in case the `template1` database is corrupted. Also, it can be used if the `template1` locale is not the required locale.

The role has several attributes, such as login, superuser, and createdb. The role is named a user in the older PostgreSQL version if it can log in to the database, and a group if it cannot. Roles can be granted to other roles; this allows the database administrators to manage permissions easily.

PostgreSQL has more than two hundred settings that control the database behavior. These settings can have different contexts, namely, internal, postmaster, backend, user, superuser, and SIGHUP. To have a quick look at these settings, one can use the view `pg_settings`, which describes all the PostgreSQL settings.

The user database is the container for schemas, tables, views, functions, ranges, domain, sequences, and indexes. The database access permissions can be controlled via the create, temporary, and connect access privileges. Several aspects of the database behavior can be controlled by the `ALTER DATABASE` statement. The `pg_database` catalog table describes all the databases in the PostgreSQL cluster.

PostgreSQL provides a rich set of data types, including numeric, text, and date/time data types. Choosing a data type is an important task; thus, one should balance between between extensibility, storage consumption and performance when choosing a data type. One should be careful when performing operations on a mixture of different data types due to implicit conversion. For example, one should know how the system behaves when comparing text data type with the `varchar` data type. This also applies to time and date data types.

Tables are the major building blocks in PostgreSQL; they are used internally to implement views as well as sequences. A table can be categorized as temporary or permanent. In streaming replication, `unlogged` tables are not replicated to the slave nodes.

In the next chapter, more building blocks will be explored such as indexes, and views after completing these chapters, one will have the basic knowledge to design and implement the physical data structure of an application.

4

PostgreSQL Advanced Building Blocks

In this chapter, the rest of the PostgreSQL building blocks, including views, indexes, functions, triggers, and rules will be introduced. In addition to that, the web car portal schema will be revised. Several **DDL** commands, such as CREATE and ALTER, will also be introduced. Since the lexical structure and several **DML** commands have not been introduced as yet, we will try to use simple **DML** commands. In this chapter the topics we will be covering include:

- **Views**: views is an important part of database modelling because the act as an interface or as an abstraction layer. The view section will discuses view synopsis, usages, and an updatable view example will be demonstrated.
- **Indexes**: indexes is the secret sauce to insure consistency and performance. Indexes types will be discussed.
- **Functions**: Functions can be used to perform very complex logic in the database, also they can be used similar as views. Functions will be discussed briefly here since functions are discussed in details in Chapter 07, *Server-Side Programming with PL/pgSQL*.
- **User-defined Data types**: One big advantage of PostgreSQL is being able to define and use new different data types, this section shows several use cases where user defined data types can be used to solve some issues.
- **Triggers and rule Systems**: Triggers and rule systems allows the developers to handle events raised triggered by INSERT, UPDATE, DELETE and so on. The trigger system is used to model complex business requirements that is difficult to achieve using plain SQL.

Views

A view can be seen as a named query, or as a wrapper around a SELECT statement. Views are essential building blocks of relational databases from the UML modeling perspective; a view can be thought of as a method for a UML class. Views share several advantages with procedures, so the following benefits are shared between views and stored procedures. Views can be used for the following purposes:

- Simplifying complex queries and increasing code modularity
- Tuning performance by caching the view results for later use
- Decreasing the amount of SQL code
- Bridging the gap between relational databases and OO languages, especially updatable views
- Implementing authorization at the row level by leaving out rows that do not meet a certain predicate
- Implementing interfaces and the abstraction layer between high-level languages and relational databases
- Implementing last-minute changes

A view should meet the current business needs instead of potential future business needs. It should be designed to provide a certain functionality or service. Note that, the more attributes in a view, the more effort is required to refactor a view. In addition to that, when a view aggregates data from many tables and is used as an interface, there might be a degradation in performance due to many factors (for example, bad execution plans due to outdated statistics for some tables, execution plan time generation, and so on).

When implementing complex business logic in a database using views and stored procedures, database refactoring, especially for base tables, might turn out to be very expensive. To solve this issue, consider migrating the business logic to the application business tier.

Some frameworks, such as object-relational mappers, might have specific needs such as a unique key. This limits the usage of views in these frameworks, however, one can mitigate these issues by faking the primary keys via window functions such as row_number.

In PostgreSQL, a view is internally modeled as a table with a _RETURN rule. So in theory, one can create a table and convert it to a view. However, this is not a recommended practice. The VIEW dependency tree is well maintained; that means one cannot drop a view or amend its structure if another view that depends on it, as follows:

```
postgres=# CREATE VIEW test AS SELECT 1 as v;
CREATE VIEW
postgres=# CREATE VIEW test2 AS SELECT v FROM test;
CREATE VIEW
postgres=# CREATE OR REPLACE VIEW test AS SELECT 1 as val;
ERROR: cannot change name of view column "v" to "val"
```

View synopsis

In the view synopsis shown below, the CREATE VIEW statement is used to create a view, if the REPLACE keyword is used, the view will be replaced if it already exists. View attribute names can be given explicitly, or they can be inherited from the SELECT statement:

```
CREATE [ OR REPLACE ] [ TEMP | TEMPORARY ] [ RECURSIVE ] VIEW name [ (
column_name [, ...] ) ]
    [ WITH ( view_option_name [= view_option_value] [, ... ] ) ]
    AS query
    [ WITH [ CASCADED | LOCAL ] CHECK OPTION ]
```

The synopsis of materialized views differs from the view synopsis. Please refer to the *Materialized views* section for the materialized view synopsis.

The following example shows how to create a view that lists only the user information without the password. This might be useful for implementing data authorization to restrict applications from accessing the password. Note that the view column names are inherited from the SELECT list, as shown by the \d in the account_information meta command:

```
car_portal=> CREATE VIEW account_information AS SELECT account_id,
first_name, last_name, email FROM account;
CREATE VIEW
car_portal=> \d account_information
        View "car_portal_app.account_information"
   Column   | Type | Collation | Nullable | Default
------------+---------+-----------+----------+---------
 account_id | integer | | |
 first_name | text | | |
```

```
last_name | text | | |
email | text | | |
```

The view column names can be assigned explicitly, as shown in the following example. This might be useful when one needs to change the view column names:

```
CREATE OR REPLACE VIEW account_information
(account_id,first_name,last_name,email) AS SELECT account_id, first_name,
last_name, email FROM account;
```

When replacing the view definition using the REPLACE keyword, the column list should be identical before and after the replacement, including the column type, name, and order. The following example shows what happens when you try to change the view column order:

```
car_portal=> CREATE OR REPLACE VIEW account_information AS SELECT
account_id, last_name, first_name, email FROM account;
ERROR: cannot change name of view column "first_name" to "last_name"
```

View categories

Views in PostgreSQL can be categorized into one of the following categories on the basis of their usage:

- **Temporary views**: A temporary view is dropped automatically at the end of a user session. If the TEMPORARY or TEMP keywords are not used, then the life cycle of the view starts with the view creation and ends with the action of dropping it.
- **Recursive views**: A recursive view is similar to recursive functions in high-level languages. The view column list should be specified in recursive views. Recursion in relational databases, such as in recursive views or recursive **common table expressions (CTEs)**, can be used to write very complex queries, specifically for hierarchical data.
- **Updatable views**: Updatable views allow the user to see the view as a table. This means that the developer can perform INSERT, UPDATE and DELETE on views similar to tables. Updatable views can help in bridging the gap between an object model and a relational model to some extent, and they can help in overcoming problems such as polymorphism.
- **Materialized views**: A materialized view is a table whose contents are periodically refreshed based on a certain query. Materialized views are useful for boosting the performance of queries that require a longer execution time and are executed frequently on static data. One could perceive materialized views as a caching technique. Since recursion will be covered in later chapters, we will focus here on the updatable and materialized views.

Materialized views

The materialized view synopsis differs a little bit from the normal view synopsis. Materialized views are a PostgreSQL extension, but several databases, such as Oracle, support it. As shown in the following synopsis, a materialized view can be created in a certain TABLESPACE, as well as storage_parameter, which is logical since materialized views are physical objects:

```
CREATE MATERIALIZED VIEW [ IF NOT EXISTS ] table_name
    [ (column_name [, ...] ) ]
    [ WITH ( storage_parameter [= value] [, ... ] ) ]
    [ TABLESPACE tablespace_name ]
    AS query
    [ WITH [ NO ] DATA ]
```

At the time of creation of a materialized view, it can be populated with data or left empty. If it is not populated, retrieving data from the unpopulated materialized view will raise an ERROR. The REFRESH MATERIALIZED VIEW statement can be used to populate a materialized view. The synopsis for the refresh command is as follows:

```
REFRESH MATERIALIZED VIEW [ CONCURRENTLY ] name  [ WITH [ NO ] DATA ]
```

The following example shows an attempt to retrieve data from an unpopulated materialized view:

```
car_portal=> CREATE MATERIALIZED VIEW test_mat AS SELECT 1 WITH NO DATA;
CREATE MATERIALIZED VIEW
car_portal=> TABLE test_mat;
ERROR: materialized view "test_mat" has not been populated
HINT: Use the REFRESH MATERIALIZED VIEW command.
```

To refresh the view, as the hint suggested, one needs to refresh the view as follows:

```
car_portal=> REFRESH MATERIALIZED VIEW test_mat;
REFRESH MATERIALIZED VIEW
car_portal=> TABLE test_mat;
 ?column?
----------
        1
(1 row)
```

> Refreshing materialized view is a blocking statement, this means concurrent selects will be blocked for a specific time period until the refresh is done. This can be solved by refreshing the materialized view concurrently. To be able to use this option, the materialized view should have a unique index.

Materialized views are often used with data warehousing. In data warehousing, several queries are required for business analysis and decision support. The data in these kinds of applications does not usually change, but the calculation and aggregation of that data is often a costly operation. In general, a materialized view can be used for the following:

- Generating summary reports
- Caching the results of recurring queries
- Optimizing performance by processing data only once

Since materialized views are tables, they can also be indexed, leading to a great performance boost.

Updatable views

By default, simple PostgreSQL views are auto-updatable. Auto-updatable means that one could use the view with the DELETE, INSERT and UPDATE statements to manipulate the data of the underlying table. If the view is not updatable (which is not simple) due to the violation of one of the following constraints, the trigger and rule systems can be used to make it updatable. The view is automatically updatable if the following conditions are met:

- The view must be built on top of one table or an updatable view.
- The view definition must not contain the following clauses and set operators at the top level: DISTINCT, WITH, GROUP BY, OFFSET, HAVING, LIMIT, UNION, EXCEPT, and INTERSECT.
- The view's select list must be mapped to the underlying table directly without using functions and expressions. Moreover, the columns in the select list should not be repeated.
- The security_barrier property must not be set. The preceding conditions promise that the view attributes can be mapped directly to the underlying table attributes.

In the web car portal, let's assume that we have an updatable view that shows only the accounts that are not seller accounts, as follows:

```
CREATE VIEW user_account AS SELECT account_id, first_name, last_name,
email, password  FROM account WHERE account_id NOT IN (SELECT account_id
FROM seller_account);
```

To test it, let's insert a row:

```
car_portal=> INSERT INTO user_account VALUES
(default,'first_name1','last_name1','test@email.com','password');
INSERT 0 1
```

In the case of an auto-updatable view, one cannot modify data not returned by the view. For example, let's insert an account with a seller account, and then try to delete it:

```
car_portal=> WITH account_info AS ( INSERT INTO user_account VALUES
(default,'first_name2','last_name2','test2@email.com','password') RETURNING
account_id)
INSERT INTO seller_account (account_id, street_name, street_number,
zip_code, city) SELECT account_id, 'street1', '555', '555', 'test_city'
FROM account_info;
INSERT 0 1
```

In the preceding example, notice that the INSERT to the user account was successful. However, even though the account was inserted successfully, one cannot delete it using the updatable view since the check constraint will be effective, as follows:

```
car_portal=> DELETE FROM user_account WHERE first_name = 'first_name2';
DELETE 0
car_portal=> SELECT * FROM account where first_name like 'first_name%';
 account_id | first_name | last_name | email | password
------------+------------+-----------+-----------------+----------
        482 | first_name1 | last_name1 | test@email.com | password
        484 | first_name2 | last_name2 | test2@email.com | password
(2 rows)
```

The view WITH CHECK OPTION is used to control the behavior of automatically updatable views. If the WITH CHECK OPTION is not specified, one can UPDATE or INSERT a record even if it is not visible in the view, which might cause a security risk. The following is a simple example to demonstrate this feature. First, let's create a table, as follows:

```
CREATE TABLE a (val INT);
CREATE VIEW test_check_option AS SELECT * FROM a WHERE val > 0 WITH CHECK
OPTION;
```

To test the CHECK OPTION, let's insert a row that violates the check condition:

```
car_portal=> INSERT INTO test_check_option VALUES (-1);
ERROR: new row violates check option for view "test_check_option"
DETAIL: Failing row contains (-1).
```

For more information about views, one can have a look at `https://www.postgresql.org/docs/current/static/sql-createview.html`. If you are uncertain whether a view is auto-updatable or not, you can verify this information using the `information_schema` by checking the value of the `is_insertable_into` flag, as follows:

```
car_portal=# SELECT table_name, is_insertable_into FROM
information_schema.tables WHERE table_name = 'user_account';
 table_name | is_insertable_into
------------+--------------------
 user_account | YES
(1 row)
```

Indexes

An index is a physical database object that is defined on a table column or a list of columns. In PostgreSQL, there are many types of indexes and several ways to use them. Indexes can be used, in general, to do the following:

- **Optimize performance**: an index allows the efficient retrieval of a small number of rows from the table. Whether or not a number of rows is considered *small* is determined by the total number of rows in the table and execution planner settings.
- **Validate constraints**: An index can be used to validate the constraints on several rows. For example, the `UNIQUE` check constraint creates a unique index on the column behind the scenes.

The following example shows how to use `GIST` to forbid overlapping between date ranges. For more information, have a look at `https://www.postgresql.org/docs/current/static/rangetypes.html`

```
CREATE TABLE no_date_overlap (
    date_range daterange,
    EXCLUDE USING GIST (date_range WITH &&)
);
```

To test date range overlapping:

```
car_portal=# INSERT INTO no_date_overlap values ('[2010-01-01,
2020-01-01)');
INSERT 0 1
car_portal=# INSERT INTO no_date_overlap values ('[2010-01-01,
2017-01-01)');
ERROR: conflicting key value violates exclusion constraint
```

```
"no_date_overlap_date_range_excl"
DETAIL: Key (date_range)=([2010-01-01,2017-01-01)) conflicts with existing
key (date_range)=([2010-01-01,2020-01-01)).
```

Index synopsis

Indexes can be created using the CREATE INDEX statement. Since an index is a physical database object, one can specify the TABLESPACE and storage_parameter options. An index can be created on columns or expressions. Index entries can be sorted in ASC or DESC order. Also, one can specify the sort order for NULL values. If an index is created for text fields, one can also specify the collation. The following is the synopsis for the index:

```
CREATE [ UNIQUE ] INDEX [ CONCURRENTLY ] [ [ IF NOT EXISTS ] name ] ON
table_name [ USING method ]
  ( { column_name | ( expression ) } [ COLLATE collation ] [ opclass ] [ ASC
| DESC ] [ NULLS { FIRST | LAST } ] [, ...] )
  [ WITH ( storage_parameter = value [, ... ] ) ]
  [ TABLESPACE tablespace_name ]
  [ WHERE predicate ]
```

Indexes are created automatically for primary keys and unique keys.

Index selectivity

Let's take a look at the account_history table in the car web portal example. The unique constraint, UNIQUE (account_id, search_key, search_date), has two purposes. The first purpose is to define the validity constraint for inserting the search key into the table only once each day, even if the user searches for the key several times. The second purpose is to retrieve data quickly. Let's assume that we would like to show the last 10 searches for a user. The query for performing this would be as follows:

```
SELECT search_key FROM account_history WHERE account_id = <account> GROUP
BY search_key ORDER BY max(search_date) limit 10;
```

The preceding query returns only 10 records containing the different search_key ordered by search_date. If we assume that the search account_history contains millions of rows, then reading all of the data will take a lot of time. In this case, this is not true, because the unique index will help us in reading the data only for this particular customer.

Indexes on tables are not used if the table size is small. The PostgreSQL planner will scan the complete table instead. To show this, the `account_history` was populated with a very small dataset, generated as follows:

```
WITH test_account AS( INSERT INTO account VALUES (1000, 'test_first_name',
'test_last_name','test@email.com', 'password') RETURNING account_id
),car AS ( SELECT i as car_model FROM (VALUES('brand=BMW'), ('brand=WV'))
AS foo(i)
),manufacturing_date AS ( SELECT 'year='|| i as date FROM generate_series
(2015, 2014, -1) as foo(i))
INSERT INTO account_history (account_id, search_key, search_date) SELECT
account_id, car.car_model||'&'||manufacturing_date.date, current_date
FROM test_account, car, manufacturing_date;
VACUUM ANALYZE;
```

To test whether the index is used, let's run the query as follows:

```
car_portal=> SELECT search_key FROM account_history WHERE account_id = 1000
GROUP BY search_key ORDER BY max(search_date) limit 10;
     search_key
--------------------
 brand=WV&year=2014
 brand=BMW&year=2014
 brand=WV&year=2015
 brand=BMW&year=2015
(4 rows)

car_portal=> EXPLAIN SELECT search_key FROM account_history WHERE
account_id = 1000 GROUP BY search_key ORDER BY max(search_date) limit 10;
                              QUERY PLAN
---------------------------------------------------------------------------
-------
 Limit (cost=1.17..1.18 rows=3 width=23)
   -> Sort (cost=1.17..1.18 rows=3 width=23)
         Sort Key: (max(search_date))
         -> HashAggregate (cost=1.12..1.15 rows=3 width=23)
               Group Key: search_key
               -> Seq Scan on account_history (cost=0.00..1.10 rows=4
width=23)
                     Filter: (account_id = 1000)
```

The index in the above example is not used; the PostgreSQL planner decides whether to use an index based on the execution plan cost. For the same query with different parameters, the planner might pick a different plan based on the data histogram. So, even if we have a big dataset, and the predicate used in the query does not filter a lot of data, the index will not be used. To create such a scenario, let's insert some entries only for another account and rerun the query as follows:

```
WITH test_account AS( INSERT INTO account VALUES (2000, 'test_first_name',
'test_last_name','test2@email.com', 'password') RETURNING account_id
),car AS ( SELECT i as car_model FROM (VALUES('brand=BMW'), ('brand=WV'),
('brand=Audi'), ('brand=MB')) AS foo(i)
),manufacturing_date AS ( SELECT 'year='|| i as date FROM generate_series
(2017, 1900, -1) as foo(i))
INSERT INTO account_history (account_id, search_key, search_date) SELECT
account_id, car.car_model||'&'||manufacturing_date.date, current_date
FROM test_account, car, manufacturing_date;
VACUUM ANALYZE;
```

To run the query for the second account:

```
car_portal=> EXPLAIN SELECT search_key FROM account_history WHERE
account_id = 2000 GROUP BY search_key ORDER BY max(search_date) limit 10;
 QUERY PLAN
-------------------------------------------------------------------------
---------
 Limit (cost=27.10..27.13 rows=10 width=23)
  -> Sort (cost=27.10..28.27 rows=468 width=23)
  Sort Key: (max(search_date))
  -> HashAggregate (cost=12.31..16.99 rows=468 width=23)
  Group Key: search_key
  -> Seq Scan on account_history (cost=0.00..9.95 rows=472 width=23)
  Filter: (account_id = 2000)
(7 rows)
```

Again, the index is not used, because we would like to read the whole table. Index selectivity here is very low since account 2000 has 427 records, where account 1000 only has four records, as shown below:

```
car_portal=> SELECT count(*), account_id FROM account_history group by
account_id;
 count | account_id
-------+------------
 472 | 2000
 4 | 1000
(2 rows)
```

Finally, let's rerun the query again for account `1000`. In this case, the selectivity is high, thus the index will be used:

```
EXPLAIN SELECT search_key FROM account_history WHERE account_id = 1000
GROUP BY search_key ORDER BY max(search_date) limit 10;
                                                          QUERY PLAN
-----------------------------------------------------------------------
-------------------------------------------------------------
 Limit (cost=8.71..8.72 rows=4 width=23)
   -> Sort (cost=8.71..8.72 rows=4 width=23)
         Sort Key: (max(search_date))
         -> GroupAggregate (cost=8.60..8.67 rows=4 width=23)
             Group Key: search_key
             -> Sort (cost=8.60..8.61 rows=4 width=23)
                 Sort Key: search_key
                 -> Bitmap Heap Scan on account_history
(cost=4.30..8.56 rows=4 width=23)
                         Recheck Cond: (account_id = 1000)
                         -> Bitmap Index Scan on
account_history_account_id_search_key_search_date_key (cost=0.00..4.30
rows=4 width=0)
                             Index Cond: (account_id = 1000)
(11 rows)
```

Index types

PostgreSQL supports different indexes; each index can be used for a certain scenario or data type:

- **B-tree index**: This is the default index in PostgreSQL when the index type is not specified with the `CREATE INDEX` command. The **B** stands for **balanced**, which means that the data on both sides of the tree is roughly equal. B-tree can be used for equality, ranges, and null predicates. The B-tree index supports all PostgreSQL data types.
- **Hash index**: Prior to PostgreSQL 10, hash indexes are not well supported. They are not transaction-safe, and are not replicated to the slave nodes in streaming replication. In PostgreSQL 10, hash index's limitations have been tackled. It is useful for equality predicates =.
- **Generalized inverted index (GIN)**: The GIN index is useful when several values need to map to one row. It can be used with complex data structures such as arrays and full-text searches.

- **Generalized search tree (GiST)**: The GiST indexes allow the building of general balanced tree structures. They are useful in indexing geometric data types, as well as full-text search.
- **Space-partitioned GiST (SP-GiST)**: They are similar to GIST and support partitioned search trees. Generally speaking, `GIST`, `GIN`, and `SP-GIST` are designed to handle complex user-defined data types.
- **Block range index (BRIN)**: This was introduced in PostgreSQL 9.5. The BRIN index is useful for very large tables where the size is limited. A BRIN index is slower than a B-tree index, but requires less space than the B-tree.

Index categories

One can classify indexes on a high level as follows:

- **Partial index**: A partial index indexes only a subset of the table data that meets a certain predicate; the `WHERE` clause is used with the index. The idea behind a partial index is to decrease the index size, thus making it more maintainable and faster to access.
- **Unique index**: The unique index guarantees the uniqueness of a certain value in a row across the whole table. In the `account` table, the `email` column has a unique check constraint. This is implemented by the unique index, as shown by the `\d` meta command:

```
\d account
                              Table "car_portal_app.account"
    Column | Type | Collation | Nullable | Default
------------+---------+-----------+----------+--------------------
------------------------
 account_id | integer | | not null |
nextval('account_account_id_seq'::regclass)
 first_name | text | | not null |
 last_name | text | | not null |
 email | text | | not null |
 password | text | | not null |
Indexes:
    "account_pkey" PRIMARY KEY, btree (account_id)
    "account_email_key" UNIQUE CONSTRAINT, btree (email)
```

- **A multicolumn index** can be used for a certain pattern of query conditions. Suppose a query has a pattern similar to the following: `SELECT * FROM table WHERE column`$_1$ = `constant`$_1$ and `column`$_2$= `constant`$_2$ `AND ... column`$_n$ = `constant`$_n$; in this case, an index can be created on `column`$_1$, `column`$_2$,..., and `column`$_n$, where n is less than or equal to 32.
- **Index on expression**: As stated earlier, an index can be created on a table column or multiple columns. One can also be created on expressions and function results.

One can also mix different categories together, for example, one can create a unique partial index, and so on. This gives the developer greater flexibility to meet business requirements or to optimize for speed. For example, as shown in later chapters, one can use index to optimize a case-insensitive search by simply creating an index using the function `lower()` or `upper()` as follows:

```
car_portal=> CREATE index on account(lower(first_name));
CREATE INDEX
```

The index we just saw, will speed the performance of searching an account by names in a case-insensitive way, as follows:

```
SELECT * FROM account WHERE lower(first_name) = lower('foo');
```

 Index on expression, will only be chosen if the PRECISELY same functional expression is used in the WHERE clause of the query.

Another usage for expression indexes is to filter rows by casting a data type to another data type. For example, the departure time of a flight can be stored as a `timestamp` ; however, we often search for a date and not a time.

As we said earlier, one can also use unique and partial indexes together. For example, let's assume that we have a table called `employee`, where each employee must have a supervisor, except for the company head. We can model this as a self-referencing table, as follows:

```
CREATE TABLE employee (employee_id INT PRIMARY KEY, supervisor_id INT);
ALTER TABLE employee ADD CONSTRAINT supervisor_id_fkey FOREIGN KEY
(supervisor_id) REFERENCES employee(employee_id);
```

To guarantee that only one row is assigned to a supervisor, we can add the following unique index:

```
CREATE UNIQUE INDEX ON employee ((1)) WHERE supervisor_id IS NULL;
```

The unique index on the constant expression (1) will allow only one row with a null value. With the first insert of a null value, a unique index will be built using the value 1. A second attempt to add a row with a null value will cause an error because the value 1 is already indexed:

```
car_portal=> INSERT INTO employee VALUES (1, NULL);
INSERT 0 1
car_portal=> INSERT INTO employee VALUES (2, 1);
INSERT 0 1
car_portal=> INSERT INTO employee VALUES (3, NULL);
ERROR: duplicate key value violates unique constraint "employee_expr_idx"
DETAIL: Key ((1))=(1) already exists.
```

Currently, only B-tree, GIN, GIST and BRIN support multi-column indexes. When creating a multi-column index, the column order is important. Since the multi-column index size is often big, the planner might prefer to perform a sequential scan rather than reading the index.

Best practices on indexes

It is often useful to index columns that are used with predicates and foreign keys. This enables PostgreSQL to use an index scan instead of a sequential scan. The benefits of indexes are not limited to the SELECT statements, DELETE and UPDATE statements can also benefit from them. There are some cases where an index is not used, and this is often due to a small table size. In big tables, one should plan the space capacity carefully, since the index size might be very big. Also note that indexes have a negative impact on INSERT statements, since amending the index comes with a cost.

There are several catalog tables and functions that help in maintaining indexes, such as pg_stat_all_indexes, which gives statistics about index usage. One can refer to the PostgreSQL system catalog chapter for index maintenance.

When creating an index, make sure that the index does not exist, otherwise one could end up with duplicate indexes. PostgreSQL does not raise a warning when creating duplicate indexes, as shown in the following example:

```
car_portal=# CREATE index on car_portal_app.account(first_name);
CREATE INDEX
car_portal=# CREATE index on car_portal_app.account(first_name);
CREATE INDEX
```

In rare cases, an index might be bloated; PostgreSQL provides the REINDEX command, which is used to rebuild the index. Note that the REINDEX command is a blocking command. To solve this, one can create another index identical to the original index concurrently to avoid locks. Creating an index concurrently is often preferred with a live system, but it requires more work than creating a normal index.

Moreover, creating an index concurrently has some caveats; in some cases, index creation might fail, leading to an invalid index. An invalid index can be dropped or rebuilt using the DROP and REINDEX statements respectively. To re-index the index account_history_account_id_search_key_search_date_key, one can run the following script. Note that this is a blocking statement:

```
car_portal=# REINDEX index
car_portal_app.account_history_account_id_search_key_search_date_key;
REINDEX
```

Alternatively, one can create a concurrent index, as follows, which is not blocking:

```
car_portal=# CREATE UNIQUE INDEX CONCURRENTLY ON
car_portal_app.account_history(account_id, search_key, search_date);
CREATE INDEX
```

Finally, to clean up, we need to drop the original index. In this particular case, we cannot use the DROP INDEX statement because the index is created via unique constraint. To Drop the index, the constraint needs to be dropped, as follows:

```
car_portal=# ALTER TABLE car_portal_app.account_history DROP CONSTRAINT
account_history_account_id_search_key_search_date_key;
ALTER TABLE
```

Finally, the unique constraint can be added as follows:

```
car_portal=> ALTER TABLE account_history ADD CONSTRAINT
account_history_account_id_search_key_search_date_key UNIQUE USING INDEX
account_history_account_id_search_key_search_date_idx;
NOTICE: ALTER TABLE / ADD CONSTRAINT USING INDEX will rename index
"account_history_account_id_search_key_search_date_idx" to
"account_history_account_id_search_key_search_date_key"
ALTER TABLE
```

Functions

A PostgreSQL function is used to provide a distinct service, and is often composed of a set of declarations, expressions, and statements. PostgreSQL has very rich built-in functions for almost all existing data types. In this chapter, we will focus on user-defined functions. However, details about the syntax and function parameters will be covered in later chapters.

PostgreSQL native programming language

PostgreSQL supports out-of-the-box user-defined functions written in C, SQL, and PL/pgSQL. There are also three other procedural languages that come with the standard PostgreSQL distribution: PL/Tcl, PL/Python, and PL/Perl. However, one needs to create the languages in order to use it, via the CREATE EXTENSION PostgreSQL command or via the createlang utility tool. The simplest way to create a language and make it accessible to all databases is to create it in template1, directly after the PostgreSQL cluster installation. Note that one does not need to perform this step for C, SQL, and PL/pgSQL.

For beginners, the most convenient languages to use are SQL and PL/pgSQL, since they are supported directly. Moreover, they are highly portable and do not need special care during the upgrading of the PostgreSQL cluster. Creating functions in the C is not as easy as creating them in SQL or PL/pgSQL, but since the C is a general programming language, one could use it to create very complex functions to handle complex data types such as images.

Creating a function in the C language

In the following example, we will create a factorial function in the C. This can be used as a template for creating more complex functions. One can create a PostgreSQL C function in four steps, as follows:

1. Install the postgresql-server-development library.
2. Define your function in C, create a make file, and compile it as a shared library (.so).
3. Specify the location of the shared library that contains your function. The easiest way to do this is to provide the library's absolute path when creating the function, or by copying the function-shared library created to the PostgreSQL library directory.
4. Create the function in your database using the CREATE FUNCTION statement.

To install the PostgreSQL development library, one can use the `apt` tool, as follows:

```
sudo  apt-get install postgresql-server-dev-10
```

In C language development, the `make` tools are often used to compile C code. The following is a simple `makefile` to compile the factorial function. The `pg_config` is used to provide information about the installed version of PostgreSQL:

```
MODULES = fact

PG_CONFIG = pg_config
PGXS = $(shell $(PG_CONFIG) --pgxs)
INCLUDEDIR = $(shell $(PG_CONFIG) --includedir-server)
include $(PGXS)

fact.so: fact.o
        cc -shared -o fact.so fact.o

fact.o: fact.c
        cc -o fact.o -c fact.c $(CFLAGS) -I$(INCLUDEDIR)
```

The source code of the factorial fact for the abbreviation C function is given as follows:

```
#include "postgres.h"
#include "fmgr.h"
#ifdef PG_MODULE_MAGIC
PG_MODULE_MAGIC;
#endif
Datum fact(PG_FUNCTION_ARGS);
PG_FUNCTION_INFO_V1(fact);
Datum
fact(PG_FUNCTION_ARGS) {
int32 fact = PG_GETARG_INT32(0);
int32 count = 1, result = 1;
for (count = 1; count <= fact; count++)
    result = result * count;
PG_RETURN_INT32(result);
}
```

The last step is to compile the code, copy the library to the PostgreSQL libraries location, and create the function as `postgres` or normal user. One can compile the code as follows:

```
$ make -f makefile
cc -o fact.o -c fact.c -Wall -Wmissing-prototypes -Wpointer-arith -
Wdeclaration-after-statement -Wendif-labels -Wmissing-format-attribute -
Wformat-security -fno-strict-aliasing -fwrapv -fexcess-precision=standard -
g -g -O2 -fstack-protector-strong -Wformat -Werror=format-security -fPIC -
pie -fno-omit-frame-pointer -fPIC -I/usr/include/postgresql/10/server
```

```
cc -shared -o fact.so fact.o
```

Now, we need to copy the file, and this requires `sudo` privileges:

```
$sudo cp fact.so $(pg_config --pkglibdir)/
```

Finally, as a `postgres` user, create the function in the `template` library, and test it:

```
$ psql -d template1 -c "CREATE FUNCTION fact(INTEGER) RETURNS INTEGER AS
'fact', 'fact' LANGUAGE C STRICT;"
CREATE FUNCTION
$ psql -d template1 -c "SELECT fact(5);"
 fact
------
  120
(1 row)
```

Writing C functions is quite complicated compared to SQL and PL/pgSQL functions. They might even cause some complications when upgrading the database if they are not well maintained.

```
CREATE OR REPLACE FUNCTION is_updatable_view (text) RETURNS BOOLEAN AS
$$
    SELECT is_insertable_into='YES' FROM information_schema.tables WHERE
table_type = 'VIEW' AND table_name = $1
$$ LANGUAGE SQL;
```

The body of the SQL function can be composed of several SQL statements; the result of the last SQL statement determines the function return type. An SQL PostgreSQL function cannot be used to construct dynamic SQL statements, since the function argument can only be used to substitute data values and not identifiers. The following snippet is not valid in an SQL function:

```
CREATE FUNCTION drop_table (text) RETURNS VOID AS
$$
    DROP TABLE $1;
$$ LANGUAGE SQL;
```

The PL/pgSQL language is full-fledged and is the preferable choice for usage on a daily basis. It can contain a variable declaration, conditional and looping construct, exception trapping, and so on. The following function returns the factorial of an integer:

```
CREATE OR REPLACE FUNCTION fact(fact INT) RETURNS INT AS
$$
DECLARE
    count INT = 1;
    result INT = 1;
```

```
BEGIN
    FOR count IN 1..fact LOOP
        result = result* count;
    END LOOP;
    RETURN result;
END;
$$ LANGUAGE plpgsql;
```

Function usages

PostgreSQL can be used in several scenarios. For example, some developers use functions as an abstract interface with higher programming languages to hide the data model. Additionally, functions can have several other usages, such as:

- Performing complex logic that is difficult to perform with SQL
- Performing actions before or after the execution of an SQL statement via the trigger system
- Cleaning SQL code by reusing the common code and bundling SQL code in modules
- Automating common tasks related to a database by utilizing dynamic SQL

Function dependency

When using PostgreSQL functions, one needs to be careful not to end up with dangling functions, since the dependency between functions is not well maintained in the PostgreSQL system catalog. The following example shows how one can end up with a dangling function:

```
CREATE OR REPLACE FUNCTION test_dep (INT) RETURNS INT AS $$
BEGIN
        RETURN $1;
END;
$$
LANGUAGE plpgsql;
CREATE OR REPLACE FUNCTION test_dep_2(INT) RETURNS INT AS
$$
BEGIN
    RETURN test_dep($1);
END;
$$
LANGUAGE plpgsql;
DROP FUNCTION test_dep(int);
```

The `test_dep_2` function is dangling. When invoking this function, an error will be raised, as follows:

```
SELECT test_dep_2 (5);
ERROR: function test_dep(integer) does not exist
LINE 1: SELECT test_dep($1)
               ^
HINT: No function matches the given name and argument types. You might
need to add explicit type casts.
QUERY: SELECT test_dep($1)
CONTEXT: PL/pgSQL function test_dep_2(integer) line 3 at RETURN
```

PostgreSQL function categories

When creating a function, it is marked as volatile by default if the volatility classification is not specified. If the created function is not volatile, it is important to mark it as stable or immutable, because this will help the optimizer to generate the optimal execution plans. PostgreSQL functions can have one of the following three volatility classifications:

- **Volatile**: The volatile function can return a different result on successive calls even if the function argument did not change, or it can change the data in the database. The `random()` function is a volatile function.
- **Stable and immutable**: These functions cannot modify the database, and are guaranteed to return the same result for the same argument. The `stable` function provides this guarantee within the statement scope, while the `immutable` function provides this guarantee globally, without any scope.

For example, the `random()` function is volatile, since it will give a different result for each call. The function `round()` is immutable because it will always give the same result for the same argument. The function `now()` is stable, since it will always give the same result within the statement or transaction, as shown next:

```
postgres=# BEGIN;
BEGIN
postgres=# SELECT now();
              now
------------------------------
 2017-10-30 22:00:04.723596+01
(1 row)

postgres=# SELECT 'Some time has passed', now();
       ?column? | now
```

```
--------------------+-------------------------------
 Some time has passed | 2017-10-30 22:00:04.723596+01
(1 row)
```

PostgreSQL anonymous functions

PostgreSQL provides the DO statement, which can be used to execute anonymous code blocks. The DO statement reduces the need to create shell scripts for administration purposes. However, one should note that all PostgreSQL functions are transactional, so if one would like to create indexes, for example, shell scripting is a better alternative. In the car portal schema, let's assume that we would like to have another user who can perform only select statements. One can create a role as follows:

```
CREATE user select_only;
```

Now we need to grant select permission on each table for the newly created role. This can be done using dynamic SQL as follows:

```
DO $$
    DECLARE r record;
BEGIN
    FOR r IN SELECT table_schema, table_name FROM information_schema.tables
WHERE table_schema = 'car_portal_app' LOOP
        EXECUTE 'GRANT SELECT ON ' || quote_ident(r.table_schema) || '.'||
quote_ident(r.table_name) || ' TO select_only';
    END LOOP;
END$$;
```

User-defined data types

PostgreSQL provides two methods for implementing user-defined data types through the following commands:

- CREATE DOMAIN: The CREATE DOMAIN command allows developers to create a user-defined data type with constraints. This helps to make the source code more modular.
- CREATE TYPE: The CREATE TYPE command is often used to create a composite type, which is useful in procedural languages, and is used as the return data type. Also, one can use the create type to create the ENUM type, which is useful to decrease the number of joins, specifically for lookup tables.

Often, developers tend not to use user-defined data types and use flat tables instead due to a lack of support on the driver side, such as JDBC and ODBC. Nonetheless, in JDBC, the composite data types can be retried as Java objects and parsed manually.

Domain objects, as with other database objects, should have a unique name within the schema scope. The first use case of domains is to use them for common patterns. For example, a text type that does not allow null values and does not contain spaces is a common pattern. In the web car portal, the `first_name` and the `last_name` columns in the account table are not null. They should also not contain spaces, and are defined as follows:

```
first_name TEXT NOT NULL,
last_name TEXT NOT NULL,
CHECK(first_name !~ '\s' AND last_name !~ '\s'),
```

One can replace the text data type and the constraints by creating a domain and using it to define the `first_name` and the `last_name` data type, as follows:

```
CREATE DOMAIN text_without_space_and_null AS TEXT NOT NULL CHECK (value!~
'\s');
```

In order to test the `text_without_space_and_null` domain, let's use it in a table definition, and execute several `INSERT` statements, as follows:

```
CREATE TABLE test_domain (
test_att text_without_space_and_null
);
```

Let's finally insert several values into the table `test_domain`:

```
postgres=# INSERT INTO test_domain values ('hello');
INSERT 0 1
postgres=# INSERT INTO test_domain values ('hello world');
ERROR: value for domain text_without_space_and_null violates check
constraint "text_without_space_and_null_check"
postgres=# INSERT INTO test_domain values (null);
ERROR: domain text_without_space_and_null does not allow null values
```

Another good use case for creating domains is to create distinct identifiers across several tables, since some people tend to use numbers instead of names to retrieve information. One can do that by creating a sequence and wrapping it with a domain:

```
CREATE SEQUENCE global_id_seq;
CREATE DOMAIN global_serial INT DEFAULT NEXTVAL('global_id_seq') NOT NULL;
```

Finally, one can alter the domain using the ALTER DOMAIN command. If a new constraint is added to a domain, it will cause all the attributes using that domain to be validated against the new constraint. One can control this by suppressing the constraint validation on old values and then cleaning up the tables individually. For example, let's assume we would like to have a constraint on the text length of the text_without_space_and_null domain, this can be done as follows:

```
ALTER DOMAIN text_without_space_and_null ADD CONSTRAINT
text_without_space_and_null_length_chk check (length(value)<=15);
```

The preceding SQL statement will fail due to data violation if an attribute is using this domain and the attribute value length is more than 15 characters. So, to force the newly created data to adhere to the domain constraints and to leave the old data without validation, one can still create it, as follows:

```
ALTER DOMAIN text_without_space_and_null ADD CONSTRAINT text_without_
space_and_null_length_chk check (length(value)<=15) NOT VALID;
```

After data clean up, one can also validate the constraint for old data by invoking the ALTER DOMAIN ... VALIDATE CONSTRAINT statement. Finally, the \dD+ psql meta-command can be used to describe the domain.

Composite data types are very useful for creating functions, especially when the return type is a row of several values. For example, let's assume that we would like to have a function that returns the seller_id, seller_name, number of advertisements, and the total rank for a certain customer account. The first step is to create a TYPE, as follows:

```
CREATE TYPE seller_information AS (seller_id INT, seller_name
TEXT,number_of_advertisements BIGINT, total_rank float);
```

Then, we can use the newly created data TYPE as the return type of the function, as follows:

```
CREATE OR REPLACE FUNCTION seller_information (account_id INT ) RETURNS
seller_information AS
$$
SELECT seller_account.seller_account_id, first_name || last_name as
seller_name, count(*), sum(rank)::float/count(*)
FROM account INNER JOIN
    seller_account ON account.account_id = seller_account.account_id LEFT
JOIN
    advertisement ON advertisement.seller_account_id =
seller_account.seller_account_id LEFT JOIN
    advertisement_rating ON advertisement.advertisement_id =
advertisement_rating.advertisement_id
WHERE account.account_id = $1
GROUP BY seller_account.seller_account_id, first_name, last_name
```

```
$$
LANGUAGE SQL;
```

CREATE TYPE could also be used to define enums; an enum type is a special data type that enables an attribute to be assigned one of the predefined constants. The usage of the enum data types reduces the number of joins needed to create some queries; thus, it makes SQL code more compact and easier to understand. In the advertisement_rating table, we have a column with the rank name, which is defined as follows:

```
-- This is a part of advertisement_rating table def.
rank INT NOT NULL,
CHECK (rank IN (1,2,3,4,5)),
```

In the preceding example, the given code is not semantically clear. For example, some people might consider 1 to be the highest rank, while others might consider 5 to be the highest rank. To solve this, one could use the lookup table, as follows:

```
CREATE TABLE rank (
    rank_id SERIAL PRIMARY KEY,
    rank_name TEXT NOT NULL
);
INSERT INTO rank VALUES (1, 'poor') , (2, 'fair'), (3, 'good') , (4,'very
good') ,( 5, 'excellent');
```

In the preceding approach, the user can explicitly see the rank table entries. Moreover, the rank table entries can be changed to reflect new business needs, such as to make the ranking from 1 to 10. Additionally, in this approach, changing the rank table entries will not lock the advertisement_rating table, since the ALTER TABLE command will not be needed to change the check constraint CHECK (rank IN (1, 2, 3, 4, 5)). The disadvantage of this approach lies in retrieving the information of a certain table that is linked to several lookup tables, since the tables need to be joined together. In our example, we need to join advertisement_rating and the rank table to get the semantic of rank_id . The more lookup tables, the more lengthy queries are.

Another approach to modeling the rank is to use the enum data types, as follows:

```
CREATE TYPE rank AS ENUM ('poor', 'fair', 'good', 'very good','excellent');
```

The psql \dT meta command is used to describe the enum data type. One could also use the function enum_range, as follows:

```
postgres=# SELECT enum_range(null::rank);
 enum_range
---------------------------------------
 {poor,fair,good,"very good",excellent}
```

The enum data type order is determined by the order of the values in the enum at the time of its creation.

```
postgres=# SELECT unnest(enum_range(null::rank)) order by 1 desc;
  unnest
-----------
 excellent
 very good
 good
 fair
 poor
(5 rows)
```

enum PostgreSQL data types are type safe, and different enum data types cannot be compared with each other. Moreover, enum data types can be altered, and new values can be added.

Triggers and rule systems

PostgreSQL provides triggers and rule systems to automatically perform a certain function when an event such as INSERT, UPDATE, or DELETE is performed. Triggers and rules cannot be defined on SELECT statements, except for _RETURN, which is used in the internal implementation of PostgreSQL views.

From a functionality point of view, the trigger system is more generic; it can be used to implement complex actions more easily than rules. However, both trigger and rule systems can be used to implement the same functionality in several cases. From the performance point of view, rules tend to be faster than triggers, but triggers tend to be simpler and more compatible with other RDBMs, since the rule system is a PostgreSQL extension.

Rule system

Creating a rule will either rewire the default rule, or create a new rule for a specific action on a specific table or view. In other words, a rule on an insert action can change the insert action behavior, or can create a new action for the insert. When using the rule system, one needs to note that it is based on the C macro system. This means one can get strange results when it is used with volatile functions such as random(), and sequence functions such as nextval(). The following example shows how tricky the rule system can be. Let's assume that we would like to audit the table for car. For this reason, a new table called car_log will be created to keep a track of all the actions on the car table, such as UPDATE, DELETE, and INSERT. One can achieve this by using the trigger system, as follows:

```
CREATE TABLE car_log (LIKE car);
ALTER TABLE car_log ADD COLUMN car_log_action varchar (1) NOT NULL, ADD
COLUMN car_log_time TIMESTAMP WITH TIME ZONE NOT NULL;

CREATE RULE car_log AS ON INSERT TO car DO ALSO
   INSERT INTO car_log (car_id, car_model_id, number_of_owners,
registration_number, number_of_doors, manufacture_year,car_log_action,
car_log_time)
   VALUES (new.car_id, new.car_model_id,new.number_of_owners,
new.registration_number, new.number_of_doors, new.manufacture_year,'I',
now());
```

The preceding code creates the car_log table, which has a structure similar to the car table. The car_log table also has two additional attributes to log the actions: such as insert (indicated in the example as I), and the action time. The preceding code also creates a rule on the car table to cascade the insert on the car table to the car_log table. To test the code, let's insert a record:

```
INSERT INTO car (car_id, car_model_id, number_of_owners,
registration_number, number_of_doors, manufacture_year) VALUES (100000, 2,
2, 'x', 3, 2017);
```

One can examine the contents of the car_log table, as follows:

```
car_portal=> SELECT to_json(car) FROM car where registration_number ='x';
to_json
---------------------------------------------------------------------------
---------------------------------------------------------------------------
{"car_id":100000,"number_of_owners":2,"registration_number":"x","manufactur
e_year":2017,"number_of_doors":3,"car_model_id":2,"mileage":null}
(1 row)

car_portal=> SELECT to_json(car_log) FROM car_log where registration_number
='x';
```

```
to_json
---------------------------------------------------------------------------
---------------------------------------------------------------------------
----------------------------------------------------------------------
{"car_id":100000,"number_of_owners":2,"registration_number":"x","manufactur
e_year":2017,"number_of_doors":3,"car_model_id":2,"mileage":null,"car_log_a
ction":"I","car_log_time":"2017-11-20T20:08:50.107895+01:00"}
(1 row)
```

As the preceding example shows, everything goes as expected. One record is inserted in the car_log table, and that record is identical to the one inserted in the car table. However, as mentioned earlier, the rules system is built on macros, which cause some issues. For example, if we use the default value, this will create a problem, as shown:

```
INSERT INTO car (car_id, car_model_id, number_of_owners,
registration_number, number_of_doors, manufacture_year) VALUES (default, 2,
2, 'y', 3, 2017);
```

Now, one can test the content of the two tables as follows:

```
car_portal=> SELECT to_json(car) FROM car where registration_number ='y';
                                                                   to_json
---------------------------------------------------------------------------
----------------------------------------------------------------------
{"car_id":230,"number_of_owners":2,"registration_number":"y","manufacture_y
ear":2017,"number_of_doors":3,"car_model_id":2,"mileage":null}
(1 row)

car_portal=> SELECT to_json(car_log) FROM car_log where registration_number
='y';
to_json
---------------------------------------------------------------------------
---------------------------------------------------------------------------
----------------------------------------------------------------
{"car_id":231,"number_of_owners":2,"registration_number":"y","manufacture_y
ear":2017,"number_of_doors":3,"car_model_id":2,"mileage":null,"car_log_acti
on":"I","car_log_time":"2017-11-20T20:14:49.820841+01:00"}
(1 row)
```

Note that the records in the car table and the car_log tables are not identical. The car_id in the car table is less than the car_id in the car_log table by one. One can notice that the DEFAULT keyword is used to assign the car_id the default value, which is nextval('car_car_id_seq'::regclass).

When creating a rule one can have a conditional rule, that is, one can rewrite the action if a certain condition is met, as shown in the following rule synopsis. However, one cannot have conditional rules for INSERT, UPDATE, and DELETE on views without having unconditional rules. To solve this problem, one can create an unconditional dummy rule. Rules on views are one way of implementing updatable views.

Trigger system

PostgreSQL triggers a function when a certain event occurs on a table, view, or foreign table. Triggers are executed when a user tries to modify the data through any of the **data manipulation language** (**DML**) events, including INSERT, UPDATE, DELETE, or TRUNCATE. The trigger synopsis is as follows:

```
CREATE [ CONSTRAINT ] TRIGGER name { BEFORE | AFTER | INSTEAD OF } { event
[ OR ... ] }
    ON table_name
    [ FROM referenced_table_name ]
    [ NOT DEFERRABLE | [ DEFERRABLE ] [ INITIALLY IMMEDIATE | INITIALLY
DEFERRED ] ]
    [ REFERENCING { { OLD | NEW } TABLE [ AS ] transition_relation_name } [
... ] ]
    [ FOR [ EACH ] { ROW | STATEMENT } ]
    [ WHEN ( condition ) ]
    EXECUTE PROCEDURE function_name ( arguments )

where event can be one of:

    INSERT
    UPDATE [ OF column_name [, ... ] ]
    DELETE
    TRUNCATE
```

The trigger time context is one of the following:

- BEFORE: This is applied on tables only, and is fired before the constraints are checked and the operation is performed. It is useful for checking data constraints on several tables when it is not possible to model using referential integrity constraints.
- AFTER: This too is applied on tables only, and is fired after the operation is performed. It is useful for cascading changes to other tables. An example use case is data auditing.
- INSTEAD OF: This is applied on views, and is used to make views updatable.

When a trigger is marked for each row, then the trigger function will be executed for each row that has been affected by the CRUD operation. A statement trigger is only executed once per operation. When the WHEN condition is supplied, then only the rows that fulfill the condition will be handled by the trigger.

Finally, triggers can be marked as CONSTRAINT to control when they can be executed; a trigger can be executed after the end of the statement or at the end of the transaction. The constraint trigger must be AFTER or FOR EACH ROW trigger, and the firing time of constraint trigger is controlled by the following options:

- DEFERRABLE: This marks the trigger as deferrable, which can be used to cause the trigger firing to be postponed till the end of the transaction.
- INITIALLY DEFERRED: This specifies the time when the trigger is to be executed. This means that the trigger will be executed at the end of the transaction. The trigger should be marked as DEFERRABLE.
- NOT DEFERRABLE: This is the default behavior of the trigger, which will cause the trigger to be fired after each statement in the transaction.
- INITIALLY IMMEDIATE: This specifies the time when the trigger is to be executed. This means that the trigger will be executed after each statement. The Trigger should be marked as DEFERRABLE.

 Trigger names define the execution order of the triggers, which have the same firing time context alphabetically.

The firing time options: DEFERRABLE, INITIALLY DEFERRED, NOT DEFERRABLE, and INITIALLY IMMEDIATE, can also be applied to constraint triggers. These options are very useful when PostgreSQL interacts with external systems such as memcached. For example, let's assume that we have a trigger on a table and this table is cached; whenever the table is updated, the cache is also updated. Since the caching system is not transactional, we can postpone the update until the end of the transaction to guarantee data consistency.

To explain the trigger system, let's redo the car_log table example using triggers. First of all, notice that the trigger type is the AFTER trigger, since data should first be checked against the car table constraint before inserting it in the new table. To create a trigger, one needs to create a function, as follows:

```
CREATE OR REPLACE FUNCTION car_log_trg () RETURNS TRIGGER AS
$$
BEGIN
IF TG_OP = 'INSERT' THEN
```

```
      INSERT INTO car_log SELECT NEW.*, 'I', NOW();
ELSIF TG_OP = 'UPDATE' THEN
      INSERT INTO car_log SELECT NEW.*, 'U', NOW();
ELSIF TG_OP = 'DELETE' THEN
      INSERT INTO car_log SELECT OLD.*, 'D', NOW();
END IF;
RETURN NULL; --ignored since this is after trigger
END;
$$
LANGUAGE plpgsql;
```

To create the TRIGGER, one needs to execute the following statement:

```
CREATE TRIGGER car_log AFTER INSERT OR UPDATE OR DELETE ON car FOR EACH ROW
EXECUTE PROCEDURE car_log_trg ();
```

The trigger function should fulfill the following requirements:

- **Return type**: The TRIGGER function should return the TRIGGER pseudo type.
- **Return value**: The TRIGGER function must return a value. The value is often NULL for AFTER ... EACH ROW, and for statement level triggers a row with the exact structure of the table that fired the trigger.
- **No arguments**: The TRIGGER function must be declared without an argument, even if one needs to pass an argument to it. The passing of an argument is achieved via the TG_ARG variable. When the trigger function is created, several variables, such as TG_ARG and NEW, are created automatically. Other variables that are created are listed in the following table:

Trigger variable	Data type	Description
NEW	RECORD	Holds the row that is inserted or updated. In the case of the statement level trigger, it is NULL.
OLD	RECORD	Holds the old row that is updated or deleted. In the case of the statement level trigger, it is NULL.
TG_NAME	NAME	The trigger name.
TG_OP	NAME	The trigger operation, which can have one of the following values: INSERT, UPDATE, DELETE, TRUNCATE
TG_WHEN	NAME	The time when the trigger is fired, which can have one of the following values: AFTER, BEFORE.

Trigger variable	Data type	Description
TG_RELID	OID	The relation OID. One can get the relation name by casting it to text using regclass::text.
TG_TABLE_NAME	NAME	The trigger table name.
TG_TABLE_SCHEMA	NAME	The trigger table schema name.
TG_ARG[]	TEXT array	The trigger argument. The indexing starts from zero and a wrong index returns NULL.
TG_NARG	INTEGER	The number of arguments passed to the trigger.

A row-level trigger, which is fired BEFORE the actual operation, returning null values will cancel the operation. This means that the next trigger will not be fired, and the affected row will not be deleted, updated, or inserted. For a trigger that is fired AFTER the operation or a statement-level trigger, the return value will be ignored; however, the operation will be aborted if the trigger function raises an exception or an error due to the relational database's transactional behavior.

In the preceding auditing example, if one changes the car table definition, such as adding or dropping a column, the trigger function on the car table will fail, leading to the ignoring of the newly inserted or updated row. One could solve this by using exception trapping in the trigger definition.

Triggers with arguments

In the following example, another general auditing technique will be presented, which can be applied to several tables, while some table columns can be excluded from auditing. The new editing techniques use the hstore extension. hstore defines a hash map data type, and provides a set of functions and operators to handle this data type. In the new auditing technique, the table rows will be stored as a hash map. The first step is to create the hstore extension and a table where the audited data will be stored, as follows:

```
SET search_path to car_portal_app;
CREATE extension hstore;
CREATE TABLE car_portal_app.log
(
    schema_name text NOT NULL,
    table_name text NOT NULL,
    old_row hstore,
    new_row hstore,
    action TEXT check (action IN ('I','U','D')) NOT NULL,
```

```
        created_by text NOT NULL,
        created_on timestamp without time zone NOT NULL
);
```

The second step is to define the TRIGGER function, as follows:

```
CREATE OR REPLACE FUNCTION car_portal_app.log_audit() RETURNS trigger AS
$$
DECLARE
    log_row log;
    excluded_columns text[] = NULL;
BEGIN
    log_row = ROW (TG_TABLE_SCHEMA::text,
TG_TABLE_NAME::text,NULL,NULL,NULL,current_user::TEXT,
current_timestamp);
    IF TG_ARGV[0] IS NOT NULL THEN excluded_columns = TG_ARGV[0]::text[];
END IF;
    IF (TG_OP = 'INSERT') THEN
        log_row.new_row = hstore(NEW.*) - excluded_columns;
        log_row.action ='I';
    ELSIF (TG_OP = 'UPDATE' AND (hstore(OLD.*) - excluded_columns!=
hstore(NEW.*)-excluded_columns)) THEN
        log_row.old_row = hstor(OLD.*) - excluded_columns;
        log_row.new_row = hstore(NEW.* )- excluded_columns;
        log_row.action ='U';
    ELSIF (TG_OP = 'DELETE') THEN
        log_row.old_row = hstore (OLD.*) - excluded_columns;
        log_row.action ='D';
    ELSE
        RETURN NULL; -- update on excluded columns
    END IF;
    INSERT INTO log SELECT log_row.*;
    RETURN NULL;
END;
$$ LANGUAGE plpgsql;
```

The preceding function defines a variable, log_row, of type log, and populates this variable with the trigger table name, trigger table schema, current user, and the current timestamp using the row construct. Moreover, the preceding trigger function parses TG_ARGV to determine whether some columns need to be excluded from auditing. Note that the excluded columns are passed as a text array. Finally, the trigger function populates log.action, log.old_row, and log.new_row based on the TG_OP variable.

To apply the preceding trigger on the `car` table, assuming that the `number_of_doors` attribute should be excluded from tracking, one can create the trigger as follows:

```
CREATE TRIGGER car_log_trg AFTER INSERT OR UPDATE OR DELETE ON
car_portal_app.car FOR EACH ROW EXECUTE PROCEDURE
log_audit('{number_of_doors}');
```

The array literal `{number_of_doors}` is passed to the function `log_audit` and accessed via the `TG_ARG` variable. Finally, the expression `hstore(NEW.*) - excluded_columns` is used to convert the `NEW` variable to the `hstore` type and then delete the keys specified in the `excluded_columns` array from the converted `hstore`. The following example shows the trigger behavior for the insert statement:

```
car_portal=# INSERT INTO car (car_id, car_model_id, number_of_owners,
registration_number, number_of_doors, manufacture_year) VALUES (default, 2,
2, 'z', 3, 2017);
INSERT 0 1
```

To display the result, let's retrieve the content of the log table in JSON format, as follows:

```
car_portal=# SELECT jsonb_pretty((to_json(log))::jsonb) FROM
car_portal_app.log WHERE action = 'I' and
new_row->'registration_number'='z';
                    jsonb_pretty
-------------------------------------------------
 { +
     "action": "I", +
     "new_row": { +
         "car_id": "235", +
         "mileage": null, +
         "car_model_id": "2", +
         "manufacture_year": "2017", +
         "number_of_owners": "2", +
         "registration_number": "z" +
     }, +
     "old_row": null, +
     "created_by": "postgres", +
     "created_on": "2017-11-20T20:42:41.132194",+
     "table_name": "car", +
     "schema_name": "car_portal_app" +
 }
(1 row)
```

Triggers and updatable views

For views that are not automatically updatable, the trigger system can be used to make them updatable. The view `seller_account_information`, which shows the information about the seller account, is not automatically updatable, as shown next:

```
CREATE OR REPLACE VIEW seller_account_info AS SELECT account.account_id,
first_name, last_name, email, password, seller_account_id, total_rank,
number_of_advertisement, street_name, street_number, zip_code , city
FROM account INNER JOIN
seller_account ON (account.account_id = seller_account.account_id);
```

To verify that the view is not updatable:

```
car_portal=# SELECT is_insertable_into FROM information_schema.tables WHERE
table_name = 'seller_account_info';
 is_insertable_into
--------------------
 NO
(1 row)
```

The following trigger function assumes that `account_id` and `seller_account_id` are always generated using the default values, which are the sequences generated automatically when creating a serial data type. This is often a good approach and relieves the developer of checking the table for a unique constraint before inserting new rows, and it keeps primary key values without big gaps. Furthermore, the trigger function assumes that primary keys cannot be changed for the same reason. Changing primary keys might also cause problems when the default foreign keys options, cascade delete and cascade update, are not used.

Finally, note that the trigger functions return NEW for the INSERT and UPDATE operations, OLD for the DELETE operation, and NULL in the case of an exception. Returning the proper value is important to detect the number of rows that are affected by the operation. It is also very important to return the proper value. Using the RETURNING keyword, as shown in the following function, is used to assign the value for
NEW.`account_id` and NEW.`seller_account_id`. Note that if the IDs are not assigned properly, this might lead to issues and hard to trace problems for object-relational mappers such as Hibernate:

```
CREATE OR REPLACE FUNCTION seller_account_info_update () RETURNS TRIGGER AS
$$
DECLARE
    acc_id INT;
    seller_acc_id INT;
BEGIN
```

```
        IF (TG_OP = 'INSERT') THEN
            WITH inserted_account AS (
                INSERT INTO car_portal_app.account (account_id, first_name,
last_name, password, email) VALUES (DEFAULT, NEW.first_name, NEW.last_name,
NEW.password, NEW.email) RETURNING account_id
            ), inserted_seller_account AS (
            INSERT INTO car_portal_app.seller_account(seller_account_id,
account_id, total_rank, number_of_advertisement, street_name,
street_number, zip_code, city)
            SELECT
nextval('car_portal_app.seller_account_seller_account_id_seq'::regclass),
account_id, NEW.total_rank, NEW.number_of_advertisement, NEW.street_name,
NEW.street_number, NEW.zip_code, NEW.city FROM inserted_account RETURNING
account_id, seller_account_id)
            SELECT account_id, seller_account_id INTO acc_id, seller_acc_id FROM
inserted_seller_account;
        NEW.account_id = acc_id;
        NEW.seller_account_id = seller_acc_id;
        RETURN NEW;
      ELSIF (TG_OP = 'UPDATE' AND OLD.account_id = NEW.account_id AND
OLD.seller_account_id = NEW.seller_account_id) THEN
        UPDATE car_portal_app.account SET first_name = new.first_name,
last_name = new.last_name, password= new.password, email = new.email WHERE
account_id = new.account_id;
        UPDATE car_portal_app.seller_account SET total_rank = NEW.total_rank,
number_of_advertisement= NEW.number_of_advertisement, street_name=
NEW.street_name, street_number = NEW.street_number, zip_code =
NEW.zip_code, city = NEW.city WHERE seller_account_id =
NEW.seller_account_id;
        RETURN NEW;
      ELSIF (TG_OP = 'DELETE') THEN
        DELETE FROM car_portal_app.seller_account WHERE seller_account_id =
OLD.seller_account_id;
        DELETE FROM car_portal_app.account WHERE account_id = OLD.account_id;
        RETURN OLD;
      ELSE
        RAISE EXCEPTION 'An error occurred for % operation', TG_OP;
        RETURN NULL;
      END IF;
END;
$$ LANGUAGE plpgsql;
```

To run and test the trigger function, let's execute the following SQL statements:

```
CREATE TRIGGER seller_account_info_trg INSTEAD OF INSERT OR UPDATE OR
DELETE ON car_portal_app.seller_account_info FOR EACH ROW EXECUTE PROCEDURE
seller_account_info_update ();
```

To test the INSERT on the view, we can run the following code:

```
car_portal=# INSERT INTO car_portal_app.seller_account_info
(first_name,last_name, password, email, total_rank,
number_of_advertisement, street_name, street_number, zip_code, city) VALUES
('test_first_name', 'test_last_name', 'test_password',
'test_email@test.com', NULL, 0, 'test_street_name', 'test_street_number',
'test_zip_code','test_city') RETURNING account_id, seller_account_id;
 account_id | seller_account_id
------------+-------------------
        482 | 147
(1 row)
```

Notice the return value; the primary keys are returned correctly to the user. To test DELETE and UPDATE, we simply run the following snippet:

```
car_portal=# UPDATE car_portal_app.seller_account_info set email =
'test2@test.com' WHERE seller_account_id=147 RETURNING seller_account_id;
 seller_account_id
-------------------
               147
(1 row)

UPDATE 1
car_portal=# DELETE FROM car_portal_app.seller_account_info WHERE
seller_account_id=147;
DELETE 1
```

Finally if we tried to delete all seller accounts , this will fail due to referential integrity constraint as follows:

```
car_portal=# DELETE FROM car_portal_app.seller_account_info;
ERROR: update or delete on table "seller_account" violates foreign key
constraint "advertisement_seller_account_id_fkey" on table "advertisement"
DETAIL: Key (seller_account_id)=(57) is still referenced from table
"advertisement".
CONTEXT: SQL statement "DELETE FROM car_portal_app.seller_account WHERE
seller_account_id = OLD.seller_account_id"
PL/pgSQL function seller_account_info_update() line 21 at SQL statement
car_portal=#
```

Summary

In this chapter, indexes, views, functions, user-defined data types, and rule and trigger systems have been discussed. A view is a named query or a wrapper around a SELECT statement. They can be used as a data access layer, provide an abstraction level, and control data privileges and permissions.

A view in PostgreSQL can be categorized as temporary, materialized, updatable, and recursive. Simple views in PostgreSQL are automatically updatable. To make complex views updatable, one can use the rule and trigger systems. Indexes are physical database objects defined on a table column, a set of columns, and expressions. Indexes are often used to optimize performance or to validate data. There are several techniques for building indexes, including B-tree, hash, GIN, GIST, and BRIN. B-tree is the default indexing method. GIN and GIST are useful for indexing complex data types and for full-text searches. There are several types of indexes; each type can be used for a different use case. For example, partial indexes index only a subset of the data that meets a certain predicate. The unique index is often used to validate data such as the uniqueness of primary keys. Finally, a multi-column index can be used for specific data retrieval scenarios.

The information about indexes can be retrieved from the pg_catalog statistics, and can be used for maintenance purposes. When an index is bloated, one can create a concurrent index instead of re-indexing it. Note that the creation of concurrent indexes will not lock the database table.

PostgreSQL functions provide distinct services, and have usages similar to views. Functions can be written in C, SQL, and PL/pgsql without extra extensions. One important usage of functions is to assist in maintaining a database. This can be done easily without using external scripting, such as Bash, by utilizing anonymous functions.

Specifying the function category as stable, volatile, or immutable is very important because it helps the optimizer to generate the optimal execution plan. Unfortunately, the interdependency between functions is not recorded in the database catalog. This means one should take great care when writing complex logic using functions. User-defined data types can be created using the CREATE DOMAIN and CREATE TYPE commands. Some user-defined data types, such as ENUM, can greatly reduce the number of joins, thus leading to more understandable and efficient SQL code. PostgreSQL triggers and rules are used to execute an action when a certain event occurs. They can be used alternately in several scenarios. One needs to be careful when using rules with volatile functions because they have some side effects.

5
SQL Language

Structured query language (SQL) is used to set up the structure of the database, manipulate the data in the database, and query the database. This chapter will be dedicated to the **data manipulation language (DML)**.

After reading the chapter, you will understand the concept of SQL and the logic of SQL statements. You will be able to write your own SQL queries and manipulate the data using this language. The complete reference of SQL can be found in the official PostgreSQL documentation at `http://www.postgresql.org/docs/current/static/sql.html`.

So the topics that we will cover in this chapter are as follows:

- SQL fundamentals
- Lexical structure
- Select
- Update
- Delete

Code examples in this chapter are based on the car portal database described in the previous chapters. The scripts to create the database and fill it with sample data can be found in the attached media. They are called `schema.sql` and `data.sql`. All the code examples from this chapter can be found in the `examples.sql` file.

Refer to the `Chapter 02`, *PostgreSQL in Action*, for details on how to use the `psql` utility.

SQL fundamentals

SQL is used to manipulate the data in the database and query the database. It is also used to define and change the structure of the data--in other words, to implement the data model. This you already know from the previous chapters.

In general, SQL consists of three parts:

- **Data definition language (DDL)**
- **Data manipulation language (DML)**
- **Data control language (DCL)**

The first part is used to create and manage the structure of the data, the second part is used to manage the data itself, and the third part—to control access to the data. Usually, the data structure is defined only once and then it is rarely changed. However, data is constantly inserted into the database, changed, or retrieved. For this reason, DML is used more often than DDL.

SQL is not an imperative programming language, which makes it different from many other languages. To be more specific, one cannot define a detailed algorithm of how the data should be processed. This might make an impression of lack of control of the data. When using imperative languages, the developer usually specifies it on a very detailed level: where to take the data from and how to do it, how to iterate through the array of records, and when and how to process them. If it is necessary to process the data from multiple sources, the developer should implement the relationship between them in the application layer rather than in the database.

SQL, in contrast, is a declarative language. In other words, to get the same result in other languages, the developer writes a whole story. In SQL, the developer writes only one major sentence and leaves details for the database. Developing SQL statements, one just defines the format in which it is needed to get the data from the database, specifies the tables where the data is stored, and states the rules to process the data. All the necessary operations and their exact order and actual algorithms to process the data are chosen by the database, and the developer is not supposed to care about it.

However, this black-box behavior should not be treated as something bad. First, the box is not completely black: there are ways to find out how the data is processed by the database engine, and there are ways to control it. Second, the logic in the SQL statement is very deterministic. Even if it is not clear how the database is processing the query on a low level, the logic of the process and the result of the query is entirely determined by the SQL statement.

This determines the size of a statement (smallest standalone element of execution). In Java, for example, every operation such as assigning a value to a variable is logically processed as a separate item of an algorithm. In contrast, the logic of SQL implies that the whole algorithm is executed all at once, as one statement. There is no way to get the state of the data at any intermediate step of the execution of the query. This does not limit the complexity of the query though. It is possible to implement any sophisticated algorithm in a single SQL statement. Usually, it takes less time to implement complex logic in SQL than in any lower-level language. Developers operate with logical relational data structures and do not need to define their own algorithms of data processing on a physical level. This is what makes SQL so powerful.

Another good thing about SQL is that there is a standard for the language and every modern relation database supports SQL. Although different databases could support different features and implement their own dialect of SQL, the basics of the language are the same. PostgreSQL also has its own SQL dialect, and we will point out some differences to the other RDBMS. By the way, at the beginning of its history, postgres did not support SQL. It was added in 1994 and, after a while, the database was renamed PostgreSQL to indicate this fact.

SQL lexical structure

The minimal SQL instruction that can be executed by the database engine is a **statement**. It can also be called a command or query. For example, each of the following is a statement:

```
SELECT car_id, number_of_doors FROM car_portal_app.car;
DELETE FROM car_portal_app.a;
SELECT now();
```

SQL commands are terminated by a semicolon ; .

> End of input also terminates a command, but that depends on the tools being used: for example, psql would not execute a command when the user presses *Enter* if there is no semicolon, it would just move to a new line. However, when psql executes a SQL script from a file, the last command is always executed, even without a semicolon.

The following elements form the lexical structure of SQL:

- **Keywords** determine what exactly is required from the database to be done
- **Identifiers** refer to the objects in the database—tables, their fields, functions, and so on

- **Constants** (or **literals**) are parts of expressions whose values are specified directly in the code
- **Operators** determine how the data is processed in the expressions
- Special characters, such as parenthesis, brackets, commas, and so on, which have other meanings than simply being an operator
- **Whitespaces** separate words from each other
- **Comments** are used to describe a particular piece of code

Keywords are words such as SELECT or UPDATE. They have special meaning in SQL. They are names of statements or parts of statements. The full list of keywords can be found in the documentation at http://www.postgresql.org/docs/current/static/sql-keywords-appendix.html.

Identifiers are the names of the database objects. Objects such as tables or views can be referred to by the name of the schema it belongs to (see Chapter 03, *PostgreSQL Basic Building Blocks*) followed by the dot symbol . and the name of the object. This is called a **qualified object name**. If the name of the schema is included in the search_path setting or if the object belongs to the current user's schema, then it is not required to use the schema name when referring to the object. In that case, it is called an unqualified object name. Names of the fields of tables are used in the same way: table name, then dot . and field name. It is not necessary to specify the table name, for example, when only one table is queried, and in other cases, it is possible to use a table alias.

SQL is not case-sensitive. Both keywords and identifiers can contain any letters (az), digits (0-9), underscores (_), or dollar signs ($). However, they cannot start with a digit or dollar sign. That makes them similar to each other and without knowing the language, sometimes it is difficult to say if some word is a keyword or an identifier. Usually, keywords are typed in uppercase.

In identifiers, it is still possible to use symbols other than those mentioned earlier, by double-quoting them. It is also possible to create objects with the same names as keywords, but, is not recommended.

Constants in SQL are also called literals. PostgreSQL supports three types of implicitly typed constants: numbers, strings, and bit strings. To use constant values of any other data type, implicit or explicit conversion should be performed.

Numeric constants contain digits and optionally a decimal point, and exponent sign. These are examples of selecting valid numeric constants:

```
SELECT 1, 1.2, 0.3, .5, 1e15, 12.65e-6;
```

String constants should be quoted. There are two kinds of syntax for string constants in PostgreSQL: single quoted constants such as in the SQL Standard, and PostgreSQL-specific dollar-quoted constants. Putting a letter E before the string constant makes it possible to use C-style backslash escaped characters such as \n for a new line or /t for tabulation. A single quote character ' inside a literal should be doubled '' or used with an escape string \'. Putting a letter U with an ampersand before the string without any spaces in between allows you to specify Unicode characters by their code after a backslash.

The examples would be as follows:

```
car_portal=> SELECT 'a', 'aa''aa', E'aa\naa', $$aa'aa$$,
U&'\041C\0418\0420';
 ?column? | ?column? | ?column? | ?column? | ?column?
----------+----------+----------+----------+----------
 a        | aa'aa    | aa      +| aa'aa    | МИР
          |          | aa       |          |
```

The first is simple—a letter a. The second will have a single quote in the middle. The third has C-style new line sequence: \n. The next string is a dollar-quoted. The last has Unicode characters (the word means *peace* in Russian).

Dollar-quoted string constants always have the same value as it was written. No escape sequences are recognized and any kind of quotes are part of the string except for dollar-quote when it is written in the same way as in the beginning. Dollar-quoted strings can have their names set between the dollar signs, which makes it possible to use one dollar-quoted string inside another, like this:

```
car_portal=> SELECT $str1$SELECT $$dollar-quoted string$$;$str1$;
 ?column?
----------------------------------
 SELECT $$dollar-quoted string$$;
```

Here, the sequences $str1$ are taking the role of quotes, and another double dollar inside the literal does not terminate the string. That's why it is very common to use dollar-quoted string to define a function body that is usually given to the PostgreSQL server as a string literal.

Bit strings are preceded by a letter B and can contain only digits 0 or 1. Alternatively, they can be preceded by a letter X and contain any digits, along with letters A-F. In that case, they are hexadecimal strings. Most of the time, bit strings are converted to a numeric data type:

```
car_portal=> SELECT B'01010101'::int, X'AB21'::int;
 int4 | int4
------+-------
   85 | 43809
```

Operators are basic elements of data processing. They are used in SQL expressions. They take one or two arguments and return a value. The examples of operators can be addition +, subtraction –, and so on. PostgreSQL supports a wide range of operators for all data types. In the statements, operators look like sequences of characters from the list: + - * / < > = ~ ! @ # % ^ & | ` ?.

When several operators are used in the same expression, they are executed in a specific order. Some operators, such as multiplication * or division /, have higher precedence among others, and some other operators such as logical or comparison operators have lower precedence. The operators with the same precedence are executed from left to right. The short list of operators and their precedence can be found in the documentation at `https://www.postgresql.org/docs/current/static/sql-syntax-lexical.html#SQL-PRECEDENCE`.

Special characters include the following:

- **Parenthesis (())**: These are used to control the precedence of operations or to group expressions. They can also have special meaning in the syntax of a particular SQL command. They are used as a part of a function name.
- **Brackets ([])**: These are used to select elements from an array.
- **Colons (:)**: These are used to access parts of arrays.
- **Double colons (::)**: These are used for type casing.
- **Commas (,)**: These are used to separate elements of a list.
- **Periods (.)**: These are used to separate schema, table, and column names from each other.
- **Semicolon (;)**: This is used to terminate a statement.
- **Asterisk (*)**: This is used to refer to all the fields of a table or all the elements of a composite value.

Whitespaces separate words from each other. In SQL, any number of spaces, new lines, or tabulations are considered as a single whitespace.

Comments can be used in any part of SQL code. The server ignores comments, treating them as whitespace. Comments are quoted in pairs of /* and */. Also, the whole line of code can be commented by using double dash --. In this case, a comment starts from the double dash and ends at the end of the line.

Simply speaking, DML has only four types of statements:

- INSERT is used to put new data into the database
- UPDATE is used to change the data
- DELETE is used to delete the data
- SELECT is used to retrieve the data

The structure of every statement is strict and human-readable, though the syntax of each statement is different. A complete list of detailed syntax diagrams can be found in the PostgreSQL documentation at http://www.postgresql.org/docs/current/static/sql-commands.html. Later in this chapter, the main elements of each statement will be described.

SELECT will be the first because it is the most used command and very often it is used as an element of other commands. SQL allows that it is possible to nest commands, using a result of one command as an input for another command. These nested queries are called **subqueries**.

Querying data with SELECT statements

SELECT statements or SELECT queries or just queries are used to retrieve data from a database. SELECT queries can have different sources: tables, views, functions, or the VALUES command. All of them are relations or can be treated as relations or return relations, which functions can do. The output of SELECT is also a relation that in general can have multiple columns and contain many rows. As the result and the source of a query have the same nature in SQL, it is possible to use one SELECT query as a source for another statement. In this case, both queries are considered as parts of one bigger query. The source of the data, output format, filters, grouping, ordering, and required transformations of the data are specified in the code of the query.

In general, SELECT queries do not change the data in the database and could be considered as read-only, but there is an exception. If a volatile function is used in the query, then the data can be changed by the function.

Structure of a SELECT query

Let's start with a simple example. We will use the sample database of the car web portal, which was described in previous chapters.

To connect to the database, the following command is used:

```
> psql -h localhost car_portal
```

There is a table called `car` that contains information about cars registered in the system. Suppose it is necessary to query the database to get the information about cars that have three doors. They should be sorted by their ID. The output should be limited to five records due to pagination in the user interface. The query will look like this:

```
SELECT car_id, registration_number, manufacture_year
  FROM car_portal_app.car
  WHERE number_of_doors=3
  ORDER BY car_id
  LIMIT 5;
```

This is the result:

```
 car_id | registration_number | manufacture_year
--------+---------------------+------------------
      2 | VSVW4565            | 2014
      5 | BXGK6290            | 2009
      6 | ORIU9886            | 2007
      7 | TGVF4726            | 2009
      8 | JISW6779            | 2013
(5 rows)
```

The syntax and the logic of the query are the following. The query starts from the keyword SELECT, which determines the type of the statement. Therefore, this keyword is always required. The keyword is followed by the comma-separated list of the fields to be retrieved from the database. Instead of the list, it is possible to use an asterisk *, which would mean that all the fields from the table are selected.

The name of the table is specified after the FROM keyword. It is possible to get the data from several tables at the same time. The filter criteria--predicate--is after the WHERE keyword. The sorting rule is at the end after ORDER BY. The LIMIT keyword makes the database return not more than five rows, even if the number of records in the table is bigger.

These parts of the query—the keywords and the following expressions--are called clauses, such as the FROM clause, the WHERE clause, and so on. All of these clauses have their own purpose and logic. They must follow each other in the specific order. None of them is mandatory. The simplified syntax diagram for the SELECT statement is as follows:

```
SELECT [DISTINCT | ALL] <expression>[[AS] <output_name>][, ...]
[FROM <table>[, <table>... | <JOIN clause>...]
[WHERE <condition>]
[GROUP BY <expression>|<output_name>|<output_number> [,...]]
[HAVING <condition>]
[ORDER BY <expression>|<output_name>|<output_number> [ASC | DESC] [NULLS
FIRST | LAST] [,...]]
[OFFSET <expression>]
[LIMIT <expression>];
```

Some elements were not included here such as the WINDOW clause, the WITH clause, or FOR UPDATE. A complete syntax diagram can be found in the documentation at http://www. postgresql.org/docs/current/static/sql-select.html.

Some of the omitted elements will be described in the next chapters.

There is no part of the SELECT statement that is always mandatory. For example, the query might be simpler if no ordering or filtering is needed:

```
SELECT * FROM car_portal_app.car;
```

Even the FROM clause is not mandatory. When one needs to evaluate an expression that does not take any data from the database, the query takes this form:

```
car_portal=> SELECT 1;
 ?column?
----------
 1
```

This can be considered as Hello world in SQL.

> The FROM clause is optional in PostgreSQL but in other RDBMS such as Oracle, the FROM keyword may be required.

Logically, the sequence of the operations performed by the SELECT query is as follows:

1. Take all the records from all the source tables. If there are subqueries in the FROM clause, they are evaluated first.
2. Build all possible combinations of those records and discard the combinations that do not follow the JOIN conditions or set some fields to NULL in case of outer joins.
3. Filter out the combinations that do not match the condition of the WHERE clause.
4. Build groups based on the values of the expressions of the GROUP BY list.
5. Filter the groups that match the HAVING conditions.
6. Evaluate expressions of the select-list.
7. Eliminate duplicated rows if DISTINCT is specified.
8. Apply the set operations UNION, EXCEPT, or INTERSECT.
9. Sort rows according to the ORDER BY clause.
10. Discard records according to OFFSET and LIMIT.

In fact, PostgreSQL optimizes that algorithm by performing the steps in a different order or even simultaneously. For example, if LIMIT 1 is specified, then it does not make sense to retrieve all the rows from the source tables, but only one that would match the WHERE condition.

Select-list

After the SELECT keyword, one should specify the list of fields or expressions to get from the database. This list is called **select-list**. It defines the structure of the query result: the number, names, and type of the selected values.

Every expression in select-list has a name in the output of the query. The names, when not provided by the user, are assigned automatically by the database and in most cases the name reflects the source of the data: a name of a column when a field from a table is selected, or a name of a function when one is used. In other cases, the name will look like ?column?. It is possible and, in many cases, it totally makes sense to provide a different name for a selected expression. This is done using the keyword AS, like this:

```
SELECT car_id AS identifier_of_the_car ...
```

In the result, the `car_id` column from the table car will be named `identifier_of_the_car`. The keyword `AS` is optional. The output column name follows the rules for any SQL identifier. It is possible to use the same name for several columns in a single `SELECT` query. Double quoted names could be used, for example, when a report is generated by a `SELECT` query without any subsequent processing. In that case, it may make sense to use more human-readable column names:

```
SELECT car_id "Identifier of the car" ...
```

In many cases, it is convenient to use an asterisk * instead of a select-list. An **asterisk** represents all the fields from all the tables specified in the `FROM` clause. It is possible to use an asterisk for each table separately, like this:

```
SELECT car.*, car_model.make ...
```

In this example, all fields are selected from table `car` and only one field--`make`--from `car_model`.

It is considered a bad practice to use * in situations where the query is used in other code: in applications, stored procedures, view definitions, and so on. It is not recommended because in the case of using *, the output format depends not on the code of the query but on the structure of the data. If the data structure changes, the output format also changes, which will break the application using it. However, if you explicitly specify all the output fields in the query and afterward add another column to the input table, this will not change the output of the query and will not break the application.

So in our example, instead of `SELECT  *  ...`, it would be safer to use the following:

```
SELECT car_id, number_of_owners, registration_number, number_of_doors,
car_model_id, mileage ...
```

SQL expressions

Expressions in the select-list are called **value expressions** or **scalar expressions**. This is because each expression in the select-list always returns only one value (but the value can be an array).

Scalar expressions can also be called SQL expressions or simply expressions. Each expression in SQL has its data type. It is determined by the data type(s) of the input. In many cases, it is possible to explicitly change the type of the data. Each item of the select-list becomes a column in the output dataset of a type that the corresponding expression has.

SQL expressions can contain the following:

- Column names (most of the cases)
- Constants
- Operator invocations
- Parentheses to control operations, precedence
- Function calls
- Aggregate expressions (we will discuss them later)
- Scalar subqueries
- Type casts
- Conditional expressions

This list is not complete. There are several other cases of using SQL expressions that are not covered by this chapter.

Column names can be qualified and unqualified. **Qualified** means that the name of the column is preceded by the table name and optionally the schema name, all separated by the period . symbol. **Unqualified** are just names of the fields without table references. Qualified column names must be used when several tables in the FROM clause have columns with the same name. Unqualified naming in this case will cause an error, **column reference is ambiguous**. This means that the database cannot understand which column is meant there. It is possible to use a table alias instead of a table name, and in case of using subqueries or functions, the alias must be used.

An example of using qualified names in a select-list is as follows:

```
SELECT car.car_id, car.number_of_owners FROM car_portal_app.car;
```

SQL supports all common operators as most of the other programming languages: logical, arithmetic, string, binary, date/time, and so on. We will discuss logical operators later in reference to SQL conditions. An example of using arithmetic operators in expressions would be as follows:

```
car_portal=> SELECT 1+1 AS two, 13%4 AS one, -5 AS minus_five, 5! AS
factorial, |/25 AS square_root;
 two | one | minus_five | factorial | square_root
-----+-----+------------+-----------+-------------
 2 | 1 | -5 | 120 | 5
```

In PostgreSQL, it is also possible to create user-defined operators.

Function calls can also be a part of a SQL expression. To call a SQL function, one should use its name and the arguments in parenthesis:

```
car_portal=> SELECT substring('this is a string constant',11,6);
 substring
-----------
 string
```

A built-in function named `substring` was executed here. Three arguments were passed to the function: a `string` and two integers. This function extracts a part from the given string starting from the character specified by the second argument and having a specified length. By default, PostgreSQL assigns to the output column the same name as the function.

If a function has no arguments, it is still necessary to use parenthesis to indicate that it is a function name and not a field name or another identifier or a keyword.

Another thing that makes SQL very flexible and powerful is scalar subqueries, which can be used as a part of the value expression. It allows the developer to combine the results of different queries together. **Scalar subqueries** or **scalar queries** are queries that return exactly one column and one or zero records. They have no special syntax and their difference from non-scalar queries is nominal.

Consider the following example:

```
car_portal=> SELECT (SELECT 1) + (SELECT 2) AS three;
 three
-----------
 3
```

Here, the result of one scalar query that returns the value of **1** is added to the result of another scalar query returning **2**. The result of the whole expression is **3**.

Type casting means changing the data type of a value. Type casts have several syntax patterns with the same meaning:

- `CAST ( <value> AS <type>)`
- `<value>::<type>`
- `<type> '<value>'`
- `<type> (<value>)`

The first is a common SQL syntax that is supported in most databases. The second is PostgreSQL specific. The third is only applicable for string constants and is usually used to define constants of other types but string or numeric. The last is function-like and can be applied only for types whose names are also existing function names, which is not very convenient. That's why this syntax is not widely used.

In many cases, PostgreSQL can do implicit type conversion. For example, the concatenation operator || (double vertical bar) takes two operands of type string. If one tries to concatenate a string with a number, PostgreSQL will convert the number to a string automatically:

```
car_portal=> SELECT 'One plus one equals ' || (1+1) AS str;
 str
-----------------------
 One plus one equals 2
```

A conditional expression is an expression returning different results depending on some condition. It is similar to an IF – THEN – ELSE statement in other programming languages. The syntax is as follows:

```
CASE WHEN <condition1> THEN <expression1> [WHEN <condition2> THEN
<expression2> ...] [ELSE <expression n>] END
```

The behavior is understandable from the syntax: if the first condition is met, then the result of the first expression is returned; if the second condition is met, then the second expression is used; and so on. If no condition is met, then the expression specified in the ELSE part is evaluated. Each <condition> is itself an expression returning Boolean (true or false) result. All expressions used after the THEN keyword should return a result of the same type or at least of compatible types.

The number of condition-expression pairs should be one or more. ELSE is optional and when ELSE is not specified and no condition's result is true, then the whole CASE expression returns NULL.

CASE can be used in any place where the SQL expression is used. CASE expressions can be nested, that is they can be put one inside another as both condition part or expression part. The order of evaluating conditions is the same as specified in the expression. This means for any condition, it is known that all preceding conditions are evaluated as false. If any condition returns true, subsequent conditions are not evaluated at all.

There is a simplified syntax for CASE expressions. When all the conditions implement checking of equality of the same expression to several values, it is possible to use it like this:

```
CASE <checked_expression> WHEN <value1> THEN <result1> [WHEN <value2> THEN
<result2> ...] [ELSE <result_n>] END
```

This means that when the value of checked_expression is equal to value1, the result1 is returned, and so on.

This is an example of using a CASE expression:

```
car_portal=> SELECT CASE WHEN now() > date_trunc('day', now()) + interval
'12 hours'
  THEN 'PM' ELSE 'AM' END;
 case
------
 PM
```

Here, the current time is compared to midday (the current time is truncated to day, which gives midnight, and then time interval of 12 hours is added). When the current time is after (operator >) midday, the expression returns the string PM, otherwise it returns AM.

A single SQL expression can have many operators, functions, type casts, and so on. The length of a SQL expression has no limits in language specification. The select-list is not the only place where SQL expressions can be used. In fact, they are used almost everywhere in SQL statements. For example, one can order the results of the query based on some SQL expression, as a sorting key. In an INSERT statement, they are used to calculate values of the fields for newly inserted records. SQL expressions that return Boolean values are often used as conditions in the WHERE clause.

PostgreSQL supports the short-circuit evaluation of the expressions and sometimes it skips the evaluation of some parts of the expression when they do not affect the result. For example, when evaluating the expression false AND z(), PostgreSQL will not call the z() function because the result of the AND operator is determined by its first operand, constant false, and it is false always, regardless of what the z() function would return.

DISTINCT

Another thing related to the select-list is pair of keywords DISTINCT and ALL, which can be used right after the SELECT keyword. When DISTINCT is specified, only unique rows from the input dataset will be returned. ALL returns all the rows, this is the default.

Consider the following examples:

```
car_portal=> SELECT ALL make FROM car_portal_app.car_model;
 marke
---------------
 Audi
 Audi
 Audi
 Audi
 BMW
 BMW
 ...
(99 rows)
```

and

```
car_portal=> SELECT DISTINCT make FROM car_portal_app.car_model;
 marke
---------------
 Ferrari
 GMC
 Citroen
 UAZ
 Audi
 Volvo
 ...
(25 rows)
```

The input in both cases is the same: the table with the car models. However, the first query returned 99 records while the second only returned 25. This is because the first returned all the rows that were in the input table. The second query selected only the unique rows. DISTINCT removes duplicate records based on the select-list, not on the data in the input table. For example, if only the first letter of the name of the manufacturer is selected the result will be even shorter because some names start with the same letter:

```
SELECT DISTINCT substring(make, 1, 1) FROM car_portal_app.car_model;
 substring
-----------
 H
 S
 C
 J
 L
 I
 ...
(21 rows)
```

DISTINCT also works when several columns are selected. In that case, DISTINCT will remove duplicated combinations of all the column values.

FROM clause

The source of the rows for the query is specified after the FROM keyword. It is called the FROM clause. The query can select rows from zero, one, or more sources. When no source is specified, the FROM keyword should be omitted. The source of the rows for the query can be any of the following:

- Table
- View
- Function
- Subquery
- VALUES

When multiple sources are specified, they should be separated by a comma or the JOIN clause should be used.

It is possible to set aliases for tables in the FROM clause. The optional keyword AS is used for that:

```
car_portal=> SELECT a.car_id, a.number_of_doors FROM car_portal_app.car AS
a;
 car_id | number_of_doors
--------+-----------------
 1 | 5
 2 | 3
 3 | 5
...
```

In the preceding example, the table name car_portal_app.car was substituted with its alias a in the select-list. If an alias is used for a table or view in the FROM clause, in the select-list (or anywhere else) it is no longer possible to refer to the table by its name. Subqueries when used in the FROM clause must have an alias. Aliases are often used when a self-join is performed, which means using the same table several times in the FROM clause.

Selecting from multiple tables

It is possible to select records from several sources at a time. Consider the following examples. There are two tables each having three rows:

```
car_portal=> SELECT * FROM car_portal_app.a;
 a_int | a_text
-------+--------
     1 | one
     2 | two
     3 | three
(3 rows)

car_portal=> SELECT * FROM car_portal_app.b;
 b_int | b_text
-------+--------
     2 | two
     3 | three
     4 | four
(3 rows)
```

When records are selected from both of them, we get the combinations of all their rows:

```
car_portal=> SELECT * FROM car_portal_app.a, car_portal_app.b;
 a_int | a_text | b_int | b_text
-------+--------+-------+--------
     1 | one    |     2 | two
     1 | one    |     3 | three
     1 | one    |     4 | four
     2 | two    |     2 | two
     2 | two    |     3 | three
     2 | two    |     4 | four
     3 | three  |     2 | two
     3 | three  |     3 | three
     3 | three  |     4 | four
(9 rows)
```

All possible combinations of records from several tables are called **Cartesian product** and usually it does not make much sense. In most cases, the user is interested in certain combinations of rows, when rows from one table match rows from another table based on some criteria. For example, it may be necessary to select only the combinations when the integer fields of both the tables have equal values. To get this, the query should be changed:

```
car_portal=> SELECT * FROM car_portal_app.a, car_portal_app.b WHERE
a_int=b_int;
 a_int | a_text | b_int | b_text
-------+--------+-------+--------
     2 | two    |     2 | two
```

```
       3 | three   |      3 | three
(2 rows)
```

This condition `a_int=b_int` joins the tables. The joining conditions could be specified in the `WHERE` clause but in most cases it is better to put them into the `FROM` clause to make it explicit that they are here for joining and not for filtering the result of the join, though there is no formal difference.

The `JOIN` keyword is used to add join conditions to the `FROM` clause. The following query has the same logic and the same results as the previous one:

```
SELECT * FROM car_portal_app.a JOIN car_portal_app.b ON a_int=b_int;
```

The `JOIN` condition may be specified using any of these three ways--using the keywords `ON`, `USING`, or `NATURAL`:

```
<first table> JOIN <second table> ON <condition>
```

The condition can be any SQL expression returning boolean result. It's not even necessary to include fields of the joined tables:

```
<first table> JOIN <second table> USING (<field list>)
```

The join is based on the equality of all the fields specified in the comma separated `<field list>`. The fields should exist in both tables with the same name. So this syntax can be not flexible enough:

```
<first table> NATURAL JOIN <second table>
```

Here, the join is based on the equality of all the fields that have the same name in both tables.

> Usage of `USING` or `NATURAL JOIN` syntax has a drawback that is similar to the usage of `*` in the select-list. It is possible to change the structure of the tables, for example, by adding another column or renaming them, in a way that does not make the query invalid but changes the logic of the query. This will cause errors that are very difficult to find.

What if not all rows from the first table can be matched to a row in the second table?

In our example, only rows with integer values 2 and 3 exist in both tables. When we join on the condition `a_int=b_int`, only those two rows are selected from the tables. The rest of the rows are not selected. This kind of join is called **inner join**.

It can be shown as a filled area on the diagram, like this:

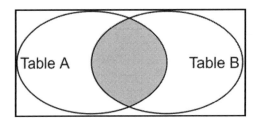

Inner join

When all the records from one table are selected, regardless of the existence of matching records in the other table, it is called an **outer join**. There are three types of outer joins. Look at the following diagrams:

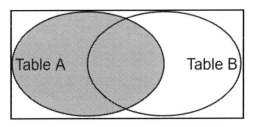

Left outer join

If all records are selected from the first table, along with only those records that match the joining condition from the second, it is a **left outer join**:

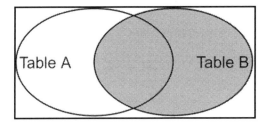

Right outer join

When all records from the second table are selected, along with only the matching records from the first table, it is a **right outer join**:

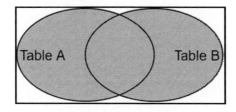

Full outer join

When all the records from both tables are selected, it is a **full outer join**.

In SQL syntax, the words inner and outer are optional. Consider the following code examples:

```
car_portal=> SELECT * FROM car_portal_app.a JOIN car_portal_app.b ON
a_int=b_int;
 a_int | a_text | b_int | b_text
-------+--------+-------+--------
     2 | two    |     2 | two
     3 | three  |     3 | three
(2 rows)

car_portal=> SELECT * FROM car_portal_app.a LEFT JOIN car_portal_app.b ON
a_int=b_int;
 a_int | a_text | b_int | b_text
-------+--------+-------+--------
     1 | one    |       |
     2 | two    |     2 | two
     3 | three  |     3 | three
(3 rows)

car_portal=> SELECT * FROM car_portal_app.a RIGHT JOIN car_portal_app.b ON
a_int=b_int;
 a_int | a_text | b_int | b_text
-------+--------+-------+--------
     2 | two    |     2 | two
     3 | three  |     3 | three
       |        |     4 | four
(3 rows)

car_portal=> SELECT * FROM car_portal_app.a FULL JOIN car_portal_app.b ON
a_int=b_int;
 a_int | a_text | b_int | b_text
-------+--------+-------+--------
```

```
   1 | one     |       |
   2 | two     |   2 | two
   3 | three   |   3 | three
     |         |   4 | four
(4 rows)
```

Note that the Cartesian product is not the same as the result of the full outer join. Cartesian product means all possible combinations of all records from the tables without any specific matching rules. Full outer join returns pairs of records when they match the join conditions. The records that do not have a pair in the other table are returned separately. Outer joins return empty values NULL in columns that correspond to the table from where no matching record is found.

As it is possible to query not only tables but also views, functions, and subqueries, it is also possible to join them using the same syntax as is used to join tables:

```
car_portal=> SELECT *
 FROM car_portal_app.a
 INNER JOIN (SELECT * FROM car_portal_app.b WHERE b_text = 'two') subq ON
a.a_int=subq.b_int;
 a_int | a_text | b_int | b_text
-------+--------+-------+--------
     2 | two    |     2 | two
```

In the example, the subquery got the alias subq and it was used in the join condition.

It is also possible to join more than two tables. In fact, every join clause joins all the tables before the JOIN keyword with one table right after the keyword.

For example, this is correct:

```
SELECT *
  FROM table_a
    JOIN table_b ON table_a.field1=table_b.field1
    JOIN table_c ON table_a.field2=table_c.field2 AND
table_b.field3=table_c.field3;
```

At the moment of joining the table table_c, the table table_a has been mentioned already in the FROM clause, therefore it is possible to refer to that table.

However, this is not correct:

```
SELECT *
  FROM table_a
    JOIN table_b ON table_b.field3=table_c.field3
    JOIN table_c ON table_a.field2=table_c.field2
```

The code will cause an error because at `JOIN table_b`, the table `table_c` has not been there yet.

The Cartesian product can also be implemented using the `JOIN` syntax. The keywords `CROSS JOIN` are used for that. See the following code:

```
SELECT * FROM car_portal_app.a CROSS JOIN car_portal_app.b;
```

The preceding code is equivalent to the following:

```
SELECT * FROM car_portal_app.a, car_portal_app.b;
```

The join condition in `INNER JOIN` in the logic of the query has the same meaning as a condition to filter the rows in the `WHERE` clause. So the two following queries are in fact the same:

```
SELECT * FROM car_portal_app.a INNER JOIN car_portal_app.b ON
a.a_int=b.b_int;
```

```
SELECT * FROM car_portal_app.a, car_portal_app.b WHERE a.a_int=b.b_int;
```

However, this is not the case for outer joins. There is no way to implement an outer join with the `WHERE` clause in PostgreSQL, though it may be possible in other databases.

Self-joins

It is possible to join a table with itself. This is called **self-join**. Self-join has no special syntax. In fact, all the data sources in a query are independent even though they could be the same physically. Suppose one wants to know about each record of the table `a` and how many records exist with a bigger value than the field `a_int`. The following query can be used for this:

```
car_portal=> SELECT t1.a_int AS current, t2.a_int AS bigger
 FROM car_portal_app.a t1
 INNER JOIN car_portal_app.a t2 ON t2.a_int > t1.a_int;
current | bigger
--------+--------
      1 |      2
      1 |      3
      2 |      3
(3 rows)
```

The table `a` is joined to itself. From the logic of the query, it does not matter if two different tables are joined or if the same table is used twice. To be able to reference the fields and distinguish the instances of the table, the table aliases are used. The first instance is called `t1` and the second `t2`. From the results, it is visible that for the value 1 there are two bigger values: 2 and 3; and for the value 2 only one bigger value exists which is 3. The examined value is in the column named `current` and the bigger values are in the column called `bigger`.

The value 3 is not selected because there are no values bigger than 3. However, if one wants to explicitly show that, `LEFT JOIN` is used:

```
car_portal=> SELECT t1.a_int AS current, t2.a_int AS bigger
 FROM car_portal_app.a t1
 LEFT JOIN car_portal_app.a t2 ON t2.a_int > t1.a_int;
current | bigger
--------+--------
      1 |      2
      1 |      3
      2 |      3
      3 |
(4 rows)
```

The WHERE clause

In many cases, after the rows are taken from the input tables, they should be filtered. It is done via the `WHERE` clause. The filtering condition is specified after the `WHERE` keyword. The condition is a SQL expression returning a Boolean value. That's why the syntax of the `WHERE` condition is the same as in the expressions in the select-list. This is specific for PostgreSQL. In other databases, it may not be possible to use Boolean values in the select-list, which makes SQL conditions different from SQL expressions. In PostgreSQL, the difference is only in the data type of a returned value.

Simple examples of the `WHERE` conditions can be as follows:

```
SELECT * FROM car_portal_app.car_model WHERE make='Peugeot';
SELECT * FROM car_portal_app.car WHERE mileage < 25000;
SELECT * FROM car_portal_app.car WHERE number_of_doors > 3 AND
number_of_owners <= 2;
```

Although there is no formal difference between SQL expressions and SQL conditions in PostgreSQL, usually all expressions returning a Boolean type are called conditional expressions or just conditions. They are mostly used in the WHERE clause or in conditional expressions such as CASE or in the JOIN clause.

Logical operators are usually used in conditional expressions. They are AND, OR and NOT. They take Boolean arguments and return Boolean values. Logical operators are evaluated in the following order: NOT, AND, OR, but they have a lower priority than any other operators. PostgreSQL tries to the optimize evaluation of logical expressions. For example, when the OR operator is evaluated, and it is known that the first operand has the true value, PostgreSQL may not evaluate the second operand at all, because the result of OR is already known. For that reason, PostgreSQL may change the actual order of evaluating expressions on purpose to get the results faster.

Sometimes this might cause problems. For example, it is not possible to divide by zero, and in case one wanted to filter rows based on the result of division, this would not be correct:

```
car_portal=> SELECT * FROM t WHERE b/a>0.5 and a<>0;
ERROR:  division by zero
```

It is not guaranteed that PostgreSQL will evaluate the condition a<>0 before the other one b/a>0.5, and in case a has a value of 0, this could cause an error. To be secure, one should use a CASE statement because the order of evaluation of CASE conditions is determined by the statement:

```
car_portal=> SELECT * FROM t WHERE CASE WHEN a=0 THEN false ELSE b/a>0.5
END;
 a | b
---+---
(0 rows)
```

There are some other operators or expressions returning Boolean values that are used in conditional expressions:

- Comparison operators
- Pattern matching operators
- The OVERLAPS operator
- Row and array comparison constructs
- Subquery expressions
- Any function returning Boolean or convertible to Boolean values

As in the select-list, functions can be used in the WHERE clause as well as anywhere in the expression. Suppose one wants to search for car models whose name is four letters long. This can be done using a length function:

```
car_portal=> SELECT * FROM car_portal_app.car_model WHERE length(model)=4;
 car_model_id |    make    | model
--------------+------------+-------
           47 | KIA        | Seed
           57 | Nissan     | GT-R
           70 | Renault    | Clio
...
```

Comparison operators

Comparison operators are < (less), > (more), <= (equal or less), >= (equal or more), = (equal) and <> or != (not equal - those two are synonyms). These operators can compare not only numbers but any values that can be compared, for example dates, or strings.
There is a BETWEEN construct that also relates to comparing the following:

```
x BETWEEN a AND b
```

The preceding code is equivalent to the following:

```
x>=a AND a<=b
```

The OVERLAPS operator checks to see whether two ranges of dates overlap or not. An example would be as follows:

```
car_portal=> SELECT 1 WHERE (date '2017-10-15', date '2017-10-31')
   OVERLAPS (date '2017-10-25', date '2017-11-15');
 ?column?
----------
        1
```

 Formally, comparison operators have different precedence: >= and <= have the highest priority. Then comes BETWEEN, then OVERLAPS, then < and >. = has the lowest priority. However, it is difficult to come up with a practical example of using several comparison operators in the same expression without any parentheses.

Pattern matching

Pattern matching is always about strings. There are two similar operators: LIKE and ILIKE. They check whether a string matches a given pattern. Only two wildcards can be used in the pattern: an underscore _ for exactly one character (or number) and percent sign % for any number of any characters, including an empty string.

LIKE and ILIKE are the same except that the first is case-sensitive and the second is not.

For example, to get car models whose names start with s and have exactly four characters, one can use the following query:

```
car_portal=> SELECT * FROM car_portal_app.car_model WHERE model ILIKE
's___';
 car_model_id |    make    | model
--------------+------------+-------
           47 | KIA        | Seed
```

There are two other pattern matching operators: SIMILAR and ~ (tilde sign). They check for pattern matching using regular expressions. The difference between them is that SIMILAR uses regular expression syntax defined in SQL standard, while ~ uses **Portable Operating System Interface (POSIX)** regular expressions.

In the following example, one selects all car models whose names consist of exactly two words:

```
car_portal=> SELECT * FROM car_portal_app.car_model WHERE model ~
'^\w+\W+\w+$';
 car_model_id |      make      | model
--------------+----------------+--------------
           21 | Citroen        | C4 Picasso
           33 | Ford           | C-Max
           34 | Ford           | S-Max
...
```

Row and array comparison constructs

Row and array comparison constructs are used to make multiple comparisons between values, groups of values, and arrays.

The expression IN is used to check whether a value equals to any of the values from a list. The expression is as follows:

```
a IN (1, 2, 3)
```

The preceding code will return true if a equals to 1, 2 or 3. It is a shorter and cleaner way of implementing the following logic:

```
(a = 1 OR a = 2 OR a = 3)
```

SQL allows the use of array types, that means several elements as a whole in one single value. You will read about arrays in detail in the Chapter 09, *Beyond Conventional Data Types*. Arrays can be used for enriching comparison conditions. For example, this checks whether a is bigger than any of x, y, or z:

```
a > ANY (ARRAY[x, y, z])
```

The preceding code is equivalent to the following:

```
(a > x OR a > y OR a > z)
```

This checks whether a is bigger than all x, y, and z:

```
a > ALL (ARRAY[x, y, z])
```

The preceding code is equivalent to the following:

```
(a > x AND a > y AND a > z )
```

The keywords IN, ALL, and ANY (which has a synonym SOME) can also be used with subquery expressions, implementing the same logic. A result of subquery can be used in any place where it is possible to use a set of values or an array. This makes it possible, for instance, to select records from one table, when some values exist in another table.

For example, here car models are selected when there is a car of that model:

```
car_portal=> SELECT * FROM car_portal_app.car_model
 WHERE car_model_id IN (SELECT car_model_id FROM car_portal_app.car);
 car_model_id |     make       | model
--------------+----------------+-------------
            2 | Audi           | A2
            3 | Audi           | A3
            4 | Audi           | A4
...
(86 rows)
```

Sometimes an IN expression can be replaced by inner join, but not always. Consider the example:

```
car_portal=> SELECT car_model.*
  FROM car_portal_app.car_model INNER JOIN car_portal_app.car USING
(car_model_id);
```

```
car_model_id |      make      |      model
-------------+----------------+---------------
           2 | Audi           | A2
           2 | Audi           | A2
           2 | Audi           | A2
           3 | Audi           | A3
           3 | Audi           | A3
           4 | Audi           | A4
           4 | Audi           | A4
...
(229 rows)
```

Although the same table is queried and the same columns are returned, the number of records is bigger. This is because there are many cars of the same model, and for them, the model is selected several times.

 The NOT IN construct with a subquery is sometimes very slow because the check for the nonexistence of a value is more expensive than the opposite.

Grouping and aggregation

In all previous examples, the number of records returned by the SELECT query is the same as the number of rows from the input table (or tables) after filtering. In other words, every row from any of the source tables (or joined tables) becomes exactly one row in the query result. Rows are processed one by one.

SQL provides a way to get some aggregated results of processing several records at a time and get the result in one single row. The easiest example would be counting the total number of records in the table. The input is all the records of a table. The output is one single record. Grouping and aggregation is used for this.

The GROUP BY clause

The GROUP BY clause is used for the grouping. **Grouping** means splitting the whole input set of records into several groups with a view to have only one result row for each group. Grouping is performed on the basis of a list of expressions. All records that have the same combination of values of grouping expressions are grouped together. This means that the groups are identified by the values of expressions defined in the GROUP BY clause. Usually, it makes sense to include these expressions in the select-list in order to make it visible which group is referred to by the result row.

For example, let us group the data set by car make and model and select the groups:

```
car_portal=> SELECT a.make, a.model
  FROM car_portal_app.car_model a
    INNER JOIN car_portal_app.car b ON a.car_model_id=b.car_model_id
  GROUP BY a.make, a.model;
     make        |     model
---------------+--------------
 Opel          | Corsa
 Ferrari       | 458 Italia
 Peugeot       | 308
 Opel          | Insignia
 ...
(86 rows)
```

Here, the list of all the car models that are used in the table car is selected. Each record in the result set represents a group of records from the source tables relating to the same car model. In fact, this query gives the same result as SELECT DISTINCT make, model..., without GROUP BY, but the logic is different. DISTINCT removes duplicated values, but GROUP BY groups duplicated values together.

It is almost useless just to group rows. Usually, it is necessary to do some computing on the groups. In the last case, it would be interesting to know how many cars of which model are in the system. This is done by **aggregation**. **Aggregation** means performing calculation on a group of records returning a single value for the whole group. This is done by the special aggregating functions that are used in the select-list. To get the number of cars, one needs to use the count function:

```
car_portal=> SELECT a.make, a.model, count(*)
  FROM car_portal_app.car_model a
    INNER JOIN car_portal_app.car b ON a.car_model_id=b.car_model_id
  GROUP BY a.make, a.model;
     make        |     model      | count
---------------+--------------+-------
 Opel          | Corsa        |     6
 Ferrari       | 458 Italia   |     4
 Peugeot       | 308          |     3
 Opel          | Insignia     |     4
 ...
(86 rows)
```

There are several aggregating functions available in PostgreSQL. The most frequently used are count, sum, max, min, and avg to compute respectively the number of records in the group, the sum of any numeric expression for all the records in the group, and the biggest, the lowest, and average value of any expression. There are some other aggregating functions such as corr, which computes the correlation coefficient of the two given arguments, stddev for standard deviation, string_agg, which concatenates the string values of an expression, and others.

When grouping and aggregation is used, the records are grouped. This means that several records become one. Therefore, no other expressions except the aggregation functions and expressions from the GROUP BY list can be included in the select-list. If it is done, the database will raise an error:

```
car_portal=> SELECT a_int, a_text FROM car_portal_app.a GROUP BY a_int;
ERROR: column "a.a_text" must appear in the GROUP BY clause or be used in
an aggregate function
```

It is possible to create new expressions based on the expressions from the GROUP BY list. For example, if we have GROUP BY a, b, it is possible to use SELECT a+b.

What if it is needed to group all of the records of the table together, not on the basis of the values of some field, but the whole table? To do this, one should include aggregating functions in the select-list (and only them!) and not use the GROUP BY clause:

```
car_portal=> SELECT count(*) FROM car_portal_app.car;
 count
-------
   229
(1 row)
```

If all the records of a table are grouped without any GROUP BY expressions, then exactly one group is created. Note that the SQL queries that have aggregating functions in the select-list and do not have the GROUP BY clause always return exactly one row, even if there are no rows in the input tables, or if all of them are filtered out:

```
car_portal=> SELECT count(*) FROM car_portal_app.car WHERE number_of_doors
= 15;
 count
-------
     0
(1 row)
```

There are no cars with 15 doors. If the table is selected with this WHERE condition, no rows will be returned. However, if one uses count(*), the aggregating function will return a row with a value of zero.

It is possible to count the number of unique values of the expression with count(DISTINCT <expression>):

```
car_portal=> SELECT count(*), count(DISTINCT car_model_id) FROM
car_portal_app.car;
 count | count
-------+-------
   229 |    86
(1 row)
```

In the preceding example, the first column has the total number of cars. The second column is the number of the car models to which the cars belong. As some cars are of the same model, the number of models is lower than the total number of the cars.

The HAVING clause

Aggregating functions are not allowed in the WHERE clause but it is possible to filter groups that follow a certain condition. This is different from filtering in the WHERE clause because WHERE filters input rows, and groups are calculated afterward.

The filtering of the groups is done by the HAVING clause. This is very similar to the WHERE clause but only aggregating functions are allowed there. The HAVING clause is specified after the GROUP BY clause. Suppose one needs to know which models have more than five cars entered in the system. This can be done using a subquery:

```
car_portal=> SELECT make, model FROM
(
  SELECT a.make, a.model, count(*) c
    FROM car_portal_app.car_model a
      INNER JOIN car_portal_app.car b ON a.car_model_id=b.car_model_id
    GROUP BY a.make, a.model
) subq
WHERE c >5;
  make   | model
---------+-------
 Opel    | Corsa
 Peugeot | 208
(2 rows)
```

A simpler and clearer way is to do it with a HAVING clause:

```
car_portal=> SELECT a.make, a.model
  FROM car_portal_app.car_model a
    INNER JOIN car_portal_app.car b ON a.car_model_id=b.car_model_id
  GROUP BY a.make, a.model
```

```
HAVING count(*)>5;
  make   | model
---------+-------
 Opel    | Corsa
 Peugeot | 208
```

Ordering and limiting the results

The results of the query are not ordered by default. The order of the rows is not defined and may depend on their physical place on the disc, the joining algorithm, or on other factors. In many cases, it is required to have the result set sorted. This is done with the ORDER BY clause. The list of expressions whose values should be sorted is specified after the ORDER BY keyword. At the beginning, the records are sorted on the basis of the first expression of the ORDER BY list. If some rows have the same value for the first expression, they are sorted by the values of the second expression, and so on.

After each item of the ORDER BY list, it is possible to specify if the order should be ascending or descending. This is done by specifying the keywords ASC or DESC after the expression. Ascending is the default. NULL values are considered larger than any other values by default but it is possible to explicitly define that NULLs should precede other rows by specifying NULLS FIRST or NULLS LAST if NULLs should be at the end.

It is not required for the ORDER BY clause to contain the same expressions as the select-list but it usually does. So, to make it more convenient, it is allowed to use in the ORDER BY list the output column names that are assigned to the expression in the select-list instead of fully qualified expressions. It is also possible to use the numbers of the columns.

So, these examples are equivalent:

```
SELECT number_of_owners, manufacture_year, trunc(mileage/1000) as kmiles
FROM car_portal_app.car
ORDER BY number_of_owners, manufacture_year, trunc(mileage/1000) DESC;

SELECT number_of_owners, manufacture_year, trunc(mileage/1000) as kmiles
FROM car_portal_app.car
ORDER BY number_of_owners, manufacture_year, kmiles DESC;

SELECT number_of_owners, manufacture_year, trunc(mileage/1000) as kmiles
FROM car_portal_app.car
ORDER BY 1, 2, 3 DESC;
```

Sometimes it is necessary to limit the output of the query to a certain number of rows and discard the rest. This is done by specifying that number after the `LIMIT` keyword:

```
car_portal=> SELECT * FROM car_portal_app.car_model LIMIT 5;
 car_model_id | make  | model
--------------+-------+-------
            1 | Audi  | A1
            2 | Audi  | A2
            3 | Audi  | A3
            4 | Audi  | A4
            5 | Audi  | A5
(5 rows)
```

The preceding code returns only five rows regardless of the fact that the actual number of records in the table is bigger. This is sometimes used in scalar subqueries that should not return more than one record.

Another similar task is to skip several rows at the beginning of the output. This is done using the keyword `OFFSET`. `OFFSET` and `LIMIT` can be used together:

```
car_portal=> SELECT * FROM car_portal_app.car_model OFFSET 5 LIMIT 5;
 car_model_id | make  | model
--------------+-------+-------
            6 | Audi  | A6
            7 | Audi  | A8
            8 | BMW   | 1er
            9 | BMW   | 3er
           10 | BMW   | 5er
(5 rows)
```

The typical use case for `OFFSET` and `LIMIT` is the implementation of paginated output in web applications. For example, if ten rows are displayed on a page, then on the third page, the rows 21-30 should be shown. Then the construct `OFFSET 20 LIMIT 10` is used. In most cases of using `OFFSET` and `LIMIT`, the rows should be ordered; otherwise, it is not determined which records are not shown. The keywords are then specified after the `ORDER BY` clause.

Subqueries

Subqueries are a very powerful feature of SQL. They can be used almost everywhere in the query. The most obvious way to use subqueries is in the FROM clause as a source for the main query:

```
car_portal=> SELECT * FROM
   (SELECT car_model_id, count(*) c FROM car_portal_app.car GROUP BY
car_model_id) subq
WHERE c = 1;
 car_model_id | c
--------------+---
            8 | 1
           80 | 1
...
(14 rows)
```

When subqueries are used in the FROM clause, they must have an alias. In the preceding example, the subquery is given the name, subq.

Subqueries are often used in SQL conditions in the IN expressions:

```
car_portal=> SELECT car_id, registration_number
FROM car_portal_app.car
WHERE car_model_id IN (SELECT car_model_id FROM car_portal_app.car_model
WHERE make='Peugeot');
 car_id | registration_number
--------+----------------------
      1 | MUWH4675
     14 | MTZC8798
     18 | VFZF9207
...
(18 rows)
```

Scalar subqueries can be used everywhere in expressions--in the select-list, WHERE clause, GROUP BY clause, and so on. Even in LIMIT:

```
car_portal=> SELECT (SELECT count(*) FROM car_portal_app.car_model)
FROM car_portal_app.car
LIMIT (SELECT MIN(car_id)+2 FROM car_portal_app.car);
count
-------
    99
    99
    99
(3 rows)
```

This is a PostgreSQL-specific feature. Not every RDBMS supports subqueries in every place where expression is allowed.

It is not possible to refer to the internal elements of one subquery from inside of another. However, subqueries can refer to the elements of the main query. For example, if it is necessary to count cars for each car model and select the top five most popular models, it can be done using a subquery in this way:

```
car_portal=> SELECT make, model,
    (SELECT count(*) FROM car_portal_app.car WHERE car_model_id =
main.car_model_id)
  FROM car_portal_app.car_model AS main
  ORDER BY 3 DESC
  LIMIT 5;
  make   |  model    | count
---------+-----------+-------
 Peugeot | 208       |     7
 Opel    | Corsa     |     6
 Jeep    | Wrangler  |     5
 Renault | Laguna    |     5
 Peugeot | 407       |     5
(5 rows)
```

In the example, the subquery in the select-list refers to the table of the main query by its alias `main`. The subquery is executed for each record received from the main table, using the value of `car_model_id` in its `WHERE` condition.

Subqueries can be nested. It means it is possible to use subqueries inside another subquery.

Set operations – UNION, EXCEPT, and INTERSECT

Set operations are used to *combine* the results of several queries. It is different from joining, although the same results often can be achieved by joining. Simply speaking, joining means placing the records of two tables besides each other horizontally. The result of joining is that the number of columns equals to the sum of the numbers of columns of the source tables, and the number of records will depend on the join conditions.

Combining, in contrast, means putting the result of one query on top of the result of another query. The number of columns stays the same, but the number of rows is the sum of the rows from the sources.

There are three set operations:

- **UNION**: This appends the result of one query to the result of another query
- **INTERSECT**: This returns the records that exist in the results of both queries
- **EXCEPT**: This returns the records from the first query that does not exist in the result of the second query--the difference

The syntax of set operations is as follows:

```
<query1> UNION <query2>;

<query1> INTERSECT <query2>;

<query1> EXCEPT <query2>;
```

It is possible to use several set operations in one statement:

```
SELECT a, b FROM t1
UNION
SELECT c, d FROM t2
INTERSECT
SELECT e, f FROM t3;
```

The priority of all set operations is the same. This means that logically they are executed in the same order as used in the code. However, the records can be returned in a different order that is not predicted, unless the ORDER BY clause is used. In this case, the ORDER BY clause is applied after all of the set operations. For this reason, it does not make sense to put ORDER BY into the subqueries.

All set operations by default remove duplicated records as if SELECT DISTINCT is used. To avoid this and return all the records, the ALL keyword should be used, which is specified after the name of the set operation:

```
<query1> UNION ALL <query2>.
```

The set operations can be used to find the difference between two tables:

```
car_portal=> SELECT 'a', * FROM
(
  SELECT * FROM car_portal_app.a
  EXCEPT ALL
  SELECT * FROM car_portal_app.b
) v1
UNION ALL
SELECT 'b', * FROM
(
  SELECT * FROM car_portal_app.b
```

```
   EXCEPT ALL
   SELECT * FROM car_portal_app.a
) v2;
?column? | a_int | a_text
---------+-------+--------
 a       |     1 | one
 b       |     4 | four
(2 rows)
```

From the results of that query, you can find out that row one exists in the table a but does not exist in the table b. Row four exists in the table b, but not in a.

It is possible to append one set of records to another only when they have the same number of columns and they have respectively the same data types, or compatible data types. The output names for the columns are always taken from the first subquery, even if they are different in subsequent queries.

 In other RDBMS, set operations can have different names; for example, in Oracle, EXCEPT is called MINUS.

Dealing with NULLs

NULL is a special value that any field or expression can have, except for when it is explicitly forbidden. NULL means the absence of any value. It can also be treated as an unknown value in some cases. In relation to logical values, NULL is neither true nor false. Working with NULLs can be confusing because almost all operators, when taking NULL as an argument, return NULL. If one tries to compare some values and one of them is NULL, the result will also be NULL, which is not true.

For example, consider the following condition:

```
WHERE a > b
```

This will return NULL if a or b have a NULL value. This can be expected, but for the following condition, this is not so clear:

```
WHERE a = b
```

Here, if both `a` and `b` have a value of NULL, the result will still be NULL. The equal operator = always returns NULL if any of the arguments is NULL. Similarly, the following will also be evaluated as NULL, even if `a` has a NULL value:

```
WHERE a = NULL
```

To check the expression for a NULL value, a special predicate is used: IS NULL.

In the previous examples, if it is necessary to find records when `a = b` or both `a` and `b` are NULL, the condition should be changed this way:

```
WHERE a = b OR (a IS NULL AND b IS NULL)
```

There is a special construct that can be used to check the equivalence of expressions taking NULL into account: IS NOT DISTINCT FROM. The preceding example can be implemented in the following way, which has the same logic:

```
WHERE a IS NOT DISTINCT FROM b
```

Logical operators are different. They can sometimes return a not NULL value even if they take NULL as an argument. For logical operators, NULL means an unknown value.

The operator AND always returns `false` when any of the operands is `false`, even if the second is NULL. OR always returns `true` if one of the arguments is `true`. In all other cases, the result is unknown, therefore NULL:

```
car_portal=> SELECT true AND NULL, false AND NULL, true OR NULL, false OR NULL, NOT NULL;
 ?column? | ?column? | ?column? | ?column? | ?column?
----------+----------+----------+----------+----------
          | f        | t        |          |
```

The subquery expression IN deals with NULLs in a way that might not seem obvious:

```
car_portal=> SELECT 1 IN (1, NULL) as in;
 in
----
 t

car_portal=> SELECT 2 IN (1, NULL) as in;
 in
----

(1 row)
```

When evaluating the `IN` expression and the value that is being checked does not appear in the list of values inside `IN` (or in the result of a subquery) but there is a `NULL` value, the result will be also `NULL` and not `false`. This is easy to understand if we treat the `NULL` value as unknown, just as the logical operators do. In the first example, it is clear that 1 is included in the list inside the `IN` expression. Therefore, the result is `true`. In the second example, 2 is not equal to 1, but it is *unknown* about the `NULL` value. That's why the result is also unknown.

Functions can treat `NULL` values differently. Their behavior is determined by their code. Most built-in functions return `NULL` if any of the arguments are `NULL`.

Aggregating functions work with `NULL` values in a different way. They work with many rows and therefore many values. In general, they ignore `NULL`. `sum` calculates the total of all not-null values and ignores `NULL`. `sum` returns `NULL` only when all the received values are `NULL`. For `avg`, `max` and `min` it is the same. But for `count` it is different. `count` returns the number of not-null values. So if all the values are `NULL`, `count` returns zero.

In contrast to some other databases in PostgreSQL, an empty string is not `NULL`.

Consider the following example:

```
car_portal=> SELECT a IS NULL, b IS NULL, a = b FROM (SELECT ''::text a,
NULL::text b) v;
 ?column? | ?column? | ?column?
----------+----------+----------
 f        | t        |
```

There are a couple of functions designed to deal with `NULL` values: `COALESCE` and `NULLIF`.

The `COALESCE` function takes any number of arguments of the same data type or compatible types. It returns the value of the first of its arguments that `IS NOT NULL`:

```
COALESCE(a, b, c)
```

The preceding code is equivalent to the following:

```
CASE WHEN a IS NOT NULL THEN a WHEN b IS NOT NULL THEN b ELSE c END
```

`NULLIF` takes two arguments and returns `NULL` if they are equal. Otherwise, it returns the value of the first argument.

This is somehow the opposite of `COALESCE`:

```
NULLIF (a, b)
```

The preceding code is equivalent to the following:

```
CASE WHEN a = b THEN NULL ELSE a END
```

Another aspect of NULL values is that they are ignored by unique constraints. This means that if a field of a table is defined as unique, it is still possible to create several records having a NULL value of that field. Additionally, b-tree indexes, which are most commonly used, do not index NULL values. Consider the following query:

```
SELECT * FROM t WHERE a IS NULL
```

The preceding code will not use an index if it is created on the column, a.

Changing the data in the database

Data can be inserted into database tables, updated or deleted from the database. Respectively, statements are used for this: INSERT, UPDATE, and DELETE.

INSERT statement

The INSERT statement is used to insert new data into tables in the database. The records are always inserted into only one table.

The INSERT statement has the following syntax:

```
INSERT INTO <table_name> [(<field_list>)]
{VALUES (<expression_list>)[,...]}|{DEFAULT VALUES}|<SELECT query>;
```

The name of the table into which the records are inserted is specified after the INSERT INTO keywords. There are two options to use the INSERT statement, which has a different syntax: to insert one or several individual records or to insert the whole dataset of many records.

To insert one or several records, the VALUES clause is used. The list of the values to insert is specified after the VALUES keyword. Items of the list correspond to the fields of the table according to their order. If it is not necessary to set the values for all the fields, the names of the fields whose values should be set are specified in parentheses after the table name. The skipped fields will then get their default values, if defined, or they will be set to NULL.

The number of items in the VALUES list must be the same as the number of fields after the table name:

```
car_portal=> INSERT INTO car_portal_app.a (a_int) VALUES (6);
INSERT 0 1
```

The output of the INSERT command when it has successfully executed is the word INSERT followed by the OID of the row that has been inserted (in case only one row was inserted and OIDs are enabled for the table, otherwise it is zero) and the number of records inserted. To know more about OIDs, refer to Chapter 12, *The PostgreSQL Catalog, and System Administration Functions.*

Another way to set default values to the field is to use the DEFAULT keyword in the VALUES list. If default is not defined for the field, a NULL value will be set:

```
INSERT INTO car_portal_app.a (a_text) VALUES (default);
```

It is also possible to set all fields to their default values using the keyword, DEFAULT VALUES:

```
INSERT INTO car_portal_app.a DEFAULT VALUES;
```

It is possible to insert multiple records using the VALUES syntax:

```
INSERT INTO car_portal_app.a (a_int, a_text) VALUES (7, 'seven'),
(8,'eight');
```

This option is PostgreSQL-specific. Some other databases allow inserting only one row at a time.

In fact, in PostgreSQL, the VALUES clause is a standalone SQL command. Therefore, it can be used as a subquery in any SELECT query:

```
car_portal=> SELECT * FROM (VALUES (7, 'seven'), (8, 'eight')) v;
 column1 | column2
---------+---------
       7 | seven
       8 | eight
(2 rows)
```

When the records to insert are taken from another table or view, a SELECT query is used instead of the VALUES clause:

```
INSERT INTO car_portal_app.a SELECT * FROM car_portal_app.b;
```

The result of the query should match the structure of the table: have the same number of columns of compatible types in the same order.

In the SELECT query, it is possible to use the table in which the records are inserted. For example, to duplicate the records in the table, the following statement can be used:

```
INSERT INTO car_portal_app.a SELECT * FROM car_portal_app.a;
```

By default, the INSERT statement returns the number of inserted records. It is also possible to return the inserted records themselves or some of their fields. The output of the statement is then similar to the output of the SELECT query. The RETURNING keyword, with the list of fields to return, is used for this:

```
car_portal=> INSERT INTO car_portal_app.a SELECT * FROM car_portal_app.b
RETURNING a_int;
  a_int
 -------
     2
     3
     4
(3 rows)

INSERT 0 3
```

In case a unique constraint is defined on the table where the rows are inserted, INSERT will fail if it tries to insert records conflicting with existing ones. However, it is possible to let INSERT ignore such records or update them instead.

Assuming that there is a unique constraint on the table b, consider the following example for the field b_int:

```
car_portal=> INSERT INTO b VALUES (2, 'new_two');
ERROR: duplicate key value violates unique constraint "b_b_int_key"
DETAIL: Key (b_int)=(2) already exists.
```

What if we want to change the record instead of inserting in case it exists already:

```
car_portal=> INSERT INTO b VALUES (2, 'new_two')
  ON CONFLICT (b_int) DO UPDATE SET b_text = excluded.b_text
  RETURNING *;
 b_int | b_text
-------+---------
     2 | new_two
(1 row)

INSERT 0 1
```

Here, the `ON CONFLICT` clause specifies what has to happen in case there is already a record with the same value in the field `a_int`. The syntax is straightforward. The table alias `excluded` refers to the values that are being inserted. If it was necessary to refer to the values that were in the table, the table name would be used.

 SQL Standard defines a special command `MERGE` for this functionality. However, in PostgreSQL, the `ON CONFLICT` clause is a part of the syntax of the `INSERT` statement. In other RDBMS, this functionality could also be implemented in different ways.

The UPDATE statement

The `UPDATE` statement is used to change the data in the records of a table without changing their number. It has the following syntax:

```
UPDATE <table_name>
SET <field_name> = <expression>[, ...]
[FROM <table_name> [JOIN clause]]
[WHERE <condition>];
```

There are two ways of using the `UPDATE` statement. The first is similar to the simple `SELECT` statement and is called **sub-select**. The second is based on other tables and is similar to the `SELECT` statement from multiple tables. In most cases, the same result can be achieved using any of these methods.
In PostgreSQL, only one table can be updated at a time. Other databases may allow the updating of multiple tables at the same time under certain conditions.

UPDATE using sub-select

The expression for a new value is the usual SQL expression. It is possible to refer to the same field in the expression. In that case, the old value is used:

```
UPDATE t SET f = f+1 WHERE a = 5;
```

It is common to use a subquery in the `UPDATE` statements. To refer to the table being updated from a subquery, the table should have an alias:

```
car_portal=> UPDATE car_portal_app.a updated SET a_text =
  (SELECT b_text FROM car_portal_app.b WHERE b_int = updated.a_int);
UPDATE 7
```

If the subquery returns no result, the field value is set to NULL.

Note that the output of the UPDATE command is the word UPDATE followed by the number of records that were updated.

The WHERE clause is similar to the one used in the SELECT statement. If the WHERE statement is not specified, all the records are updated.

UPDATE using additional tables

The second way of updating rows in the table is to use the FROM clause in a similar manner as it is done in the SELECT statement:

```
UPDATE car_portal_app.a SET a_int = b_int FROM car_portal_app.b WHERE
a.a_text=b.b_text;
```

All rows from a, for which there are rows in b with the same value of the text field, were updated. The new value for the numeric field was taken from the table b. Technically, it is nothing but an inner join of the two tables. However, the syntax here is different. As table a is not a part of the FROM clause, using the usual join syntax is not possible and the tables are joined on the condition of the WHERE clause. If another table was used, it would be possible to join it to the table b using the join syntax, inner or outer.

The FROM syntax of the UPDATE statement can seem more obvious in many cases. For example, the following statement performs the same changes to the table as the previous, but it is less clear:

```
UPDATE car_portal_app.a SET a_int = (SELECT b_int FROM car_portal_app.b
WHERE a.a_text=b.b_text)
   WHERE a_text IN (SELECT b_text FROM car_portal_app.b);
```

Another advantage of the FROM syntax is that in many cases, it is much faster. On the other hand, this syntax can have unpredictable results in cases when, for a single record of the updated table, there are several matching records from the tables of the FROM clause:

```
UPDATE car_portal_app.a SET a_int = b_int FROM car_portal_app.b;
```

This query is syntactically correct. However, it is known that in the table b, there is more than one record. Which of them will be selected for every updated row is not determined, as no WHERE condition is specified. The same happens when the WHERE clause does not define the one-to-one matching rule:

```
car_portal=> UPDATE car_portal_app.a SET a_int = b_int FROM
car_portal_app.b WHERE b_int>=a_int;
UPDATE 6
```

For each record of table a, there is more than one record from table b where b_int is more than or equal to a_int. That's why the result of this update is undefined. However, PostgreSQL will allow this to be executed.

For this reason, one should be careful when using this way of doing updates.

The update query can return updated records if the RETURNING clause is used as it is in the INSERT statement:

```
car_portal=> UPDATE car_portal_app.a SET a_int = 0 RETURNING *;
 a_int | a_text
-------+--------
     0 | one
     0 | two
...
```

The DELETE statement

The DELETE statement is used to remove records from the database. As with UPDATE, there are two ways of deleting: using sub-select or using another table or tables. The sub-select syntax is as follows:

```
DELETE FROM <table_name> [WHERE <condition>];
```

Records that follow the condition will be removed from the table. If the WHERE clause is omitted, then all the records will be deleted.

DELETE based on another table is similar to using the FROM clause of the UPDATE statement. Instead of FROM, the USING keyword should be used because FROM is already used in the syntax of the DELETE statement:

```
car_portal=> DELETE FROM car_portal_app.a USING car_portal_app.b WHERE
a.a_int=b.b_int;
DELETE 6
```

The preceding statement will delete all the records from a when there is a record in b with the same value of the numeric field. The output of the command indicates the number of records that were deleted.

The previous command is equivalent to the following:

```
DELETE FROM car_portal_app.a WHERE a_int IN (SELECT b_int FROM
car_portal_app.b);
```

As well as UPDATE and INSERT, the DELETE statement can return deleted rows when the RETURNING keyword is used:

```
car_portal=> DELETE FROM car_portal_app.a RETURNING *;
 a_int | a_text
-------+--------
     0 | one
     0 | two
...
```

The TRUNCATE statement

Another statement that can also change the data but not the data structure is TRUNCATE. It clears the table completely and almost instantly. It has the same effect as the DELETE statement without the WHERE clause. So, it is useful on large tables:

```
car_portal=> TRUNCATE TABLE car_portal_app.a;
TRUNCATE TABLE
```

Summary

SQL is used to interact with the database: create and maintain the data structures, put data into the database, change it, retrieve it, and delete it. SQL has commands related to DDL (Data Definition Language), DML (Data Manipulation Language), and DCL (Data Control Language). The four SQL statements form the basis of DML: SELECT, INSERT, UPDATE, and DELETE, which were described in this chapter.

The SELECT statement was examined in detail to explain SQL concepts such as grouping and filtering to show SQL expressions and conditions, and to explain how to use subqueries. Additionally, some relational algebra topics were covered in the section about joining tables.

In the next chapters, the more complicated topics will be covered--some advanced SQL features and techniques and the programming language PL/pgSQL, which can be used to implement functions in PostgreSQL.

6
Advanced Query Writing

In this chapter, we will discuss some more advanced SQL features supported by PostgreSQL that were not covered in the previous chapters. Some query writing techniques will also be described.

In this chapter, we will cover the following topics:

- Common table expressions
- Window functions
- Advanced SQL techniques

The same sample database `car_portal` is used in the code examples here. It is recommended though to recreate the sample database in order to get the same results as shown in the code examples. The scripts to create the database and fill it with data (`schema.sql` and `data.sql`) can be found in the attached code bundle for this chapter. All the code examples of this chapter can be found in the `examples.sql` file.

Common table expressions

Although SQL is a declarative language, it provides a way of implementing the logic of sequential execution of code or of reusing code.

Common table expressions (CTE) is a feature that makes it possible to define a subquery once, give it a name, and then use it at several places in the main query.

The simplified syntax diagram for CTE is as follows:

```
WITH <subquery name> AS (<subquery code>) [, ...]
SELECT <Select list> FROM <subquery name>;
```

In the preceding syntax diagram, `subquery code` is a query whose results will be used later in the primary query as if it was a real table. The subquery in parentheses after the `AS` keyword is a common table expression. It can also be called a substatement or an auxiliary statement. The query after the `WITH` block is the primary or main query. The whole statement itself is called a `WITH` query.

It is possible to use not only the `SELECT` statements in a CTE, but also the `INSERT`, `UPDATE`, or `DELETE` statements.

It is also possible to use several CTEs in one `WITH` query. Every CTE has its name defined before the keyword, `AS`. The main query can reference a CTE by its name. A CTE can also refer to another CTE by the name. A CTE can refer only to the CTEs that were defined before the referencing one.

The references to CTEs in the primary query can be treated as table names. In fact, PostgreSQL executes the CTEs only once, caches the results, and reuses them instead of executing subqueries each time they occur in the main query. This makes them similar to tables.

CTEs may help developers in organizing SQL code. Suppose we want to find car models of the cars in the sample database that are built after 2010, and find out what is the minimal number of owners for these cars. Consider the following code:

```
car_portal=> WITH pre_select AS
(
  SELECT car_id, number_of_owners, car_model_id
    FROM car_portal_app.car WHERE manufacture_year >= 2010
),
joined_data AS
(
  SELECT car_id, make, model, number_of_owners
    FROM pre_select
      INNER JOIN car_portal_app.car_model ON pre_select.car_model_id=
car_model.car_model_id
),
minimal_owners AS (SELECT min(number_of_owners) AS min_number_of_owners
FROM pre_select)
SELECT car_id, make, model, number_of_owners
  FROM joined_data INNER JOIN minimal_owners
    ON joined_data.number_of_owners = minimal_owners.min_number_of_owners;
 car_id |     make     |   model   | number_of_owners
--------+--------------+-----------+------------------
      2 | Opel         | Corsa     |                1
      3 | Citroen      | C3        |                1
     11 | Nissan       | GT-R      |                1
     36 | KIA          | Magentis  |                1
```

```
...
(25 rows)
```

In the example, the logical part of the query is presented as a sequence of actions--filtering in `pre_select` and then joining in `joined_data`. The other part, that is, calculating the minimal number of owners, is executed in a dedicated subquery, `minimal_owners`. This makes the implementation of the query logic similar to that of an imperative programming language.

The use of CTEs in the preceding example does not make the whole query faster. However, there are situations where the use of CTEs can increase performance. Moreover, sometimes it is not possible to implement the logic in any other way except by CTEs. In the following sections, some of these situations are discussed in detail.

The order of execution of the CTEs is not defined. PostgreSQL aims to execute only the main query. If the main query contains references to the CTEs, then PostgreSQL will execute them `first`. If a `SELECT` CTE is not referenced by the main query, directly or indirectly, then it is not executed at all. Data-changing substatements are always executed.

Reusing SQL code with CTE

When the execution of a subquery takes a lot of time, and the subquery is used in the statement more than once, it makes sense to put it into a `WITH` clause to reuse its results. This makes the query faster because PostgreSQL executes the subqueries from the `WITH` clause only once, caches the results in the memory or on disk--depending on their size--and then reuses them.

For example, let's take the car portal database. Suppose it is required to find newer car models. This would require calculating the average age of the cars of each model and then selecting the models with the average age lower than the average age among all the models.

This can be done in the following way:

```
car_portal=> SELECT make, model, avg_age FROM
(
  SELECT car_model_id, avg(EXTRACT(YEAR FROM now())-manufacture_year) AS
avg_age
    FROM car_portal_app.car
    GROUP BY car_model_id
) age_subq1
INNER JOIN car_portal_app.car_model ON car_model.car_model_id =
age_subq1.car_model_id
  WHERE avg_age < (SELECT avg(avg_age) FROM
    (
```

```
        SELECT avg(EXTRACT(YEAR FROM now()) - manufacture_year) avg_age
          FROM car_portal_app.car
          GROUP BY car_model_id
      ) age_subq2
    );
       make       |    model    |     avg_age
----------------+-------------+------------------
 BMW            | 1er         |                1
 BMW            | X6          |              2.5
 Mercedes Benz  | A klasse    |              1.5
 ...
(41 rows)
```

The EXTRACT function used in the query returns the integer value of the given part of the date expression. In the preceding example, the function is used to retrieve the year from the current date. The difference between the current year and manufacture_year is the age of a car.

There are two subqueries that are similar: the same table is queried and the same grouping and aggregation are performed. This makes it possible to use the same subquery twice by using a CTE:

```
car_portal=> WITH age_subq AS
(
  SELECT car_model_id, avg(EXTRACT(YEAR FROM now())-manufacture_year) AS
avg_age
    FROM car_portal_app.car
    GROUP BY car_model_id
)
SELECT make, model, avg_age
  FROM age_subq
    INNER JOIN car_portal_app.car_model ON car_model.car_model_id =
age_subq.car_model_id
  WHERE avg_age < (SELECT avg(avg_age) FROM age_subq);
       make       |    model    |     avg_age
----------------+-------------+------------------
 BMW            | 1er         |                1
 BMW            | X6          |              2.5
 Mercedes Benz  | A klasse    |              1.5
 ...
(41 rows)
```

The result of both the queries is the same. However, the `first` query took 1.9 milliseconds to finish and the second one took 1.0 milliseconds. Of course, in absolute values, the difference is nothing, but relatively, the `WITH` query is almost twice as fast. If the number of records in the tables was in the range of millions, then the absolute difference would be substantial.

Another advantage of using a CTE in this case is that the code became smaller and easier to understand. That is another use case for the `WITH` clause. Long and complicated subqueries can be formatted as CTEs in order to make the whole query smaller and more understandable, even if it does not affect the performance.

Sometimes though, it is better not to use a CTE. For example, one could try to preselect some columns from the table thinking it would help the database to perform the query faster because of the reduced amount of information to process. In that case, the query would be the following:

```
WITH car_subquery AS
    (SELECT number_of_owners, manufacture_year, number_of_doors FROM
car_portal_app.car)
SELECT number_of_owners, number_of_doors FROM car_subquery WHERE
manufacture_year = 2008;
```

This has the opposite effect. PostgreSQL does not push the `WHERE` clause from the primary query to the substatement. The database will retrieve all the records from the table, take three columns from them, and store this temporary dataset in memory. Then, the temporary data will be queried using the predicate, `manufacture_year = 2008`. If there was an index on `manufacture_year`, it would not be used because it is the temporary data being queried and not the real table.

For this reason, the following query is executed five times faster than the preceding one even though it seems to be almost the same:

```
SELECT number_of_owners, manufacture_year, number_of_doors
 FROM car_portal_app.car
 WHERE manufacture_year = 2008;
```

Recursive and hierarchical queries

It is possible to refer to a CTE from itself. Statements like this are called **recursive queries**. Recursive queries must have a special structure that indicates to the database that the subquery is recursive. The structure of a recursive query is as follows:

```
WITH RECURSIVE <subquery_name> (<field list>) AS
(
    <non-recursive term>
    UNION [ALL|DISTINCT]
    <recursive term>
)
[,...]
<main query>
```

Both non-recursive and recursive terms are subqueries that must return the same number of fields of the same types. The names for the fields are specified in the declaration of the whole recursive query; therefore, it does not matter which names are assigned to the fields in the subqueries.

The non-recursive term is also called an anchor subquery while the recursive term is also known as an iterating subquery.

A non-recursive or anchor subquery is a starting point of the execution of a recursive query. It cannot refer to the name of the recursive subquery. It is executed only once. The results of the non-recursive term are passed again to the same CTE and then the recursive term is executed. It references the recursive subquery by its name. If the recursive term returns rows, they are passed to the CTE again. This is called iteration. Iteration is repeated as long as the result of the recursive term is not empty. The result of the whole query is all the rows returned by the non-recursive term and all the iterations of the recursive term. If the keywords UNION ALL are used, then all the rows are returned. If UNION DISTINCT or just UNION is used, then the duplicated rows are removed from the result set.

Note that the algorithm of a recursive subquery implies iterations but not recursion. However, in SQL Standard, these kind of queries are called recursive. In other databases, the same logic can be implemented in a similar manner, but the syntax can be slightly different.

For example, the following recursive query can be used to calculate factorial values:

```
car_portal=> WITH RECURSIVE subq (n, factorial) AS
(
    SELECT 1, 1
    UNION ALL
    SELECT n + 1, factorial * (n + 1) from subq WHERE n < 5
```

```
)
SELECT * FROM subq;
 n | factorial
---+-----------
 1 |         1
 2 |         2
 3 |         6
 4 |        24
 5 |       120
(5 rows)
```

Here, SELECT 1, 1 is the anchor subquery. It returns one row (the fields n and factorial have values of 1 and 1), which is passed to the subsequent iterating subquery. The first iteration adds one to the value of the field n and multiplies the value of the factorial by (n+1), which gives the values 2 and 2. Then it passes this row to the next iteration. The second iteration returns the values 3 and 6, and so on. The last iteration returns a row where the value of the field n equals 5.

This row is filtered out in the WHERE clause of the iterating subquery; that's why the following iteration returns nothing and the execution stops at this point. So, the whole recursive subquery returns a list of five numbers, from 1 to 5, and their factorial values.

> Note that if no WHERE clause was specified, the execution would never stop, which would cause an error at the end.

The preceding example is quite easy to implement without recursive queries. PostgreSQL provides a way to generate a series of numeric values and use them in subqueries. However, there is a task that cannot be solved without recursive queries, and that is querying a hierarchy of objects.

There is no hierarchical data in the car portal database, so in order to illustrate the technique, we need to create some sample data. A typical hierarchy implies the existence of a parent-child relationship between objects, where an object can be a parent and a child at the same time.

Suppose there is a family--Alan has two children: Bert and Bob. Bert also has two children: Carl and Carmen. Bob has one child: Cecil, who has two children, Dave and Den. The relationships are shown in the next image. The arrows go from each person to his parent:

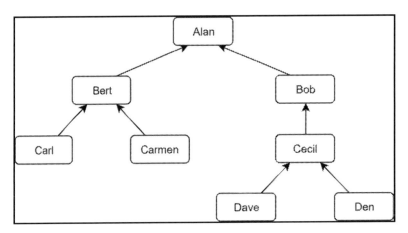

Hierarchical relationship

In the database, the hierarchy can be stored in a simple table with two columns: person and parent. The first will be the primary key and the second will be a foreign key referencing the same table:

```
car_portal=>CREATE TABLE family (person text PRIMARY KEY, parent text
REFERENCES family);
CREATE TABLE
car_portal=> INSERT INTO family VALUES ('Alan', NULL),
  ('Bert', 'Alan'), ('Bob', 'Alan'), ('Carl', 'Bert'), ('Carmen', 'Bert'),
('Cecil', 'Bob'),
  ('Dave', 'Cecil'), ('Den', 'Cecil');
INSERT 0 8
```

The first inserted record with a NULL value for parent indicates that there is no information about Alan's parent.

Suppose it is required to build a full bloodline for all the children in the family. It is not possible to do so by just joining tables, because each join will handle only one level of hierarchy, but in general, the number or levels is not given.

The following recursive query will solve the problem:

```
car_portal=> WITH RECURSIVE genealogy (bloodline, person, level) AS
(
   SELECT person, person, 0 FROM family WHERE parent IS NULL
   UNION ALL
   SELECT g.bloodline || ' -> ' || f.person, f.person, g.level + 1
     FROM family f, genealogy g WHERE f.parent = g.person
)
SELECT bloodline, level FROM genealogy;
          bloodline           | level
------------------------------+-------
 Alan                         |     0
 Alan -> Bert                 |     1
 Alan -> Bob                  |     1
 Alan -> Bert -> Carl         |     2
 Alan -> Bert -> Carmen       |     2
 Alan -> Bob -> Cecil         |     2
 Alan -> Bob -> Cecil -> Dave |     3
 Alan -> Bob -> Cecil -> Den  |     3
(8 rows)
```

In the non-recursive term, the start of the hierarchy is selected. Here, it is a person who has no parent. His name is an initial value for the bloodline. On the `first` iteration in the recursive term, his children are selected (the persons whose parent is the person selected in the non-recursive term). Their names are added to the bloodline field with a separator `->`. On the second iteration, the children of the children are selected, and so on. When no more children are found, the execution stops. The value in the field level is incremented on each iteration so that the number of iterations is visible in the results.

There is a potential problem with these hierarchical queries. If the data contained cycles, the recursive query would never stop if used in the same way as the preceding code. For example, let's change this record in the table, `family`:

```
UPDATE family SET parent = 'Bert' WHERE person = 'Alan';
```

Now there is a cycle in the data: `Alan` is a child of his own child. If we run the previous bloodline query as is, it would process this cycle until it would eventually fail. To use the query, it is necessary to somehow make the query stop. This can be done by checking whether the person that is being processed by the recursive term was already included in the bloodline, as follows:

```
car_portal=> WITH RECURSIVE genealogy (bloodline, person, level, processed)
AS
(
   SELECT person, person, 0, ARRAY[person] FROM family WHERE person = 'Alan'
```

```
    UNION ALL
    SELECT g.bloodline || ' -> ' || f.person, f.person, g.level + 1,
processed || f.person
        FROM family f, genealogy g
        WHERE f.parent = g.person AND NOT f.person = ANY(processed)
)
SELECT bloodline, level FROM genealogy;
            bloodline             | level
---------------------------------+-------
 Alan                            |    0
 Alan -> Bert                    |    1
 Alan -> Bob                     |    1
 Alan -> Bert -> Carl            |    2
 Alan -> Bert -> Carmen          |    2
 Alan -> Bob -> Cecil            |    2
 Alan -> Bob -> Cecil -> Dave    |    3
 Alan -> Bob -> Cecil -> Den     |    3
(8 rows)
```

The result is the same as in the previous example. The `processed` field that is used in the CTE, but not selected in the main query, is an array that contains the names of all the processed persons. In fact, it has the same data as the field bloodline, but in a way this is more convenient to use in the WHERE clause. In each iteration, the name of the processed person is added to the array. Additionally, in the WHERE clause of the recursive term, the name of the person is checked so that it is not equal to any element of the array.

There are some limitations to the implementation of recursive queries. The use of aggregation is not allowed in the recursive term. Moreover, the name of the recursive subquery can be referenced only once in the recursive term.

Changing data in multiple tables at a time

Another very useful application of CTEs is performing several data-changing statements at once. This is done by including the INSERT, UPDATE, and DELETE statements in the CTEs. The results of any of these statements can be passed to the following CTEs or to the primary query by specifying the RETURNING clause. As well as for SELECT statements, the maximal number of common table expressions that change data is not defined.

For example, suppose one wants to add a new car to the car portal database and there is no corresponding car model in the table `car_model`. To do this, one needs to enter a new record into `car_model`, take the ID of the new record, and use this ID to insert the data into the table `car`:

```
car_portal=> INSERT INTO car_portal_app.car_model (make, model) VALUES
('Ford','Mustang') RETURNING car_model_id;
 car_model_id
--------------
          100
(1 row)
INSERT 0 1
car_portal=> INSERT INTO car_portal_app.car (number_of_owners,
registration_number, manufacture_year, number_of_doors, car_model_id,
mileage)
VALUES (1, 'GTR1231', 2014, 4, 100, 10423);
INSERT 0 1
```

Sometimes, it is not convenient to perform two statements storing the intermediate ID number somewhere. The `WITH` queries provide a way to make the changes in both the tables at the same time:

```
car_portal=# WITH car_model_insert AS
(
   INSERT INTO car_portal_app.car_model (make, model) VALUES
('Ford','Mustang')
   RETURNING car_model_id
)
INSERT INTO car_portal_app.car
   (number_of_owners, registration_number, manufacture_year,
number_of_doors, car_model_id, mileage)
SELECT 1, 'GTR1231', 2014, 4, car_model_id, 10423 FROM car_model_insert;
INSERT 0 1
```

As mentioned earlier, the CTEs that change the data are always executed. It does not matter if they are referenced in the primary query directly or indirectly. However, the order of their execution is not determined. One can influence that order by making them dependent on each other.

What if several CTEs change the same table or use the results produced by each other? There are some principles for their isolation and interaction:

- For sub-statements:
    - All the sub-statements work with the data as it was at the moment of the start of the whole `WITH` query.
    - They don't see the results of each other's work. For example, it is not possible for the `DELETE` sub-statement to remove a row that was inserted by another `INSERT` sub-statement.
    - The only way to pass information of the processed records from a data changing CTE to another CTE is with the `RETURNING` clause.

- For triggers defined on the tables being changed:
    - For `BEFORE` triggers: Statement-level triggers are executed just before the execution of each sub-statements. Row-level triggers are executed just before the changing of every record. This means that a row-level trigger for one sub-statements can be executed before a statement-level trigger for another sub-statement even if the same table is changed.
    - For `AFTER` triggers: Both statement-level and row-level triggers are executed after the whole `WITH` query. They are executed in groups per every sub-statement: `first` row-level and then statement-level. This means that a statement-level trigger for one sub-statement can be executed before a row-level trigger for another sub-statement, even if the same table is changed.
    - The statements inside the code of the triggers do see the changes in data that were made by other sub-statements.
- For the constraints defined on the tables being changed, assuming they are not set to `DEFERRED`:
    - `PRIMARY KEY` and `UNIQUE` constraints are validated for every record at the moment of insert or update of the record. They take into account the changes made by other sub-statements.
    - `CHECK` constraints are validated for every record at the moment of insert or update of the record. They do not take into account the changes made by other sub-statements.
    - `FOREIGN KEY` constraints are validated at the end of the execution of the whole `WITH` query.

A simple example of dependency and interaction between CTEs would be as follows:

```
car_portal=> CREATE TABLE t (f int UNIQUE);
CREATE TABLE
car_portal=> INSERT INTO t VALUES (1);
INSERT 0 1
car_portal=> WITH del_query AS (DELETE FROM t) INSERT INTO t VALUES (1);
ERROR: duplicate key value violates unique constraint "t_f_key"
```

The last query failed because PostgreSQL tried to execute the main query before the CTE. If one creates a dependency that will make the CTE execute first, then the record will be deleted and the new record will be inserted. In that case, the constraint will not be violated:

```
car_portal=> WITH del_query AS (DELETE FROM t RETURNING f)
INSERT INTO t SELECT 1 WHERE (SELECT count(*) FROM del_query) IS NOT NULL;
INSERT 0 1
```

In the preceding code snippet, the WHERE condition in the main query does not have any practical meaning because the result of count is never NULL. However, as the CTE is referenced in the query, it is executed before the execution of the main query.

Window functions

Apart from grouping and aggregation, PostgreSQL provides another way to perform computations based on the values of several records. It can be done using **Window functions**. Grouping and aggregation implies the output of a single record for every group of input records. Window functions can do similar things, but they are executed for every record, and the number of records in the output and the input is the same:

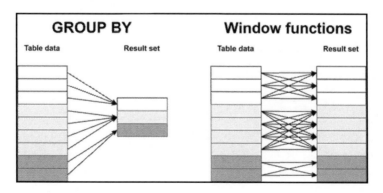

GROUP BY and window functions

In the preceding diagram, the rectangles represent the records of a table. Let's assume that the color of the rectangles indicates the value of a field used to group the records. When GROUP BY is used in a query, each distinct value of that field will create a group and each group will become a single record in the results of the query. This was explained in Chapter 05, *SQL Language*. Window functions provide access to the values of all the records of the group (which is called a partition in this case), although the number of records in the result set stays the same. When window functions are used, no grouping is necessary, although possible.

Window functions are evaluated after grouping and aggregation. For this reason, the only places in the SELECT query where the window functions are allowed are select-list and the ORDER BY clause.

Window definition

The syntax of the window functions is as follows:

```
<function_name> (<function_arguments>)
OVER (
  [PARTITION BY <expression_list>]
  [ORDER BY <order_by_list>]
  [{ROWS | RANGE} <frame_start> |
  {ROWS | RANGE} BETWEEN <frame_start> AND <frame_end>])
```

The construct in the parentheses after the OVER keyword is called the **window definition**. The last part of the window definition, which starts with ROWS, is called the **frame clause**. The syntax of frame_start and frame_end will be described later.

Window functions, in general, work like aggregating functions. They process sets of records. These sets are built separately for each processed record. That's why, unlike the normal aggregating functions, window functions are evaluated for each row.

For each record, a set of rows to be processed by a window function is built in the following way.

At the beginning, the PARTITION BY clause is processed. All the records that have the same values after evaluating the expressions from the expression_list as the current row is taken. The set of these rows is called the **partition**. The current row is also included in the partition. In fact, the PARTITION BY clause has the same logic and syntax as the GROUP BY clause of the SELECT statement, except that it is not possible to refer to the output column names or numbers in PARTITION BY.

In other words, while processing each record, a window function will take a look at all the other records to check if any of them falls into the same partition as the current one. If no PARTITION BY is specified, it means that all the rows will be included in a single partition at this step.

Next, the partition is sorted according to the ORDER BY clause, which has the same syntax and logic as the ORDER BY clause in the SELECT statement. Again, no references to the output column names or numbers are allowed here. If the ORDER BY clause is omitted, then all the records of the set are considered to have the same position.

In the end, the frame clause is processed. It means taking a subset from the whole partition to pass it to the window function.

The subset is called the **window frame**. The frame has its starting and ending points. The start of the frame, which is referenced by frame_start in the preceding syntax diagram, can be any of the following:

- UNBOUNDED PRECEDING: The very first record of the partition.
- <N> PRECEDING: A record that is placed N records before the current one in the ordered partition. <N> is an integer expression that cannot return a negative value and which cannot use aggregating functions or other window functions. 0 PRECEDING points to the current row.
- CURRENT ROW: The current row itself.
- <N> FOLLOWING: A record that is placed N records after the current record in the ordered partition.

The ending point--frame_end--can be any one of the following:

- <N> PRECEDING
- CURRENT ROW
- <N> FOLLOWING
- UNBOUNDED FOLLOWING, the very last record of the partition

The starting point should precede the ending point. That's why, for example, ROWS BETWEEN CURRENT ROW AND 1 PRECEDING is not correct.

A window frame can be defined using the ROWS mode or the RANGE mode. It affects the meaning of the CURRENT ROW. In the ROWS mode, the CURRENT ROW points to the current record itself. In the RANGE mode, the CURRENT ROW points to the first or to the last record that has the same position when sorted according to the ORDER BY clause.

First or last will be chosen with a view to make the frame wider. In the RANGE mode only UNBOUNDED ... is used or CURRENT ROW can be used in the frame clause, <N> PRECEDING will not work.

If frame_end is omitted, then CURRENT ROW is used instead.

If the whole frame clause is omitted, then the frame will be built using the RANGE UNBOUNDED PRECEDING definition.

Look at the following example of a window definition:

```
OVER (PARTITION BY a ORDER BY b ROWS BETWEEN UNBOUNDED PRECEDING AND 5
FOLLOWING)
```

The preceding definition means that for every row, all the records with the same value of the field a will form the partition. Then, the partition will be ordered in an ascending manner by the values of the field b, and the frame will contain all the records from the first one to the fifth following the current row.

The WINDOW clause

The window definitions can be quite long, and in many cases, it is not convenient to use them in the select-list. PostgreSQL provides a way to define windows and give them names that can be used in the OVER clause in window functions. This is done using the WINDOW clause of the SELECT statement, which is specified after the HAVING clause, as follows:

```
SELECT count() OVER w, sum(b) OVER w,
  avg(b) OVER (w ORDER BY c ROWS BETWEEN 1 PRECEDING AND 1 FOLLOWING)
FROM table1
WINDOW w AS (PARTITION BY a)
```

The predefined window can be used as is. In the preceding example, the window functions count and sum do so. The window definition can also be further detailed like it is for the function avg in the example. The syntactical difference is the following: to reuse the same window definition, the window name should be specified after the OVER keyword without parentheses. To extend the window definition with the ORDER BY or frame clause, one should use the name of the window inside the parentheses.

When the same window definition is used several times, PostgreSQL will optimize the execution of the query by building partitions only once and then reusing the results.

Using window functions

All aggregating functions can be used as window functions, with the exception of ordered-set and hypothetical-set aggregates. User-defined aggregating functions can also be used as window functions. The presence of the OVER clause indicates that the function is used as a window function.

When the aggregating function is used as a window function, it will aggregate the rows that belong to the window frame of a current row. The typical use cases for the window functions are computing statistical values of different kinds. Take the car portal database for example. There is a table called **advertisement** that contains information about the advertisements that users create.

Suppose it is required to analyze the quantity of advertisements that the users create over a period of time. The query that generates the report would be as follows:

```
car_portal=> WITH monthly_data AS (
  SELECT date_trunc('month', advertisement_date) AS month, count(*) as cnt
    FROM car_portal_app.advertisement GROUP BY date_trunc('month',
advertisement_date)
)
SELECT to_char(month,'YYYY-MM') as month, cnt,
  sum(cnt) OVER (w ORDER BY month) AS cnt_year,
  round(avg(cnt) OVER (ORDER BY month ROWS BETWEEN 2 PRECEDING AND 2
FOLLOWING), 1) AS mov_avg,
  round(cnt / sum(cnt) OVER w * 100,1) AS ratio_year
FROM monthly_data WINDOW w AS (PARTITION BY date_trunc('year',month));
```

month	cnt	cnt_year	mov_avg	ratio_year
2014-01	42	42	40.3	5.8
2014-02	49	91	44.5	6.7
2014-03	30	121	56.8	4.1
2014-04	57	178	69.0	7.8
2014-05	106	284	73.0	14.6
2014-06	103	387	81.0	14.2
2014-07	69	456	86.0	9.5
2014-08	70	526	74.0	9.6
2014-09	82	608	60.6	11.3
2014-10	46	654	54.2	6.3
2014-11	36	690	49.8	5.0
2014-12	37	727	35.2	5.1
2015-01	48	48	32.5	84.2
2015-02	9	57	31.3	15.8

```
(14 rows)
```

In the `WITH` clause, the data is aggregated on a monthly basis. In the main query, the window `w` is defined, implying partitioning by year. This means that every window function that uses the window `w` will work with the records of the same year as the current record.

The `first` window function, `sum`, uses the window `w`. As `ORDER BY` is specified, each record has its place in the partition. The frame clause is omitted, therefore the frame, `RANGE BETWEEN UNBOUNDED PRECEDING AND CURRENT ROW`, is applied. This means that the function calculates the `sum` of the values for the records from the beginning of each year till the current month. It is the cumulative total on a yearly basis.

The second function, `avg`, calculates the moving average. For each record, it calculates the average value of five records—ranging from the second preceding the current record to the second following the current one. It does not use a predefined window, because the moving average does not take the year into account. Only the order of the values matters.

The `third` window function, `sum`, uses the same window definition again. It calculates the total `sum` of the values for the whole year. This value is used as denominator in the expression calculating the share of the current month over the year.

There are several window functions that are not aggregating functions. They are used to get the values of other records within the partition, calculate the rank of the current row among all rows, and generate row numbers.

For example, let's change the report from the previous example. Suppose it is necessary to calculate the difference in the quantity of advertisements for each month against the previous months and against the same month of the previous year. Suppose it is also required to get the rank of the current month. The query would be as follows:

```
car_portal=> WITH monthly_data AS (
  SELECT date_trunc('month', advertisement_date) AS month, count(*) as cnt
    FROM car_portal_app.advertisement GROUP BY date_trunc('month',
advertisement_date)
)
SELECT to_char(month,'YYYY-MM') as month, cnt,
    cnt - lag(cnt) OVER (ORDER BY month) as prev_m,
    cnt - lag(cnt, 12) OVER (ORDER BY month) as prev_y,
    rank() OVER (w ORDER BY cnt DESC) as rank
  FROM monthly_data
  WINDOW w AS (PARTITION BY date_trunc('year',month))
  ORDER BY month DESC;
  month  | cnt | prev_m | prev_y | rank
---------+-----+--------+--------+------
 2015-02 |   9 |    -39 |    -40 |   2
 2015-01 |  48 |     11 |      6 |   1
```

```
2014-12 |  37 |    1 |       |  10
2014-11 |  36 |  -10 |       |  11
2014-10 |  46 |  -36 |       |   8
2014-09 |  82 |   12 |       |   3
2014-08 |  70 |    1 |       |   4
2014-07 |  69 |  -34 |       |   5
2014-06 | 103 |   -3 |       |   2
2014-05 | 106 |   49 |       |   1
2014-04 |  57 |   27 |       |   6
2014-03 |  30 |  -19 |       |  12
2014-02 |  49 |    7 |       |   7
2014-01 |  42 |      |       |   9
```

(14 rows)

The `lag` function returns the value of a given expression for the record, which is the given number of records before the current one (default is 1). In the `first` occurrence of the function in the example, it returns the value of the field `cnt` from the previous record, which corresponds to the previous month. You may see that the number of advertisements for February 2015 is 9, which is lower than in January 2015 by 39.

The second `lag` returns the value of `cnt` for the record that is 12 records before the current one--meaning a year ago. The number for February 2015 is lower than the number for February 2014 by 42.

The rank function returns the rank of the current row within the partition. It returns the rank with gaps. This means that if two records have the same position according to the ORDER BY clause, both of them will get the same rank. The next record will get the rank after the next rank. For example, two `first` records followed by a `third` one.

Other window functions are as follows:

- `lead`: Similar to lag, but returning the value of a given expression evaluated for the record that is the given number of records after the current row.
- `first_value`, `last_value`, `nth_value`: These return the value of a given expression evaluated for the `first` record, last record, or nth record of the frame respectively.
- `row_number`: Returns the number of the current row within the partition.
- `dense_rank`: Returns the rank of the current row without gaps.

- percent_rank and cume_dist: Return the relative rank of the current row. The difference is that the first function uses rank and the second uses row_number as a numerator for the calculations.
- ntile: Divides the partition into the given number of equal parts and returns the number of the part where the current record belongs.

A more detailed description of these functions is available in the documentation at http:// www.postgresql.org/docs/current/static/functions-window.html.

Window functions with grouping and aggregation

As window functions are evaluated after grouping, it is possible to use aggregating functions as arguments for window functions, but not the other way around.

A code like the following is correct: sum(count(*)) OVER()

This will also work: sum(a) OVER(ORDER BY count(*))

However, the code, sum(count(*) OVER()), is wrong.

For example, to calculate the rank of the seller accounts by the number of advertisements they give, the following query can be used:

```
car_portal=> SELECT seller_account_id, dense_rank() OVER(ORDER BY count(*)
DESC)
 FROM car_portal_app.advertisement
 GROUP BY seller_account_id;
 seller_account_id | dense_rank
-------------------+------------
                26 |          1
               128 |          2
                28 |          2
               126 |          2
...
```

Advanced SQL techniques

In the following section, some other advanced SQL techniques will be introduced:

- The DISTINCT ON clause, which helps in finding the first records in groups
- Selecting sample data from a big table

- The set returning functions, which are functions that return relations
- LATERAL joins, which allow subqueries to reference each other
- Advanced grouping techniques that can be used in generating reports
- Some special aggregating functions

Selecting the first records

Quite often, it is necessary to find the first records based on some criteria. For example, let's take the car_portal database; suppose it is required to find the first advertisement for each car_id in the advertisement table.

Grouping can help in this case. It requires a subquery to implement the logic:

```
SELECT advertisement_id, advertisement_date, adv.car_id, seller_account_id
  FROM car_portal_app.advertisement adv
  INNER JOIN
  (SELECT car_id, min(advertisement_date) min_date FROM
car_portal_app.advertisement GROUP BY car_id) first
    ON adv.car_id=first.car_id AND adv.advertisement_date = first.min_date;
```

However, if the ordering logic is complex and cannot be implemented using the min function, this approach will not work.

Although window functions can solve the problem, they are not always convenient to use:

```
SELECT DISTINCT first_value(advertisement_id) OVER w AS advertisement_id,
    min(advertisement_date) OVER w AS advertisement_date,
    car_id, first_value(seller_account_id) OVER w AS seller_account_id
  FROM car_portal_app.advertisement
  WINDOW w AS (PARTITION BY car_id ORDER BY advertisement_date);
```

In the preceding code, DISTINCT is used to remove the duplicates that were grouped together in the previous example.

PostgreSQL provides an explicit way of selecting the first record within each group. The DISTINCT ON keywords are used for this. The syntax is as follows:

```
SELECT DISTINCT ON (<expression_list>) <Select-List>
...
ORDER BY <order_by_list>
```

In the preceding code snippet, for each distinct combination of values of expression_list, only the first record will be returned by the SELECT statement. The ORDER BY clause is used to define a rule to determine which record is the first.

expression_list from DISTINCT ON must be included in the order_by_list list.

For the task being discussed, it can be applied in the following way:

```
SELECT DISTINCT ON (car_id) advertisement_id, advertisement_date, car_id,
seller_account_id
 FROM car_portal_app.advertisement
 ORDER BY car_id, advertisement_date;
```

This code is much clearer, easier to read and understand, and in fact works faster in most of the cases.

Selecting a data sample

Suppose the car_portal database is huge and there is a task to collect some statistics about the data. The statistics do not have to be exactly accurate, some estimation is good enough. It is rather important to collect it quickly. PostgreSQL provides a way to query not a whole table but a random fraction of its records.

The syntax is as follows:

```
SELECT ... FROM <table> TABLESAMPLE <sampling_method> ( <argument> [, ...]
) [ REPEATABLE ( <seed> ) ]
```

The sampling_method can be any of BERNOULLI or SYSTEM. They are provided with a standard PostgreSQL installation. More sampling methods could be available as extensions. Both of the sampling methods take one argument which is a probability that a row will be selected in percent. The difference between the two methods is that BERNOULLI implies a full table scan and the algorithm will decide if a row should be selected or not for each individual row. The SYSTEM method does the same but on the level of blocks of rows. The latter is significantly faster, but the results are less accurate because of the different number of rows in different blocks. The REPEATABLE keyword is used to specify the seed value used by the random functions in the sampling algorithm. The results of queries with the same seed value is the same, as long as the data in the table does not change.

The sampling is happening at the moment of reading the data from a table, before any filtering, grouping, or other operations are performed.

To illustrate the sampling, let's increase the number of records in the `advertisement` table, executing the following query:

```
car_portal=> INSERT INTO advertisement (advertisement_date, car_id,
seller_account_id)
   SELECT advertisement_date, car_id, seller_account_id from advertisement;
INSERT 0 784
```

This simply duplicates the number of records in the table. If this is executed many times, the table will be pretty big. For the following example that query was executed 12 more times. Now if we try to select the total count of records, it takes quite some time:

```
car_portal=> \timing
Timing is on.
car_portal=> SELECT count(*) FROM advertisement;
  count
----------
 6422528
(1 row)
Time: 394.577 ms
```

Now let's try sampling:

```
car_portal=> SELECT count(*) * 100 FROM advertisement TABLESAMPLE SYSTEM
(1);
 ?column?
----------
 6248600
(1 row)
Time: 8.344 ms
```

The second query is much faster; however, the result is not very accurate. Multiplication of the `count` function by 100 is done because only one percent of the rows are selected.

If this query is performed several times, the results will always be different and sometimes it can be quite far away from the real count of rows in the table. To improve the quality, the fraction of the rows that are selected can be increased:

```
car_portal=> SELECT count(*) * 10 from advertisement TABLESAMPLE SYSTEM
(10);
 ?column?
----------
 6427580
(1 row)
Time: 92.793 ms
```

The time increased proportionally.

Set returning functions

Functions in PostgreSQL can return not only single values, but also relations. Such functions are called **set returning functions**.

There is a quite typical task for every SQL developer: to generate a sequence of integers, each in a separate record. This sequence or relation can have many use cases. For example, suppose it is necessary to select data from the car_portal database to count the number of cars for each year of manufacture, from 2010 till 2015, and it is required to show zero for the years where no cars exist in the system at all. A simple SELECT query from the only table car cannot be used to implement this logic. It is not possible to see the records that are absent from the table data itself.

That's why it would be useful if there was a table with the numbers from 2010 to 2015. Then it could be outer-joined to the results of the query.

One could create this table in advance, but it is not a very good idea, because the number of records necessary in the table is not known in advance, and if one created a very big table, it would be just a waste of disk space in most cases.

There is a function, generate_series, which serves exactly this purpose. It returns a set of integers with the given start and stop values. The query for the example would be as follows:

```
car_portal=> SELECT years.manufacture_year, count(car_id)
 FROM generate_series(2010, 2015) as  years (manufacture_year)
   LEFT JOIN car_portal_app.car ON car.manufacture_year =
years.manufacture_year
 GROUP BY years.manufacture_year
 ORDER BY 1;
manufacture_year | count
-----------------+-------
            2010 |    11
            2011 |    12
            2012 |    12
            2013 |    21
            2014 |    16
            2015 |     0
(6 rows)
```

In the preceding query, the generate_series function returns six integers from 2010 to 2015. This set has an alias years. The table car is left-joined to this set of integers and then, all the years can be seen in the output result set.

It is possible to specify a step when calling `generate_series`:

```
car_portal=> SELECT * FROM generate_series(5, 11, 3);
 generate_series
-----------------
               5
               8
              11
(3 rows)
```

The `generate_series` function can also return a set of `timestamp` values:

```
car_portal=> SELECT * FROM generate_series('2015-01-01'::date,
'2015-01-31'::date, interval '7 days');
 generate_series
----------------------
 2015-01-01 00:00:00-05
 2015-01-08 00:00:00-05
 2015-01-15 00:00:00-05
 2015-01-22 00:00:00-05
 2015-01-29 00:00:00-05
(5 rows)
```

There are a couple of other set-returning functions designed to work with arrays:

- `generate_subscripts`: This generates numbers that can be used to reference the elements in a given array for the given dimension(s). This function is useful to enumerate the elements of an array in a SQL statement.
- `unnest`: This transforms a given array into a set or rows where each record corresponds to an element of the array.

Set-returning functions are also called **table functions**.

Table functions can return sets of rows of a predefined type, like `generate_series` returns a set of `int` or `bigint` (depending on the type of input argument). Moreover, they can return a set of abstract type records. This allows a function to return different numbers of columns depending on their arguments. SQL requires that the row structure of all input relations is defined so that the structure of the result set will also be defined. That's why table functions that return sets of records, when used in a query, can be followed by a definition of their row structure:

```
function_name (<arguments>) [AS] alias (column_name column_type [, ...])
```

The output of several set-returning functions can be combined together as if they were joined on the position of each row. The syntax construct ROWS FROM is used for this, as follows:

```
ROWS FROM (function_call [,...]) [[AS] alias (column_name [,...])]
```

The preceding construct will return a relation, therefore can be used in a FROM clause as any other relation. The number of rows is equal to the largest output of the functions. Each column corresponds to the respective function in the ROWS FROM clause. If a function returns fewer rows than other functions, the missing values will be set to NULL:

```
car_portal=> SELECT foo.a, foo.b FROM
ROWS FROM (generate_series(1,3), generate_series(1,7,2)) AS foo(a, b);
 a | b
---+---
 1 | 1
 2 | 3
 3 | 5
   | 7
(4 rows)
```

Lateral subqueries

Subqueries were discussed in the previous chapter. However, it is worth mentioning one specific pattern of using them in more detail.

It is very convenient to use subqueries in the select-list. They are used in the SELECT statements, for example, to create calculated attributes when querying a table. Let's take the car portal database again. Suppose it is required to query the table car and, for each car, it is required to assess its age by comparing it with the age of the other cars of the same model. Furthermore, we want to query the number of cars of the same model.

These two additional fields can be generated by scalar subqueries, as follows:

```
car_portal=> SELECT car_id, manufacture_year,
  CASE WHEN manufacture_year <= (
    SELECT avg(manufacture_year) FROM car_portal_app.car WHERE car_model_id
= c.car_model_id)
    THEN 'old' ELSE 'new' END as age,
  (SELECT count(*) FROM car_portal_app.car WHERE car_model_id =
c.car_model_id)
    AS same_model_count
  FROM car_portal_app.car c;
 car_id | manufacture_year | age | same_model_count
--------+------------------+-----+------------------
```

```
         1 |                 2008 | old |                    3
         2 |                 2014 | new |                    6
         3 |                 2014 | new |                    2
 . . .
(229 rows)
```

The power of these subqueries is that they can refer to the main table in their WHERE clause.
This makes them easy. It is also very simple to add more columns in the query by adding
other subqueries. On the other hand, there is a problem here: performance. The table car is
scanned by the database server once for the main query, and then it is scanned another two
times for each retrieved row, that is, for the age and same_model_count columns.

It is possible, of course, to calculate these aggregates once for each car model
independently and then join the results with the car table:

```
car_portal=> SELECT car_id, manufacture_year,
    CASE WHEN manufacture_year <= avg_year THEN 'old' ELSE 'new' END as
age,
    same_model_count
  FROM car_portal_app.car
    INNER JOIN (
       SELECT car_model_id, avg(manufacture_year) avg_year, count(*)
same_model_count
       FROM car_portal_app.car GROUP BY car_model_id) subq USING
(car_model_id);
 car_id | manufacture_year | age | same_model_count
--------+------------------+-----+------------------
      1 |             2008 | old |                3
      2 |             2014 | new |                6
      3 |             2014 | new |                2
 . . .
(229 rows)
```

The result is the same and the query is 20 times faster. However, this query is only good to
retrieve many rows from the database. If it is required to get the information about only one
car, the first query will be faster.

One could see that the first query could perform better if it was possible to select two
columns in the same subquery in the select-list, but this is not possible. Scalar queries can
return only one column.

There is yet another way of using subqueries. It combines the advantages of the subqueries in the select-list, which can refer to the main table in their WHERE clause, with the subqueries in the FROM clause, which can return multiple columns. This can be done via lateral subqueries. Putting the keyword LATERAL before a subquery in the FROM clause makes it possible to reference any preceding item of the FROM clause from that subquery.

The query would be as follows:

```
car_portal=> SELECT car_id, manufacture_year,
    CASE WHEN manufacture_year <= avg_year THEN 'old' ELSE 'new' END as
age,
    same_model_count
  FROM car_portal_app.car c,
    LATERAL (
      SELECT avg(manufacture_year) avg_year,count(*) same_model_count
        FROM car_portal_app.car
        WHERE car_model_id = c.car_model_id) subq;
 car_id | manufacture_year | age | same_model_count
--------+------------------+-----+------------------
      1 |             2008 | old |                3
      2 |             2014 | new |                6
      3 |             2014 | new |                2
...
(229 rows)
```

This query is approximately two times faster than the `first` one, and is the best one to retrieve only one row from the `car` table.

The JOIN syntax is also possible with LATERAL subqueries, though in many cases, the join condition is somehow included into the WHERE clause of the subqueries.

When it comes to set-returning functions, it is not necessary to use the LATERAL keyword. All functions that are mentioned in the FROM clause can already use the output of any preceding functions or subqueries:

```
car_portal=> SELECT a, b FROM generate_series(1,3) AS a, generate_series(a,
a+2) AS b;
 a | b
---+---
 1 | 1
 1 | 2
 1 | 3
 2 | 2
 2 | 3
 2 | 4
 3 | 3
```

```
 3 | 4
 3 | 5
(9 rows)
```

In the preceding query, the `first` function that has the alias a returns three rows. For each of these three rows, the second function is called, returning three more rows.

Advanced grouping

Databases are often used as a data source for any kind of reporting. In reports, it is quite common to show in the same table subtotals, totals, and grand totals that summarize the data rows implying in fact grouping and aggregation. Consider the following report displaying the number of advertisements by `car` make and quarter, displaying also the totals for each quarter (aggregating all makes), and the grand total. Here is how to select the data for the report:

```
car_portal=> SELECT to_char(advertisement_date, 'YYYY-Q') as quarter, make,
count(*)
   FROM advertisement a
     INNER JOIN car c ON a.car_id = c.car_id
     INNER JOIN car_model m ON m.car_model_id = c.car_model_id
   GROUP BY quarter, make;
 quarter |      make       | count
---------+-----------------+-------
 2014-4  | Peugeot         |    12
 2014-2  | Daewoo          |     8
 2014-4  | Skoda           |     5
...
```

To make the subtotals, one would need to do additional queries, like this:

```
SELECT to_char(advertisement_date, 'YYYY-Q') as quarter, count(*)
 FROM advertisement a
 INNER JOIN car c ON a.car_id = c.car_id
 INNER JOIN car_model m ON m.car_model_id = c.car_model_id
 GROUP BY quarter;

SELECT count(*)
 FROM advertisement a
 INNER JOIN car c ON a.car_id = c.car_id
 INNER JOIN car_model m ON m.car_model_id = c.car_model_id;
```

The joins in these queries are redundant, they do not affect the results, but we leave them here to illustrate that the queries are actually the same as the `first` one, only the grouping makes the difference.

PostgreSQL provides a way to combine the three queries in a single one using a special construct, GROUP BY GROUPING SETS, as follows:

```
SELECT to_char(advertisement_date, 'YYYY-Q') as quarter, make, count(*)
  FROM advertisement a
    INNER JOIN car c ON a.car_id = c.car_id
    INNER JOIN car_model m ON m.car_model_id = c.car_model_id
  GROUP BY GROUPING SETS ((quarter, make), (quarter), ())
  ORDER BY quarter NULLS LAST, make NULLS LAST;
  quarter |     make       | count
 ---------+----------------+-------
  2014-1 | Alfa Romeo     |    2
  2014-1 | Audi           |    5
 ...
  2014-1 | Volvo          |    9
  2014-1 |                |  121     <- This is the subtotal for the quarter
2014-1
  2014-2 | Audi           |   18
  2014-2 | Citroen        |   40
 ...
  2014-2 | Volvo          |   12
  2014-2 |                |  266     <- This is the subtotal for the quarter
2014-2
  2014-3 | Audi           |   11
 ...
  2015-1 | Volvo          |    4
  2015-1 |                |   57     <- This is the subtotal for the quarter
2015-1
         |                |  784     <- This is the grand total for the
whole report
```

The construct GROUPING SETS ((quarter, make), (quarter), ()) makes the query work as a UNION ALL of the same queries with different GROUP BY clauses:

- GROUP BY quarter, make
- GROUP BY quarter--here, the make field will get the NULL value
- All the rows grouped into a single group, both fields quarter and make will get NULL values

Generally speaking, the GROUP BY clause takes not just expressions, but **grouping elements** that could be expressions or constructs like GROUPING SETS.

Other possible grouping elements are ROLLUP and CUBE:

- ROLLUP (a, b, c) is equivalent to GROUPING SETS ((a, b, c), (a, b), (c), ())
- CUBE (a, b, c) is equivalent to GROUPING SETS ((a, b, c), (a, b), (a, c), (b, c), (a), (b), (c), ())--all possible combinations of the argument expressions

It is also possible to use CUBE and ROLLUP inside GROUPING SETS, as well as combine different grouping elements in one GROUP BY clause like this: GROUP BY a, CUBE (b, c). This would be equivalent to GROUP BY GROUPING SETS ((a, b, c), (a, b), (a, c), (a))--basically a combination of the grouping elements.

Although GROUPING SETS implements the logic of UNION ALL of the results of queries with different GROUP BY clauses, in the background, it works differently from the set operation. PostgreSQL will scan the tables and perform joining and filtering only once. This means that the usage of these grouping techniques can help optimize the performance of your solutions.

The documentation about GROUPING SETS is available at https://www.postgresql.org/docs/current/static/queries-table-expressions.html#QUERIES-GROUPING-SETS.

Advanced aggregation

There are several aggregating functions that are executed in a special way.

The first group of such aggregating functions are called **ordered-set aggregates**. They take into account not just the values of the argument expressions, but also their order. They are related to statistics and calculate percentile values.

The percentile is the value of a group in which the given percentage of other values is less than that. For example, if a value is at the 95th percentile, it means that it is higher than 95 percent of the other values. In PostgreSQL, one can calculate a continuous or discrete percentile using the functions percentile_cont or percentile_disc respectively. A discrete percentile is one of the actual values of a group, while a continuous percentile is an interpolated value between two actual values. It is possible to calculate the percentile for a given fraction, or several percentile values for a given array of fractions.

For example, this is the query regarding the distribution of the number of advertisements per `car`:

```
car_portal=> SELECT percentile_disc(ARRAY[0.25, 0.5, 0.75]) WITHIN GROUP
(ORDER BY cnt)
  FROM (SELECT count(*) cnt FROM car_portal_app.advertisement GROUP BY
car_id) subq;
 percentile_disc
-----------------
 {2,3,5}
(1 row)
```

The result means that there are, at most, two advertisements for 25 percent of the cars, three advertisements for 50 percent of the cars, and five advertisements for 75 percent of the cars in the database.

The syntax of the ordered-set aggregating functions differs from the normal aggregates and uses a special construct, `WITHIN GROUP (ORDER BY expression)`. The expression here is actually an argument of a function. Here, not just the order of the rows but the values of the expressions as well affect the result of the function. In contrast to the `ORDER BY` clause of the `SELECT` query, only one expression is possible here and no references to the output column numbers are allowed.

Another ordered-set aggregating function is `mode`. It returns the most frequently appearing value of the group. If two values appear the same number of times, then the `first` of them will be returned.

For example, the following query gets the ID of the most frequent car model in the database:

```
car_portal=> SELECT mode() WITHIN GROUP (ORDER BY car_model_id) FROM
car_portal_app.car;
 mode
------
   64
(1 row)
```

To get the same result without this function will require self-join or ordering and limiting the result. Both are more expensive operations.

Another group of aggregates that use the same syntax are the **hypothetical-set aggregating functions**. They are `rank`, `dense_rank`, `percent_rank`, and `cume_dist`. There are window functions with the same names. Window functions take no argument and they return the result for the current row. Aggregate functions have no current row because they are evaluated for a group of rows. However, they take an argument: the value for the hypothetical current row.

For example, the aggregate function rank returns the rank of a given value in the ordered set as if that value existed in the set:

```
car_portal=> SELECT rank(2) WITHIN GROUP (ORDER BY a) FROM
generate_series(1,10,3) a;
 rank
------
    2
(1 row)
```

In the preceding query, the value 2 does not exist in the output of `generate_series` (it returns 1..4..7..10). If it existed, it would take the second position in the output.

Another topic worth mentioning about aggregating functions is the `FILTER` clause.

The `FILTER` clause filters the rows that are passed to the particular aggregating function based on a given condition. For example, suppose it is required to count the number of cars in the database for each `car` model separately, for each number of doors. If one groups the records by these two fields, the result will be correct but not very convenient to use in reporting:

```
car_portal=> SELECT car_model_id, number_of_doors, count(*)
  FROM car_portal_app.car
  GROUP BY car_model_id, number_of_doors;
 car_model_id | number_of_doors | count
--------------+-----------------+-------
           47 |               4 |     1
           42 |               3 |     2
           76 |               5 |     1
           52 |               5 |     2
...
```

The `FILTER` clause makes the output much clearer:

```
car_portal=> SELECT car_model_id,
    count(*) FILTER (WHERE number_of_doors = 2) doors2,
    count(*) FILTER (WHERE number_of_doors = 3) doors3,
    count(*) FILTER (WHERE number_of_doors = 4) doors4,
    count(*) FILTER (WHERE number_of_doors = 5) doors5
  FROM car_portal_app.car GROUP BY car_model_id;
 car_model_id | doors2 | doors3 | doors4 | doors5
--------------+--------+--------+--------+--------
           43 |      0 |      0 |      0 |      2
            8 |      0 |      0 |      1 |      0
           11 |      0 |      2 |      1 |      0
           80 |      0 |      1 |      0 |      0
...
```

Note that the cars with a number of doors other than from 2 to 5 will not be counted by the query.

The same result can be achieved by calling functions, as follows:

```
count(CASE WHEN number_of_doors = 2 THEN 1 END) doors2
```

However, the `FILTER` clause is easier and shorter.

Summary

This chapter described the advanced SQL concepts and features such as common table expressions and window functions. These features, for example, allow implementing a logic that would not be possible otherwise, that is, recursive queries.

The other techniques explained here, like the `DISTINCT ON` clause, grouping sets, the `FILTER` clause, or lateral subqueries, are not that irreplaceable. However, they can help in making a query smaller, easier, and faster.

SQL can be used to implement a very complicated logic. However, in difficult cases, the queries can become overcomplicated and very hard to maintain. Moreover, sometimes it is not possible to do some things in pure SQL. In these cases, one needs a procedural language to implement an algorithm. The next chapter will introduce one of them: PL/pgSQL.

7
Server-Side Programming with PL/pgSQL

The ability to write functions in PostgreSQL is an amazing feature. One can perform any task within the scope of the database server. These tasks might be related directly to data manipulation such as data aggregation and auditing, or used to perform miscellaneous services such as statistics collection, monitoring, system information acquisition, and job scheduling. In this chapter, our focus is on the PL/pgSQL language. PL/pgSQL is the default procedural language for PostgreSQL and it is full featured. As mentioned earlier, in `Chapter 04`, *PostgreSQL Advanced Building Blocks*, PL/pgSQL is installed by default in PostgreSQL.

PL/pgSQL has been influenced by the PL/SQL language, which is the Oracle stored procedural language. PL/pgSQL is a complete procedural language with rich control structures and full integration with the PostgreSQL trigger, index, rule, user-defined data type, and operator objects. There are several advantages to using PL/pgSQL; they are as follows:

- It is easy to learn and use
- It has very good support and documentation
- It has very flexible result data types, and it supports polymorphism
- It can return scalar values and sets using different return methods

The topics that will be covered in this chapter include:

- SQL language and PL/pgSQL – a comparison
- PostgreSQL function parameters
- The PostgreSQL PL/pgSQL control statements

- Function predefined variables
- Exception handling
- Dynamic SQL

SQL language and PL/pgSQL – a comparison

As shown in `Chapter 04`, *PostgreSQL Advanced Building Blocks*, one can write functions in C, SQL, and PL/pgSQL. There are some pros and cons to each approach. One can think of an SQL function as a wrapper around a parameterized `SELECT` statement. SQL functions can be inlined into the calling subquery leading to better performance. Also, since the SQL function execution plan is not cached as in PL/pgSQL, it often behaves better than PL/pgSQL. Moreover, caching in PL/ pgSQL can have some surprisingly bad side effects such as the caching of sensitive `timestamp` values, as shown in the documentation that can be found at `http://www.postgresql.org/docs/current/interactive/plpgsql-implementation.html`. Finally, with the introduction of CTE, recursive CTE, window functions, and `LATERAL JOINS`, one can perform complex logic using only SQL. If function logic can be implemented in SQL, use an SQL function instead of PL/PGSQL.

The PL/pgSQL function execution plan is cached; caching the plan can help to reduce execution time, but it can also hurt it if the plan is not optimal for the provided function parameters. From a functionality point of view, PL/pgSQL is much more powerful than SQL. PL/pgSQL supports several features that SQL functions cannot support, including the following:

- It provides the ability to raise exceptions as well as raise messages at different levels, such as notice and debug.
- It supports the construction of dynamic SQL using the `EXECUTE` command.
- It provides `EXCEPTION` handling.
- It has a complete set of assignment, control, and loop statements.
- It supports cursors.
- It is fully integrated with the PostgreSQL trigger system. SQL functions cannot be used with triggers.

PostgreSQL function parameters

In Chapter 04, *PostgreSQL Advanced Building Blocks*, we discussed the function categories immutable, stable, and volatile. In this section, we will continue with other function options. These options are not PL/pgSQL language-specific.

Function authorization-related parameters

The first parameters are related to security , when functions are called, they are executed within a security context that determines their privileges. The following options controls the function privileges context:

- SECURITY DEFINER
- SECURITY INVOKER

The default value for this option is SECURITY INVOKER, which indicates that the function will be executed with the privileges of the user who calls it. The SECURITY DEFINER functions will be executed using the privileges of the user who created it. For the SECURITY INVOKER functions, the user must have the permissions to execute the CRUD operations that the function implements; otherwise, the function will raise an error. The SECURITY DEFINER functions are very useful in defining triggers, or for temporarily promoting the user to perform tasks only supported by the function.

To test these security parameters, let's create two dummy functions using postgres user, and execute them in different sessions, as follows:

```
CREATE FUNCTION test_security_definer () RETURNS TEXT AS $$
   SELECT format ('current_user:%s session_user:%s', current_user,
session_user);
$$ LANGUAGE SQL SECURITY DEFINER;

CREATE FUNCTION test_security_invoker () RETURNS TEXT AS $$
   SELECT format ('current_user:%s session_user:%s', current_user,
session_user);
$$ LANGUAGE SQL SECURITY INVOKER;
```

To test the functions, let's execute them using a session created by postgres user, as follows:

```
$ psql -U postgres car_portal
psql (10.0)
Type "help" for help.
car_portal=# SELECT test_security_definer() , test_security_invoker();
             test_security_definer | test_security_invoker
----------------------------------------------------+---------------------------
----------------
 current_user:postgres session_user:postgres | current_user:postgres
session_user:postgres
(1 row)
```

Now, let's use another session created by the car_portal_app user, as follows:

```
psql -U car_portal_app car_portal
psql (10.0)
Type "help" for help.
car_portal=> SELECT test_security_definer() , test_security_invoker();
             test_security_definer | test_security_invoker
----------------------------------------------------+--------------------
-------------------------------------
 current_user:postgres session_user:car_portal_app |
current_user:car_portal_app session_user:car_portal_app
(1 row)
```

The two functions test_security_definer and test_security_invoker are identical except for the security parameter. When the two functions are executed by a postgres user, the result of the two functions is identical. This is simply because the one who created the function and the one who called it is the same user.

When the user car_portal_app executes the two preceding functions, the result of the test_security_definer function is current_user:postgres session_user:car_portal_app. In this case, the session_user is car_portal_app, since it has started the session using a psql client. However, the current_user who executes the SELECT statement is postgres.

Function planner-related parameters

Function planer related parameters helps in giving the planner information about the function execution cost, this helps the planner to generate a good execution plans. The following three parameters are used by the planner to determine the cost of executing the function, the number of rows that are expected to be returned, and whether the function pushes down when evaluating predicates. These parameters are:

- Leakproof: Leakproof means that the function has no side effects. It does not reveal any information about its argument. For example, it does not throw error messages about its argument. This parameter affects views with the security_barrier parameter.
- Cost: Declares the execution cost per row; the default value for the C language function is 1, and for PL/pgSQL it is 100. The cost is used by the planner to determine the best execution plan.
- Rows: The estimated number of rows returned by the function if the function is set-returning. The default value is 1000.

To understand the effect of the rows configuration parameter, let's consider the following example:

```
CREATE OR REPLACE FUNCTION a() RETURNS SETOF INTEGER AS $$
    SELECT 1;
$$ LANGUAGE SQL;
```

Now, let's execute the following query:

```
car_portal=> EXPLAIN SELECT * FROM a() CROSS JOIN (Values(1),(2),(3)) as
foo;
                            QUERY PLAN
---------------------------- ---------------------------------------------
 Nested Loop (cost=0.25..47.80 rows=3000 width=8)
   -> Function Scan on a (cost=0.25..10.25 rows=1000 width=4)
   -> Materialize (cost=0.00..0.05 rows=3 width=4)
        -> Values Scan on "*VALUES*" (cost=0.00..0.04 rows=3 width=4)
(4 rows)
```

The SQL function return type is SETOF INTEGER, which means that the planner expected more than one row to be returned from the function. Since the ROWS parameter is not specified, the planner uses the default value, which is 1000. Finally, due to CROSS JOIN, the total estimated number of rows is 3000, which is calculated as 3 * 1000.

In the preceding example, an incorrect estimation is not critical. However, in a real-life example, where one might have several joins, the error of rows estimation will be propagated and amplified, leading to bad execution plans.

The COST function parameter determines when the function will be executed, such as:

- It determines the function execution order
- It determines whether the function call can be pushed down

The following example shows how the execution order for functions is affected by the function COST. Let's assume we have two functions, as follows:

```
CREATE OR REPLACE FUNCTION slow_function (anyelement) RETURNS BOOLEAN AS $$
BEGIN
  RAISE NOTICE 'Slow function %', $1;
  RETURN TRUE;
END; $$ LANGUAGE PLPGSQL COST 10000;

CREATE OR REPLACE FUNCTION fast_function (anyelement) RETURNS BOOLEAN AS $$
BEGIN
  RAISE NOTICE 'Fast function %', $1;
  RETURN TRUE;
END; $$ LANGUAGE PLPGSQL COST 0.0001;
```

The fast_function and the slow_function are identical except for the cost parameter:

```
car_portal=> EXPLAIN SELECT * FROM pg_language WHERE fast_function(lanname)
AND slow_function(lanname) AND lanname ILIKE '%sql%';
 QUERY PLAN
-------------------------------------------------------------------------------
--------------------
 Seq Scan on pg_language (cost=0.00..101.05 rows=1 width=114)
 Filter: (fast_function(lanname) AND (lanname ~~* '%sql%'::text) AND
slow_function(lanname))
(2 rows)
car_portal=# EXPLAIN SELECT * FROM pg_language WHERE slow_function(lanname)
AND fast_function(lanname) AND lanname ILIKE '%sql%';
                                   QUERY PLAN
-------------------------------------------------------------------------------
--------------------
 Seq Scan on pg_language (cost=0.00..101.05 rows=1 width=114)
   Filter: (fast_function(lanname) AND (lanname ~~* '%sql%'::text) AND
slow_function(lanname))
(2 rows)
```

The preceding two SQL statements are identical, but the predicates are shuffled. Both statements give the same execution plan. Notice how the predicates are arranged in the filter execution plane node. The `fast_function` is evaluated first, followed by the `ILIKE` operator, and finally, the `slow_function` is pushed. When executing one of the preceding statements, one will get the following result:

```
car_portal=> SELECT lanname FROM pg_language WHERE lanname ILIKE '%sql%'
AND slow_function(lanname)AND fast_function(lanname);
NOTICE: Fast function internal
NOTICE: Fast function c
NOTICE: Fast function sql
NOTICE: Slow function sql
NOTICE: Fast function plpgsql
NOTICE: Slow function plpgsql
 lanname
---------
 sql
 plpgsql
(2 rows)
```

Notice that `fast_function` was executed four times, and `slow_function` was executed only twice. This behavior is known as **short circuit** evaluation. `slow_function` is executed only when `fast_function` and the `ILIKE` operator have returned true.

> In PostgreSQL, the `ILIKE` operator is equivalent to the `~~*` operator, and `LIKE` is equivalent to the `~~` operator.

As discussed in Chapter 04, *PostgreSQL Advanced Building Blocks*, views can be used to implement authorization, and they can be used to hide data from some users. The function `cost` parameter can be exploited in earlier versions of `postgres` to crack views; however, this has been improved by the introduction of the `LEAKPROOF` and `SECURITY_BARRIER` flags.

To be able to exploit the function `cost` parameter to get data from a view, several conditions should be met, some of which are as follows:

- The function `cost` should be very low.
- The function should be marked as `LEAKPROOF`. Note that only superusers are allowed to mark functions as `LEAKPROOF`.
- The view security barrier flag should not be set.

- The function should be executed and not ignored due to short-circuit evaluation.
- Meeting all these conditions is very difficult.

The following code shows a hypothetical example of exploiting views. First, let's create a view, alter the function `fast_function`, and set it as LEAKPROOF.

```
CREATE OR REPLACE VIEW pg_sql_pl AS SELECT lanname FROM pg_language WHERE
lanname ILIKE '%sql%';
ALTER FUNCTION fast_function(anyelement) LEAKPROOF;
```

To exploit the function, let's execute the following query:

```
car_portal=# SELECT * FROM pg_sql_pl WHERE fast_function(lanname);
NOTICE: Fast function internal
NOTICE: Fast function c
NOTICE: Fast function sql
NOTICE: Fast function plpgsql
 lanname
---------
 sql
 plpgsql
(2 rows)
```

In the preceding example, the view itself should not show c and `internal`. By exploiting the function `cost`, the function was executed before executing the filter `lanname ILIKE '%sql%'`, exposing information that will never be shown by the view.

Since only superusers are allowed to mark a function as LEAKPROOF, exploiting the function `cost` in newer versions of `postgres` is not possible.

Function configuration-related parameters

PostgreSQL configuration can be configured per a session as well as within a function scope. This is quiet useful in particular cases when one wants to override the session settings in the function. Settings parameters can be used to determine resources, such as the amount of memory required to perform an operation such as `work_mem`, or they can be used to determine execution behavior, such as disabling a sequential scan or nested loop joins. Only parameters that have the context of the user can be used, which means only settings parameters that can be assigned to the user session.

The SET clause causes the specified setting parameter to be set with a specified value when the function is entered; the same setting parameter value is reset back to its default value when the function exits. The parameter configuration setting can be set explicitly for the whole function, or can be overwritten locally inside the function, and can inherit the value from the session setting using the CURRENT clause.

These configuration parameters are often used to tweak function performance in the case of limited resources, legacy code, bad design, wrong statistics estimation, and so on. For example, let's assume that a function behaves badly due to database normalization. In this case, refactoring the database might be an expensive action to perform. To solve this problem, one could alter the execution plan by enabling or disabling some settings. Let us assume , a developer would like to quickly fix the following statement which uses external merge sort method without altering the session work_mem :

```
car_portal=# EXPLAIN (analyze, buffers) SELECT md5(random()::text) FROM
generate_series(1, 1000000) order by 1;
                                                           QUERY PLAN
--------------------------------------------------------------------------
------------------------------------------------------------
 Sort (cost=69.83..72.33 rows=1000 width=32) (actual
time=7324.824..9141.209 rows=1000000 loops=1)
    Sort Key: (md5((random())::text))
    Sort Method: external merge Disk: 42056kB
    Buffers: temp read=10114 written=10113
    -> Function Scan on generate_series (cost=0.00..20.00 rows=1000
width=32) (actual time=193.730..1774.369 rows=1000000 loops=1)
          Buffers: temp read=1710 written=1709
 Planning time: 0.055 ms
 Execution time: 9192.393 ms
(8 rows)
```

The select statement in the preceding example can be wrapped in a function and the function can be assigned a specific work_mem as follows:

```
CREATE OR REPLACE FUNCTION configuration_test () RETURNS TABLE (md5 text) AS
$$
    SELECT md5(random()::text) FROM generate_series(1, 1000000) order by 1;
$$ LANGUAGE SQL
SET enable_seqscan FROM current
SET work_mem = '100MB';
```

Now let's run the function to see the result of `work_mem` setting effect:

```
car_portal=# EXPLAIN (ANALYZE ,BUFFERS) SELECT * FROM configuration_test();
                                                           QUERY PLAN
--------------------------------------------------------------------------------
--------------------------------------------------------------
 Function Scan on configuration_test (cost=0.25..10.25 rows=1000 width=32)
(actual time=7377.196..7405.635 rows=1000000 loops=1)
 Planning time: 0.028 ms
 Execution time: 7444.426 ms
(3 rows)

Time: 7444.984 ms
```

When the function is entered, the `work_mem` is assigned a value of 100Mib, this has affected the execution plane and the sorting now is done in memory. The function execution time is faster than the query. To confirm this result, let us change the `work_mem` for the session in order to compare the results as follows:

```
car_portal=# set work_mem to '100MB';
SET
Time: 0.343 ms
car_portal=# EXPLAIN (analyze, buffers) SELECT md5(random()::text) FROM
generate_series(1, 1000000) order by 1;
                                                           QUERY PLAN
--------------------------------------------------------------------------------
----------------------------------------------------------
 Sort (cost=69.83..72.33 rows=1000 width=32) (actual
time=7432.831..7615.666 rows=1000000 loops=1)
    Sort Key: (md5((random())::text))
    Sort Method: quicksort Memory: 101756kB
    -> Function Scan on generate_series (cost=0.00..20.00 rows=1000
width=32) (actual time=104.305..1626.839 rows=1000000 loops=1)
 Planning time: 0.050 ms
 Execution time: 7662.650 ms
(6 rows)

Time: 7663.269 ms
```

The PostgreSQL PL/pgSQL control statements

The PostgreSQL control structure is an essential part of the PL/pgSQL language; it enables developers to code very complex business logic inside PostgreSQL.

Declaration statements

The general syntax of a variable declaration is as follows:

```
name [ CONSTANT ] type [ COLLATE collation_name ] [ NOT NULL ] [ { DEFAULT
| := | = } expression ];
```

- `name`: The name should follow the naming rules discussed in `Chapter 03`, *PostgreSQL Basic Building Blocks*. For example, the name should not start with an integer.
- `CONSTANT`: The variable cannot be assigned another value after the initialization. This is useful in defining constant variables such as PI.
- `type`: The `type` of variable can be simple, such as an integer, user-defined data type, pseudo type, record, and so on. Since a type is created implicitly when creating a table, one can use this `type` to declare a variable.

> In PostgreSQL, the following two declarations are equivalent; however, the second declaration is more portable with Oracle. Additionally, it is more descriptive of the intent; and it can not be confused as a reference to the actual table. This is the preferred type declaration style.
>
> - `myrow tablename;`
> - `myrow tablename%ROWTYPE;`

- `NOT NULL`: `NOT NULL` causes a runtime error to be raised if the variable is assigned a null. `NOT NULL` variables must be initialized.
- `DEFAULT`: Causes the initialization of the variable to be delayed until the block is entered. This is useful in defining a timestamp variable to indicate when the function is called, but not the function precompilation time.
- An expression is a combination of one or more explicit values, operators, and functions that can be evaluated to another value.

The PostgreSQL PL/pgSQL function body is composed of nested blocks with an optional declaration section and a label. Variables are declared in the declare section of the block, shown as follows:

```
[ <<label>> ]
[ DECLARE
    declarations ]
BEGIN
    statements
END [ label ];
```

The BEGIN and END keywords are not used in this context to control transactional behavior, but only for grouping. The declaration section is used for declaring variables, and the label is used to give a name to the block, as well as to give fully qualified names to the variables. Finally, in each PL/pgSQL function, there is a hidden block labeled with a function name that contains predefined variables, such as FOUND. To understand the function block, let's take a look at the following code, which defines the `factorial` function in a recursive manner:

```
CREATE OR REPLACE FUNCTION factorial(INTEGER ) RETURNS INTEGER AS $$
BEGIN
  IF $1 IS NULL OR $1 < 0 THEN RAISE NOTICE 'Invalid Number';
    RETURN NULL;
  ELSIF $1 = 1 THEN
    RETURN 1;
  ELSE
    RETURN factorial($1 - 1) * $1;
END IF;
END;
$$ LANGUAGE 'plpgsql';
```

The block defines the variable scope; in our example, the scope of the argument variable $1 is the whole function. Also, as shown in the example, there is no declaration section. To understand the scope between different code blocks, let's write the `factorial` function in a slightly different manner, which is as follows:

```
CREATE OR REPLACE FUNCTION factorial(INTEGER ) RETURNS INTEGER AS $$
  DECLARE
    fact ALIAS FOR $1;
  BEGIN
  IF fact IS NULL OR fact < 0 THEN
    RAISE NOTICE 'Invalid Number';
    RETURN NULL;
  ELSIF fact = 1 THEN
    RETURN 1;
  END IF;
  DECLARE
    result INT;
  BEGIN
    result = factorial(fact - 1) * fact;
    RETURN result;
  END;
END;
$$ LANGUAGE 'plpgsql';
```

The preceding function is composed of two blocks: the variable fact is an alias for the first argument. In the subblock, the result variable is declared with a type integer. Since the fact variable is defined in the upper block, it can also be used in the subblock. The result variable can be used only in the subblock.

Assignment statements

The assignment operators := and = are used to assign an expression to a variable, as follows:

```
variable { := | = } expression;
```

For variable names, one should choose names that do not conflict with column names. This is important when writing parameterized SQL statements. The = operator is supported not only for PostgreSQL version 10, but also for previous versions. Unfortunately, the documentation for previous versions does not mention it. Moreover, since the = operator is used in SQL for equality comparison, it is preferable to use the := operator to reduce confusion.

In certain contexts, it is important to pick up the right assignment operator:

- When assigning a default value, one should use the = operator, as indicated in the documentation at http://www.postgresql.org/docs/current/interactive/sql-createfunction.html.
- For named notations in a function call, one should use the := operator.

The following example shows a case when one cannot use = and := interchangeably:

```
CREATE OR REPLACE FUNCTION cast_numeric_to_int (numeric_value numeric,
round boolean = TRUE /*correct use of "=". Using ":=" will raise a syntax
error */)
RETURNS INT AS
$$
  BEGIN
  RETURN (CASE WHEN round = TRUE THEN CAST (numeric_value AS INTEGER)
  WHEN numeric_value>= 0 THEN CAST (numeric_value -.5 AS INTEGER)
  WHEN numeric_value< 0 THEN CAST (numeric_value +.5 AS INTEGER)
  ELSE NULL
  END);
END;
$$ LANGUAGE plpgsql;
```

To test the assignment:

```
car_portal=# SELECT cast_numeric_to_int(2.3, round:= true);
 cast_numeric_to_int
---------------------
                   2
(1 row)

car_portal=# SELECT cast_numeric_to_int(2.3, round= true);
ERROR: column "round" does not exist
LINE 1: SELECT cast_numeric_to_int(2.3, round= true);
```

The assignment expression can be a single atomic value such as $pi = 3.14$, or it can be a row:

```
DO $$
  DECLARE
    test record;
  BEGIN
    test = ROW (1,'hello', 3.14);
    RAISE notice '%', test;
  END;
$$ LANGUAGE plpgsql;

DO $$
DECLARE
  number_of_accounts INT:=0;
BEGIN
  number_of_accounts:= (SELECT COUNT(*) FROM car_portal_app.account)::INT;
  RAISE NOTICE 'number_of accounts: %', number_of_accounts;
END;$$
LANGUAGE plpgsql;
```

There are other techniques for assigning values to variables from a query that returns a single row:

```
SELECT select_expressions INTO [STRICT] targets FROM ...;
 INSERT ... RETURNING expressions INTO [STRICT] targets;
 UPDATE ... RETURNING expressions INTO [STRICT] targets;
 DELETE ... RETURNING expressions INTO [STRICT] targets;
```

Often, expressions are column names, while targets are variable names. In the case of SELECT INTO, the target can be of the type record. The query INSERT ... RETURNING is often used to return the default value of a certain column; this can be used to define the ID of a primary key using the SERIAL and BIGSERIAL data types, which is shown as follows:

```
CREATE TABLE test (
 id SERIAL PRIMARY KEY,
 name TEXT NOT NULL
 );
```

To test the assignment, let's run the following code:

```
DO $$
  DECLARE
    auto_generated_id INT;
  BEGIN
    INSERT INTO test(name) VALUES ('Hello World') RETURNING id INTO
auto_generated_id;
    RAISE NOTICE 'The primary key is: %', auto_generated_id;
END
$$;
NOTICE: The primary key is: 1
DO
```

One could get the default value when inserting a row in plain SQL using CTE, as follows:
```
WITH get_id AS (
INSERT INTO test(name) VALUES ('Hello World')
RETURNING id
) SELECT * FROM get_id;
```

Finally, one could use qualified names to perform assignment; in trigger functions, one could use NEW and OLD to manipulate the values of these records.

Conditional statements

PostgreSQL supports the IF and CASE statements, which allow execution based on a certain condition. PostgreSQL supports the IF statement construct, as follows:

- IF ... THEN ... END IF
- IF ... THEN ... ELSE ... END IF
- IF ... THEN ... ELSIF ... THEN ... ELSE ... END IF

The case statement comes in two forms, as follows:

- CASE ... WHEN ... THEN ... ELSE ... END CASE
- CASE WHEN ... THEN ... ELSE ... END CASE

To understand the IF statement, let's assume that we would like to convert the advertisement **rank** to text:

```
CREATE OR REPLACE FUNCTION cast_rank_to_text (rank int) RETURNS TEXT AS $$
DECLARE
  rank ALIAS FOR $1;
  rank_result TEXT;
BEGIN
  IF rank = 5 THEN rank_result = 'Excellent';
  ELSIF rank = 4 THEN rank_result = 'Very Good';
  ELSIF rank = 3 THEN rank_result = 'Good';
  ELSIF rank = 2 THEN rank_result ='Fair';
  ELSIF rank = 1 THEN rank_result ='Poor';
  ELSE rank_result ='No such rank';
  END IF;
  RETURN rank_result;
END;
$$ Language plpgsql;
 --- to test the function
 SELECT n,cast_rank_to_text(n) FROM generate_series(1,6) as foo(n);
```

When any branch of the IF statement is executed due to the IF condition being met, then the execution control returns to the first statement after END IF, assuming the RETURN statement is not executed inside this branch. If none of the conditions are met for IF or ELSIF, then the ELSE branch will be executed. Also note that one could nest all the control structures; so, one can have an IF statement inside another one.

The following code snippet implements the preceding function using the CASE statement:

```
CREATE OR REPLACE FUNCTION cast_rank_to_text (rank int) RETURNS TEXT AS
$$
DECLARE
  rank ALIAS FOR $1;
  rank_result TEXT;
BEGIN
  CASE rank
    WHEN 5 THEN rank_result = 'Excellent';
    WHEN 4 THEN rank_result = 'Very Good';
    WHEN 3 THEN rank_result = 'Good';
    WHEN 2 THEN rank_result ='Fair';
    WHEN 1 THEN rank_result ='Poor';
```

```
      ELSE rank_result ='No such rank';
    END CASE;
    RETURN rank_result;
END;$$ Language plpgsql;
```

In the CASE statement, if any branch of the case matches the selector, the execution of the case is terminated and the execution control goes to the first statement after CASE. Moreover, in the previous form of CASE, one cannot use it to match NULL values, since NULL equality is NULL. To overcome this limitation, one should specify the matching condition explicitly using the second form of the CASE statement, as follows:

```
CREATE OR REPLACE FUNCTION cast_rank_to_text (rank int) RETURNS TEXT AS $$
DECLARE
    rank ALIAS FOR $1;
    rank_result TEXT;
BEGIN
    CASE
        WHEN rank=5 THEN rank_result = 'Excellent';
        WHEN rank=4 THEN rank_result = 'Very Good';
        WHEN rank=3 THEN rank_result = 'Good';
        WHEN rank=2 THEN rank_result ='Fair';
        WHEN rank=1 THEN rank_result ='Poor';
        WHEN rank IS NULL THEN RAISE EXCEPTION 'Rank should be not NULL';
        ELSE rank_result ='No such rank';
    END CASE;
    RETURN rank_result;
END;
$$ Language plpgsql;
--- to test
SELECT cast_rank_to_text(null);
```

Finally, the CASE statement raises an exception if no branch is matched and the ELSE branch is not specified, as follows:

```
DO $$
DECLARE
    i int := 0;
BEGIN
    case WHEN i=1 then
        RAISE NOTICE 'i is one';
    END CASE;
END;
$$ LANGUAGE plpgsql;
ERROR: case not found
HINT: CASE statement is missing ELSE part.
CONTEXT: PL/pgSQL function inline_code_block line 5 at CASE
```

Iteration

Iteration is used to repeat a block of statements to achieve a certain goal. With iteration, one often needs to specify the starting point and the ending condition. In PostgreSQL, there are several statements for iterating through the results and for performing looping, including LOOP, CONTINUE, EXIT, FOR, WHILE, and FOR EACH.

Loop statement

The basic LOOP statement has the following structure:

```
[ <<label>> ]
LOOP
    statements
END LOOP [ label ];
```

To understand the LOOP statement, let's rewrite the factorial function, as follows:

```
DROP FUNCTION IF EXISTS factorial (int);
CREATE OR REPLACE FUNCTION factorial (fact int) RETURNS BIGINT AS $$
DECLARE
  result bigint = 1;
BEGIN
  IF fact = 1 THEN RETURN 1;
  ELSIF fact IS NULL or fact < 1 THEN RAISE EXCEPTION 'Provide a positive
integer';
  ELSE
    LOOP
      result = result*fact;
      fact = fact-1;
      EXIT WHEN fact = 1;
    END Loop;
  END IF;
  RETURN result;
END; $$ LANGUAGE plpgsql;
```

In the preceding code, the conditional EXIT statement is used to prevent infinite looping by exiting the LOOP statement. When an EXIT statement is encountered, the execution control goes to the first statement after the LOOP. To control the execution of the statements inside the LOOP statement, PL/pgSQL also provides the CONTINUE statement, which works somewhat like the EXIT statement. Thus, instead of forcing termination, the CONTINUE statement forces the next iteration of the loop to take place, skipping any code in between.

The usage of the CONTINUE and EXIT statements, especially in the middle of a code block, is not encouraged because it breaks the execution order, which makes the code harder to read and understand.

While loop statement

The WHILE statement keeps executing a block of statements while a particular condition is met. Its syntax is as follows:

```
[ <<label>> ]
WHILE boolean-expression LOOP
    statements
END LOOP [ label ];
```

The following example uses the while loop to print the days of the current month:

```
DO $$
DECLARE
  first_day_in_month date := date_trunc('month', current_date)::date;
  last_day_in_month date := (date_trunc('month', current_date)+ INTERVAL '1
MONTH - 1 day')::date;
  counter date = first_day_in_month;
BEGIN
  WHILE (counter <= last_day_in_month) LOOP
    RAISE notice '%', counter;
    counter := counter + interval '1 day';
  END LOOP;
END;
$$ LANGUAGE plpgsql;
```

For loop statement

PL/pgSQL provides two forms of the FOR statement, and they are used to:

- Iterate through the rows returned by an SQL query
- Iterate through a range of integer values

The syntax of the FOR loop statement is:

```
[ <<label>> ]
FOR name IN [ REVERSE ] expression1 .. expression2 [ BY expression ] LOOP
    statements
END LOOP [ label ];
```

The `name` is the name of a local variable of the type integer. This local variable scope is the `FOR` loop. Statements inside the loop can read this variable, but cannot change its value. Finally, one can change this behavior by defining the variable in the declaration section of the outer block. `expression1` and `expression2` must be evaluated to integer values; if `expression1` equals `expression2` then the `FOR` loop is run only once.

The `REVERSE` keyword is optional, and it is used to define the order in which the range will be generated (ascending or descending). If `REVERSE` is omitted, then `expression1` should be smaller than `expression2`, otherwise the loop will not be executed. Finally, `BY` defines the steps between two successive numbers in the range. Note that the `BY` `expression` value should always be a positive integer. The following example shows a `FOR` loop iterating over a negative range of numbers in the reverse order, the following example will print the values $-1, -3,...,-9$.

```
DO $$
BEGIN
  FOR j IN REVERSE -1 .. -10 BY 2 LOOP
      Raise notice '%', j;
  END LOOP;
END; $$ LANGUAGE plpgsql;
```

To iterate through the result of a set query, the syntax is different, as follows:

```
[ <<label>> ]
FOR target IN query LOOP
    statements
END LOOP [ label ];
```

`target` is a local variable in the outer block. Its type is not restricted to simple types such as integer and text. However, its type might be a composite or a `RECORD` data type. In PL/pgSQL, one could iterate over a `CURSOR` result or over a `SELECT` statement result. Cursor is a special data object that can be used to encapsulate a `SELECT` query, and then to read the query result a few rows at a time. The following example shows all the database names:

```
DO $$
DECLARE
  database RECORD;
BEGIN
  FOR database IN SELECT * FROM pg_database LOOP
    RAISE notice '%', database.datname;
  END LOOP;
END; $$;
----- output
NOTICE: postgres
NOTICE: template1
```

```
NOTICE: template0
....
DO
```

Returning from the function

The PostgreSQL return statement is used for terminating the function, and for returning the control to the caller. The return statement has different forms, such as RETURN, RETURN NEXT, RETURN QUERY, RETURN QUERY EXECUTE, and so on. The RETURN statement can return a single value or a set to the caller, as will be shown in this chapter. In this context, let's consider the following anonymous function:

```
DO $$
BEGIN
  RETURN;
  RAISE NOTICE 'This statement will not be executed';
END
$$
LANGUAGE plpgsql;
--- output
DO
```

As shown in the preceding example, the function is terminated before the execution of the RAISE statement due to the RETURN statement.

Returning void

A void type is used in a function to perform some side effects, such as logging; the built-in function pg_sleep is used to delay the execution of a server process in seconds:

```
postgres=# \df pg_sleep
                         List of functions
   Schema  | Name  | Result data type | Argument data types | Type
-----------+----------+------------------+---------------------+--------
 pg_catalog | pg_sleep | void | double precision | normal
(1 row)
```

Returning a single row

PL/pgSQL can be used to return a single row from a function; an example of this type is the factorial function.

Some developers refer to PL/pgSQL and SQL functions returning a single-row, single-column scalar variable as scalar functions.

The RETURN type can be base, composite, domain, pseudo type, or domain data type. The following function returns a JSON representation of a certain account:

```sql
-- in sql
CREATE OR REPLACE FUNCTION car_portal_app.get_account_in_json (account_id
INT) RETURNS JSON AS $$
  SELECT row_to_json(account) FROM car_portal_app.account WHERE account_id
= $1;
$$ LANGUAGE SQL;

--- in plpgsql
CREATE OR REPLACE FUNCTION car_portal_app.get_account_in_json1 (acc_id INT)
RETURNS JSON AS $$
BEGIN
  RETURN (SELECT row_to_json(account) FROM car_portal_app.account WHERE
account_id = acc_id);
END;
$$ LANGUAGE plpgsql;
```

Returning multiple rows

Set returning functions (SRFs) can be used to return a set of rows. The row type can either be a base type such as integer, composite, table type, pseudo type, or domain type. To return a set from a function, the keyword SETOF is used to mark the function as an SRF, as follows:

```sql
-- In SQL
CREATE OR REPLACE FUNCTION car_portal_app.car_model(model_name TEXT)
RETURNS SETOF car_portal_app.car_model AS $$
  SELECT car_model_id, make, model FROM car_portal_app.car_model WHERE
model = model_name;
$$ LANGUAGE SQL;

-- In plpgSQL
CREATE OR REPLACE FUNCTION car_portal_app.car_model1(model_name TEXT)
RETURNS SETOF car_portal_app.car_model AS $$
BEGIN
  RETURN QUERY SELECT car_model_id, make, model FROM
car_portal_app.car_model WHERE model = model_name;
END;
$$ LANGUAGE plpgsql;
```

To test the previous functions, let's run them. Note the caching effect of `plpgsql` on performance:

```
car_portal=> \timing
Timing is on.
car_portal=> SELECT * FROM car_portal_app.car_model('A1');
 car_model_id | make | model
--------------+------+-------
            1 | Audi | A1
(1 row)

Time: 1,026 ms
car_portal=> SELECT * FROM car_portal_app.car_model1('A1');
 car_model_id | make | model
--------------+------+-------
            1 | Audi | A1
(1 row)

Time: 0,546 ms
```

If the return type is not defined, one could:

- Define a new data type and use it
- Use a return table
- Use output parameters and record the datatype

Let's assume that we would like to return only the `car_model_id` and the `make`, as in this case, we do not have a data type defined. Thus, the preceding function can be written as:

```
-- SQL
CREATE OR REPLACE FUNCTION car_portal_app.car_model2(model_name TEXT)
RETURNS TABLE (car_model_id INT , make TEXT) AS $$
  SELECT car_model_id, make FROM car_portal_app.car_model WHERE model =
model_name;
$$ LANGUAGE SQL;

-- plpgSQL
CREATE OR REPLACE FUNCTION car_portal_app.car_model3(model_name TEXT)
RETURNS TABLE (car_model_id INT , make TEXT) AS $$
BEGIN
  RETURN QUERY SELECT car_model_id, make FROM car_portal_app.car_model
WHERE model = model_name;
END;
$$ LANGUAGE plpgsql;
```

To test the functions:

```
car_portal=> SELECT * FROM car_portal_app.car_model2('A1');
 car_model_id | make
--------------+------
            1 | Audi
(1 row)

Time: 0,797 ms
car_portal=> SELECT * FROM car_portal_app.car_model3('A1');
ERROR: column reference "car_model_id" is ambiguous
LINE 1: SELECT car_model_id, make FROM car_portal_app.car_model WHE...
               ^
DETAIL: It could refer to either a PL/pgSQL variable or a table column.
QUERY: SELECT car_model_id, make FROM car_portal_app.car_model WHERE model
= model_name
CONTEXT: PL/pgSQL function car_model3(text) line 3 at RETURN QUERY
Time: 0,926 ms
```

Note that, in the preceding function, an error is raised because `plpgsql` was confusing the column name with the table definition. The reason behind this is that the return table is a shorthand for writing OUTPUT parameters. To fix this, we need to rename the attribute names, as follows:

```
CREATE OR REPLACE FUNCTION car_portal_app.car_model3(model_name TEXT)
RETURNS TABLE (car_model_id INT , make TEXT) AS $$
BEGIN
  RETURN QUERY SELECT a.car_model_id, a.make FROM car_portal_app.car_model
a WHERE model = model_name;
END;
$$ LANGUAGE plpgsql;
car_portal=> SELECT * FROM car_portal_app.car_model3('A1');
 car_model_id | make
--------------+------
            1 | Audi
(1 row)
```

The preceding function can also be written using the OUT variables; actually, the return table is implemented internally, as indicated by the error using the OUT variables, as follows:

```
CREATE OR REPLACE FUNCTION car_portal_app.car_model4(model_name TEXT, OUT
car_model_id INT, OUT make TEXT ) RETURNS SETOF RECORD AS $$
BEGIN
  RETURN QUERY SELECT a.car_model_id, a.make FROM car_portal_app.car_model
a WHERE model = model_name;
END;
$$ LANGUAGE plpgsql;
```

```
car_portal=> SELECT * FROM car_portal_app.car_model4('A1'::text);
 car_model_id | make
--------------+------
            1 | Audi
(1 row)
```

Function predefined variables

The PL/pgSQL functions have several special variables that are created automatically in the top-level block. For example, if the function returns a trigger, then several variables, such as NEW, OLD, and TG_OP, are created.

In addition to the trigger special values, there is a Boolean variable called FOUND. This is often used in combination with DML and PERFORM statements to conduct sanity checks. The value of the FOUND variable is affected by the SELECT, INSERT, UPDATE, DELETE, and PERFORM statements. These statements set FOUND to true if at least one row is selected, inserted, updated, or deleted.

The PERFORM statement is similar to the SELECT statement, but it discards the result of the query. Finally, the EXECUTE statement does not change the value of the FOUND variable. The following examples show how the FOUND variable is affected by the INSERT and PERFORM statements:

```
DO $$
BEGIN
  CREATE TABLE t1(f1 int);

  INSERT INTO t1 VALUES (1);
  RAISE NOTICE '%', FOUND;

  PERFORM* FROM t1 WHERE f1 = 0;
  RAISE NOTICE '%', FOUND;
  DROP TABLE t1;
END;
$$LANGUAGE plpgsql;
--- output
NOTICE: t
NOTICE: f
```

In addition to the preceding query, one could get the last OID--object identifier--for an inserted row, as well as the affected number of rows, by using the INSERT, UPDATE, and DELETE statements via the following commands:

```
GET DIAGNOSTICS variable = item;
```

Assuming that there is a variable called i of type integer, one can get the affected number of rows, as follows:

```
GET DIAGNOSTICS i = ROW_COUNT;
```

Exception handling

One could trap and raise errors in PostgreSQL using the exception and raise statements. Errors can be raised by violating data integrity constraints, or by performing illegal operations such as assigning text to integers, dividing an integer or float by zero, out-of-range assignments, and so on. By default, any error occurrence inside a PL/pgSQL function causes the function to abort the execution and roll back the changes. To be able to recover from errors, PL/pgSQL can trap the errors using the EXCEPTION clause. The syntax of the exception clause is very similar to PL/pgSQL blocks. Moreover, PostgreSQL can raise errors using the RAISE statement. To understand exception handling, let's consider the following helping function:

```
CREATE OR REPLACE FUNCTION check_not_null (value anyelement ) RETURNS VOID
AS
$$
BEGIN
  IF (value IS NULL) THEN RAISE EXCEPTION USING ERRCODE =
'check_violation'; END IF;
END;
$$ LANGUAGE plpgsql;
```

The check_not_null statement is a polymorphic function, which simply raises an error with a check_violation SQLSTATE. Calling this function and passing the NULL value as an argument will cause an error, as follows:

```
car_portal=> SELECT check_not_null(null::text);
ERROR: check_violation
CONTEXT: PL/pgSQL function check_not_null(anyelement) line 3 at RAISE
Time: 0,775 ms
```

In order to properly determine when the exception is raised and why, PostgreSQL defines several categories of error codes. PostgreSQL error codes can be found at http://www. postgresql.org/docs/current/interactive/errcodes-appendix.html. For example, raising an exception by the user without specifying the ERRCODE will set the SQLSTATE to P001, while a unique violation exception will set the SQLSTATE to 23505.

Errors can be matched in the EXCEPTION clause either by the SQLSTATE or by the condition name, as follows:

```
WHEN unique_violation THEN ...
WHEN SQLSTATE '23505' THEN ...
```

Finally, one could provide a customized error message and SQLSTATE when raising an exception such that the ERRCODE should be five digits and/or uppercase ASCII letters other than 00000, as follows:

```
DO $$
BEGIN
  RAISE EXCEPTION USING ERRCODE = '1234X', MESSAGE = 'test customized
SQLSTATE:';
  EXCEPTION WHEN SQLSTATE '1234X' THEN
    RAISE NOTICE '% %', SQLERRM, SQLSTATE;
END;
$$ LANGUAGE plpgsql;
```

The output of executing the previous anonymous function is as follows:

```
NOTICE: test customized SQLSTATE: 1234X
DO
Time: 0,943 ms
```

To trap an exception, let's rewrite the factorial function, and let's assume that the factorial function should return null if the provided argument is null:

```
DROP FUNCTION IF EXISTS factorial( INTEGER );
CREATE OR REPLACE FUNCTION factorial(INTEGER ) RETURNS BIGINT AS $$
DECLARE
  fact ALIAS FOR $1;
BEGIN
  PERFORM check_not_null(fact);
  IF fact > 1 THEN RETURN factorial(fact - 1) * fact;
  ELSIF fact IN (0,1) THEN RETURN 1;
  ELSE RETURN NULL;
  END IF;

  EXCEPTION
    WHEN check_violation THEN RETURN NULL;
    WHEN OTHERS THEN RAISE NOTICE '% %', SQLERRM, SQLSTATE;
END;
$$ LANGUAGE 'plpgsql';
```

To test the function:

```
car_portal=> \pset null 'null'
Null display is "null".
car_portal=> SELECT * FROM factorial(null::int);
 factorial
-----------
      null
(1 row)

Time: 1,018 ms
```

The `factorial` function did not raise an error, because the error is trapped in the `EXCEPTION` clause and a `NULL` value is returned instead. Notice that the matching is performed using the condition name instead of `SQLSTATE`. The special condition name `OTHERS` matches any error; this is often used as a safe fallback when unexpected errors occur.

In handling exceptions, if `SQLERRM` and `SQLSTATE` are not deterministic enough to know the exception cause, one could get more information about the exception using `GET STACKED DIAGNOSTICS`:

```
GET STACKED DIAGNOSTICS variable { = | := } item [ , ... ];
```

The item is a keyword identifying a status value related to the exception. For example, the item keywords `COLUMN_NAME`, `TABLE_NAME`, and `SCHEMA_NAME` indicate the names of the column, table, and schema involved in the exception.

Dynamic SQL

Dynamic SQL is used to build and execute queries on the fly. Unlike the static SQL statement, a dynamic SQL statement's full text is unknown and can change between successive executions. These queries can be **DDL**, **DCL**, and **DML** statements. Dynamic SQL is used to reduce repetitive tasks. For example, one could use dynamic SQL to create table partitioning for a certain table on a daily basis, to add missing indexes on all foreign keys, or add data auditing capabilities to a certain table without major coding effects. Another important use of dynamic SQL is to overcome the side effects of PL/pgSQL caching, as queries executed using the `EXECUTE` statement are not cached.

Dynamic SQL is achieved via the EXECUTE statement. The EXECUTE statement accepts a string and simply evaluates it. The synopsis to execute a statement is given as follows:

```
EXECUTE command-string [ INTO [STRICT] target ] [ USING expression [, ...]
];
```

Executing DDL statements in dynamic SQL

In some cases, one needs to perform operations at the database object level, such as tables, indexes, columns, roles, and so on. For example, a database developer would like to vacuum and analyze a specific schema object, which is a common task after the deployment in order to update the statistics. For example, to analyze the car_portal_app schema tables, one could write the following script:

```
DO $$
DECLARE
  table_name text;
BEGIN
    FOR table_name IN SELECT tablename FROM pg_tables WHERE schemaname
='car_portal_app' LOOP
        RAISE NOTICE 'Analyzing %', table_name;
        EXECUTE 'ANALYZE car_portal_app.' || table_name;
    END LOOP;
END;
$$;
```

Executing DML statements in dynamic SQL

Some applications might interact with data in an interactive manner. For example, one might have billing data generated on a monthly basis. Also, some applications filter data on different criteria defined by the user. In such cases, dynamic SQL is very convenient. For example, in the car portal application, the search functionality is needed to get accounts using the dynamic predicate, as follows:

```
CREATE OR REPLACE FUNCTION car_portal_app.get_account (predicate TEXT)
RETURNS SETOF car_portal_app.account AS
$$
BEGIN
  RETURN QUERY EXECUTE 'SELECT * FROM car_portal_app.account WHERE ' ||
predicate;
END;
$$ LANGUAGE plpgsql;
```

To test the previous function:

```
car_portal=> SELECT * FROM car_portal_app.get_account ('true') limit 1;
 account_id | first_name | last_name | email | password
------------+------------+-----------+-----------------+--------------------
---------------
          1 | James | Butt | jbutt@gmail.com |
1b9ef408e82e38346e6ebebf2dcc5ece
(1 row)
car_portal=> SELECT * FROM car_portal_app.get_account
(E'first_name=\'James\'');
 account_id | first_name | last_name | email | password
------------+------------+-----------+-----------------+--------------------
---------------
          1 | James | Butt | jbutt@gmail.com |
1b9ef408e82e38346e6ebebf2dcc5ece
(1 row)
```

Dynamic SQL and the caching effect

As mentioned earlier, PL/pgSQL caches execution plans. This is quite good if the generated plan is expected to be static. For example, the following statement is expected to use an index scan because of selectivity. In this case, caching the plan saves some time and thus increases performance:

```
SELECT * FROM account WHERE account_id =<INT>
```

In other scenarios, however, this is not true. For example, let's assume we have an index on the advertisement_date column and we would like to get the number of advertisements since a certain date, as follows:

```
SELECT count (*) FROM car_portal_app.advertisement WHERE advertisement_date
>= <certain_date>;
```

In the preceding query, the entries from the advertisement table can be fetched from the hard disk either by using the index scan or using the sequential scan based on selectivity, which depends on the provided certain_date value. Caching the execution plan of such a query will cause serious problems; thus, writing the function as follows is not a good idea:

```
CREATE OR REPLACE FUNCTION car_portal_app.get_advertisement_count
(some_date timestamptz ) RETURNS BIGINT AS $$
BEGIN
  RETURN (SELECT count (*) FROM car_portal_app.advertisement WHERE
advertisement_date >=some_date)::bigint;
```

```
END;
$$ LANGUAGE plpgsql;
```

To solve the caching issue, one could rewrite the previous function either using the SQL language function or by using the PL/pgSQL execute command, as follows:

```
CREATE OR REPLACE FUNCTION car_portal_app.get_advertisement_count
(some_date timestamptz ) RETURNS BIGINT AS $$
DECLARE
  count BIGINT;
BEGIN
  EXECUTE 'SELECT count (*) FROM car_portal_app.advertisement WHERE
advertisement_date >= $1' USING some_date INTO count;
  RETURN count;
END;
$$ LANGUAGE plpgsql;
```

Recommended practices for dynamic SQL usage

Dynamic SQL can cause security issues if not handled carefully; dynamic SQL is vulnerable to the SQL injection technique. SQL injection is used to execute SQL statements that reveal secure information, or even to destroy data in a database. A very simple example of a PL/pgSQL function vulnerable to SQL injection is as follows:

```
CREATE OR REPLACE FUNCTION car_portal_app.can_login (email text, pass text)
RETURNS BOOLEAN AS $$
DECLARE
  stmt TEXT;
  result bool;
BEGIN
  stmt = E'SELECT COALESCE (count(*)=1, false) FROM car_portal_app.account
WHERE email = \''|| $1 || E'\' and password = \''||$2||E'\'';
  RAISE NOTICE '%' , stmt;
  EXECUTE stmt INTO result;
  RETURN result;
END;
$$ LANGUAGE plpgsql;
```

The preceding function returns true if the email and the password match. To test this function, let's insert a row and try to inject some code, as follows:

```
car_portal=> SELECT car_portal_app.can_login('jbutt@gmail.com',
md5('jbutt@gmail.com'));
NOTICE: SELECT COALESCE (count(*)=1, false) FROM account WHERE email =
'jbutt@gmail.com' and password = '1b9ef408e82e38346e6ebebf2dcc5ece'
 can_login
```

```
-----------
 t
(1 row)

car_portal=> SELECT car_portal_app.can_login('jbutt@gmail.com',
md5('jbutt@yahoo.com'));
NOTICE: SELECT COALESCE (count(*)=1, false) FROM account WHERE email =
'jbutt@gmail.com' and password = '37eb43e4d439589d274b6f921b1e4a0d'
 can_login
-----------
 f
(1 row)

car_portal=> SELECT car_portal_app.can_login(E'jbutt@gmail.com\'--', 'Do
not know password');
NOTICE: SELECT COALESCE (count(*)=1, false) FROM account WHERE email =
'jbutt@gmail.com'--' and password = 'Do not know password'
 can_login
-----------
 t
(1 row)
```

Notice that the function returns true even when the password does not match the password stored in the table. This is simply because the predicate was commented, as shown by the raise notice:

```
SELECT COALESCE (count(*)=1, false) FROM account WHERE email =
'jbutt@gmail.com'--' and password = 'Do not know password'
```

To protect code against this technique, one could follow these practices:

- For parameterized dynamic SQL statements, use the USING clause.
- Use the format function with appropriate interpolation to construct your queries. Note that %I escapes the argument as an identifier and %L as a literal.
- Use quote_ident(), quote_literal(), and quote_nullable() to properly format your identifiers and literal.

One way to write the preceding function is as follows:

```
CREATE OR REPLACE FUNCTION car_portal_app.can_login (email text, pass text)
RETURNS BOOLEAN AS
$$
DECLARE
  stmt TEXT;
result bool;
BEGIN
```

```
    stmt = format('SELECT COALESCE (count(*)=1, false) FROM
car_portal_app.account WHERE email = %Land password = %L', $1,$2);
    RAISE NOTICE '%' , stmt;
    EXECUTE stmt INTO result;
    RETURN result;
END;
$$ LANGUAGE plpgsql;
```

Summary

PostgreSQL provides a complete programming language called PL/pgSQL, which is integrated with the PostgreSQL trigger system. The PL/pgSQL and SQL languages can be used to code very complex logic. One should use the SQL functions when possible. With the introduction of advanced query writing techniques such as window functions and lateral Join in PostgreSQL, one can write very complex logic using only the standard SQL language.

There are several parameters in PostgreSQL for controlling function behavior; these parameters are applicable to the PL/pgSQL and SQL functions as well. For example, SECURITY DEFINER and SECURITY INVOKER define the execution security context and privileges. Function's planner parameters help the planner to generate execution plans. These parameters are COST, LEAKPROOF, and ROWS. Configuration related parameters can also be applied to functions.

PL/pgSQL is a fully fledged language, there are statements for assignment, conditionals, iterations, and for exception handling. Functions can return VOID pseudo type, scalar values , records, and so on. Also function supports IN, OUT and INOUT parameters.

The dynamic SQL technique enables developers to build SQL statements dynamically at runtime. One can create general purpose, flexible functions because the full text of an SQL statement may be unknown at the time of compilation. Dynamic SQL needs careful handling because it is exposed to SQL injection attacks.

In the next Chapter 08, *OLAP and Data Warehousing*, we will discuss modeling strategies for **OLAP** applications, also we will discuss some features that makes PostgreSQL a good candidate for **OLAP** applications. These features includes SQL statements such as COPY statement as well as data partitioning strategies via inheritance.

8
OLAP and Data Warehousing

A database usually performs the role of a storage component of a complex software solution. Depending on the type of the solution and what problem it aims to solve, the configuration of database and the data structure can be different. It is common to set up a database in regard to configuration and data structure in one of the two ways: **online transaction processing (OLTP)** and **online analytical processing (OLAP)**.

When a database works as a backend for an application, it implements an OLTP solution. This means that the database is supposed to perform a lot of small transactions on a regular basis. The car portal database we used as an example in previous chapters can be an example of a typical OLTP data structure. The application working with this database executes a transaction each time a user does something: creates an account, modifies the password, enters a car into the system, creates or changes an advertisement, and so on. Every action like that would cause a transaction in the database that would imply creating, changing, or deleting a row or a couple of rows in one or more tables. The more users work with the system, the more often the transactions are performed. The database should be able to handle the load, and its performance is measured by the number of transactions per second it can handle. The amount of the data is usually not a concern.

The key characteristics of an OLTP database are as follows:

- Normalized structure
- Relatively small amount of data
- Relatively big number of transactions
- Each transaction is small, affecting one or several records in the database
- The users typically do all the operations on the data: select, insert, delete, and update

When a database is working as a data source for a reporting software and its data is used for analysis, it implements an OLAP solution. It implies the opposite compared to OLTP: a lot of data, but it is rarely changed. The number of queries is relatively small, but the queries are big and complex and they usually do reading and aggregation of a huge numbers of records. The performance of database solutions of this kind is measured by the amount of time the queries take. OLAP solutions are often called **data warehouses**.

The OLAP databases normally have the following characteristics:

- Denormalized structure
- Relatively big amount of data
- Relatively small number of transactions
- Each transaction is big, affecting millions of records
- The users usually do only SELECT queries

In this chapter, we will discuss some features of PostgreSQL that help implement a data warehouse solution based on a PostgreSQL database, namely:

- Online analytical processing: what it is and why it is special
- Partitioning: a way to physically organize and manage huge tables
- Parallel query: a feature increasing the speed of query execution
- Index-only scans: a way to improve performance by building indexes in a right way

We will extend the database car_portal by adding another schema to the database, dwh, and creating some tables there. The schema itself and the sample data can be found in the attached media for this chapter, in schema.sql and data.sql respectively. All the code examples are in the examples.sql file.

Online analytical processing

A company running such a car portal website could store the HTTP access log in a database table. This can be used to analyze users' activity. For example, to measure the performance of the application, identify the patterns in the users' behavior, or simply to collect statistics about which car models are of the most interest. This data would be inserted into the table and never deleted or changed, or maybe deleted only when it is too old. However, the amount of data would be much bigger than the actual business data in the car portal database, but the data would be accessed only from time to time by internal users for performing analysis and creating reports.

These users are not expected to execute many queries per second, rather the opposite, but those queries will be big and complex, therefore the time that each query can take matters.

Another thing about OLAP databases is that they are not always up to date. As the analysis is performed on a basis of weeks and months (for example, comparing the number of requests in the current month with the previous month), it is not worth it to invest the effort to make the data of the very last second available in the data warehouse in real time. The data can be loaded into the data warehouse periodically; for example, daily or several times per day.

Extract, transform, and load

Let's consider the task of loading HTTP logs in the database and preparing it for analysis. Such tasks in data warehouse solutions are called **extract, transform, and load** (ETL).

Suppose the HTTP server that runs the car portal application is writing access logs in files and they are recreated every day. Assuming that the server runs nginx, a popular HTTP server software, lines in such log files by default should look similar to this:

```
94.31.90.168 - - [01/Jul/2017:01:00:22 +0000] "GET / HTTP/1.1" 200 227 "-"
"Mozilla/5.0 (Windows NT 10.0; Win64; x64) AppleWebKit/537.36 (KHTML, like
Gecko) Chrome/55.0.2883.87 Safari/537.36"
```

It has the given fields, separated by a space: remote address, remote user, timestamp, access method and resource URL, status code, body size, bytes, HTTP referer, and HTTP user agent.

The setup process and configuration of a HTTP server is out of the scope of this book. However, it is worth mentioning that to make it easier to load into a PostgreSQL database, it would make sense to change the log file format. To make it contain comma-separated values, one should change the directive log_format in the configuration file, nginx.conf, to make it look like this:

```
log_format main '$time_local;$remote_addr;$remote_user;'
                '"$request";$status;$body_bytes_sent;'
                '"$http_referer";"$http_user_agent"'
```

Now the logs are produced as CSV files containing the following lines:

```
01/Jul/2017:01:00:22 +0000;94.31.90.168;-;"GET / HTTP/1.1";200;227;"-
";"Mozilla/5.0 (Windows NT 10.0; Win64; x64) AppleWebKit/537.36 (KHTML,
like Gecko) Chrome/61.0.3163.79 Safari/537.36"
```

The file has the same fields as before, just the timestamp field is moved to the first position. All the fields are separated by a semicolon (;). In the database, there is a table named called dwh.access_log with the following structure:

```
CREATE TABLE dwh.access_log
(
    ts timestamp with time zone,
    remote_address text,
    remote_user text,
    url text,
    status_code int,
    body_size int,
    http_referer text,
    http_user_agent text
);
```

PostgreSQL provides a way to load data into tables quickly, many rows at a time, instead of executing INSERT commands row by row. There is a command named COPY that loads data into a table. The data can be taken from a file that is located on the database server in a place accessible by the PostgreSQL server process or from a stream. The data by default should look like a tab-separated list of fields; with records separated by a new line. However, this is customizable. The command is not included in the SQL standard. Here is a simplified syntax diagram for this command:

```
COPY <table name> [(column [, ...])] FROM { <file name> | STDIN } [[WITH]
(<options>)]
```

options here is used to specify data format, delimiters, quotations, escape characters, and some other parameters. STDIN can be specified instead of the filename to copy the data from standard input. The column list can be provided when the file does not have the data for all the columns or they are given in a different order.

To load the data into the database, one should somehow copy the file to the server and then execute a command such as this:

```
COPY dwh.access_log FROM '/tmp/access.log';
```

This would load the contents of the file located at /tmp/access.log to the dwh.access_log table. However, this is not a good idea for several reasons:

- Only a superuser can execute the COPY command to read or write from files.
- As the PostgreSQL server process needs to access the file, it would be necessary to either place the file in the location where other database files are stored, or allow the PostgreSQL process to access other locations. Both may be considered issues from a security point of view.

- Copying the file to the server may be the issue by itself: it would be necessary to allow the user (or the application) to access the filesystem on the server or mount shared network locations to the server.

To avoid these issues, one should use the COPY command to load the data from a stream, namely standard input. To do so, it may be necessary to write an application that would connect to the database, execute the COPY command, and then stream the data to the server. Luckily, the psql console can do this.

Let's try to load the sample file access.log that is provided in the attached media.

Suppose the file is located in the current directory. The database is running on localhost and the database user car_portal_app is allowed to connect. The following command will load the data from the file to the dwh.access_log table on a Linux system:

```
user@host:~$ cat access.log | psql -h localhost -U car_portal_app -d
car_portal -c "COPY dwh.access_log FROM STDIN WITH (format csv, delimiter
';')"
COPY 15456
```

The cat command prints the file to the console. Its output is piped to psql that is executing the COPY command loading the data from standard input. The output of the command is the word COPY followed by the number of rows copied.

On Windows, the command is similar:

```
c:\Users\user> psql -h localhost -U car_portal_app -d car_portal -c "COPY
dwh.access_log FROM STDIN WITH (format csv, delimiter ';')" < access.log
COPY 15456
```

It is also possible to execute this operation interactively from the psql console. There is a \copy command provided by psql, which has a similar syntax to the SQL command COPY: \copy dwh.access_log FROM 'access.log' WITH csv delimiter ';'. In the background, it is still the same. On the server, the COPY ... FROM STDIN command is executed and psql reads the file and sends its contents to the server.

Using this approach, it is very easy to organize a simple ETL process. It may be executed once per day and would just execute the preceding command. The prerequisite for this would be setting up log rotation for the HTTP server to make sure that the same data is not loaded twice.

The COPY command can not only load data into tables, but it can also copy the data the other way round: from tables to files or to standard output. This feature can be used again in ETL processes that can be organized in the form of simple bash scripts instead of complex software that would use high-level access to the database using JDBC or other APIs.

Here is an example of how to copy data table from one server to another (supposing the structure of the table is identical):

```
$ psql -h server1 -d database1 -c "COPY table1 TO STDOUT"
| psql -h server2 -d database2 -c "COPY table2 FROM
STDIN"
```

Here, the first psql command will read the table and output it to standard output. This stream is piped to the second psql command that writes the data from standard input to the other table.

ETL can also include enriching the input raw data with additional attributes or preprocessing it to make it easier to query. For example, the entries could be mapped to the records in the car_portal database. Let's say, API calls to /api/cars/30 could be mapped to the record in the table car with car_id = 30. Such processing can be done in the database, as follows:

```
car_portal=> ALTER TABLE dwh.access_log ADD car_id int;
ALTER TABLE

car_portal=> UPDATE dwh.access_log
  SET car_id = (SELECT regexp_matches(url, '/api/cars/(\d+)\W'))[1]::int
  WHERE url like '%/api/cars/%';
UPDATE 2297
```

In a similar way, the access_log table can be enriched by another attribute and can be joined to other tables.

In real life, ETL is usually more complex. It would normally include checking whether the data that is being loaded exists already in the destination table and would clean it before loading. This will make the process idempotent. Additionally, the process could identify which data to load and locate the input data. For example, consider an ETL job that loads some dataset every day. If it has failed for some reason, then when started the next day it should recognize that the failure has occurred and load two sets of data instead of only one. Notifying the right systems or people in case of failure can also be done by the ETL process.

There are a lot of different ETL tools available on the market, and as open source software.

Data modeling for OLAP

The big table containing the data that is the subject of analysis in a data warehouse is usually called the **fact table**. The HTTP access log that we discussed in the previous section plays the role of a fact table in those examples.

It does not make sense to perform any analytical queries on the fact table, grouping the data by car_id without knowing what the values in the field car_id actually mean. Therefore, the table car should also be available in the data warehouse. The difference between this table and the fact table is that the data is always loaded into the fact table, but the table car is quite static. The number of records in this table is many times smaller. Such tables that are used to resolve IDs into names are called **lookup tables** or **dimension tables**. The table car has a reference key car_model_id that points to records in the table car_model, which is used to resolve the ID of the car model into the name of the car make and the model.

The typical usage pattern for a fact table includes big SELECT queries that are not executed very often, but read large numbers of records, sometimes millions or tens of millions. In this case, any additional operation performed by the server could cost a lot of time. This includes the joining of fact tables to dimension tables.

For this reason, it is quite common to denormalize the data. Practically, it means joining the source tables in advance and storing the result of the join in a table. For example, if the access log entries we discussed in the previous section were mapped to car_id and the analytical task would imply calculating some statistics on car makes, this would mean performing two joins: the access_log is joined to the car table, which would be joined to the car_model table. This can be expensive.

To save time, it could make sense to join the car and car_model tables and store the result in another table. This table would not be in a normal form because the same car model would appear in the table many times. This would consume some extra disk space, of course. However, this may be a good compromise to make, as querying the fact table would be faster when this new lookup table is joined instead of both car and car_model.

Alternatively, the car_model_id field could be created in the fact table and filled when data is loaded by the ETL process. This structure would also be denormalized, consuming more disk space, but easier to query.

A fact table can reference dimension tables. A dimension table in turn could have references to other dimension tables. This is called a **snowflake schema** in OLAP terminology. It could like this:

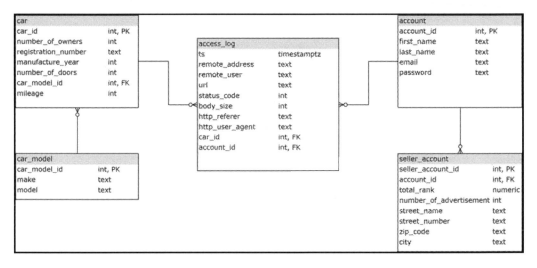

Snowflake data warehouse model

If the structure is denormalized and the dimension tables are not joined to each other, that is called a **star schema**. It could look like this:

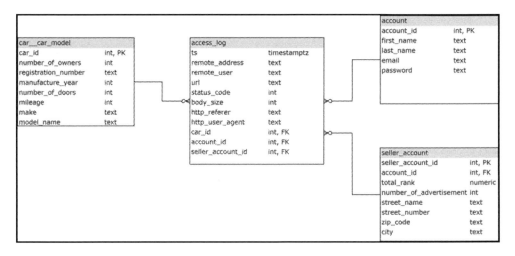

Star data warehouse model

There are advantages and disadvantages in both, and of course hybrid schemas, that combine both star and snowflake models for different dimension tables, are also possible. So usually it is a trade-off between complexity, maintainability, and performance.

Aggregation

Storing individual entries in a data warehouse could be too expensive. The number of HTTP requests for a big web application could be huge, and nobody would care for the individual entries in such a dataset. The individual records are used for troubleshooting the system, but in this case it would not make sense to keep them for longer than several days.

The table containing the information about the HTTP API calls could have the following fields: the amount of bytes sent, the response time, the URL of the API endpoint, the date and time of the request, and the user ID. In this case, the amount of bytes sent and the response time would be measures, and the URL of the API endpoint, HTTP status code, user ID, and date and time of the request are dimensions.

The data is grouped by the dimension fields and the measure fields are aggregated. The meaningful aggregation functions for the measures in the example would be `sum` for the amount of bytes sent and `avg` for the response time. Additionally, the total number of requests could be counted. For grouping, the date and time of the request could be truncated to hours. The result of this aggregation is stored in the data warehouse. The amount of data in the aggregated table is much smaller than individual entries would take, and therefore it works much faster. The aggregation could be a part of the ETL process.

When the amount of data is very big, it is possible to exchange granularity for performance. This means dropping one dimension in order to reduce the number of possible combinations of values in the grouping. For example, group by day instead of by hour, or remove the user ID from the table so that the number of rows will be reduced because all the users will be grouped together. It may make sense to keep different levels of aggregation in different tables at the same time and use the most suitable table for a particular report.

Partitioning

Data is constantly or periodically loaded into a data warehouse. The database can grow very big. The bigger it gets, the slower it works. The size of the database is limited by the capacity of the disk storage, so the needs to be deleted from time to time. Deletion from a very big table can also be quite slow.

The data that is newer is usually queried more often. Business users could check the reports of the last day every morning, of the last week every Monday, and of the month at the beginning of the next month. It is common to compare results of a time period with a corresponding previous period. For example, the current month as compared to the previous month, or to the respective month one year ago. It is unlikely that somebody would query data that is ten years old.

It would be nice to keep the newer, more queried data in one table that is relatively small and the old data in a different table or tables, and query only the table that has the data for a report that is required. On the other hand, it would be quite complex to implement a reporting tool that would query different tables depending on the parameters of the query.

PostgreSQL provides a way of keeping data in different tables and using a common name when querying them. This is called **partitioning**. Partitioning is implemented through the mechanism of table inheritance. This was mentioned in Chapter 03, *PostgreSQL Basic Building Blocks*. When a table inherits another table or tables, it is called a **child table**. The table that is inherited is a **parent table**. When a parent table is queried, the data from all the child tables is returned. In the context of partitioning, child tables are called **partitions**.

To define partitions for a table, it is necessary to choose a **partition key**. The partition key is a field or expression (or list of them) whose value will define to which partition a record belongs. In PostgreSQL, it is possible to create two different partitioning schemes: *range* and *list*. Range means that all the values within a certain range will belong to a partition. List means that only a specific value or values will belong to a partition.

Let's now define a partitioned data structure to store the data for the HTTP access log we imported in the previous section. We will only use a subset of fields for simplicity.

Firstly, create the parent table, as follows:

```
CREATE TABLE dwh.access_log_partitioned (ts timestamptz, url text,
status_code int)
PARTITION BY RANGE (ts);
```

This creates a table and defines the field `ts` as the partition key for a range partitioning scheme.

Now create partitions for ranges of values of the `ts` field for July, August, and September 2017, as follows:

```
CREATE TABLE dwh.access_log_2017_07 PARTITION OF dwh.access_log_partitioned
FOR VALUES FROM ('2017-07-01') TO ('2017-08-01');

CREATE TABLE dwh.access_log_2017_08 PARTITION OF dwh.access_log_partitioned
FOR VALUES FROM ('2017-08-01') TO ('2017-09-01');
```

```
CREATE TABLE dwh.access_log_2017_09 PARTITION OF dwh.access_log_partitioned
FOR VALUES FROM ('2017-09-01') TO ('2017-10-01');
```

 The lower bound for a range partition is inclusive and the upper bound is exclusive. In the preceding example, the partition `access_log_2017_07` will contain the records that satisfy the predicate `ts >= '2017-07-01'` `AND ts < '2017-08-01'`.

When such a structure is defined, it is possible to insert data into the parent table `access_log_partitioned`. Records will be automatically distributed into the correct partitions depending on the values of the partition key.

What if somebody tries to insert a record where the value of the partition key is outside any of the existing partition ranges? PostgreSQL will return an error, as follows:

```
car_portal=> INSERT INTO dwh.access_log_partitioned values ('2017-02-01',
'/test', 404);
 ERROR: no partition of relation "access_log_partitioned" found for row
 DETAIL: Partition key of the failing row contains (ts) = (2017-02-01
00:00:00+00).
```

To make it possible to insert such rows, one would need to create another partition for February. Alternatively, it is possible to create a partition for all rows over some value or below some value. To do this, the keywords MAXVALUE and MINVALUE are used. This command will create a partition for all the records before July 1, 2017:

```
CREATE TABLE dwh.access_log_min PARTITION OF dwh.access_log_partitioned
FOR VALUES FROM (MINVALUE) TO ('2017-07-01');
```

The partition scheme by list can be used with fields that do not have too many distinct values that are known in advance. For example, for the HTTP status code, it is possible to combine those partitioning schemes by creating sub-partitions for existing partitions, as follows:

```
CREATE TABLE dwh.access_log_2017_10 PARTITION OF dwh.access_log_partitioned
FOR VALUES FROM ('2017-10-01') TO ('2017-11-01')
PARTITION BY LIST (status_code);

CREATE TABLE dwh.access_log_2017_10_200 PARTITION OF dwh.access_log_2017_10
FOR VALUES IN (200);

CREATE TABLE dwh.access_log_2017_10_400 PARTITION OF dwh.access_log_2017_10
FOR VALUES IN (400);
```

We have now a partition for October that has two sub-partitions for the HTTP status codes 200 and 400. Note that it will not be possible to insert other status codes into the table with such a configuration. It is however possible to give a list of values of the partition key when creating a partition.

Alternatively, it is possible to define the partitioning scheme not just on a field, but on an expression. Here, partitions are created based on the first digit of the status code:

```
CREATE TABLE dwh.access_log_2017_11 PARTITION OF dwh.access_log_partitioned
FOR VALUES FROM ('2017-11-01') TO ('2017-12-01')
PARTITION BY LIST (left(status_code::text, 1));

CREATE TABLE dwh.access_log_2017_11_2XX PARTITION OF dwh.access_log_2017_11
FOR VALUES IN ('2');

CREATE TABLE dwh.access_log_2017_11_4XX PARTITION OF dwh.access_log_2017_11
FOR VALUES IN ('4');
```

More complicated partitioning strategies are still possible using the traditional table inheritance feature. This will require some manual effort to create tables, define an inheritance relationships, create check constraints to make PostgreSQL aware of which data is stored in which partition when necessary, and set up triggers or rules to distribute the records into proper partitions when inserted into the parent table.

It's possible to delete a partition by simply deleting the table. It is also possible to detach a partition from the parent table so that it is not a partition anymore but just a standalone table:

```
car_portal=> ALTER TABLE dwh.access_log_partitioned DETACH PARTITION
dwh.access_log_2017_11;
ALTER TABLE
```

It is also possible to make an existing table a partition of some other table:

```
car_portal=> ALTER TABLE dwh.access_log_partitioned ATTACH PARTITION
dwh.access_log_2017_11
FOR VALUES FROM ('2017-11-01') TO ('2017-12-01');
ALTER TABLE
```

To illustrate the benefits of partitioning, let's see an example. First, create a non-partitioned table to compare the results, with the same structure as the partitioned one:

```
car_portal=> CREATE TABLE dwh.access_log_not_partitioned (LIKE
dwh.access_log_partitioned);
CREATE TABLE
```

Insert the data into both the partitioned and non-partitioned tables, duplicating the contents of the table `dwh.access_log` 1,000 times, as follows:

```
car_portal=> INSERT INTO dwh.access_log_not_partitioned SELECT ts, url,
status_code FROM dwh.access_log, generate_series(1, 1000);
INSERT 0 15456000
car_portal=> INSERT INTO dwh.access_log_partitioned SELECT ts, url,
status_code FROM dwh.access_log, generate_series(1, 1000);
INSERT 0 15456000
```

Now let's count the number of records for the last 10 days of August, measuring the time the query takes, as follows:

```
car_portal=> \timing
Timing is on.

car_portal=> SELECT count(*) FROM dwh.access_log_not_partitioned
  WHERE ts >= '2017-08-22' AND ts < '2017-09-01';
 count
---------
 1712000
(1 row)
Time: 921.122 ms

car_portal=> SELECT count(*) FROM dwh.access_log_partitioned
  WHERE ts >= '2017-08-22' AND ts < '2017-09-01';
 count
---------
 1712000
(1 row)
Time: 336.221 ms
```

Querying the partitioned table was about three times quicker. That is because PostgreSQL knows which partition has the data for August and only scans that one. This is also visible in the execution plan:

```
car_portal=> EXPLAIN SELECT count(*) FROM dwh.access_log_partitioned
  WHERE ts >= '2017-08-22' AND ts < '2017-09-01';
QUERY PLAN
-------------------------------------------------------------------------
-------------------------------------------------------------------------
--------
 Finalize Aggregate (cost=82867.96..82867.97 rows=1 width=8)
  -> Gather (cost=82867.75..82867.96 rows=2 width=8)
    Workers Planned: 2
     -> Partial Aggregate (cost=81867.75..81867.76 rows=1 width=8)
       -> Append (cost=0.00..80149.89 rows=687141 width=0)
         -> Parallel Seq Scan on access_log_2017_08 (cost=0.00..80149.89
```

```
rows=687141 width=0)
          Filter: ((ts >= '2017-08-22 00:00:00+00'::timestamp with time
zone) AND (ts < '2017-09-01
          00:00:00+00'::timestamp with time zone))
(7 rows)
```

The sequential scan is performed on the partition table `access_log_2017_08`.

Partitioning is described in detail in the PostgreSQL documentation at `https://www.postgresql.org/docs/current/static/ddl-partitioning.html`.

Parallel query

PostgreSQL creates a server process for each client connection. This means that only one CPU core will be used to perform all the work. Of course, when multiple connections are active, the resources of the server machine will be used intensively. However, in the data warehouse solutions, the number of concurrent sessions is usually not very big. They tend to perform big complex queries. It makes sense to utilize multiple CPU cores to process the queries of a single client connection.

PostgreSQL supports a feature called **parallel query** that makes it possible to use multiple CPUs for one query. Certain operations like table scans, joins, or aggregation can be executed in several processes concurrently. The administrator can configure the number of workers that the PostgreSQL server will create for parallel query execution. When the query optimizer can detect a benefit from parallel execution, it will request some workers, and if they are available the query (or a part of it) will be executed in parallel.

To see the benefits of the parallel query execution, let's show an example using the HTTP access log table used in the previous sections. At first, disable the parallel query feature for the current session by changing the configuration parameter `max_parallel_workers_per_gather` to zero. Note that this is not the total number of processes performing the queries, but the number of *extra* processes. The main server process that serves the current client session is always there. The parameter is changed as follows:

```
car_portal=> SET max_parallel_workers_per_gather = 0;
SET
```

Assuming timing is still enabled, query the table:

```
car_portal=> SELECT count(*) FROM dwh.access_log_not_partitioned WHERE url
~ 'car';
 count
```

```
  ---------
  7030000
  (1 row)
Time: 10876.095 ms (00:10.876)
```

Now enable the parallel query again by setting the `max_parallel_workers_per_gather` to one. This will effectively make the query execute in two parallel processes. Run the query again:

```
car_portal=> SET max_parallel_workers_per_gather = 1;
SET

car_portal=> SELECT count(*) FROM dwh.access_log_not_partitioned WHERE url
~ 'car';
  count
  ---------
  7030000
  (1 row)
Time: 6435.174 ms (00:06.435)
```

The query is now almost two times faster!

The query that we just saw is CPU intensive because it uses a regular expression match in its WHERE clause. Otherwise, the hard disk would be a bottleneck and the effect of multiple CPUs being used would not be that explicit.

More information on parallel query can be found in the PostgreSQL documentation at `https://www.postgresql.org/docs/current/static/parallel-query.html`.

Index-only scans

Indexes have already been described in Chapter 04, *PostgreSQL Advanced Building Blocks*. Simply speaking, indexes work like a glossary at the end of a book. When searching for a keyword in a book, to make it faster one can look it up in the glossary and then go to the page specified. The glossary is alphabetically organized; that's why searching in it is fast. However, when it is necessary just to find out if a keyword exists in the book, there is no need to go to the page. Just looking in the glossary is enough.

PostgreSQL can do the same. If all the information that is needed for a query is contained in the index, the database will not perform the scan on the table data and only use the index. This is called an **index-only scan**.

To demonstrate how it works, let's create an index for the table
dwh.access_log_not_partitioned, as follows:

```
CREATE INDEX on dwh.access_log_not_partitioned (ts, status_code);
```

Now, suppose we want to find out when the first HTTP request that resulted in a status
code 201 happened on August 1. The query will be as follows:

```
car_portal=> SELECT min(ts) FROM dwh.access_log_not_partitioned
  WHERE ts BETWEEN '2017-08-01' AND '2017-08-02' AND status_code = '201';
 min
------------------------
 2017-08-01 01:30:57+00
(1 row)
Time: 0.751 ms
```

The query took less than a millisecond. From the execution plan, it is clear that PostgreSQL
did not scan the table and performed an index-only scan:

```
car_portal=> EXPLAIN SELECT min(ts) FROM dwh.access_log_not_partitioned
  WHERE ts BETWEEN '2017-08-01' AND '2017-08-02' AND status_code = '201';
QUERY PLAN
-----------------------------------------------------------------------
-----------------------------------------------------------------------
---------------------------------------------------------
 Result (cost=4.23..4.24 rows=1 width=8)
   InitPlan 1 (returns $0)
     -> Limit (cost=0.56..4.23 rows=1 width=8)
       -> Index Only Scan using
access_log_not_partitioned_ts_status_code_idx on
         access_log_not_partitioned (cost=0.56..135923.57 rows=37083
width=8)
             Index Cond: ((ts IS NOT NULL) AND (ts >= '2017-08-01
00:00:00+00'::timestamp with time zone)
             AND (ts <= '2017-08-02 00:00:00+00'::timestamp with time zone)
AND (status_code = 201))
(5 rows)
```

To see the benefit of applying this feature, let's switch it off and check the timing again, as
follows:

```
car_portal=> SET enable_indexonlyscan = off;
SET

car_portal=> SELECT min(ts) FROM dwh.access_log_not_partitioned
  WHERE ts BETWEEN '2017-08-01' AND '2017-08-02' AND status_code = '201';
 min
------------------------
```

```
 2017-08-01 01:30:57+00
 (1 row)
Time: 1.225 ms
```

Now the query is almost two times slower. The execution plan is slightly different (though the total cost is the same):

```
car_portal=> EXPLAIN SELECT min(ts) FROM dwh.access_log_not_partitioned
   WHERE ts BETWEEN '2017-08-01' AND '2017-08-02' AND status_code = '201';
 QUERY PLAN
-----------------------------------------------------------------------------
-----------------------------------------------------------------------------
-------------------------------------------------
 Result  (cost=4.23..4.24 rows=1 width=8)
   InitPlan 1 (returns $0)
     -> Limit  (cost=0.56..4.23 rows=1 width=8)
       -> Index Scan using access_log_not_partitioned_ts_status_code_idx on
          access_log_not_partitioned  (cost=0.56..135923.57 rows=37083
width=8)
             Index Cond: ((ts IS NOT NULL) AND (ts >= '2017-08-01
00:00:00+00'::timestamp with time zone)
             AND (ts <= '2017-08-02 00:00:00+00'::timestamp with time zone)
AND (status_code = 201))
(5 rows)
```

This feature can only work if all the fields that are referenced in a query are part of an index. In some cases, the optimizer may conclude that a sequential scan on the table will be cheaper, even if the index has all the data. This is usually true when a big number of records are supposed to be returned.

Index-only scans have certain limitations due to how PostgreSQL maintains transaction isolation. For details, see Chapter 10, *Transactions and Concurrency Control*. In short, PostgreSQL checks the visibility maps for the table to decide whether certain data should be visible to the current transaction. If it cannot find this information there, checking the table data is necessary.

Not all index types support index-only scans. B-tree indexes always support them, GiST and SP-GiST support then only for certain operators, and GIN indexes do not support this feature.

This topic does not belong specifically to OLAP solutions. However, in data warehouses, it is common to create multiple indexes on different combinations of fields, sometimes overlapping each other. Understanding how index-only scans work can help with designing a better structure for a database.

More on index-only scans can be found in the PostgreSQL documentation at `https://www.postgresql.org/docs/current/static/indexes-index-only-scans.html`.

Summary

OLAP and data warehousing are both used in the context of specific database design patterns, where a database is used for analysis and reporting. OLAP stands for online analytical processing. In contrast to OLTP, OLAP implies bigger amounts of data, a smaller number of concurrent sessions and transactions, but the size of the transactions is bigger. The database structure is often denormalized to improve query performance. A database that is a part of an OLAP solution is often called a data warehouse.

In this chapter, we covered how to structure data in a data warehouse, how to load data there, and how to optimize the database performance by applying partitioning, using parallel query execution, and index-only scans.

In the next chapter, we will discuss the extended data types supported by PostgreSQL such as arrays, JSON, and others. These data types make it possible to implement complicated business logic using native database support.

Beyond Conventional Data Types

9

PostgreSQL can handle rich data types due to its powerful extensions. Data that does not fit the relational model inherently, such as semi-structured data, can be stored and manipulated, either using out-of-the-box data types or extensions. Also, the PostgreSQL community focuses not only on enhancing relational database features, but also on supporting rich data types such as arrays, XMLs, hash stores, and JSON documents. The focus shift is a result of embracing changes in the software development process's life cycle, such as agile development methods, and supporting unknown and rapid software requirements.

Non-conventional data types allow PostgreSQL to store different data types such as geographical, binary, as well as schema-less data, such as JSON documents and hash stores. PostgreSQL supports some of these data types out of the box, including JSON, JSONB, XML, array, byte, and BLOB. More data types are available via extensions such as `hstore` and PostGIS.

JSON, JSONB, and HStore allow PostgreSQL to handle schema-less models, which in turn allow developers to make real-time adjustments to data in an automatic and transparent way. Using JSON, JSONB, and `hstore` allows developers to change the data structure without changing the table structure using the `ALTER` command. Also, it allows them to have a flexible data model without using the **entity-attribute-value** (**EAV**) model, which is difficult to handle in the relational model. However, developers should take care handling data integrity in the business logic to ensure that the data is clean and error free.

In this chapter the following data types will be covered:

- Array datatype.
- Hstore datatype which is used as a key/value store.
- JSON datatype
- Full text search datatypes including tsquery and tsvector.

It would be nice to have a look also at the PostGIS extension, knowing that PostGIS supports raster and vector formats, and provides very rich functions to manipulate data. Other interesting datatype is range datatype which can be used in defining range interval such as date range.

Arrays

An array is a data structure consisting of a collection of elements (values or variables), the order of the elements in the array is significant and each element in the array is identified by an index. The index of the the array is often started by 1, but in some programming languages such as C and C++, the index starts at 0. Array elements should have the same type such as INT or TEXT.

Multidimensional arrays are supported; here, the array type can be a base, enum, or composite type. Array elements should have only one data type. PostgreSQL arrays allow duplicate values as well as null values. The following example shows how to initialize a one-dimensional array and get the first element:

```
car_portal=> SELECT ('{red, green, blue}'::text[])[1] as red ;
 red
-----
 red
(1 row)
```

The array length, by default, is not bound to a certain value, but this can also be specified when using arrays to define a relation. By default, an array index, as shown in the preceding example, starts from index one; however, this behavior can be changed by defining the dimension when initializing the array, as follows:

```
car_portal=> WITH test AS (SELECT '[0:1]={1,2}'::INT[] as arr) SELECT arr,
arr[0] from test;
     arr     | arr
-------------+-----
 [0:1]={1,2} | 1
(1 row)
```

Arrays can be initialized using the { } construct. Another way to initialize an array is as follows:

```
car_portal=> SELECT array['red','green','blue'] AS primary_colors;
  primary_colors
-----------------
 {red,green,blue}
(1 row)
```

PostgreSQL provides many functions to manipulate arrays, such as `array_remove` to remove a certain element. The following are some of the array functions:

```
car_portal=> SELECT
 array_ndims(two_dim_array) AS "Number of dimensions",
 array_dims(two_dim_array) AS "Dimensions index range",
 array_length(two_dim_array, 1) AS "The array length of 1st dimension",
 cardinality(two_dim_array) AS "Number of elements",
 two_dim_array[1][1] AS "The first element"
FROM
(VALUES ('{{red,green,blue}, {red,green,blue}}'::text[][])) AS
foo(two_dim_array);
-[ RECORD 1 ]--------------------+-----------
Number of dimensions | 2
Dimensions index range | [1:2][1:3]
The array length of 1st dimension | 2
Number of elements | 6
The first element | red
```

A very common use case of arrays is to model multi-valued attributes. For example, a dress can have more than one color, and a newspaper article can have several tags. Another use case is to model a hash store. This is achieved by having two arrays—one with the keys and another with the values—and the array index is used to associate the key with the value. For example, `pg_stats` uses this approach to store information about the common values histogram. The `most_common_vals` and the `most_common_freqs` columns are used to list the most common values in a certain column and the frequencies of these most common values, respectively, as shown in the following example:

```
car_portal=> SELECT tablename, attname, most_common_vals, most_common_freqs
FROM pg_stats WHERE array_length(most_common_vals,1) < 10 AND schemaname
NOT IN ('pg_catalog','information_schema') LIMIT 1;
-[ RECORD 1 ]-----+-----------------------------------------------------
tablename | seller_account
attname | zip_code
most_common_vals | {10011,37388,94577,95111,99501}
most_common_freqs | {0.0136986,0.0136986,0.0136986,0.0136986,0.0136986}
```

Also, arrays can be used to facilitate coding and in performing some SQL tricks, such as passing several arguments to the function using the VARIADIC array option or performing loops using the generate_series function. This allows developers to perform complex tasks without using the PL/pgSQL language. For example, let's assume that we want to have at least one column as not null out of several columns. This, in reality, can be used to check for disjoint attributes or model inheritance.

Let us see another example, let's assume we have a table called vehicle that contains a vehicle's common attributes. Also, let's assume that we have several types of vehicles, such as trucks, cars, sport cars, and so on. One could model this by having several columns referencing the car, truck, and sport car tables. To understand how one can use the VARIADIC function, let's model the vehicle inheritance example, as follows:

```
CREATE OR REPLACE FUNCTION null_count (VARIADIC arr int[]) RETURNS INT AS
$$
   SELECT count(CASE WHEN m IS NOT NULL THEN 1 ELSE NULL END)::int FROM
unnest($1) m(n)
$$ LANGUAGE SQL
```

To use the preceding function, one needs to add a check to the table, as follows:

```
CREATE TABLE public.car (
   car_id SERIAL PRIMARY KEY,
   car_number_of_doors INT DEFAULT 5
);
CREATE TABLE public.bus (
   bus_id SERIAL PRIMARY KEY,
   bus_number_of_passengers INT DEFAULT 50
);
CREATE TABLE public.vehicle (
   vehicle_id SERIAL PRIMARY KEY,
   registration_number TEXT,
   car_id INT REFERENCES car(car_id),
   bus_id INT REFERENCES bus(bus_id),
   CHECK (null_count(car_id, bus_id) = 1)
);
INSERT INTO public.car VALUES (1, 5);
INSERT INTO public.bus VALUES (1, 25);
```

When inserting now to the vehicle table one should specify either car_id or bus_id as follows:

```
car_portal=> INSERT INTO public.vehicle VALUES (default, 'a234', null,
null);
ERROR: new row for relation "vehicle" violates check constraint
"vehicle_check"
```

```
DETAIL: Failing row contains (1, a234, null, null).
Time: 1,482 ms
car_portal=> INSERT INTO public.vehicle VALUES (default, 'a234', 1, 1);
ERROR: new row for relation "vehicle" violates check constraint
"vehicle_check"
DETAIL: Failing row contains (2, a234, 1, 1).
Time: 0,654 ms
car_portal=> INSERT INTO public.vehicle VALUES (default, 'a234', null, 1);
INSERT 0 1
Time: 1,128 ms
car_portal=> INSERT INTO public.vehicle VALUES (default, 'a234', 1, null);
INSERT 0 1
Time: 1,217 ms
```

Note that to call the null_count function, we need to add VARIADIC to the function's argument, as follows:

```
car_portal=> SELECT * FROM null_count(VARIADIC ARRAY [null, 1]);
 null_count
------------
          1
(1 row)
```

Another trick is to generate the substring of a text; this comes in handy when one would like to get the longest prefix match. The longest prefix match is very important in areas such as telecommunication, such as mobile operators or telephone companies. Longest prefix matching is used to determine networks. The following example shows how we can achieve this:

```
CREATE TABLE prefix (
  network TEXT,
  prefix_code TEXT NOT NULL
);

INSERT INTO prefix VALUES ('Palestine Jawwal', 97059), ('Palestine
Jawwal',970599), ('Palestine watania',970597);

CREATE OR REPLACE FUNCTION prefixes(TEXT) RETURNS TEXT[] AS $$
   SELECT ARRAY(SELECT substring($1,1,i) FROM generate_series(1,length($1))
g(i))::TEXT[];
$$ LANGUAGE SQL IMMUTABLE;
```

The function prefixes will return an array with the prefix substring. To test whether longest prefix matching worked, let's get the longest prefix for the number 97059973456789 through the following code:

```
car_portal=> SELECT * FROM prefix WHERE prefix_code = any
(prefixes('97059973456789')) ORDER BY length(prefix_code) DESC limit 1;
    network | prefix_code
------------------+-------------
 Palestine Jawwal | 970599
(1 row)
```

Common functions of arrays and their operators

Array operators are similar to other data type operators. For example, the = sign is used for equality comparison, and the || operator is used for concatenation. Also, in previous chapters, we saw some operators similar to &&, which returns true if the arrays are overlapping. Finally, the @> and <@ operators are used if an array contains or is contained by another array, respectively. The unnest function is used to return a set of elements from an array. This is quite useful when one would like to use set operations on arrays, such as distinct, order by, intersect, union, and so on. The following example is used to remove the duplicates and sort the array in an ascending order:

```
SELECT array(SELECT DISTINCT unnest (array [1,1,1,2,3,3]) ORDER BY 1);
```

In the preceding example, the result of the unnest function is sorted and duplicates are removed using ORDER BY and DISTINCT, respectively. The array() function is used to construct the array from a set. Also, arrays can be used to aggregate the date, for example, if I would like to get all the models of a certain make, array_agg can be used as follows:

```
car_portal=> SELECT make, array_agg(model) FROM car_model group by make;
    make | array_agg
---------------+---------------------------------------------------------
 Volvo | {S80,S60,S50,XC70,XC90}
 Audi | {A1,A2,A3,A4,A5,A6,A8}
 UAZ | {Patriot}
 Citroen | {C1,C2,C3,C4,"C4 Picasso",C5,C6}
```

The array `ANY` function is similar to the SQL `IN ()` construct and is used to compare containment, as shown in the following example:

```
car_portal=> SELECT 1 in (1,2,3), 1 = ANY ('{1,2,3}'::INT[]);
 ?column? | ?column?
----------+----------
 t | t
(1 row)
```

The full list of arrays functions and operator is quite long, and it can be found in the official documentation `https://www.postgresql.org/docs/current/static/functions-array.html`. Up till now we have demonstrated several functions including `unnest`, `array_agg`, `any`, `array_length`, and so on. The following list of functions is often used in daily development:

function	Return Type	Description	Example	Result
array_to_string(anyarray, text [, text])	text	convert an array to a text based . One can specify the delimiter as well as NULL value substitution.	array_to_string(ARRAY[1, NULL, 5], ',', 'x')	'1,,x,5'
array_remove(anyarray, anyelement)	anyarray	remove all elements based on element value	array_remove(ARRAY[1,2,3], 2)	{1,3}
array_replace(anyarray, anyelement, anyelement)	anyarray	replace all array elements equal to the given value with a new value	array_replace(ARRAY[1,2,5,4], 5, 3)	{1,2,3,4}

Modifying and accessing arrays

An array element can be accessed via an index; if the array does not contain an element for this index, the NULL value is returned, as shown in the following example:

```
CREATE TABLE color(
  color text []
);
INSERT INTO color(color) VALUES ('{red, green}'::text[]);
INSERT INTO color(color) VALUES ('{red}'::text[]);
```

To confirm that NULL is returned, let's run the following:

```
car_portal=> SELECT color [3]IS NOT DISTINCT FROM null FROM color;
 ?column?
----------
 t
 t
(2 rows)
```

Also, an array can be sliced by providing a lower and upper bound, as follows:

```
car_portal=> SELECT color [1:2] FROM color;
    color
-------------
 {red,green}
 {red}
(2 rows)
```

When updating an array, one could completely replace the array, get a slice, replace an element, or append the array using the || concatenation operator as shown in the below example. The full set of array functions can be found at: https://www.postgresql.org/docs/current/static/functions-array.html-

```
car_portal=> SELECT ARRAY ['red', 'green'] || '{blue}'::text[] AS append;
     append
-----------------
 {red,green,blue}
(1 row)

Time: 0,848 ms
car_portal=> UPDATE color SET color[1:2] = '{black, white}';
UPDATE 2
car_portal=> table color ;
    color
---------------
 {black,white}
```

```
{black,white}
(2 rows)
```

The `array_remove` function can be used to remove all the elements that are equal to a certain value, as follows:

```
car_portal=> SELECT array_remove ('{Hello, Hello, World}'::TEXT[],
'Hello');
 array_remove
--------------
 {World}
(1 row)
```

To remove a certain value based on an index, one can use the `WITH ORDINALITY` clause. So, let's assume that we want to remove the first element of an array; this can be achieved as follows:

```
car_portal=> SELECT ARRAY(SELECT unnest FROM unnest ('{Hello1, Hello2,
World}'::TEXT[]) WITH ordinality WHERE ordinality <> 1);
     array
----------------
 {Hello2,World}
(1 row)
```

Indexing arrays

The GIN index can be used to index arrays; standard PostgreSQL distributions have the GIN operator class for one-dimensional arrays. The GIN index is supported for the following operators:

- The **contains** operator @>
- The **is contained by** operator <@
- The **overlapping** operator &&
- The **equality** operators =

The following code shows how to create an Index on color column using GIN function :

```
CREATE INDEX ON color USING GIN (color);
```

The `index` function can be tested by using the following code:

```
car_portal=> SET enable_seqscan TO off; -- To force index scan
SET
car_portal=> EXPLAIN SELECT * FROM color WHERE '{red}'::text[] && color;
                            QUERY PLAN
----------------------------------------------------------------------
---
 Bitmap Heap Scan on color (cost=8.00..12.01 rows=1 width=32)
   Recheck Cond: ('{red}'::text[] && color)
   -> Bitmap Index Scan on color_color_idx (cost=0.00..8.00 rows=1 width=0)
         Index Cond: ('{red}'::text[] && color)
(4 rows)
```

The hash store data structure

A hash store, also known as key-value store, or associative array is a famous data structure in modern programming languages such as **Java**, **Python**, and **Node.js**. Also, there are dedicated database frameworks to handle this kind of data, such as the `Redis` database.

PostgreSQL has supported hash store—`hstore`—since PostgreSQL version 9.0. The `hstore` extension allows developers to leverage the best of both worlds. It increases the developer's agility without sacrificing the powerful features of PostgreSQL. Also, `hstore` allows the developer to model semistructured data and sparse arrays in a relational model.

To create the `hstore`, one simply needs to execute the following command as a superuser:

```
CREATE EXTENSION hstore;
```

The textual representation of `hstore` includes a zero or higher `key=>` `value` pair followed by a comma. An example of the `hstore` data type is as follows:

```
SELECT 'tires=>"winter tires", seat=>leather'::hstore;
                   hstore
-------------------------------------------
 "seat"=>"leather", "tires"=>"winter tires"
(1 row)
```

One could also generate a single value hstore using the hstore(key, value) function as shown below:

```
SELECT hstore('´Hello', 'World');
      hstore
------------------
 "´Hello"=>"World"
(1 row)
```

Note that, in hstore, keys are unique, as shown in the following example:

```
SELECT 'a=>1, a=>2'::hstore;
   hstore
----------
 "a"=>"1"
(1 row)
```

In the car web portal, let's assume that the developer wants to support several other attributes, such as airbags, air conditioning, power steering, and so on. The developer, in the traditional relational model, should alter the table structure and add new columns. Thanks to hstore, the developer can store this information using the key-value store without having to keep altering the table structure, as follows:

```
car_portal=# ALTER TABLE car_portal_app.car ADD COLUMN features hstore;
ALTER TABLE
```

One limitation of the hstore is that it is not a full document store, so it is difficult to represent nested objects in an hstore. The other problem is maintaining the set of keys, since a hstore key is case sensitive.

```
car_portal=# SELECT 'color=>red, Color=>blue'::hstore;
               hstore
----------------------------------
 "Color"=>"blue", "color"=>"red"
(1 row)
```

The -> operator is used to get a value for a certain key. To append an hstore, the || concatenation operator can be used. Furthermore, the minus sign – is used to delete a key-value pair. To update an hstore, the hstore can be concatenated with another hstore that contains the updated value. The following example shows how hstore keys can be inserted, updated, and deleted:

```
CREATE TABLE features (
        features hstore
);
```

The following example demonstrates insert, update and delete operations:

```
car_portal=# INSERT INTO features (features) VALUES
('Engine=>Diesel'::hstore) RETURNING *;
      features
--------------------
 "Engine"=>"Diesel"
(1 row)

INSERT 0 1
car_portal=# -- To add a new key
car_portal=# UPDATE features SET features = features || hstore ('Seat',
'Lethear') RETURNING *;
                features
---------------------------------------
 "Seat"=>"Lethear", "Engine"=>"Diesel"
(1 row)

UPDATE 1
car_portal=# -- To update a key, this is similar to add a key
car_portal=# UPDATE features SET features = features || hstore ('Engine',
'Petrol') RETURNING *;
                features
---------------------------------------
 "Seat"=>"Lethear", "Engine"=>"Petrol"
(1 row)

UPDATE 1
car_portal=# -- To delete a key
car_portal=# UPDATE features SET features = features - 'Seat'::TEXT
RETURNING *;
      features
--------------------
 "Engine"=>"Petrol"
(1 row)
```

> The hstore data type is very rich in functions and operators; there are several operators to compare hstore content. For example, the ?, ?&, and ?| operators can be used to check whether hstore contains a key, set of keys, or any of the specified keys, respectively. Also, an hstore can be cast to arrays, sets, and JSON documents.

As an hstore data type can be converted to a set using each (hstore) function, this allows the developer to use all the relational algebra set operators on an hstore, such as DISTINCT, GROUP BY, and ORDER BY.

The following example shows how to get distinct `hstore` keys; this could be used to validate `hstore` keys:

```
car_portal=# SELECT DISTINCT (each(features)).key FROM features;
   key
 --------
 Engine
(1 row)
```

To get the `hstore` as a set, one can simply use each function again:

```
car_portal=# SELECT (each(features)).* FROM features;
 key | value
 --------+--------
 Engine | Petrol
(1 row)
```

Indexing an hstore

An hstore data type can be indexed using the GIN and GIST indexes, and picking the right index type depends on several factors, such as the number of rows in the table, available space, index search and update performance, the queries pattern, and so on. To properly pick up the right index, it is good to perform benchmarking

The following example shows the effect of using the GIN index to retrieve a record that has a certain key. The ? operator returns true if hstore contains a key:

```
CREATE INDEX ON features USING GIN (features);
```

To `index` function can be tested by using the following code::

```
SET enable_seqscan to off;
car_portal=# EXPLAIN SELECT features->'Engine' FROM features WHERE features
? 'Engine';
                              QUERY PLAN
-------------------------------------------------------------------------
---------
 Bitmap Heap Scan on features (cost=8.00..12.02 rows=1 width=32)
    Recheck Cond: (features ? 'Engine'::text)
    -> Bitmap Index Scan on features_features_idx (cost=0.00..8.00 rows=1
width=0)
          Index Cond: (features ? 'Engine'::text)
(4 rows)
```

Certainly, if an operator is not supported by the GIN index, such as the -> operator, one can still use the B-tree index, as follows:

```
CREATE INDEX ON features ((features->'Engine'));
car_portal=# EXPLAIN SELECT features->'Engine' FROM features WHERE
features->'Engine'= 'Diesel';
                                QUERY PLAN
-------------------------------------------------------------------
--------
 Index Scan using features_expr_idx on features (cost=0.12..8.14 rows=1
width=32)
   Index Cond: ((features -> 'Engine'::text) = 'Diesel'::text)
(2 rows)
```

The JSON data structure

JSON is a universal data structure that is human and machine-readable. JSON is supported by almost all modern programming languages, embraced as a data interchange format and heavily used in RESTful web services.

JSON and XML

XML and JSON are both used to define the data structure of exchanged documents. JSON grammar is simpler than that of XML, and JSON documents are more compact. JSON is easier to read and write. On the other hand, XML can have a defined data structure enforced by the **XML schema definition (XSD)** schema. Both JSON and XML have different usages as exchange formats; based on personal experience, JSON is often used within organizations themselves or with web services and mobile applications due to its simplicity, while XML is used to define highly structured documents and formats to guarantee interoperability with data exchange between different organizations. For example, several **Open Geospatial Consortium (OGC)** standards, such as web map services, use XML as an exchange format with a defined XSD schema.

JSON data types for PostgreSQL

PostgreSQL supports two JSON data types, mainly JSON and JSONB, both of which are implementations of RFC 7159. Both types can be used to enforce JSON rules. Both types are almost identical. However, JSONB is more efficient, as it stores JSON documents in a binary format and also supports indexes.

When using JSON, it is preferable to have UTF8 as the database encoding to ensure that the JSON type conforms to RFC 7159 standards. On one hand, when storing data as a JSON document, the JSON object is stored in a textual format. On the other hand, when storing a JSON object as JSONB, the JSON primitive data types, mainly string, Boolean, and number, will be mapped to text, Boolean, and numeric respectively.

Modifying and accessing JSON types

When casting text as a json type, the text is stored and rendered without any processing; so, it will preserve the whitespace, numeric formatting, and element's order details. JSONB does not preserve these details, as shown in the following example:

```
car_portal=# SELECT '{"name":"some name", "name":"some name" }'::json;
                          json
----------------------------------------------
 {"name":"some name", "name":"some name" }
(1 row)

car_portal=#
car_portal=# SELECT '{"name":"some name", "name":"some name" }'::jsonb;
          jsonb
----------------------
 {"name": "some name"}
(1 row)
```

JSON objects can contain other nested JSON objects, arrays, nested arrays, arrays of JSON objects, and so on. JSON arrays and objects can be nested arbitrarily, allowing the developer to construct complex JSON documents. The array elements in JSON documents can be of different types. The following example shows how to construct an account with name as text value, address as JSON object, and rank as an array:

```
car_portal=# SELECT '{"name":"John", "Address":{"Street":"Some street",
"city":"Some city"}, "rank":[5,3,4,5,2,3,4,5]}'::JSONB;
                                            jsonb
--------------------------------------------------------------------------
----------------------------------------
 {"name": "John", "rank": [5, 3, 4, 5, 2, 3, 4, 5], "Address": {"city":
"Some city", "Street": "Some street"}}
(1 row)
```

One could get the JSON object field as a JSON object or as text. Also, JSON fields can be retrieved using the index or the field name. The following table summarizes the JSON retrieval operators:

Json	Text	Description
->	->>	This returns a JSON field either using the field index or field name
#>	#>>	This returns a JSON field defined by a specified path

To get the address and city from the JSON object created before, one could use two methods as follows (note that the field names of JSON objects are case sensitive):

```
CREATE TABLE json_doc ( doc jsonb );
INSERT INTO json_doc SELECT '{"name":"John", "Address":{"Street":"Some
street", "city":"Some city"}, "rank":[5,3,4,5,2,3,4,5]}'::JSONB ;
```

To return the city from the previous `json` doc in TEXT format, one can use either the ->> or #>> operators, as follows:

```
SELECT doc->'Address'->>'city', doc#>>'{Address, city}' FROM json_doc WHERE
doc->>'name' = 'John';
 ?column? | ?column?
-----------+-----------
 Some city | Some city
(1 row)
```

In older version of Postgres, such as 9.4, it is quite difficult to manipulate JSON documents. However, in the newer version, a lot of operators were introduced such as || to concatenate two JSON objects, and – which is used to delete a key-value pair. A simple approach to manipulating a JSON object in older versions of PostgreSQL is to convert it to text then use regular expressions to replace or delete an element, and finally, cast the text to JSON again. To delete the rank from the account object one can do the following:

```
SELECT (regexp_replace(doc::text, '"rank":(.*)],',''))::jsonb FROM json_doc
WHERE doc->>'name' = 'John';
```

The functions `jsonb_set` and `json_insert` were introduced in PostgreSQL 9.5 and PostgreSQL 9.6 respectively. These functions allow us to amend a JSON object to insert into a JSON key-value pair:

```
car_portal=# update json_doc SET doc = jsonb_insert(doc,
'{hobby}','["swim", "read"]', true) RETURNING * ;
                                                                       doc
---------- ---------------------------------------------------------------------
------------------------------------------------------------------ --------
```

```
{"name": "John", "rank": [5, 3, 4, 5, 2, 3, 4, 5], "hobby": ["swim",
"read"], "Address": {"city": "Some city", "Street": "Some street"}}
```

To amend an existing key-value pair one can do the following:

```
car_portal=# update json_doc SET doc = jsonb_set(doc, '{hobby}','["read"]',
true) RETURNING * ;
 doc
-------------------------------------------------------------------------
-------------------------------------------------------


 {"name": "John", "rank": [5, 3, 4, 5, 2, 3, 4, 5], "hobby": ["read"],
"Address": {"city": "Some city", "Street": "Some street"}}
```

The following code shows how to delete a key-value pair:

```
car_portal=# update json_doc SET doc = doc -'hobby' RETURNING * ;
                                                    doc
-------------------------------------------------------------------------
------------------------------------


 {"name": "John", "rank": [5, 3, 4, 5, 2, 3, 4, 5], "Address": {"city":
"Some city", "Street": "Some street"}}
```

The full list of JSON functions and operators can be found at: `https://www.postgresql.org/docs/current/static/functions-json.html`

Indexing a JSON data type

JSONB documents can be indexed using the GIN index, and the index can be used for the following operators:

- @>: Does the left JSON value contain the right value?
- ?: Does the key string exist in the JSON doc?
- ?&: Do any of the elements in the text array exist in the JSON doc?
- ?|: Do all the keys/elements in the text array exist in the JSON doc?

To see the effect of indexing on the `json_doc` table, let's create an index and disable sequential scan as follows:

```
CREATE INDEX ON json_doc(doc);
SET enable_seqscan = off;
```

We can use the following code to test the `index` function:

```
car_portal=# EXPLAIN SELECT * FROM json_doc WHERE doc @> '{"name":"John"}';
                                QUERY PLAN
-------------------------------------------------------------------------
-------------
 Index Only Scan using json_doc_doc_idx on json_doc (cost=0.13..12.16
rows=1 width=32)
    Filter: (doc @> '{"name": "John"}'::jsonb)
(2 rows)
```

A JSON document can be converted into a set using the `json_to_record()` function. This is quite useful since we can sort and filter data as in normal tables. In addition to that, one can aggregate data from several rows and construct an array of JSON objects via the `jsosn_agg()` function.

Providing a RESTful API interface for PostgreSQL

It is convenient to provide an interface to share data commonly used by several applications via a RESTful API. Let's assume we have a table that is used by several applications; one way to make these applications aware of that table is to create a **data access object (DAO)** for that table, wrap it in a library, and then reuse that library in those applications. This approach has some disadvantages, such as resolving library dependency and mismatching library versions. Also, deploying new versions of a library requires a lot of effort because applications using that library need to be compiled, tested, and deployed.

The advantage of providing a `RESTful` API interface for the PostgreSQL database is to allow easy access to data. Also, it allows the developer to utilize microservice architecture, which leads to better agility.

There are several open source frameworks to set up a `RESTful` API interface for PostgreSQL such as `psql-api`, and `PostgREST`. To set up a complete CRUD API using Nginx, one can use the Nginx PostgreSQL upstream module, `ngx_postgres`, which is very easy to use and well supported. Unfortunately, it is not available as a `Debian` package, which means that one needs to compile Nginx and install it manually.

In the following example, a `RESTful` API to retrieve data is presented using Nginx and memcached, assuming that the data can fit completely in the memory. PostgreSQL pushes data to the memcached server, and Nginx pulls the data from the memcached server. Memcached is used to cache data and as an intermediary layer between Postgres and Nginx.

As memcached uses the key-value data structure, one needs to identify the key to get data. Nginx uses the URI and passed arguments to map a certain request to a memcached value. In the following example, RESTful API best practices are not covered, as this is only for a technical demonstration. Also, in a production environment, one could combine caching and the PostgreSQL Nginx upstream module, ngx_postgres, to achieve a highly performant CRUD system. By combining memcached and ngx_postgres, one could get rid of the limitation of **RAM** size.

In order to push data to a memcached server, the PostgreSQL pgmemcache module is required. To install pgmemcache one can add it to the template1 to be available for the new databases. Also, let's add it to the car_portal database:

```
$sudo apt-get install -y postgresql-10-pgmemcache
$psql template1 -c "CREATE EXTENSION pgmemcache"
$psql car_portal -c "CREATE EXTENSION pgmemcache"
```

To install the Nginx and memcached server on Ubuntu or Debian OS, one can execute the following commands:

```
$sudo apt-get install -y nginx
$sudo apt-get install -y memcached
```

Also, to add the memcached server permanently to the PostgreSQL server, one can add the following custom variable in the customized options settings block in the PostgreSQL.conf file:

```
$echo "pgmemcache.default_servers =
'localhost'">>/etc/postgresql/10/main/postgresql.conf
$/etc/init.d/postgresql reload
```

To test the memcached and pgmemcache extensions, one can use the memcached_add(key,value) and memcached_get(key) functions to populate and retrieve a dictionary memcached value, as follows:

```
car_portal=# SELECT memcache_add('/1', 'hello');
 memcache_add
--------------
 t
(1 row)

car_portal=# SELECT memcache_get('/1');
 memcache_get
--------------
 hello
(1 row)
```

We have used Linux for demonstrating this use case due to the simplicity of installation. If you are working with windows machine, one can easily install a Linux flavor via virtual box. Finally, Nginx can be installed on windows , but the functionality is limited. For more information `http://nginx.org/en/docs/windows.html`.

To get a full list of `memcache` functions, one can run the following meta command `\df memcache_*`.

In order to allow Nginx to access memcached, the Nginx server needs to be configured, and the Nginx server configuration needs to be reloaded in order for the configuration to take effect. The following is a minimal Nginx configuration file, `nginx.conf`, to allow access to the memcached server. Note that in Ubuntu, the Nginx configuration file is located under `/etc/nginx/nginx.conf`:

```
# cat /etc/nginx/nginx.conf
user www-data;
worker_processes 4;
pid /run/nginx.pid;
events {
  worker_connections 800;
}

http {
  server {
    location / {
      set $memcached_key "$uri";
      memcached_pass 127.0.0.1:11211;
      default_type application/json;
      add_header x-header-memcached true;
    }
  }
}
```

In the preceding example, the Nginx web server is used to serve the responses from the memcached server defined by the `memcached_pass` variable. The response from memcached is obtained by the key, which is the **uniform resource identifier** (URI). The default response type is JSON. Finally, the `x-header-memcached` header is set to true to enable troubleshooting.

To test the Nginx server setting, let's retrieve the value of the /1 key generated by the pgmemcache PostgreSQL extension, as follows:

```
curl -I -X GET http://127.0.0.1/1
HTTP/1.1 200 OK
Server: nginx/1.10.3 (Ubuntu)
Date: Wed, 01 Nov 2017 17:29:07 GMT
Content-Type: application/json
Content-Length: 5
Connection: keep-alive
x-header-memcached: true
Accept-Ranges: bytes
```

Note that the server responded successfully to the request, the response type is marked as JSON and the response is obtained by memcached as shown by the header. Let's assume that we want to have a RESTful web service to present user account information, including the account ID, first name, last name, and email from the account table. The functions row_to_json (), to_jason(), and to_jsonb() can be used to construct a JSON document from a relational row, as follows:

```
car_portal=# SELECT to_json (row(account_id,first_name, last_name, email))
FROM car_portal_app.account LIMIT 1;
                            to_json
------------------------------------------------------------
 {"f1":1,"f2":"James","f3":"Butt","f4":"jbutt@gmail.com"}
(1 row)

car_portal=# SELECT to_json (account) FROM car_portal_app.account LIMIT 1;
                                                            to_json
------------------------------------------------------------------------
------------------------------------------------------------
{"account_id":1,"first_name":"James","last_name":"Butt","email":"jbutt@gmai
l.com","password":"1b9ef408e82e38346e6ebebf2dcc5ece"}
(1 row)
```

In the preceding example, the usage of the row (account_id, first_name, last_ name, email) construct caused the to_jsonb function to be unable to determine the attribute names, and the names were replaced with f1, f2, and so on.

To work around this, one needs to give a name to the row. This can be done in several ways, such as using subqueries or giving an alias to the result; the following example shows one way to resolve the issue by specifying aliases using CTE:

```
WITH account_info(account_id, first_name, last_name, email) AS ( SELECT
account_id,first_name, last_name, email FROM car_portal_app. account LIMIT
1 ) SELECT to_json(account_info) FROM account_info;
                              to_json
-----------------------------------------------------------------------
---------
{"account_id":1,"first_name":"James","last_name":"Butt","email":"jbutt@gmai
l.com"}
(1 row)
```

To generate entries for the `account` table using `account_id`, the primary key, as the hash key, one can use the following:

```
SELECT memcache_add('/'||account_id, (SELECT to_json(foo) FROM (SELECT
account_id, first_name,last_name, email ) AS FOO )::text) FROM
car_portal_app.account;
```

Note that at this point, one can access data from the Nginx server. To test this, let's get the JSON representation for the account with `account_id` equaling 1 as follows:

```
$ curl -sD - -o -X GET http://127.0.0.1/2
HTTP/1.1 200 OK
Server: nginx/1.10.3 (Ubuntu)
Date: Wed, 01 Nov 2017 17:39:37 GMT
Content-Type: application/json
Content-Length: 103
Connection: keep-alive
x-header-memcached: true
Accept-Ranges: bytes

{"account_id":2,"first_name":"Josephine","last_name":"Darakjy","email":"jos
ephine_darakjy@darakjy.org"}
```

Also, one needs to be careful with handling transaction rollbacks and have the appropriate caching strategy to decrease data inconsistency between the cache and database system. The following example shows the effect of a rollback on memcached data:

```
BEGIN
car_portal=# SELECT memcache_add('is_transactional?', 'No');
 memcache_add
--------------
 t
(1 row)
```

```
car_portal=# Rollback;
ROLLBACK
car_portal=# SELECT memcache_get('is_transactional?');
 memcache_get
--------------
 No
(1 row)
```

To ensure that the account table data is consistent with the memcached server data, one can add an `AFTER INSERT OR UPDATE OR DELETE` trigger to reflect the changes performed on the table on memcached. This trigger can be marked as `DEFERRABLE INITIALLY DEFERRED` to postpone amending memcache. In other words, memcache is manipulated if all the changes by a certain transaction succeed.

A PostgreSQL full text search

PostgreSQL provides a full text search capability, which is used to overcome SQL pattern matching operators, including `LIKE` and `ILIKE`, boosting the performance of the text search. For example, even though an index on text using the `text_pattern_op` class is supported, this index cannot be used to match a non-anchored text search.

Another issue with the traditional `LIKE` and `ILIKE` operators is the ranking based on similarity and natural language linguistic support. The `LIKE` and `ILIKE` operators always evaluate a Boolean value: either as `TRUE` or as `FALSE`.

In addition to ranking and non-anchored text search support, PostgreSQL full text search provides many other features. Full text search supports dictionaries, so it can support language, such as synonyms.

The tsquery and tsvector data types

The full text search is based on the `tsvector` and `tsquery` datatypes. Here, `tsvector` represents a document in a normalized state and `tsquery` represents the query.

The tsvector data type

The `tsvector` datatype is a sorted list of distinct lexeme. Lexeme is the fundamental unit of word, simply speaking one can see a lexeme as the word root without a suffix or inflectional forms or grammatical variants . The following example shows casting a text to a `tsvector` as follows:

```
car_portal=# SELECT 'A wise man always has something to say, whereas a fool
always needs to say something'::tsvector;
                                    tsvector
----------------------------------------------------------------------
------------------
 'A' 'a' 'always' 'fool' 'has' 'man' 'needs' 'say' 'say,' 'something' 'to'
'whereas' 'wise'
(1 row)
```

Casting a text to `tsvector` does not normalize the document completely due to the lack of linguistic rules. To normalize the preceding example, one can use the `to_tsvector()` function to normalize the text properly, as follows:

```
car_portal=# SELECT to_tsvector('english', 'A wise man always has something
to say, whereas a fool always needs to say something');
                                  to_tsvector
----------------------------------------------------------------------
-----------
 'alway':4,12 'fool':11 'man':3 'need':13 'say':8,15 'someth':6,16
'wherea':9 'wise':2
(1 row)
```

As shown in the preceding example, the `to_tsvector` function stripped some letters, such as s from `always`, and also generated the integer position of lexemes, which can be used for proximity ranking.

The tsquery data type

The `tsquery` data type is used to search for certain lexeme. Lexeme can be combined with the & (AND), | (OR), and ! (NOT) operators. Note that the NOT operator has the highest precedence, followed by AND and then OR. Also, parentheses can be used to group lexemes and operators to force a certain order. The following example shows how we can search for certain lexemes using `tsquery`, `tsvector`, and the match operator @@:

```
car_portal=# SELECT 'A wise man always has something to say, whereas a fool
always needs to say something'::tsvector @@ 'wise'::tsquery;
 ?column?
----------
```

```
t
(1 row)
```

The tsquery also has the to_tsquery function to convert text to lexemes, as shown here:

```
car_portal=# SELECT to_tsquery('english', 'wise & man');
   to_tsquery
----------------
 'wise' & 'man'
(1 row)
```

Searching for phrases in tsquery is possible by using the followed by tsquery operator <->, this means the result is matched if the two words are adjacent and in the given order:

```
car_portal=# SELECT to_tsvector('A wise man always has something to say,
whereas a fool always needs to say something') @@ to_tsquery('wise <->
man');
 ?column?
----------
 t
(1 row)
```

Pattern matching

pattern matching is the act of checking a given sequence of words for the presence of the constituents of some pattern. There are several factors affecting the result of pattern matching, including:

- Text normalization
- Dictionary
- Ranking

If the text is not normalized, a text search might not return the expected result. The following examples show how pattern matching can fail with unnormalized text:

```
car_portal=# SELECT 'elephants'::tsvector @@ 'elephant';
 ?column?
----------
 f
(1 row)
```

In the preceding query, casting elephants to `tsvector` and the implicit casting of elephant to the query does not generate normalized lexemes due to missing information about the dictionary. To add dictionary information, `to_tsvector` and `to_tsquery` can be used as follows:

```
car_portal=# SELECT to_tsvector('english', 'elephants') @@
to_tsquery('english', 'elephant');
 ?column?
----------
 t
(1 row)

car_portal=#
car_portal=# SELECT to_tsvector('simple', 'elephants') @@
to_tsquery('simple', 'elephant');
 ?column?
----------
 f
(1 row)
```

Full text search supports pattern matching based on ranks. The `tsvector` lexemes can be marked with the labels A, B, C, and D; where D is the default and A has the highest rank. The set weight function can be used to assign a weight to `tsvector` explicitly, as follows:

```
car_portal=# SELECT setweight(to_tsvector('english', 'elephants'),'A') ||
setweight(to_tsvector('english', 'dolphin'),'B');
         ?column?
-------------------------
 'dolphin':2B 'eleph':1A
(1 row)
```

For ranking, there are two functions: `ts_rank` and `ts_rank_cd`. The `ts_rank` function is used for standard ranking, while `ts_rank_cd` is used for the cover density ranking technique. The following example shows the result of `ts_rank_cd` when used to search `eleph` and `dolphin`, respectively:

```
car_portal=# SELECT ts_rank_cd
(setweight(to_tsvector('english','elephants'),'A') ||
setweight(to_tsvector('english', 'dolphin'),'B'),'eleph' );
 ts_rank_cd
------------
          1
(1 row)

car_portal=# SELECT ts_rank_cd
(setweight(to_tsvector('english','elephants'),'A') ||
```

```
setweight(to_tsvector('english', 'dolphin'),'B'),'dolphin' );
 ts_rank_cd
------------
        0.4
(1 row)
```

Ranking is often used to enhance, filter out, and order the result of pattern matching. In real-life scenarios, different document sections can have different weights. For example, when searching for a movie, the highest weight could be given to the movie title and main character, and less weight could be given to the summary of the movie plot.

Full text search indexing

GIN indexes are the preferred indexes for full text search, one can simply create an index on the document using the to_tsvector function, as follows:

```
CREATE INDEX ON <table_name> USING GIN (to_tsvector('english', <attribute
name>));
-- OR
CREATE INDEX ON <table_name> USING GIN (to_tsvector(<attribute name>));
```

The query predicated is used to determine the index definition, for example, if the predicate looks like to_tsvector('english',..)@@ to_tsquey (.., then the first index will be used to evaluate the query.

GIST can be used to index tsvector and tsquery, while GIN can be used to index tsvector only. The GIST index is lossy and can return false matches, so PostgreSQL automatically rechecks the returned result and filters out false matches. False matches can reduce performance due to the records' random access cost. The GIN index stores only the lexemes of tsvector and not the weight labels. Due to this, the GIN index could also be considered lossy if weights are involved in the query.

The performance of the GIN and GIST indexes depends on the number of unique words, so it is recommended to use dictionaries to reduce the total number of unique words. The GIN index is faster to search and slower to build and requires more space than GIST. Increasing the value of maintenance_work_mem setting can improve the GIN index's build time, but this does not work for the GIST index.

Summary

PostgreSQL is very rich in built-in data types and external extensions. It can be easily extended using the C and C++ languages. In fact, PostgreSQL provides an extension-building infrastructure called PGXS so that extensions can be built against an installed server. Some PostgreSQL extensions, such as PostGIS, require complete chapters to be discussed.

PostgreSQL provides a very rich set of data types, such as XML, `hstore`, JSON, array, and so on. These data types can be used to ease the developer's life by not reinventing the wheel and utilizing their very rich set of functions and operators. Also, several PostgreSQL data types, such as `hstore` and JSON, can increase the developer's agility because the database's physical design is not often amended.

PostgreSQL arrays are very mature; they have a rich set of operators and functions. PostgreSQL can handle multidimensional arrays with different base types. Arrays are useful when modeling multi-valued attributes, as well as when performing several tasks that are difficult to achieve using only the pure relational model.

Hash store has been supported in PostgreSQL since version 9.0; it allows the developer to store key values in the data structure. Hash store is very useful when modeling semi-structured data, as well as at increasing the developer's agility.

Both JSON and XML documents are supported, allowing PostgreSQL to support different document exchange formats. PostgreSQL provides several JSON functions to convert rows to JSON and vice versa. This allows PostgreSQL to server also `RESTful` web services easily.

PostgreSQL also supports full text search. Full text search solves several problems related to linguistics, as well as non-anchored text search performance, and enhances the end user's experience and satisfaction.

The next chapter, discusses in a greater detail the ACID properties and the relation between these properties and concurrency controls. This chapter also discusses several concepts such as isolation levels and their side effects and it shows these side effects using SQL examples. Finally, the chapters discusses different locking methods including pessimistic locking strategies such as row locking and advisory locks.

10
Transactions and Concurrency Control

The relational model describes the logical unit of processing data as the *transaction*; transactions can be defined as a set of operations performed in sequence. Relational databases provide a locking mechanism to ensure the integrity of transactions.

In this chapter, we focus on the basic concepts that guarantee the correct execution of transactions. Also, we will discuss the concurrency control problems, locking systems, dead locks, and advisory locks.

Transactions

A transaction is a set of operations which might include updating, deleting, inserting, and retrieving data. These operations are often embedded in a higher level language, or can be explicitly wrapped in a transaction block using BEGIN and END statements. A transaction is successfully executed if all the operations in the transaction are successfully executed. If an operation in a transaction fails, the effect of the partially executed operation on the transaction can be undone.

To control the beginning and the end of a transaction explicitly, one can use the BEGIN statement to mark the the start of transaction , and the statements END or COMMIT to mark the end of the transaction. The following example shows how to explicitly execute an SQL statement in a transaction:

```
BEGIN;
CREATE TABLE employee (id serial primary key, name text, salary numeric);
COMMIT;
```

One usage of transactions, other than ensuring data integrity, is to provide an easy way to undo changes to the database in development and testing mode. A transaction block can be combined with a SAVEPOINT statement to work with data interactively; a SAVEPOINT is a mark inside a transaction block where the state is saved. Savepoints undo parts of a transaction instead of the whole transaction. The following example shows how a SAVEPOINT can be used:

```
BEGIN;
UPDATE employee set salary = salary*1.1;
SAVEPOINT increase_salary;
UPDATE employee set salary = salary + 500 WHERE name ='john';
ROLLBACK to increase_salary;
COMMIT;
```

In the preceding example, the UPDATE employee set salary = salary*1.1; statement is committed to the database, while the UPDATE employee set salary = salary + 500 WHERE name ='john'; statement is rolled back.

All statements executed by PostgreSQL are transactional, even if you do not open a transaction block explicitly. For example, if you execute several statements without wrapping them in a transaction block, then each statement is executed in a separate transaction.

The transaction behavior can be controlled by the database driver and application frameworks such as Java EE or Spring. For example, in JDBC, one can specify whether he or she would like to set the autocommit property or not.

Check your client tools to check whether BEGIN and COMMIT are issued automatically.

Transaction and ACID properties

A fundamental precept of relational databases is the concept of guaranteeing Atomicity, Consistency, Isolation, and Durability (**ACID**) of its operations. This is referred to as ACID compliance.

A transaction is a logical execution unit and is indivisible, which means all-or-none, also known as **atomicity**; this statement holds true regardless of the failure reason. For example, a transaction might fail due to an error such as a mathematical error, the misspelling of a relation name, or even an operating system crash.

After the transaction is successfully committed, the transaction effect must persist even against hardware crashes; this property is referred to as **durability**. Furthermore, in a multi-user environment several users can execute several transactions, and each transaction contains a set of actions or operations. Each transaction should be executed without interference from concurrently running transactions; this property is called **isolation**.

Finally, the **consistency** property is not a property of a transaction itself but rather a desirable effect of transaction isolation and atomicity. Database consistency is concerned with business requirements, which are defined via rules, including triggers, constraints, and any combination thereof. If the database state is consistent immediately before executing a transaction, then the database state must also be consistent after executing the transaction. Database consistency is the responsibility of the developer who codes the transaction.

ACID properties are not easily met. For example, **durability** has heavy requirements because there are a lot of factors that might cause data loss, such as an operating system crash, power outage, hard disk failure, and so on. Also, computer architecture is quite complex, for example, the data can flow through several layers of storage, such as memory, IO buffers, and the disk cache, until it is persisted on the hard disk.

By default, PostgreSQL uses `fsync`, which transfers all modified buffer cache pages to a file on the disk so that changes can be retrieved in the event of a system crash or reboot.

Transaction and concurrency

Concurrency can be defined as the interleaving of actions in time to give the appearance of simultaneous execution. Concurrency tries to solve several issues, including sharing global resources safely, and handling errors in multiple execution contexts.

Concurrency is pervasive in computing, occurring everywhere from low-level hardware design to worldwide access of shared data. Examples of concurrency handling can be found in instruction pipe-lining in CPU micro-architecture and threading in operating system design. Even in our daily lives, we can encounter concurrency when using tools such as Git. A common scenario is when several developers are sharing the same code base, introducing conflicts, and finally resolving these conflicts by doing merges.

Concurrency and parallelism can be confused. Parallelism is distinguished by using extra computational units to do more work per unit time, while concurrency manages access to shared resources; thus, parallelism is often easier to handle. Concurrency is a more generalized form of parallelism, which can include time-slicing as a form of virtual parallelism.

Many databases utilize parallelism in addition to concurrency. PostgreSQL in fact has also utilized parallelism since version 9.6 to increase query performance. **Greenplum**, which is a fork of PostgreSQL, also uses **massively parallel processing (MPP)** to increase performance and to handle data warehousing loads.

A fundamental problem in concurrency is actions meddling with each other while accessing a shared global resource. No conflict will occur if developers do not write code in a concurrent manner but rather in a serial manner, one after the other. However, in reality, this is not practical and causes a lot of delay in completing tasks.

Concurrency control coordinates the execution of concurrent transactions in a multiuser environment and handles potential problems such as lost updates, uncommitted data, and inconsistent data retrieval.

Concurrency is a good selling point for PostgreSQL, because PostgreSQL is able to handle concurrency even on significant read and write activity. In PostgreSQL, write activity does not block read activity and vice versa. PostgreSQL uses a technique called **multiversion concurrency control (MVCC)**; this technique is also used by several commercial and non-commercial databases, such as Oracle, MySQL with InoDB engine, Informix, Firebird, and CouchDB.

Note that MVCC is not the only way to handle concurrency in RDBMS; SQL Server uses another technique called **strong strict two-phase locking (SS2PL)**.

MVCC in PostgreSQL

Accessing the same data at the same time for read and write purposes might cause an inconsistent data state or wrong reads. For example, the reader might get partially written data. The simplest technique to solve this is to lock the reader from reading the data until the writer finishes writing the data. This solution causes a lot of contention, thus the performance penalty, and causes the reader to wait until the writer is done with the job.

In MVCC, when the data is updated, a newer version of the data is created, and the original data is not overwritten. That means there are several versions of data, hence the name multiversion. Each transaction can access a version of the data based on the transaction isolation level, current transaction status, and tuple versions.

Each transaction in PostgreSQL is assigned to a transaction ID called **XID**. The **XID** is incremented whenever a new transaction is started. The transaction IDs are 4 byte unsigned integers, that is around 4.2 billion compilations. New transaction assignments are based on a modular arithmetic function, which means the normal **XID** space is circular with no endpoint, and all transactions -around two billion- before a certain transaction are considered old and are visible to that particular transaction.

The following example shows how transaction IDs are incremented; note that, without opening an explicit transaction, each statement caused the XID to be incremented:

```
test=# SELECT txid_current();
 txid_current
--------------
          682
(1 row)

test=# SELECT 1;
 ?column?
----------
        1
(1 row)

test=# SELECT txid_current();
 txid_current
--------------
          683

(1 row)
test=# BEGIN;
BEGIN
test=# SELECT txid_current();
 txid_current
--------------
          684
(1 row)

test=# SELECT 1;
 ?column?
----------
        1
(1 row)
test=# SELECT txid_current();
 txid_current
--------------
          684
(1 row)
```

Due to the nature of transaction ID assignments, one needs to be careful when handling them. First of all, never disable the vacuum process, otherwise your database will shut down due to a transaction wraparound issue. Also, when you have bulk insert and update wrap the statements in an explicit transaction block. Finally, heavily updated tables might get bloated due to dead rows.

Internally, PostgreSQL assigns the transaction ID which creates a tuple to `xmin`, and the transaction ID of the transaction deletes the tuple to `xmax`. The update is handled internally in MVCC as `DELETE` and `INSERT` and, in this case, another version of the tuple is created. PostgreSQL uses the information about the tuple's creation and deletion, transaction status - `committed`, `in progress`, and `rolled back`, `isolation levels`, and `transaction visibility` to handle concurrency issues. The following example shows how transaction IDs are assigned to the tuple `XMIN` column in the case of an insert scenario:

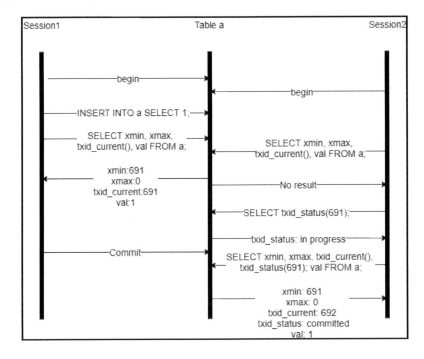

Transaction isolation levels

A transaction isolation level can be set by the developer by invoking the following SQL statement:

```
SET TRANSACTION ISOLATION LEVEL { SERIALIZABLE | REPEATABLE READ | READ
COMMITTED | READ UNCOMMITTED}
```

The SET TRANSACTION ISOLATION LEVEL statement should be called inside a transaction block before any query, otherwise, it will have no effect. An alternative is to use the following syntax:

```
BEGIN TRANSACTION ISOLATION LEVEL { SERIALIZABLE | REPEATABLE READ | READ
COMMITTED | READ UNCOMMITTED}
```

Finally, one can change the whole default database isolation level to SERIALIZABLE as follows:

```
ALTER DATABASE <DATABASE NAME> SET DEFAULT_TRANSACTION_ISOLATION TO
SERIALIZABLE ;
```

As shown by the preceding SQL statement, the transaction isolation levels are:

- SERIALIZABLE: The SERIALIZABLE isolation level is the strongest consistency level; it relieves the developer of planning for concurrency effects. The cost of using the serialize isolation model is often performance. In the SQL standard, SERIALIZABLE is the default isolation model. In PostgreSQL, the default isolation model is READ COMMITTED.

- REPEATABLE READ: REPEATABLE READ is the second strongest transaction isolation level; it is similar to READ COMMITTED in that it allows only the reading of committed data. It also guarantees that any data read cannot be changed.

- READ COMMITTED: This is the default PostgreSQL model; it allows committed data to be read by the transaction. In this level, performance is favored over preciseness.

- READ UNCOMMITTED: This is the weakest transaction isolation level. It allows uncommitted data to be read.

> READ UNCOMMITTED is not supported in PostgreSQL and is treated as READ COMMITTED. PostgreSQL only supports three levels.

The transaction isolation level can be explained by having a look at the side effects of each level, which are:

- Dirty read: A dirty read occurs when a transaction reads data from a tuple that has been modified by another running transaction and not yet committed. In PostgreSQL, this cannot happen since READ UNCOMMITTED is unsupported.
- Nonrepeatable read: A nonrepeatable read occurs when, during the course of a transaction, a row is retrieved twice and the values within the row differ between reads. A nonrepeatable read occurs in the READ COMMITTED isolation level and is often a result of updating a row several times with other transactions.
- Phantom read: A phantom read occurs when a new row (or rows) disappears since the beginning of the transaction. This is often a result of committed inserts followed by committed deletes. A phantom read occurs when you select a set of rows several times and a different result is returned within the same transaction. A phantom read occurs in the READ COMMITTED and REPEATABLE READ levels based on the SQL standard definition. In PostgreSQL, a phantom read occurs only in READ COMMITTED.
- Serialization anomaly: The result of executing a group of transactions is inconsistent with all possible ordering of running these transactions. This can occur only in REPEATABLE READ.

SQL standard allows phantom read in the REPEATABLE READ isolation level. In PostgreSQL, that is not allowed. That means that only a serialization anomaly can happen in REPEATABLE READ.

To understand different transaction isolation side effects, let's show the nonrepeatable read side effect; for that, we will use a test_tx_level table, which is defined as follows:

```
postgres=# CREATE TABLE test_tx_level AS SELECT 1 AS val;
SELECT 1
postgres=# TABLE test_tx_level ;
 val
-----
   1
(1 row)
```

To test repeatable read, the default transaction isolation model READ COMMITTED will be used; the **T** as in **T1** is used to indicate the execution time in ascending order, as follows:

	Session 1	Session 2

T1	`postgres=# BEGIN;`
	`BEGIN`
	`postgres=# SELECT * FROM test_tx_level ;`
	` val`
	`-----`
	` 1`
	`(1 row)`	

T2		`postgres=# BEGIN;`
		`BEGIN`
		`postgres=# UPDATE`
		`test_tx_level SET val = 2;`
		`UPDATE 1`
		`postgres=# COMMIT;`
		`COMMIT`

T3	`postgres=# SELECT * FROM test_tx_level ;`
	`val`
	`-----`
	` 2`
	`(1 row)`
	`postgres=# COMMIT;`
	`COMMIT`	

The `val` value has changed from 1 to 2 in **session 1**. The change that are committed by **session 2** are reflected in **session 1**. This is called a nonrepeatable read. Also notice that we have used BEGIN without specifying the transaction isolation level, and in this case, the default isolation level is used.

To check phantom read, again, the default transaction isolation level will be used, as follows:

	Session 1	Session 2

T1	`postgres=# BEGIN;`
	`BEGIN`
	`postgres=# SELECT count(*) FROM`
	`test_tx_level ;`
	`count`
	`-------`
	` 1`
	`(1 row)`	

| T2 | | ```
postgres=# BEGIN;
BEGIN
postgres=# INSERT INTO
test_tx_level SELECT 2;
INSERT 0 1
postgres=# COMMIT;
COMMIT
``` |
| T3 | ```
postgres=# SELECT count(*) FROM
test_tx_level ;
 count
 -------
 2
(1 row)
postgres=# COMMIT;
``` | |

Phantom read and nonrepeatable read can occur, as shown in the preceding examples, in the READ COMMITTED transaction isolation level. The scope of nonrepeatable read is often a certain row or set of rows, while the scope of phantom read is all the table. Nonrepeatable read occurs when the transaction reads committed **updates** from another transaction, while phantom read happens as a result of committed **inserts** and **deletes**.

If one runs the same preceding examples with the SERIALIZABLE and REPEATABLE READ isolation level, we will see that the result of **session 1** is not affected by **session 2,** as shown in the following example:

	Session 1	**Session 2**
| T1 | ```
BEGIN TRANSACTION ISOLATION LEVEL
SERIALIZABLE ;
BEGIN
postgres=# SELECT count(*) FROM
test_tx_level ;
 count
 -------
     2
(1 row)
``` | |
| T2 | | ```
postgres=# BEGIN;
BEGIN
postgres=# INSERT INTO
test_tx_level SELECT 2;
INSERT 0 1
postgres=# COMMIT;
COMMIT
``` |

| T3 | postgres=# SELECT count(*) FROM test_tx_level ;
 count

     2
(1 row) | |

In PostgreSQL versions prior to 9.1, PostgreSQL has only two transaction isolation levels. This changed with the introduction of PostgreSQL 9.1, where a true SERIALIZABLE transaction isolation model is submitted. The SERIALIZABLE transaction isolation level protects data against many anomalies, such as write skew. Write skew happens when two transactions read overlapping data, concurrently make updates, and finally commit the data. For example, let's assume we have a table containing ones and zeros; the first transaction wants to change the ones to zeros, and the second transaction wants to change the zeros to ones. If transactions are executed in a serial manner, we should get either ones or zeros based on which transaction is executed first. To demonstrate this anomaly, let's create a table, as follows:

```
postgres=# CREATE TABLE zero_or_one (val int);
CREATE TABLE
postgres=# INSERT INTO zero_or_one SELECT n % 2 FROM generate_series(1,10)
as foo(n) ;
INSERT 0 10
postgres=# SELECT array_agg(val) FROM zero_or_one ;
      array_agg
---------------------
 {1,0,1,0,1,0,1,0,1,0}
(1 row)
```

To see the effect of write skew, let's start two sessions with the REPEATABLE isolation level, as follows:

	Session 1	Session 2

T1	postgres=# BEGIN TRANSACTION ISOLATION LEVEL REPEATABLE READ ;
	BEGIN
	postgres=# UPDATE zero_or_one SET val = 1 WHERE val = 0;
	UPDATE 5	

T2		`postgres=# BEGIN TRANSACTION`
		`ISOLATION LEVEL REPEATABLE READ ;`
		`BEGIN`
		`postgres=# UPDATE zero_or_one SET`
		`val =0 WHERE val =1;`
		`UPDATE 5`
		`postgres=# COMMIT;`
		`COMMIT`

T3	`postgres=# COMMIT;` `COMMIT`	

Let's now have a look at the final result of the table:

```
postgres=# SELECT array_agg(val) FROM zero_or_one ;
       array_agg
----------------------
 {1,1,1,1,1,0,0,0,0,0}
(1 row)
```

To see what happens in the serializable transaction mode, let's truncate the tables and rerun the example:

```
postgres=# truncate zero_or_one ;
TRUNCATE TABLE
postgres=# INSERT INTO zero_or_one SELECT n % 2 FROM generate_series(1,10)
as foo(n) ;
INSERT 0 10
```

	Session 1	**Session 2**

T1	`postgres=# BEGIN TRANSACTION ISOLATION LEVEL`
	`SERIALIZABLE ;`
	`BEGIN`
	`postgres=# UPDATE zero_or_one SET val = 1`
	`WHERE val = 0;`
	`UPDATE 5`	

T2		`postgres=# BEGIN`
		`TRANSACTION ISOLATION LEVEL`
		`SERIALIZABLE ;`
		`BEGIN`
		`postgres=# UPDATE`
		`zero_or_one SET val =0`
		`WHERE val =1;`
		`UPDATE 5`
		`postgres=# COMMIT;`

| T3 | `postgres=# COMMIT ;`
`ERROR: could not serialize access due to`
`read/write dependencies among transactions`
`DETAIL: Reason code: Canceled on`
`identification as a pivot, during commit`
`attempt.`
`HINT: The transaction might succeed if`
`retried.` | |

In the repeatable read isolation mode, both transactions were executed without an error. However, the end result was wrong. In the case of the serializable isolation level, when there is write skew, transactions will proceed until one transaction commits. The first committer wins and other transactions are rolled back. The first committer wins rule guarantees that we will make progress. Finally, note that only one transaction succeeded and the other has failed. Also note the hint **the transaction might succeed if retried**, to see the final result:

```
postgres=# SELECT array_agg(val) FROM zero_or_one ;
        array_agg
-----------------------
 {0,0,0,0,0,0,0,0,0,0}
(1 row)
```

More information on the REPEATABLE READ and SERIALIZABLE transaction isolation levels can be found on the **serializable snapshot isolation (SSI)** wiki page at `https://wiki.postgresql.org/wiki/SSI`.

Explicit locking

In addition to MVCC locking, one can control locking explicitly when MVCC does not provide a desirable behavior. Generally speaking, PostgreSQL provides three locking mechanisms, which are:

- Table-level locks
- Row-level locks
- Advisory locks

Table-level locks

Tables can be locked in several locking modes; the syntax of the LOCK statement is as follows:

```
LOCK [ TABLE ] [ ONLY ] name [ * ] [, ...] [ IN lockmode MODE ] [ NOWAIT ]

where lockmode is one of:

    ACCESS SHARE | ROW SHARE | ROW EXCLUSIVE | SHARE UPDATE EXCLUSIVE
    | SHARE | SHARE ROW EXCLUSIVE | EXCLUSIVE | ACCESS EXCLUSIVE
```

PostgreSQL locks the table implicitly when invoking an SQL command. It locks the table using the least restrictive mode to increase concurrency. When the developer desires a more restrictive lock, then the LOCK statement can be used.

Table locking modes

Table locks are often acquired automatically, but they can also be acquired explicitly with the LOCK command. The following is the list of locking modes:

- ACCESS SHARE: This mode is acquired by the SELECT statement.
- ROW SHARE: The SELECT FOR UPDATE and SELECT FOR SHARE commands acquire this lock.
- ROW EXCLUSIVE: The statements UPDATE, DELETE, and INSERT acquire this lock mode.
- SHARE UPDATE EXCLUSIVE: This mode is used to protect a table against concurrent schema changes. Acquired by VACUUM (without FULL), ANALYZE, CREATE INDEX CONCURRENTLY, CREATE STATISTICS, and ALTER TABLE VALIDATE and other ALTER TABLE variants.
- SHARE: This mode is used to protect a table against concurrent data changes. Acquired by CREATE INDEX (without CONCURRENTLY).
- SHARE ROW EXCLUSIVE: This mode protects a table against concurrent data changes, and is self-exclusive, so that only one session can hold it at a time. Acquired by CREATE COLLATION, CREATE TRIGGER, and many forms of ALTER TABLE.
- EXCLUSIVE: This is acquired by REFRESH MATERIALIZED VIEW CONCURRENTLY. This mode only allows reading data for the table.

- ACCESS EXCLUSIVE: This mode guarantees that the holder is the only transaction accessing the table in any way. Acquired by the DROP TABLE, TRUNCATE, REINDEX, CLUSTER, VACUUM FULL, and REFRESH MATERIALIZED VIEW (without CONCURRENTLY) commands. Many forms of ALTER TABLE also acquire a lock at this level. This is also the default lock mode for LOCK TABLE statements that do not specify a mode explicitly.

A very important thing to note for each mode is the list of modes that are in conflict with that specific mode. Transactions can't hold locks on conflicting modes on the same table.

Conflicting?	ACCESS SHARE	ROW SHARE	ROW EXCLUSIVE	SHARE UPDATE EXCLUSIVE	SHARE	SHARE ROW EXCLUSIVE	EXCLUSIVE	ACCESS EXCLUSIVE
ACCESS SHARE								yes
ROW SHARE							yes	yes
ROW EXCLUSIVE					yes	yes	yes	yes
SHARE UPDATE EXCLUSIVE				yes	yes	yes	yes	yes
SHARE			yes	yes	yes	yes	yes	yes
SHARE ROW EXCLUSIVE			yes	yes	yes	yes	yes	yes
EXCLUSIVE		yes	yes	yes	yes	yes	yes	yes
ACCESS EXCLUSIVE	yes	yes	yes	yes	yes	yes	yes	yes

As shown in the preceding table, ACCESS EXCLUSIVE conflicts with ACCESS SHARE, which means one cannot perform the SELECT statement on a table if the table is locked in ACCESS EXCLUSIVE mode. Also, one cannot DROP a table if one is reading it. Also note that one can execute SELECT statements in all other modes. So the only mode where a SELECT statement can be blocked is the ACCESS EXCLUSIVE mode.

The following example shows what will happen in the case of dropping a table while another transaction is reading from it:

	Session 1	Session 2

T1	```
	BEGIN;
	BEGIN
	postgres=# SELECT COUNT(*) FROM test_tx_level ;
	 count
	------- 	
	     3
	(1 row)
	
	postgres=# SELECT mode, granted FROM pg_locks where
	relation ='test_tx_level'::regclass::oid;
	     mode
		granted
		-----------------+---------
		 AccessShareLock
			t
			(1 row)
			``	

T2		BEGIN postgres=# DROP TABLE test_tx_level;
T3	postgres=# SELECT mode, granted FROM pg_locks where relation ='test_tx_level'::regclass::oid; mode | granted ---------------------+--------- AccessShareLock | t AccessExclusiveLock | f (2 rows)	

The preceding example shows that the lock is acquired when the data is selected from the table in **session 1** and they are not released. So, once a lock is acquired, the lock is normally held till the end of the transaction. The `pg_locks` table is very handy for understanding locks. It is often used to detect bottlenecks in high concurrency systems. The following view shows lock information in a human-friendly way:

```
CREATE OR REPLACE VIEW lock_info AS
SELECT
    lock1.pid as locked_pid,
    stat1.usename as locked_user,
    stat1.query as locked_statement,
    stat1.state as locked_statement_state,
    stat2.query as locking_statement,
    stat2.state as locking_statement_state,
    now() - stat1.query_start as locking_duration,
    lock2.pid as locking_pid,
    stat2.usename as locking_user
FROM pg_catalog.pg_locks lock1
    JOIN pg_catalog.pg_stat_activity stat1 on lock1.pid = stat1.pid
    JOIN pg_catalog.pg_locks lock2 on
(lock1.locktype,lock1.database,lock1.relation,lock1.page,lock1.tuple,lock1.
virtualxid,lock1.transactionid,lock1.classid,lock1.objid,lock1.objsubid) IS
NOT DISTINCT FROM
(lock2.locktype,lock2.DATABASE,lock2.relation,lock2.page,lock2.tuple,lock2.
virtualxid,lock2.transactionid,lock2.classid,lock2.objid,lock2.objsubid)
    JOIN pg_catalog.pg_stat_activity stat2 on lock2.pid = stat2.pid
WHERE NOT lock1.granted AND lock2.granted;
```

To check the locks:

```
postgres=# SELECT * FROM lock_info ;
-[ RECORD 1 ]-----+-----------------------------------------------------
--------------- -----------
locked_pid | 3736
```

```
locked_user | postgres
locked_statement | DROP TABLE test_tx_level;
locked_statement_state | active
locking_statement | SELECT mode, granted FROM pg_locks where relation
='test_tx_level'::regclass::oid;
locking_statement_state| idle in transaction
locking_duration | 00:09:57.32628
locking_pid | 3695
locking_user | postgres
```

The view shows that the process 3736 tries to execute the DROP TABLE statement and is waiting for the transaction issued by the process ID 3695. Since the process 3695 is doing nothing at the time of running the preceding query, the state of the process is idle in transaction. Finally, the preceding view is a bit misleading, as it shows the locking statement is SELECT mode, granted ..; which is not true. Simply, the pg_state_activity shows the last statement executed by the process. As we said earlier, once the lock is acquired, it is held by the transaction. So the process 3736 is waiting for the transaction started by process 3695 to finish.

Row-level locks

Row-level locking doesn't lock SELECT statements at all, they are used to lock UPDATE and DELETE statements. As in table-level locks, no two transactions can lock a row in conflicting row-level lock mode. Row locking is useful in a scenario where the application inspects the value of the row before updating it. Another scenario is to lock users from updating an old value; for example, if one is editing a document, the application should forbid users from editing it. In PostgreSQL 9.5, the SKIP LOCKED option was introduced, which changes the behavior of row locking. The SKIP LOCKED option is useful in handling batch processing without introducing a high wait time, or handling queues and pools on the database's side.

Row-level lock modes

In older versions, as in PostgreSQL 9.3, there are only two locking modes, which are FOR UPDATE and FOR SHARE. FOR UPDATE is used to acquire an exclusive lock on the row and does not allow other transactions to update or delete it; FOR SHARE is less restrictive, allows other transactions to lock the ROW in FOR SHARE mode, and still does not it allow other transactions to delete or update the row. FOR SHARE is used to handle a nonrepeatable read scenario in a READ COMMITTED transaction isolation level. For example, one could lock the row's FOR SHARE and this will guarantee that the value will not change until the transaction is committed.

FOR SHARE does not handle the lost update problem, since FOR SHARE allows other transactions to lock the row in the same mode. To handle a lost update problem, FOR UPDATE can be used.

 Lost updates happen when two transactions try to update the same row concurrently. See the deadlock section, which presents a lost update scenario.

PostgreSQL also provides the FOR NO KEY UPDATE, which is similar to the FOR UPDATE but the lock is weaker, and FOR KEY SHARE, which is again a weaker form of FOR SHARE. The row-level locking mode conflicts are given in the following table:

Conflicting?	FOR KEY SHARE	FOR SHARE	FOR NO KEY UPDATE	FOR UPDATE
FOR KEY SHARE				yes
FOR SHARE			yes	yes
FOR NO KEY UPDATE		yes	yes	yes
FOR UPDATE	yes	yes	yes	yes

To test row-level locking, let's truncate the `test_tx_level` and populate a new record, as follows:

```
postgres=# truncate test_tx_level ;
TRUNCATE TABLE
postgres=# insert into test_tx_level Values(1), (2);
INSERT 0 2
```

To test for an updated row-level lock:

	Session 1	Session 2

T1	`postgres=# BEGIN;`
	`BEGIN`
	`postgres=# SELECT * FROM`
	`test_tx_level WHERE val = 1 FOR`
	`update;`
	`  val`
	`  -----`
	`    1`
	`(1 row)`	

T2		`postgres=# BEGIN;`
		`BEGIN`
		`postgres=# update test_tx_level SET`
		`val =2 WHERE val =1;`

Session 2 is waiting for **session 1,** since it has acquired a FOR UPDATE lock.

```
postgres=# SELECT * FROM lock_info ;
-[ RECORD 1 ]-----+----------------------------------------------------
locked_pid | 3368
locked_user | postgres
locked_statement | update test_tx_level SET val =2 WHERE val =1;
state | active
locking_statement | SELECT * FROM test_tx_level WHERE val = 1 FOR update;
state | idle in transaction
locking_duration | 00:04:04.631108
locking_pid | 3380
locking_user | postgres
```

Deadlocks

Deadlocks occur when two or more transactions each hold locks that the other wants. Using explicit locking can increase deadlocks. To simulate a deadlocks scenario, let's use FOR SHARE row-level locking, as follows:

	Session 1	Session 2

T1	`postgres=# begin;`
	`BEGIN`
	`postgres=# SELECT * FROM`
	`test_tx_level WHERE val = 1 FOR`
	`SHARE;`
	` val`
	`-----`
	`    1`
	`(1 row)`	

T2		`postgres=# begin;`
		`BEGIN`
		`postgres=# SELECT * FROM test_tx_level`
		`WHERE val = 1 FOR SHARE;`
		` val`
		`-----`
		`    1`
		`(1 row)`

T3	`postgres=# UPDATE test_tx_level` `SET val = 2 WHERE val=1;`	

| T4 | | ```
postgres=# UPDATE test_tx_level SET val
= 2 WHERE val=1;
ERROR: deadlock detected
DETAIL: Process 3368 waits for
ExclusiveLock on tuple (0,1) of relation
139530 of database 13014; blocked by
process 3380.
Process 3380 waits for ShareLock on
transaction 121862; blocked by process
3368.
HINT: See server log for query details.
``` |
|---|---|---|
| T5 | `UPDATE 1` | |

To avoid deadlocks, one should also ensure that the first lock acquired in a transaction is the most restrictive mode. For example, if **session 1** has used `FOR UPDATE`, then **session 2** will be blocked instead of failing due to deadlocks.

> As mentioned earlier, to avoid deadlocks, one can use a more restrictive mode. This forces other transactions to wait until the lock is removed. If the locking transaction is kept open for a long period, that means the application will suffer long delay.

Advisory locks

Advisory locks are application enforced locks. Advisory locks are used to emulate pessimistic locking strategies. Advisory locks are acquired at session level or at transaction level and are released when the session ends or the transaction commits.

Advisory locks can be used to limit the concurrency to one process, for example, when the process starts, it tries to acquire a lock; if it acquires it successfully, it continues, otherwise it exits. Advisory locks enable the developers to treat the database system as a single user environment and relieves them from the complexity of the locking system.
```

Advisory locks are stored in memory, so one needs to be careful not to exhaust the database cluster resources when using them. Finally, the full list of advisory locks can be found at https://www.postgresql.org/docs/current/static/functions-admin.html#functions-advisory-locks-table.

Session 1	Session2
postgres=# SELECT pg_try_advisory_lock(1); pg_try_advisory_lock ---------------------- t (1 row)	
	postgres=# SELECT pg_try_advisory_lock(1); pg_try_advisory_lock ---------------------- f (1 row)
postgres=# select pg_advisory_unlock(1); pg_advisory_unlock -------------------- t (1 row)	
	postgres=# SELECT pg_try_advisory_lock(1); pg_try_advisory_lock ---------------------- t (1 row)

In the same session, one can acquire the same advisory lock several times. However, it should be released the same number of times as it has been acquired, for example:

```
SELECT pg_try_advisory_lock(1);
SELECT pg_try_advisory_lock(1);
-- To release
select pg_advisory_unlock(1);
select pg_advisory_unlock(1);
```

Summary

PostgreSQL provides several locking mechanisms to increase concurrency and performance, including implicit locking via MVCC and explicit locking via table-level locks, row-level locks, and advisory locks.

The MVCC model is one of the biggest selling factors of PostgreSQL, since one can achieve high performance. In general, the MVCC model is suitable for most common database access patterns and it is better to use the MVCC model instead of explicit locking where possible.

Using explicit locking via table-level or row-level locks enables the user to solve several data inconsistency issues. However, explicit locking, if not planned carefully, might increase the chances of having deadlocks. Finally, PostgreSQL provides advisory locks, which are used to emulate pessimistic locking strategies.

The next chapter, covers the concepts of authentication and authorization. It describes PostgreSQL authentication methods and explains the structure of a PostgreSQL host-based authentication configuration file. It also discusses the permissions that can be granted to database building objects such as schemas, tables, views, indexes, and columns. Finally, it shows how sensitive data, such as passwords, can be protected using different techniques, including one-way and two-way encryption.

11
PostgreSQL Security

Data protection and security are essential for the continuity of business. Data protection is not nice to have, but it is required by the legal system. Sensitive data, such as user information, email addresses, geographical addresses, and payment information, should be protected against any data breach. There are several other topics related to data security, such as data privacy, retention, and loss prevention.

There are several levels of data protection, often defined in the data protection policy and by the country's legal system. Data protection policy often defines data dissemination to other parties, users authorized to access the data, and so on. Data should be protected on different levels, including transferring and encrypting data on storage devices. Data security is a huge topic and often there are data security managers dedicated only to these tasks.

In this chapter we will discuss the following topics:

- Authentication in PostgreSQL including PostgreSQL host based authentication and best practices.
- Default access privileges and the privileges on the public schema.
- Proxy authentication strategy.
- PostgreSQL security levels including database, schema, table , column and row privileges.
- Data encryption and decryption including one-way and two-way encryption.

Authentication in PostgreSQL

Authentication answers the question: who is the user? PostgreSQL supports several authentication methods, including

- **trust:** anyone who can connect to the server is authorized to access the database / databases as specified in the `pg_hba.conf` configuration file. Often used to allow connection using Unix-domain socket on a single user machine to access the database. One can also use this method with TCP/IP , but it is rare to allow connection from any IP address other than localhost.
- ident: it works by getting the client's operating system user name from an ident server and then using it in accessing the database server. This method is recommend only for closed networks where client machines has a tight control by system administrators.
- peer: it works similar to ident, but the client's operating system user name is obtained from the kernel.
- **GSSAPI:** GSSAPI is an industry standard defined in RFC 2743, it provides automatic authentication (single sign-on).
- **LDAP: LDAP (Lightweight Directory Access Protocol)** server is used only to validate the user name/password pairs.
- **Password authentication**: There are three methods as follows:
  - **scram-sha-256**: The strongest password authentication method, introduced in PostgreSQL 10. this method prevents password sniffing on untrusted connections
  - **md5**: Second strongest method, for new applications it is recommend to use scram-sha-256. Also PostgreSQL, provide the mean to migrate from md5 to scram-sha-256
  - **password**: This is not recommended to use since password are sent to server in a clear text format.

There are other authentication methods not covered , and the full list of supported authentication can be found at `https://www.postgresql.org/docs/current/static/auth-methods.html`.

To understand authentication, one needs to have the following information:

- Authentication is controlled via a `pg_hba.conf` file, where **hba** stands for **host-based authentication**.
- It is good to know the default initial authentication settings shipped with PostgreSQL distribution.
- The `pg_hba.conf` file is often located in the data directory, but it also can be specified in the `postgresql.conf` configuration file.
- When changing the authentication, one needs to send a **SIGHUP** signal, and this is done via several methods based on the PostgreSQL platform. Note that the user who sends the signal should be a superuser or the `postgres` or a `root` system user on the Linux distribution; again, this depends on the platform. Here is an example of several ways to reload PostgreSQL configuration:

```
psql -U postgres -c "SELECT pg_reload_conf();"
sudo service postgresql reload
sudo /etc/init.d/postgresql reload
sudo Kill -HUP <postgres process id>
```

- The order of `pg_hba.conf` records matters. The session connection is compared with `pg_hba.conf` records one by one until it is rejected or the end of the configuration file is reached.
- Finally, it is important to check the PostgreSQL log files to determine whether there are errors after configuration reload.

PostgreSQL pg_hba.conf

As in `postgresql.conf`, the `pg_hba.conf` file is composed of a set of records, lines can be commented using the hash sign, and spaces are ignored. The structure of the `pg_hba.conf` file record is as follows:

```
host_type database user [IP-address| address] [IP-mask] auth-method [auth-options]
```

The `host_type` part of this query can be the following:

- `Local`: This is used in Linux systems to allow users to access PostgreSQL using socket connections
- `Host`: This is to allow connections from other hosts, either based on the address or IP address, using TCP/IP with and without SSL encryption

- `Hostssl`: This is similar to host, but the connection should be encrypted using SSL in this case
- `Hostnossl`: This is also similar to host, but the connection should not be encrypted in this case

The database part of the query is the name of the database that the user would like to connect to. For flexibility, one could also use a comma-separated list to specify several databases, or one could use `all` to indicate that the user can access all the databases in the database cluster. Also, the `sameuser` and `samerole` values can be used to indicate that the database name is the same as the username or the user is a member of a role with the same name as the database.

The user part of the query specifies the database user's name; again, the `all` value matches all users. The IP address, address, and IP subnet mask are used to identify the host where the user tries to connect from. The IP address can be specified using a **CIDR (Classless Inter-Domain Routing)** or dot decimal notation. Finally, the password authentication methods can be trust, MD5, reject, and so on.

The following are some typical examples of configuring a PostgreSQL authentication:

- **Example 1**: Any USER on the PostgreSQL cluster can access any database using the Unix domain socket, as shown in the following database table:

#TYPE	DATABASE	USER	ADDRESS	METHOD
Local	all	all		trust

- **Example 2**: Any USER on the PostgreSQL cluster can access any database using the local loop back IP address:

#TYPE	DATABASE	USER	ADDRESS	METHOD
Host	all	all	127.0.0.1/32	trust
host	all	all	::1/128	trust

- **Example 3**: All connections that come from `92.168.0.53` are rejected, and the connections that come from the range `192.168.0.1/24` are accepted:

#TYPE	DATABASE	USER	ADDRESS	METHOD
Host	all	all	92.168.0.53/32	reject
Host	all	all	92.168.0.1/24	trust

PostgreSQL provides a very convenient way to view the rules defined in the pg_hba.conf file by providing a view called pg_hba_file_rules as follows:

```
postgres=# SELECT * FROM pg_hba_file_rules limit 1;
 line_number | type | database | user_name | address | netmask |
auth_method | options | error
-------------+-------+----------+------------+---------+---------+-
------------+---------+-------
          85 | local | {all} | {postgres} | | | peer | |
(1 row)
```

Listen addresses

The listen_addresses are defined in postgresql-conf. The PostgreSQL listen_addresses connection setting is used to identify the list of IP addresses that the server should listen to from client applications. The listen_addresses are comma-separated lists of hostnames or IP addresses. Changing this value requires a server restart. In addition to the preceding, one should note the following:

- The default value is localhost
- Giving an empty list means that the server should accept only a Unix socket connection
- The value * indicates all

It is a common mistake for people new to PostgreSQL users to forget to change the listen_address.

Authentication best practices

Authentication best practices depend on the whole infrastructure setup, the application's nature, the user's characteristics, data sensitivity, and so on. For example, the following setup is common for start-up companies: the database application, including the database server, is hosted on the same machine and only used from one physical location by intracompany users.

Often, database servers are isolated from the world using firewalls; in this case, one can use the **scram-sha-256** authentication method and limit the IP addresses so that the database server accepts connections within a certain range or set. Note that it is important not to use a superuser or database owner account to connect to the database, because if this account were hacked, the whole database cluster would be exposed.

If the application server—business logic—and database server are not on the same machine, one can use a strong authentication method, such as **LDAP (Lightweight Directory Access Protocol)** and **Kerberos**. However, for small applications where the database server and application are on the same machine, the **scram-sha-256** authentication method and limiting the listen address to the localhost might be sufficient.

To authenticate an application, it is recommended to use only one user and try to reduce the maximum number of allowed connections using a connection pooling software to better tune PostgreSQL resources. Another level of security might be needed in the application business logic to distinguish between different login users. For real-world users, LDAP or Kerberos authentication is more desirable.

Furthermore, if the database server is accessed from the outer world, it is useful to encrypt sessions using SSL certificates to avoid packet sniffing.

One should also remember to secure database servers, which trust all localhost connections as anyone who accesses the localhost can access the database server.

PostgreSQL default access privileges

By default, PostgreSQL users—also known as roles with the login option—can access the public schema. Additionally, note that the default PostgreSQL authentication policy allows users to access all databases from the localhost using peer authentication on a Linux system. Users can create database objects -tables, views, functions and so on- in the public schema of any database that they can access by default. Finally, the user can alter some settings regarding sessions such as `work_mem`.

The user cannot access other user objects in the public schema or create databases and schemas. However, the user can sniff data about the database objects by querying the system catalog. Unprivileged users can get information about other users, table structure, table owner, some table statistics, and so on.

The following example shows how the user `test_user` is able to get information about a table, which is owned by a `postgres` user; to simulate this situation, let's create a test database as follows:

```
psql -U postgres -c 'CREATE ROLE test_user LOGIN;';
psql -U postgres -c 'CREATE DATABASE test;';
psql -U postgres -d test -c'CREATE TABLE test_permissions(id serial , name
text);'
```

The user `test_user` does not have permissions to the table itself, but he has permissions to access the system catalog; to see this, connect to the database using `test_user`:

```
test=# SET ROLE test_user;
SET
test=> \d
 List of relations
 Schema | Name | Type | Owner
--------+------------------------+----------+----------
 public | test_permissions | table | postgres
 public | test_permissions_id_seq | sequence | postgres
(2 rows)
test=> \du
                            List of roles
 Role name | Attributes | Member of
-----------+-------------------------------------------------------------+--
---------
 postgres | Superuser, Create role, Create DB, Replication, Bypass RLS | {}
 test_user | | {}
```

The user can also access functions that are created in the public schema by other users as long as this function does not access objects that the user cannot access.

For mistrusted languages, such as **plpythonu**, the user cannot create functions unless he/she is a superuser. If anyone who is not a superuser tries to create a function using C language or **plpythonu**, an error will be raised.

To prevent the user from accessing the public schema, the public schema privileges should be revoked, as follows:

```
test=# SELECT session_user;
 session_user
--------------
 postgres
(1 row)
test=# REVOKE ALL PRIVILEGES ON SCHEMA PUBLIC FROM public;
REVOKE
test=# SET ROLE test_user;
```

```
SET
test=> CREATE TABLE b();
ERROR: no schema has been selected to create in
LINE 1: create table b();
```

 The user test_user has explicit privileges on the public schema; the user inherits these privileges from the public role.

For views, the view owner cannot execute a view unless he/she has permission to access the base tables used in the view.

Role system and proxy authentication

Often, when designing an application, a user is used to configure database connections and connection tools. Another level of security needs to be implemented to ensure that the user who uses the application is authorized to perform a certain task. This logic is often implemented in application business logic. The database's role system can also be used to partially implement this logic by delegating the authentication to another role after the connection is established or reused, using the SET SESSION AUTHORIZATION statement or SET ROLE command in a transaction block:

```
postgres=# SELECT session_user, current_user;
 session_user | current_user
--------------+--------------
 postgres | postgres
(1 row)

postgres=# SET SESSION AUTHORIZATION test_user;
SET
postgres=> SELECT session_user, current_user;
 session_user | current_user
--------------+--------------
 test_user | test_user
(1 row)
```

The SET ROLE requires a role membership, while SET SESSION AUTHORIZATION requires superuser privileges. Allowing an application to connect as a superuser is dangerous because the SET SESSION AUTHORIZATION and SET ROLE commands can be reset using the RESET ROLE and RESET SESSION commands, respectively, allowing the application to gain superuser privileges.

To understand how the PostgreSQL role system can be used to implement authentication and authorization, we will use the role system in the car portal app. In the car portal application, several groups of users can be classified as web_app_user, public_user, registered_user, seller_user, and admin_user. The web_app_user is used to configure business logic connection tools; the public_user, registered_user, and seller_user are used to distinguish users. The public_user group can access only public information, such as advertisements, but cannot add ratings as registered_user nor create advertisements as seller_user. admin_user is a super role to manage all of the application's content, such as filtering out spams and deleting the users that do not adhere to the website's policies. When the car web portal application connects to the database, the web_app_user user is used. After this, car_portal invokes the SET ROLE command based on the user class. This authentication method is known as **proxy authentication**.

The following examples demonstrate how a role system can be used to implement proxy authentication. The first step is to create roles and assign role memberships and privileges:

```
CREATE ROLE web_app_user LOGIN NOINHERIT;
CREATE ROLE public_user NOLOGIN;
GRANT SELECT ON car_portal_app.advertisement_picture,
car_portal_app.advertisement_rating , car_portal_app.advertisement TO
public_user;
GRANT public_user TO web_app_user;
GRANT USAGE ON SCHEMA car_portal_app TO web_app_user, public_user;
```

The NOINHERIT option for the web_app user does not allow the user to inherit the permissions of role membership; however, web_app can change the role to public user, as in the following example:

```
$ psql car_portal -U web_app_user
psql (10.0)
Type "help" for help.

car_portal=> SELECT * FROM car_portal_app.advertisement;
ERROR: permission denied for relation advertisement
car_portal=> SET ROLE public_user;
SET
car_portal=> SELECT * FROM car_portal_app.advertisement;
 advertisement_id | advertisement_date | car_id | seller_account_id
```

```
-------------------+--------------------+--------+-------------------
(0 rows)

car_portal=> SELECT session_user, current_user;
 session_user | current_user
--------------+--------------
 web_app_user | public_user
(1 row)
```

PostgreSQL security levels

PostgreSQL has different security levels defined on PostgreSQL objects, including tablespace, database, schema, table, foreign data wrapper, sequence, domain, language, and large object. One can have a peek into different privileges by running the \h meta command in psql, as follows:

```
Command: GRANT
Description: define access privileges
Syntax:
GRANT { { SELECT | INSERT | UPDATE | DELETE | TRUNCATE | REFERENCES |
TRIGGER }
    [, ...] | ALL [ PRIVILEGES ] }
    ON { [ TABLE ] table_name [, ...]
        | ALL TABLES IN SCHEMA schema_name [, ...] }
    TO role_specification [, ...] [ WITH GRANT OPTION ]
```

Database security level

To disallow users from connecting to the database by default, one needs to revoke the default database permissions from public, as follows:

```
$ psql car_portal -U postgres
psql (10.0)
Type "help" for help.
car_portal=# REVOKE ALL ON DATABASE car_portal FROM public;
REVOKE
car_portal=# \q
$ psql car_portal -U web_app_user
psql: FATAL: permission denied for database "car_portal"
DETAIL: User does not have CONNECT privilege.
```

To allow the user to connect to the database, the connect permissions should be granted, as follows:

```
postgres=# GRANT CONNECT ON DATABASE car_portal TO web_app_user;
GRANT
postgres=# \l car_portal
List of databases
-[ RECORD 1 ]-----+----------------------------------
Name | car_portal
Owner | car_portal_app
Encoding | UTF8
Collate | en_US.UTF-8
Ctype | en_US.UTF-8
Access privileges | car_portal_app=CTc/car_portal_app+
                  | web_app_user=c/car_portal_app
```

One also could revoke the default permissions from template databases to ensure that all newly-created databases do not allow users to connect by default. If the database permissions are empty when using the \l meta command, this indicates that the database has the default permissions.

> Be careful when dumping and restoring your database using pg_dump and pg_restore. The database access privileges are not restored and need to be handled explicitly.

Schema security level

Users can CREATE or access objects in a schema; to allow a user access to a certain schema, the usage permissions should be granted, as seen in the following examples:

```
GRANT USAGE ON SCHEMA car_portal_app TO web_app_user, public_user;
```

Table-level security

The table permissions are INSERT, UPDATE, DELETE, TRIGGER, REFERENCES, and TRUNCATE. One can also use the keyword ALL to grant all privileges at once, as follows:

```
GRANT ALL ON <table_name> TO <role>;
```

REFERENCES and TRIGGER permissions allow the creation of foreign key reference to the table and triggers. Apart from this, one could use a comma-separated list for both tables and roles or even grant permissions on all relations in a schema to a certain role.

Column-level security

PostgreSQL allows permissions to be defined on the column level. To explore this feature, let's create a table and role, as follows:

```
CREATE DATABASE test_column_acl;
\c test_column_acl;
CREATE TABLE test_column_acl AS SELECT * FROM (values (1,2), (3,4)) as
n(f1, f2);
CREATE ROLE test_column_acl;
GRANT SELECT (f1) ON test_column_acl TO test_column_acl;
```

To check column permissions, let's try to get all the data from the table as follows:

```
test_column_acl=# SET ROLE test_column_acl ;
SET
test_column_acl=> TABLE test_column_acl;
ERROR: permission denied for relation test_column_acl
test_column_acl=> SELECT f1 from test_column_acl ;
 f1
----
  1
  3
(2 rows)
```

Row-level security

Row-level security (RLS), also known as **row security policy**, is used to control access to the table rows including INSERT, UPDATE, SELECT, and DELETE. Table truncate as well as referential integrity constraints such as the primary key and unique and foreign keys are not subject to row security. In addition to this, superusers bypass the row-level security. To enable row security, one needs to use the ALTER statement for each table as follows:

```
ALTER TABLE <table_name> ENABLE ROW LEVEL SECURITY
```

In order to use RLS, one needs to define some polices on how a certain role or roles in the database can access a certain set of rows. For this reason, often the role is embedded in the tables. The following sample code creates two users and a table and enables RLS for that table:

```
CREATE DATABASE test_rls;
\c test_rls
CREATE USER admin;
CREATE USER guest;
CREATE TABLE account (
```

```
    account_name NAME,
    password TEXT
    );
INSERT INTO account VALUES('admin', 'admin'), ('guest', 'guest');
GRANT ALL ON  account to admin, guest;
ALTER TABLE account ENABLE ROW LEVEL SECURITY;
```

By default, if no policy is defined, then the user will be restricted to access the rows as follows:

```
test_rls=# SET ROLE admin;
test_rls=> table account;
 account_name | password
--------------+----------
(0 rows)
```

One could define a policy as follows:

```
CREATE POLICY account_policy_user ON account USING (account_name =
current_user);
test_rls=# SET ROLE admin;
test_rls=> Table account;
 account_name | password
--------------+----------
 admin | admin
(1 row)
```

The preceding code simply matches each row `account_name` and `current_user` and if the match returned true, then the row is returned. Note that this policy is not restricted for a certain operation, so the policy is applicable for `INSERT`, `UPDATE`, and `DELETE` as well.

```
test_rls=# SET ROLE admin;
test_rls=> INSERT INTO account values('guest', 'guest');
ERROR: new row violates row-level security policy for table "account"
```

The syntax to create a policy is as follows:

```
CREATE POLICY name ON table_name
    [ FOR { ALL | SELECT | INSERT | UPDATE | DELETE } ]
    [ TO { role_name | PUBLIC | CURRENT_USER | SESSION_USER } [, ...] ]
    [ USING ( using_expression ) ]
    [ WITH CHECK ( check_expression ) ]
```

The create policy is very flexible, one can creates policy for a certain operation or a certain condition, using any expression returning a Boolean value. WITH CHECK is used to validate new inserted or updated rows. For example, we would like the users to see all the content of the account table but only modify their own rows:

```
CREATE POLICY account_policy_write_protected ON account USING (true) WITH
CHECK (account_name = current_user);

test_rls=# SET ROLE admin;
test_rls=> Table account;
 account_name | password
--------------+----------
 admin | admin
 guest | guest
(2 rows)

test_rls=> INSERT INTO account values('guest', 'guest');
ERROR: new row violates row-level security policy for table "account"
```

The policies by default are *permissive policies*, which means that they are combined using the OR operator. Two polices were created as shown, one allows the users to see their own rows and one allows the users to see all rows, in total the user will be able to see all rows:

```
\d account
                Table "public.account"
    Column | Type | Collation | Nullable | Default
--------------+------+-----------+----------+---------
 account_name | name | | |
 password | text | | |
Policies:
    POLICY "account_policy_write_protected"
      USING (true)
      WITH CHECK ((account_name = CURRENT_USER))
    POLICY "account_user"
      USING ((account_name = CURRENT_USER))
```

Restrictive polices are supported in PostgreSQL, that is, the policies are combined using the AND logical operator. Let's now restrict table access based on working hours:

```
CREATE POLICY account_policy_time ON account AS RESTRICTIVE USING (
date_part('hour', statement_timestamp()) BETWEEN 8 AND 16 ) WITH CHECK
(account_name = current_user);
test_rls=# set role admin;
test_rls=# select now();
                now
```

```
-------------------------------
 2017-10-07 17:42:34.663909+02
(1 row)
test_rls=> table account;
 account_name | password
--------------+----------
(0 rows)
```

As seen in the example, no rows were returned due to adding the *restrictive policy*. The rows are filtered out by the expression; the filtering of rows is calculated using admin as the role:

tuple	account_policy	account_policy_write_protected	account_policy_time	Final result
(admin, admin)	True	True	False	False
(guest, guest)	False	True	False	False

All the tuples or rows are filtered out because of the account_policy_time policy , in the preceding example the final result for the tuple (admin, admin) is calculated as True OR True AND False which evaluates to False.

Encrypting data

By default, PostgreSQL internally encrypts sensitive data, such as roles' passwords. However, database users can also encrypt and decrypt sensitive data using the pgcrypto extension.

PostgreSQL role password encryption

When creating a role with password and login options, one can see the role's details in the pg_shadow catalog relation. Note that it is not recommended to use the following format to create the password:

```
CREATE ROLE <role_name> <with options> PASSWORD 'some_password';
```

The CREATE ROLE statement can appear in pg_stat_activity as well as the server logs, as follows:

```
postgres=# SELECT query FROM pg_stat_activity;
                   query
-------------------------------------


   SELECT query FROM pg_stat_activity;
   create role c password 'c';
```

All passwords stored in pg_shadow are encrypted with salt; finally, renaming an account will rest the password as follows:

```
postgres=# ALTER ROLE a RENAME TO b;
NOTICE: MD5 password cleared because of role rename
```

When creating a user with a password, it is recommended to use the \password psql meta command because it ensures that the password does not appear in clear text form in the psql history command, server log files, or elsewhere. To change the password, one can invoke the meta command using a superuser role as follows:

```
postgres=#\password <some_role_name>
Enter new password:
Enter it again:
ERROR: role "<some_role_name>" does not exist
```

pgcrypto

The pgcrypto extension provides a cryptographic functionality. Data encryption and decryption consume hardware resources, so it is important to have a balance between data sensitivity and decryption complexity. There are two kinds of data encryption:

- One-way data encryption uses a function to generate a hash, which cannot be reversed. The resulting encrypted text has often a fixed length; for example, MD5 encryption generates 16 bytes of hashes. A good hash function should be quick to compute and not produce the same hash for a different input.
- Two-way data encryption allows the data to be encrypted and decrypted. pgcrypto comes with functions to support one-way and two-way encryption. It supports several hashing algorithms. pgcrypto can be installed using the CREATE EXTENSION command, as follows:

```
CREATE EXTENSION pgcrypto;
```

One-way encryption

In **one-way encryption**, retrieving data in a clear text form is not important. The encrypted text (digest) is used to verify that the user knows the secret text. One-way encryption is often used to store passwords. PostgreSQL supports out-of-the-box MD5 encryption; however, as MD5 can be cracked easily, one could use MD5 with salt, as seen in the preceding `pg_shadow` example.

The common scenario of validating a password is comparing the generated MD5 digest with the stored one, as follows:

```
CREATE TABLE account_md5 (id INT, password TEXT);
INSERT INTO account_md5 VALUES (1, md5('my password'));
SELECT (md5('my password') = password) AS authenticated FROM account_md5;
 authenticated
---------------
 t
(1 row)
```

`pgcrypto` provides two functions to encrypt the password. These functions are `crypt` and `gen_salt`; also, the `pgcrypto` extension relieves the user from maintaining the salt. `crypt` and `gen_salt` can be used almost in the same way as MD5 to store the password, as follows:

```
CREATE TABLE account_crypt (id INT, password TEXT);
INSERT INTO account_crypt VALUES (1, crypt ('my password',
gen_salt('md5')));
INSERT INTO account_crypt VALUES (2, crypt ('my password',
gen_salt('md5')));
SELECT * FROM account_crypt;
 id | password
----+-----------------------------------
  1 | $1$ITT7yisa$FdRe4ihZ9kep1oU6wBr090
  2 | $1$HT2wH3UL$8DRdP6kLz5LvTXF3F2q610
(2 rows)
SELECT crypt ('my password', password) = password AS authenticated FROM
account_crypt;
 authenticated
----------
 t
 t
(2 rows)
```

As shown in the example, the passwords' digest differ due to a different generated salt. Also, note that salt does not need to be maintained. Finally, one could have a stronger password by tuning the salt generation. For example, one could use blowfish hashing and specify the iteration count. Note that the more the iteration counts, the slower the decryption, and more time is subsequently required to break it, as shown in the following example:

```
\timing
SELECT crypt('my password', gen_salt('bf',4));
                         crypt
----------------------------------------------------------------
 $2a$04$RZ5KWnI.IB4eLGNnT.37kuui4.Qi4Xh4TZmL7SOB6YW4LRpyZlP/K
(1 row)

Time: 1,801 ms

SELECT crypt('my password', gen_salt('bf',16));
                         crypt
----------------------------------------------------------------
 $2a$16$/cUY8PX7v2GLPCQBCbnL6OtlFm4YACmShZaH1gDNZcHyAYBvJ.9jq
(1 row)

Time: 4686,712 ms (00:04,687)
```

Two-way encryption

Two-way encryption is used to store sensitive information, such as payment information. pgcrypto provides two functions—mainly encrypt and decrypt—as shown in the following script:

```
test=# \df encrypt
                     List of functions
 Schema | Name | Result data type | Argument data types | Type
--------+---------+------------------+--------------------+--------
 public | encrypt | bytea | bytea, bytea, text | normal
(1 row)

test=# \df decrypt
                     List of functions
 Schema | Name | Result data type | Argument data types | Type
--------+---------+------------------+--------------------+--------
 public | decrypt | bytea | bytea, bytea, text | normal
(1 row)
```

The `encrypt` and `decrypt` functions require three arguments: the data to encrypt, the key, and the encryption algorithm. The following example shows how to `encrypt` and `decrypt` the string `Hello World` using the `aes` encryption algorithm:

```
test=# SELECT encrypt ('Hello World', 'Key', 'aes');
                 encrypt
------------------------------------
 \xf9d48f411bdee81a0e50b86b501dd7ba
(1 row)
test=# SELECT decrypt(encrypt ('Hello World', 'Key', 'aes'),'Key','aes');
         decrypt
--------------------------
 \x48656c6c6f20576f726c64
(1 row)
test=# SELECT convert_from(decrypt(encrypt ('Hello World', 'Key',
'aes'),'Key','aes'), 'utf-8');
 convert_from
--------------
 Hello World
(1 row)
```

The preceding form of encryption has some limitations; for example, the statement can appear in `pg_stat_activity` or in the database server log, and thus, one could get the key.

Two-way encryption can be achieved in two ways: symmetric and asymmetric encryption. The preceding example shows how symmetric encryption works, where there is a key used to `encrypt` and `decrypt` data. Asymmetric encryption uses public and private keys; the public key is used to `encrypt` the data and the private key is used to `decrypt` it. Asymmetric encryption is more secure than symmetric encryption but harder to set up. To set up asymmetric encryption and decryption, one needs to generate a public key via the `gpg` tool. Note that the `gpg` command asks for a passphrase; in this example, the passphrase should not be provided, also for simplicity, follow the default settings:

```
gpg --gen-key
```

Now, to extract the public and private keys, one could execute the following commands; note that if you use the `root` user to generate the key, you need to change the generated keys ownership to `postgres` user:

```
$ gpg --list-secret-key
/var/lib/postgresql/.gnupg/secring.gpg
---------------------------------------
sec 2048R/28502EEF 2017-10-08
uid Salahaldin Juba <juba@example.com>
ssb 2048R/D0B149A9 2017-10-08
```

```
$ gpg -a --export 28502EEF>/var/lib/postgresql/10/main/public.key
$ gpg -a --export-secret-key
D0B149A9>/var/lib/postgresql/10/main/secret.key
```

The gpg option, --list-secret-key, is used to determine the key IDs, and the options, --export-secret-key and --export, are used to export the public and the private keys respectively. The -a option is used to dump the keys in copy and paste formats. On the PostgreSQL cluster, we need to run the dearmor function. Also, the keys were moved to the database cluster folder for convenience purposes to use the pg_read_file function. After the generation of the keys, one could create a wrapper around pgp_pub_encrypt and pgp_pub_decrypt to hide the location of the keys, as follows:

```
CREATE OR REPLACE FUNCTION encrypt (text) RETURNS bytea AS
$$
BEGIN
  RETURN pgp_pub_encrypt($1, dearmor(pg_read_file('public.key')));
END;
$$ LANGUAGE plpgsql;
CREATE OR REPLACE FUNCTION decrypt (bytea) RETURNS text AS
$$
BEGIN
  RETURN pgp_pub_decrypt($1, dearmor(pg_read_file('secret.key')));
END;
$$ LANGUAGE plpgsql;
```

To test our functions, let's encrypt Hello World as follows:

```
test=# SELECT substring(encrypt('Hello World'), 1, 50);
                                          substring
----------------------------------------------------------------------
------------------------------
\xc1c04c034db92a51d0b149a90107fe3dc44ec5dccc039aea2a44e1d811426583a265feb22
f68421355a3b4755a6cb19eb3fa
(1 row)

test=#
test=# SELECT decrypt(encrypt('Hello World'));
   decrypt
-------------
 Hello World
(1 row)
```

Summary

In this chapter, PostgreSQL security is tackled from the authorization, authentication, and data encryption aspects; however, one also should protect the code against SQL injection and other known security issues, such as function cost, and the security barrier options. PostgreSQL provides several authentication methods, such as password and trust. Also, it provides security levels on all database objects including the database itself, schemas, tables, views, function, columns, and rows. Finally, one can also store sensitive data in the database in an encrypted format using pgcrypto extension.

The next chapter will focus on the PostgreSQL system catalog and introduce several recipes to maintain the database. The recipes will be used to extract potential problems in the database, such as missing indexes, and introduce the solutions to tackle these problems.

12
The PostgreSQL Catalog

The PostgreSQL system catalog and system administration functions can aid both developers and administrators to keep the database clean and performant. System catalogs can be used to automate several tasks, such as finding tables without indexes, finding dependencies between database objects, and extracting information about the database using health checks such as table bloats, database size, and so on. Information extracted from the system catalog can be employed in monitoring solutions such as Nagios and in dynamic SQL. This chapter will discuss some tasks a developer and administrator needs to do on a daily basis, such as cleaning up database data and unused objects, building an index automatically, and monitoring database objects access. The following topics will be covered in this chapter:

- An overview of the system catalog
- System catalog for administrators
- Using system catalog for database clean up.
- The usage of system catalog for performance tuning
- Selective dump for a certain view dependency tree

The system catalog

PostgreSQL describes all database objects using the meta information stored in database relations. These relations hold information about tables, views, functions, indexes, **foreign data wrappers (FDWs)**, triggers, constraints, rules, users, groups, and so on. This information is stored in the `pg_catalog` schema, and to make it more readable by humans, PostgreSQL also provides the `information_schema` schema, in which the meta information is wrapped and organized into views.

In the `psql` client, one can see exactly what is happening behind the scenes when a certain meta command is executed, such as `\z`, by enabling ECHO_HIDDEN. The ECHO_HIDDEN or –E switch allows users to study the system catalog tables of PostgreSQL. You need to run the following command:

```
postgres=# \set ECHO_HIDDEN
postgres=# \d
********* QUERY **********
SELECT n.nspname as "Schema",
  c.relname as "Name",
  CASE c.relkind WHEN 'r' THEN 'table' WHEN 'v' THEN 'view' WHEN 'm' THEN
'materialized view' WHEN 'i' THEN 'index' WHEN 'S' THEN 'sequence' WHEN 's'
THEN 'special' WHEN 'f' THEN 'foreign table' WHEN 'p' THEN 'table' END as
"Type",
  pg_catalog.pg_get_userbyid(c.relowner) as "Owner"
FROM pg_catalog.pg_class c
     LEFT JOIN pg_catalog.pg_namespace n ON n.oid = c.relnamespace
WHERE c.relkind IN ('r','p','v','m','S','f','')
     AND n.nspname <> 'pg_catalog'
     AND n.nspname <> 'information_schema'
     AND n.nspname !~ '^pg_toast'
  AND pg_catalog.pg_table_is_visible(c.oid)
ORDER BY 1,2;
**************************
Did not find any relations.
```

As seen in the preceding example, when the `\d` meta command is used, the query is sent to the database server backend. In addition to ECHO_HIDDEN, one can have a peek at the `information_schema` and `pg_catalog` views, as follows:

```
SELECT * FROM information_schema.views where table_schema IN ('pg_catlog',
'information_schema');
```

The `pg_catalog` and `information_schema` views contain hundreds of views, tables, and administration functions; for this reason, only some of the common and heavily used catalog tables will be described.

The `pg_class` table is one of the main tables in `pg_catalog`; it stores information about various relation types, including tables, indexes, views, sequences, and , composite types. The `relkind` attribute in `pg_class` specifies the relation type. The following characters are used to identify relations:

- `r`: Ordinary table
- `i`: Index
- `S`: Sequence

- t: TOAST table
- v: View
- m: Materialized view
- c: Composite type
- f: Foreign table
- p: Partitioned table

As this table is used to describe all relations, some columns are meaningless for some relation types.

One could think of **The Oversized-Attribute Storage Technique (TOAST)** as a vertical partitioning strategy. PostgreSQL does not allow tuples to span multiple pages where the page size is often 8 KB. Therefore, PostgreSQL stores, breaks, and compresses large objects into several chunks and stores them in other tables called TOAST tables.

The relations are identified by object identifiers. These identifiers are used as primary keys in the pg_catalog schema, so it is important to know how to convert **object identifiers (OID)** into text to get the relation name. Also, note that the OIDs have types; for example, the regcalss type is used to identify all relations stored in pg_class, while the regprocedure type is used to identify functions. The following example shows how to convert a table name to OID and vice versa:

```
postgres=# SELECT 'pg_catalog.pg_class'::regclass::oid;
 oid
------
 1259
(1 row)

postgres=# SELECT 1259::regclass::text;
  text
----------
 pg_class
(1 row)
```

Another approach is to use pg_class and pg_namespace to get the oid as follows:

```
SELECT c.oid FROM pg_class c join pg_namespace n ON (c.relnamespace =
n.oid) WHERE relname ='pg_class' AND nspname ='pg_catalog';
 oid
------
 1259
(1 row)
```

Another important table is `pg_attribute`; this table stores information about tables and other `pg_class` object columns. The `pg_index` table, as the name suggests, stores information about indexes. In addition, `pg_depend` and `pg_rewrite` are used to store information about dependent objects and rewrite rules for tables and views.

Another important set of tables and views are `pg_stat<*>` relations; these tables and views provide statistics about tables, indexes, columns, sequences, and so on. Information stored in these tables is highly valuable for debugging performance issues and usage patterns. The following query shows some of the static relations:

```
SELECT relname, case relkind when 'r' then 'table' WHEN 'v' THEN 'VIEW' END
as type FROM pg_class WHERE relname like 'pg_sta%' AND relkind IN ('r','v')
LIMIT 5 ;
          relname | type
--------------------------------+-------
 pg_statistic | table
 pg_stat_user_tables | VIEW
 pg_stat_xact_user_tables | VIEW
 pg_statio_all_tables | VIEW
 pg_statio_sys_tables | VIEW
```

System catalog for administrators

The following section introduces some functions and system information that are often used by database administrators. Some of these functions might be used on a daily basis, such as `pg_reload_conf()`, which is used to reload the database cluster after amending `pg_hba.conf` or `postgresql.conf`, and `pg_terminate_backend(pid)`, which is used to kill a certain process.

Getting the database cluster and client tools version

The PostgreSQL version allows the user to know the supported features and helps them to write compatible SQL queries for different versions. For example, the process ID attribute name in the `pg_stat_activity` view in PostgreSQL versions older than 9.2 is `procpid`; in PostgreSQL version 9.2, this attribute name is `pid`.

In addition, the version information provides compatibility information to client tools and the backend version. To get the database cluster, one can use the version function as follows:

```
postgres=# SELECT version();
                                                              version
--------------------------------------------------------------------------------
------------------------------------
 PostgreSQL 10.0 on x86_64-pc-linux-gnu, compiled by gcc (Ubuntu
5.4.0-6ubuntu1~16.04.4) 5.4.0 20160609, 64-bit
(1 row)
```

It is also important to check the client tools version, whether it is pg_restore, pg_dumpall or psql, in order to check its compatibility with the server. This can be done as follows:

```
$ pg_dump --version
pg_dump (PostgreSQL) 10.0
```

The pg_dump utility generates dumps that can be restored on newer versions of PostgreSQL. Also, pg_dump can dump data from PostgreSQL versions older than its own version but, logically, not for a PostgreSQL server with a version newer than its own version.

Terminating and canceling user sessions

Database administrators often need to kill server processes for various reasons. For example, in certain scenarios, very slow queries running on the slave or master, which are configured using streaming replication, can break the replication.

Database connection can be terminated for several reasons, as follows:

- **The maximum number of connections is exceeded** in some cases where connections are misconfigured, such as when keeping IDLE connections open for a very long time, or when some sessions are opened but in a stale state.
- Dropping the database, one can not drop a database if someone is connected to it. This is sometimes necessary in testing scenarios.
- **Very slow queries**: Very slow queries can have a cascading effect on streaming replication as well as other transactions.

PostgreSQL provides the `pg_terminate_backend(pid)` and `pg_cancel_backend(pid)` functions, while `pg_cancel_backend` only cancels the current query and `pg_terminate_backend` kills the entire connection. The following query terminates all connections to the current database except the session connection:

```
SELECT pg_terminate_backend(pid) FROM pg_stat_activity WHERE datname =
current_database() AND pid <> pg_backend_pid();
```

The `pg_cancel_backend` function cancels the current query, but the application may run the same query again. The `pg_terminate_backend` function terminates the connection, and this can also be done via the kill Linux command. However, the kill command may be dangerous if one kills the PostgreSQL server process instead of the connection process.

When combining the `pg_stat_activity` view and the `pg_terminate_backend` function, one can achieve greater flexibility. For example, in streaming replication, one can detect queries that spend a lot of time on the slaves and thus cause a replication lag. Also, if a certain application is not configured properly and has a big number of idle connections, one can kill them to free memory and allow other clients to connect to the database.

Also, PostgreSQL allows for terminating the SQL statement due to timeouts. For example, in several cases, long running statements can have very bad side effects such as blocking other statements. Statement timeout can be set globally in `postgresql.conf` or can be set to each session as follows:

```
SET statement_timeout to 1000;
SELECT pg_sleep(1001);
ERROR: canceling statement due to statement timeout
```

Defining and getting database cluster settings

The PostgreSQL configuration settings control several aspects of the PostgreSQL cluster. From an administration perspective, one can define the statement timeout, memory settings, connections, logging, vacuum, and planner settings. From a development point of view, these settings can help a developer optimize queries. One can use the `current_settings` function or the `show` statement for convenience:

```
SELECT current_setting('work_mem');
 current_setting
-----------------
 4MB
(1 row)

show work_mem;
```

```
 work_mem
----------
 4MB
(1 row)
```

In order to change a certain configuration value, the function
`set_config(setting_name, new_value, is_local)` can be utilized. If `is_local` is
true, the new value will only apply to the current transaction, otherwise to the current
session:

```
SELECT set_config('work_mem', '8 MB', false);
```

The `set_config` function can raise an error if the setting cannot be set to the session
context such as the number of allowed connections and shared buffers, as follows:

```
SELECT set_config('shared_buffers', '1 GB', false);
ERROR: parameter "shared_buffers" cannot be changed without restarting the
server
```

In addition to `set_config`, PostgreSQL provides the `ALTER SYSTEM` command used to
change PostgreSQL configuration parameters. The synopsis for the `ALTER SYSTEM` is:

```
ALTER SYSTEM SET configuration_parameter { TO | = } { value | 'value' |
DEFAULT }
ALTER SYSTEM RESET configuration_parameter
ALTER SYSTEM RESET ALL
```

In case the setting value requires a system reload or restart, the setting will take effect after
the system reload or restart, respectively. The `ALTER SYSTEM` command requires superuser
privileges. The `ALTER SYSTEM` command amends a file called `postgresql.auto.conf`.
The `ALTER SYSTEM` name indicates that it has a global effect, and one needs to reload the
server configuration as follows:

```
postgres=# ALTER SYSTEM SET work_mem TO '8MB';
ALTER SYSTEM
postgres=# SHOW work_mem;
 work_mem
----------
 4MB
(1 row)

postgres=# SELECT pg_reload_conf();
 pg_reload_conf
----------------
 t
(1 row)
```

```
postgres=# SHOW work_mem;
 work_mem
----------
 8MB
(1 row)
```

The following command shows the content of `postgresql.auto.conf`:

```
$cat postgresql.auto.conf
# Do not edit this file manually!
# It will be overwritten by ALTER SYSTEM command.
work_mem = '8MB'
```

Finally, browsing the `postgresql.conf` file is a bit tricky due to the big number of PostgreSQL settings. Also, most settings have the default boot values. Therefore, getting the server configuration settings that are not assigned the default values in `postgresql.conf` can be easily done, as follows:

```
SELECT name, current_setting(name), source FROM pg_settings WHERE source IN
('configuration file');
            name | current_setting | source
------------------------------+----------------------------------------+----
----------------
 cluster_name | 10/main | configuration file
 DateStyle | ISO, DMY | configuration file
```

Getting the database and database object size

Managing disk space and assigning table spaces to tables as well as databases requires knowledge about the size of the database and database objects. When performing a logical restore of a certain table, one could get information about the progress by comparing the original database table size to the one which is being restored. Finally, the database object size often gives information about bloats.

> Bloats are wasted disk space due to concurrent data manipulation, heavily updated system often gets bloated due the nature of MVCC. Bloats are often cleaned up by vacuum, thus disabling auto vacuum is not recommended.

To get the database size, one can get the `oid` database from the `pg_database` table and run the `du -h /data_directory/base/oid` Linux command. `data_directory` is the database cluster folder specified in the `postgresql.conf` configuration file.

A quick look at the PostgreSQL cluster folders can be quite useful to get familiar with PostgreSQL's main concepts and operations such as configuration files. For example, to determine the creation date of a certain database, one could have a look at the PG_VERSION file creation date located in the database directory.

In addition to this, PostgreSQL provides the pg_database_size function to get the database size and the pg_size_pretty function to display the size in a human readable form, as follows:

```
SELECT pg_database.datname,
pg_size_pretty(pg_database_size(pg_database.datname)) AS size FROM
pg_database;
    datname | size
-----------------+---------
 postgres | 8093 kB
 template1 | 7481 kB
 template0 | 7481 kB
```

One can get the table size, including indexes and TOAST tables, using the pg_total_relation_size function. If one is interested only in the table size, one can use the pg_relation_size function. This information helps manage table growth as well as tablespaces. Take a look at the following query:

```
SELECT tablename,
pg_size_pretty(pg_total_relation_size(schemaname||'.'||tablename)) FROM
pg_tables LIMIT 2;
   tablename | pg_size_pretty
--------------+-----------------
 pg_statistic | 280 kB
 pg_type | 184 kB
(2 rows)
```

Finally, to get the index size, one could use the pg_relation_size function, as follows:

```
SELECT indexrelid::regclass,
pg_size_pretty(pg_relation_size(indexrelid::regclass)) FROM pg_index LIMIT
2;
           indexrelid | pg_size_pretty
-----------------------------+-----------------
 pg_toast.pg_toast_2604_index | 8192 bytes
 pg_toast.pg_toast_2606_index | 8192 bytes
(2 rows)
```

For simplicity, the `psql` tool also provides meta commands to get the size of the database, table, and index as follows:

- `\l+`: To list database information including size.
- `\dtis+`: The letters `t`, `i`, and `s` stand for table, index, and sequence respectively. This meta command lists database objects including tables, indexes and sequences. The + is used to show the object size on the hard disk.

The table size on the hard disk gives you hints about restoring the data progress of the table. Let us assume you are moving a table from one database to another using the copy command; you cannot see how many rows were inserted, but you can compare the two table sizes, which indicates your progress.

Cleaning up the database

Often, a database can contain several unused objects or very old data. Cleaning up these objects helps administrators perform a backup of images more quickly. From a development point of view, unused objects are noise because they affect the refactoring process.

In database applications, one needs to keep the database clean as unused database objects might hinder quick development due to those objects' dependencies. To clean the database, one needs to identify the unused database objects, including tables, views, indexes, and functions.

Table statistics, such as the number of live rows, index scans, and sequential scans, can help identify empty and unused tables. Note that the following queries are based on statistics, so the results need to be validated. The `pg_stat_user_tables` table provides this information, and the following query shows empty tables by checking the number of tuples:

```
SELECT relname FROM pg_stat_user_tables WHERE n_live_tup= 0;
```

All information based on PostgreSQL statistics are not one hundred percent bulletproof, because the statistics might not be up to date.

To find the empty columns or unused columns, one can have a look at the `null_fraction` attribute of the `pg_stats` table. If the `null_fraction` equals one, then the column is completely empty:

```
SELECT schemaname, tablename, attname FROM pg_stats WHERE null_frac= 1 and
schemaname NOT IN ('pg_catalog', 'information_schema');
```

To find the useless indexes, two steps can be applied:

1. The first technique is to determine whether an index is duplicated or overlapped with another index,
2. and the second t step is to assess whether the index is used based on the index statistics.

The following query can be used to assess whether an index is used based on catalog statistics. Note that , the constraint indexes--the unique constraints and primary keys--are excluded because we need these indexes even though they are not used:

```
SELECT schemaname, relname, indexrelname FROM pg_stat_user_indexes s JOIN
pg_index i ON s.indexrelid = i.indexrelid WHERE idx_scan=0 AND NOT
indisunique AND NOT indisprimary;
```

Overlapping index attributes can be used to identify duplicate indexes. The following SQL code compares the index attributes with each other and return indexes that overlap attributes:

```
WITH index_info AS (
SELECT
    pg_get_indexdef(indexrelid) AS index_def,
    indexrelid::regclass
    index_name ,
    indrelid::regclass table_name, array_agg(attname order by attnum) AS
index_att
 FROM
    pg_index i JOIN
    pg_attribute a ON i.indexrelid = a.attrelid
GROUP BY
    pg_get_indexdef(indexrelid), indrelid, indexrelid
 ) SELECT DISTINCT
    CASE WHEN a.index_name > b.index_name THEN a.index_def ELSE b.index_def
END AS index_def,
    CASE WHEN a.index_name > b.index_name THEN a.index_name ELSE
b.index_name END AS index_name,
    CASE WHEN a.index_name > b.index_name THEN b.index_def ELSE a.index_def
END AS overlap_index_def,
    CASE WHEN a.index_name > b.index_name THEN b.index_name ELSE
```

```
    a.index_name END AS overlap_index_name,
        a.index_att = b.index_att as full_match,
        a.table_name
  FROM
        index_info a INNER JOIN
        index_info b ON (a.index_name != b.index_name AND a.table_name =
  b.table_name AND a.index_att && b.index_att );
```

To test the preceding query, let us create an overlapping index as follows and execute the query :

```
CREATE TABLE test_index_overlap(a int, b int);
CREATE INDEX ON test_index_overlap (a,b);
CREATE INDEX ON test_index_overlap (b,a);
```

The result of the preceding query is as follows:

```
-[ RECORD 1 ]------+-------------------------------------------------------
----------------------------------------------------------------------------
index_def | CREATE INDEX test_index_overlap_b_a_idx ON test_index_overlap
USING btree (b, a)
index_name | test_index_overlap_b_a_idx
overlap_index_def | CREATE INDEX test_index_overlap_a_b_idx ON
test_index_overlap USING btree (a, b)
overlap_index_name | test_index_overlap_a_b_idx
full_match | f
table_name | test_index_overlap
```

Cleaning up unused views and functions is a little bit tricky. By default, PostgreSQL collects statistics about indexes and tables but not functions. To enable statistics collection on functions, the track_functions setting needs to be enabled. The statistics on functions can be found in the pg_stat_user_functions table.

For views, there are no statistics collected unless the views are materialized. In order to assess whether a view is used, we need to do this manually. This can be done by rewriting the view and joining it with a function with a certain side effect, the joined function for example update a table and increase the number of times the view is accessed, or raise a certain log message. To test this technique, let's write a simple function that raises a log, as follows:

```
CREATE OR REPLACE FUNCTION monitor_view_usage (view_name TEXT) RETURNS
BOOLEAN AS $$
BEGIN
    RAISE LOG 'The view % is used on % by % ', view_name, current_time,
session_user;
```

```
    RETURN TRUE;
END;
$$LANGUAGE plpgsql cost .001;
```

Now, let's assume that we want to drop the dummy_view view, however, there is uncertainty regarding whether a certain application depends on it, as follows:

```
CREATE OR REPLACE VIEW dummy_view AS
SELECT dummy_text FROM (VALUES('dummy')) as dummy(dummy_text);
```

To ensure that the view is not used, the view should be rewritten as follows, with the monitor_view_usage function used:

```
-- Recreat the view and inject the monitor_view_usage
CREATE OR REPLACE VIEW dummy_view AS
SELECT dummy_text FROM (VALUES('dummy')) as dummy(dummy_text) cross join
monitor_view_usage('dummy_view');
```

If the view is accessed, an entry in the log file should appear, as follows:

```
$ tail /var/log/postgresql/postgresql-10-main.log
2017-10-10 16:54:15.375 CEST [21874] postgres@postgres LOG: The view
dummy_view is used on 16:54:15.374124+02 by postgres
```

Cleaning up the database data

Cleaning up bloated tables and indexes can be simply done by invoking the VACUUM statement; you can take a look at the Bucardo check_postgres Nagios plugin code at https://bucardo.org/wiki/Check_postgres to understand how bloats in tables and indexes can be calculated.

Cleaning up data is an important topic; often, the data life cycle is not defined when creating a database application. This leads to tons of outdated data. Unclean data hinders several processes, such as database refactoring. Also, it can create side effects for all processes in the company, such as inaccurate report results, billing issues, unauthorized access, and so on.

Several examples were introduced to determine unused objects, but that is not all. The data itself should be cleaned, and the data life cycle should be defined. For unclean data, there are several options; however, let's focus only on duplicated rows here, due to the missing unique and primary key constraints. The first step is to identify the tables that do not have unique and primary key constraints. This is quite easy using the information schema, as follows:

```
SELECT table_catalog, table_schema, table_name
FROM
  information_schema.tables
WHERE
table_schema NOT IN ('information_schema','pg_catalog')
EXCEPT
SELECT
  table_catalog, table_schema, table_name
FROM
  information_schema.table_constraints
WHERE
  constraint_type IN ('PRIMARY KEY', 'UNIQUE') AND table_schema NOT IN
('information_schema', 'pg_catalog');
```

The second step is to identify the tables that really contain duplicates; this can be done by aggregating the data in the table. To do this, let's create a table with some duplicates.

```
CREATE TABLE duplicate AS SELECT (random () * 9 + 1)::INT as f1 , (random
() * 9 + 1)::INT as f2 FROM generate_series (1,40);
SELECT count(*), f1, f2 FROM duplicate GROUP BY f1, f2;

 count | f1 | f2
-------+----+----
     2 | 7 | 4
     3 | 5 | 4
     2 | 2 | 6
(3 rows)
```

The tricky part is deleting the duplicates, as the rows are identical. To delete duplicates, a certain row needs to be marked to stay, and the rest need to be deleted. This can be achieved using the ctid column. In PostgreSQL, each row has a header, and the ctid column is the physical location of the row version within the table. Thus, the ctid column can be used as a temporarily row identifier because this identifier may change after running maintenance commands such as CLUSTER.

To delete the duplicate, one can use the `DELETE USING` statement as follows:

```
SELECT ctid, f1, f2 FROM duplicate where (f1, f2) =(7,4)
 ctid | f1 | f2
--------+----+----
 (0,11) | 7 | 4
 (0,40) | 7 | 4
(2 rows)
BEGIN;
DELETE FROM duplicate a USING duplicate b WHERE a.f1= b.f1 and a.f2= b.f2
and a.ctid > b.ctid;
SELECT ctid, f1, f2 FROM duplicate where (f1, f2) =(7,4);
 ctid | f1 | f2
--------+----+----
 (0,11) | 7 | 4
(1 row)
```

> Do not forget to use an explicit transaction block when manipulating data.
> This will allow you to rollback changes if you make an error.

There are several other approaches to clean up duplicate rows. For example, one can use the `CREATE TABLE` and `SELECT DISTINCT` statements to create a table with a unique set of rows. Then, one can drop the original table and rename the created table after the original table, as shown in the following example:

```
CREATE TABLE <tmp> AS SELECT DISTINCT * FROM <orig_tbl>;
DROP TABLE <orig_tbl>;
ALTER TABLE <tmp> RENAME TO <orig_tbl>;
```

or

```
CREATE UNLOGGED TABLE <tmp> AS SELECT DISTINCT * FROM <orig_tbl>;
DROP TABLE <orig_tbl>;
ALTER TABLE <tmp> RENAME TO <orig_tbl>;
ALTER TABLE <tmp> SET LOGGED;
```

Note that this approach might be faster than the approach represented in the preceding example; however, this technique may not work if there are other objects depending on the table that needs to be dropped, such as views, indexes, and so on.

If you are unfamiliar with the `DELETE USING` statement, here is another way to do the same trick using CTEs (however, note that the first query should be faster):

```
with should_not_delete as (
SELECT min(ctid) FROM duplicate group by f1, f2
) DELETE FROM duplicate WHERE ctid NOT IN (SELECT min FROM
should_not_delete);
```

Tuning for performance

High performance in PostgreSQL can be achieved by having good configuration settings and proper physical schema including indexes. Execution plans depend on the statistics gathered from the tables; fortunately, in PostgreSQL, one can control the behavior of the statistic collection.

For developers, it is important to get good performance. When handling foreign keys, there are two recommendations to increase performance, which are as follows:

- **Always index foreign keys**: Indexing a table foreign keys allows PostgreSQL to fetch data from the table using an index scan.
- **Increase the column statistic target on foreign keys**: This is also applicable to all predicates because it allows PostgreSQL to have a better estimation of the number of rows. The default statistic target is 100, and the maximum is 10,000. Increasing the statistics target makes the `ANALYZE` command slower.

Both of the preceding approaches require the identifying of foreign keys. The `pg_catalog.pg_constraint` table can be used to look up table constraints. To get all foreign key constrains, one can simply run the following query:

```
SELECT * FROM pg_constraint WHERE contype = 'f';
```

Also, from the previous examples, we can see how to get overlapping indexes; one can combine information from both tables to get foreign keys that do not have indexes, as follows:

```
SELECT
 conrelid::regclass AS relation_name,
 conname AS constraint_name,
 reltuples::bigint AS number_of_rows,
 indkey AS index_attributes,
 conkey AS constraint_attributes,
 CASE WHEN conkey && string_to_array(indkey::text, ' ')::SMALLINT[] THEN
FALSE ELSE TRUE END as might_require_index
```

```
FROM
  pg_constraint JOIN pg_class ON (conrelid = pg_class.oid) JOIN
  pg_index ON indrelid = conrelid
WHERE
  contype = 'f';
```

Note that if `indkey` overlaps with `conkey`, we might not need to add an index; however, this should be validated by the usage pattern . Also, in the preceding example, the number of `reltuples` is selected, as this is an important factor to determine index creation because performing sequential scans on big tables is quite costly. In addition to this, another option is to use the table statistics for sequential scan.

After identifying the foreign keys, one can use the CREATE INDEX command and ALTER TABLE to create indexes and alter default statistics, respectively.

Selective dump

When refactoring a certain view, including adding a new column or changing the column type, one needs to refactor all the views that depend on this particular view. Unfortunately, PostgreSQL does not provide the means to create a logical dump of a dependent object.

PostgreSQL provides `pg_dump` to dump a certain database or a specific set of objects in a database. Also, in development, it is recommended that you keep the code in a Git repository.

Plan your development cycle in advance, including development, testing, staging, and production. Use code versioning tools such as Git and database migration tools such as flyway to define your processes. This will save you a lot of time.

Unfortunately, often the SQL code for legacy applications is not maintained in the version control system and in migration tools such as flyway. In this case, if you need to change a certain view definition or even a column type, it is necessary to identify the affected views, dump them, and then restore them.

The first step is to identify the views to be dropped and restored. Depending on the task, one can write different scripts; a common pattern is to drop the views depending on a certain view, table, or table column. The base `pg_catalog` tables, `pg_depend` and `pg_rewrite`, store the dependency information and view rewriting rules. More human readable information can be found in `information_schema.view_table_usage`.

Let's assume that there are several views that depend on each other, as shown in the following figure, and the base view **a** needs to be refactored, which means dropped and created:

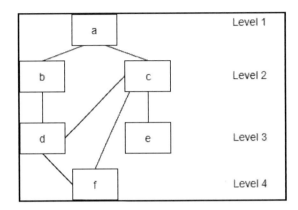

To generate this tree of dependency, one can execute the following queries:

```
CREATE TABLE test_view_dep AS SELECT 1;
CREATE VIEW a AS SELECT 1 FROM test_view_dep;
CREATE VIEW b AS SELECT 1 FROM a;
CREATE VIEW c AS SELECT 1 FROM a;
CREATE VIEW d AS SELECT 1 FROM b,c;
CREATE VIEW e AS SELECT 1 FROM c;
CREATE VIEW f AS SELECT 1 FROM d,c;
```

Now, to solve the dependency tree, a recursive query will be used, as follows:

```
CREATE OR REPLACE FUNCTION get_dependency (schema_name text, view_name
text) RETURNS TABLE (schema_name text, view_name text, level int) AS $$
WITH RECURSIVE view_tree(parent_schema, parent_view, child_schema,
child_view, level) as
(
    SELECT parent.view_schema, parent.view_name ,parent.table_schema,
parent.table_name, 1
    FROM information_schema.view_table_usage parent
    WHERE parent.view_schema = $1 AND parent.view_name = $2
    UNION ALL
    SELECT child.view_schema, child.view_name, child.table_schema,
child.table_name, parent.level + 1
    FROM view_tree parent JOIN information_schema.view_table_usage child ON
child.table_schema =          parent.parent_schema AND child.table_name
= parent.parent_view
)
SELECT DISTINCT
```

```
        parent_schema, parent_view, level
FROM (
  SELECT parent_schema, parent_view, max (level) OVER (PARTITION BY
parent_schema, parent_view) as max_level,level
  FROM view_tree) AS FOO
WHERE level = max_level
ORDER BY 3 ASC;
$$
LANGUAGE SQL;
```

In the preceding query, the inner part of the query is used to calculate dependency levels, while the outer part of the query is used to eliminate duplicates. The following shows the dependencies for the view **a** in the right order. The result for executing the previous function for the view **a** is as follows:

```
SELECT * FROM get_dependency('public', 'a');
 schema_name | view_name | level
-------------+-----------+-------
 public | a | 1
 public | b | 2
 public | c | 2
 public | d | 3
 public | e | 3
 public | f | 4
(6 rows)
```

To dump the view's definition based on the defined level, one can use pg_dump with the −t option, which is used to dump a certain relation. So, to dump the views in the previous example, one can use the following trick in bash:

```
$relations=$(psql -t -c "SELECT string_agg (' -t ' ||
quote_ident(schema_name) || '.' || quote_ident(view_name), ' ' ORDER BY
level ) FROM get_dependency ('public'::text, 'a'::text)")
$echo $relations
-t public.a -t public.b -t public.c -t public.d -t public.e -t public.f
$pg_dump -s  $relations
  --
-- PostgreSQL database dump
  --

-- Dumped from database version 10.0
-- Dumped by pg_dump version 10.0

SET statement_timeout = 0;
SET lock_timeout = 0;
SET idle_in_transaction_session_timeout = 0;
SET client_encoding = 'UTF8';
```

```
SET standard_conforming_strings = on;
SET check_function_bodies = false;
SET client_min_messages = warning;
SET row_security = off;

SET search_path = public, pg_catalog;


--
-- Name: a; Type: VIEW; Schema: public; Owner: postgres
--

CREATE VIEW a AS
 SELECT 1
   FROM test_view_dep;
...
```

The `psql` uses the `-t` option to return tuples only, and the string aggregate function is used to generate the list of views that need to be dumped based on the level order. In this case, we can guarantee the generation of an SQL script with the correct order of view creation.

Summary

Catalog tables provides invaluable information to maintain and automate database administration tasks. For example, in the previous section, we were able to dump a tree of dependent objects in the correct order. In addition to that, one can automate daily tasks checks such as bloats, locks, size, and database health. Also, with the usage of statistical table, we were able to detect unused indexes, as well as potential columns which require indexing such as foreign keys columns.

The PostgreSQL catalog contains meta information about PostgreSQL databases and objects. This information can be retrieved and manipulated using SQL statements. However, it is not recommended to manipulate the data directly in a catalog schema. PostgreSQL also provides a convenient way to extract data by providing user friendly information in `information_schema`.

With the help of the PostgreSQL catalog, one can write a complete book of recipes, and one can have recipes in his backlog for database cluster health including memory consumption, idle connections, database size, and processes status. In addition to that, one can have recipes to handle roles and role membership, objects permissions, locks detection, and streaming replication health.

The next chapter, discusses several approaches to optimize performance. It presents PostgreSQL cluster configuration settings, which are used in tuning the whole cluster's performance. Also, it presents common mistakes in writing queries and discusses several approaches to increase performance, such as using indexes or table partitioning and constraint exclusion.

13
Optimizing Database Performance

There are several aspects of optimizing database performance, such as hardware configuration, network settings, database configuration, rewriting of SQL queries, maintenance of indexes, and so on. In this chapter, we will focus only on basic configuration and query rewriting.

Generally speaking, tuning database performance requires knowledge about the system's nature; for example, we need to know whether the database system can be used for **online analytical processing (OLAP)** or **online transactional processing (OLTP)**. The database system may be **IO** or **CPU** bound; these define the whole database cluster setup, such as the number of **CPU**s, **CPU** power, **RAID** configuration, amount of **RAM**, and the database's cluster configuration. After the database server is configured, one could use a benchmark framework, such as pgbench, to calculate the number of **transactions per second (TPS)** for the database server setup.

The second step in optimizing database performance is carried out after the system is up and running, and often periodically. In this state, one could set up a monitoring system, such as a pgbadger monitoring tool, **PostgreSQL Workload Analyzer (PoWA)**, and pg_stat_statements, to find bottlenecks and slow queries.

To optimize a slow query, it should be analyzed first. If the query is poorly written, rewriting it might be enough. Otherwise, missing indexes can be created, server configuration settings can be amended, the physical structure can be refactored, and so on.

The topics we will be covering in this chapter are :

- PostgreSQL configuration tuning
- Tuning performance for write
- Tuning performance for read
- Detecting problems in query plans
- Common mistakes in writing queries
- Table partitioning
- Query rewriting

PostgreSQL configuration tuning

PostgreSQL's default configuration values are not suitable for a production environment; several default values are often undersized. In developing PostgreSQL applications, it is a good idea to have a test system that is configured very closely to a production environment to get accurate performance measures. In any PostgreSQL environment, the following configuration should be reviewed.

Maximum number of connections

The maximum number of connections is an important parameter in configuring a database. Each client connection consumes memory, thus also affecting the total amount of memory that can be allocated for other purposes. The `max_connections` configuration parameter's default value is `100`; lowering this value allows the database administrator to increase the `work_mem` setting. In general, it is good practice to use connection-pooling software to reduce the amount of memory used and increase performance, as killing and establishing a connection wastes time. There are a lot of connection-pooling tools, but the most mature ones are:

- PgBouncer
- Pgpool-II

Also, one could use connection pooling on the business level. For example, for Java there are many alternatives for connection pooling, such as Hikari, the Apache Tomcat connection pool, dbcp2, and c3p0.

Memory settings

There are several settings for controlling memory consumption and the way memory is consumed, and these settings are:

Shared buffers (`shared_buffers`**):** The default value for shared buffers is 32 MB; however, it is recommended to set it at around 25 percent of the total memory, but not more than 8 GB on Linux systems and 512 MB on Windows operating system. Sometimes, increasing `shared_buffers` to a very high value leads to an increase in performance, because the database can be cached completely in the RAM. However, the drawback of increasing this value too much is that one can't allocate memory for CPU operations such as sorting and hashing.

Working memory (`work_mem`**):** The default value is 4 MB; for CPU-bound operations, it is important to increase this value. The `work_mem` setting is linked with the number of connections, so the total amount of RAM used equals the number of connections multiplied by `work_mem`. Working memory is used to sort and hash, so it affects queries that use the ORDER BY, DISTINCT, UNION, and EXCEPT constructs. To test your working method, you could analyze a query that uses sort and take a look at whether the sort operation uses the memory or hard disk, as follows:

```
EXPLAIN ANALYZE SELECT n FROM generate_series(1,5) as foo(n) order by n;
Sort (cost=59.83..62.33 rows=1000 width=4) (actual
time=0.075..0.075 rows=5 loops=1)
Sort Key: n
Sort Method: quicksort Memory: 25kB
-> Function Scan on generate_series foo (cost=0.00..10.00
rows=1000 width=4) (actual time=0.018..0.018 rows=5 loops=1)"
Total runtime: 0.100 ms
```

Hard disk settings

There are several hard disk settings that can boost IO performance; however, this boost comes with a penalty. For example, the `fsync` setting forces each transaction to be written to the hard disk after each commit. Turning this off will increase performance, especially for bulk upload operations. A `max_wal_size` or `checkpoint_segments` of small value might lead to a performance penalty in write-heavy systems; on the other hand, increasing the `max_wal_size` or `checkpoint_segments` setting to a high value will increase recovery time.

In specific cases, such as bulk upload operations, performance can be increased by altering hard disk settings, changing the logging configuration to log minimal info, and finally, disabling autovacuuming; however, after the bulk operation is over, one should not forget to reset the server configurations and run the VACUUM ANALYZE command.

Planner-related settings

Effective cache size (effective_cache_size) should be set to an estimate of how much memory is available for disk caching in the operating system, and within the database, after taking into account what is used by the operating system and other applications. This value for a dedicated postgres server is around 50 percent to 70 percent of the total RAM.

Also, one could play with a planner setting, such as random_page_cost, to favor an index scan over sequential scans. The random_page_cost setting's default value is 4.0. In high-end SAN/NAS technologies, one could set this value to 3, and for SSD, one could use a random page cost of 1.5 to 2.5. The preceding list of parameters is minimal; in reality, one needs to also configure the logging, checkpoint, WAL settings, and vacuum settings.

Note that some parameters cannot be changed easily on production systems because they require a system restart, such as max_connections, shared_buffers, and fsync. In other cases, such as work_mem, it can be specified in the session, giving the developer the option of tuning queries that need specific work_mem.

Bench marking is your friend

pgbench is a simple program used to execute a prepared set of SQL commands to calculate the average transaction rate (transactions per second). pgbench is an implementation of the **Transaction Processing Performance Council (TPC) TPC-B** standard. pgbench can also be customized with scripts. In general, when using a benching framework, one needs to set it up on a different client in order to not steal the RAM and CPU from the tested server. Also, one should run pgbench several times with different load scenarios and configuration settings. Finally, in addition to pgbench, there are several open source implementations for different benchmarking standards, such as **TPC-C** and **TPC-H**. The pgbench synopsis is as follows: pgbench [options] dbname. The -i option is used to initialize the database with test tables, and the -s option determines the database scale factor, also known as the number of rows in each table.

A default output of `pgbench` using a default scale factor on a virtual machine with one CPU looks similar to the following:

```
$pgbench -i test_database
  creating tables...
  100000 of 100000 tuples (100%) done (elapsed 0.71 s, remaining 0.00 s).
  vacuum...
```

Finally, the `pgbench` manual pages (`pgbench --help`) explain the different query options.

Tuning performance for write

High write loads can have different patterns. For example, this can be a result of writing events to PostgreSQL or it can be a result of a bulk load from a database dump or an **ETL** job. One can tune PostgreSQL for high write loads by doing the following:

- Hardware configuration:
    - One should use RAID 1+0 instead of RAID 5 or 6. RAID 10 has much better performance for heavy writes. Also it is better to store transaction logs (`pg_xlog`) on a separate hard disk.
    - One can use SSD hard disks with **Write-back cache (WBC)**, which significantly increases write performance. Also make sure your SSDs can persist cached data on power failure.
- PostgreSQL server setting:
    - `fsync`: By default, `fsync` is on. This parameter makes sure that the database can be recovered in the event of a hardware crash. `fsync` makes sure that the data is actually written on the hard disk. You can disable this option if you can trust your hardware. Hardware failure might lead to corrupt data if this option is disabled.
    - `synchronous_commit` and `commit_delay`: When `synchronous_commit` is enabled by default, the transaction will wait until the WAL file is written to the hard disk to report `success` to the client. This will help to boost the performance of systems that have heavy concurrent small transactions. `commit_delay` is used to delay WAL flushing in microseconds. Combining both will reduce the effect off `fsync`. Unlike disabling `fsync`, a hardware crash will not cause data to be corrupted, but might cause data to be lost.

- `max_wal_size` or `checkpoint_segments` (in PostgreSQL 9.4 and older): the `checkpoint_segments` setting was deprecated in PostgreSQL 9.5 and replaced with `min_wal_size` and `max_wal_size`. The relation between `max_wal_size` and `checkpoint_segment` can be given as: `max_wal_size = (3 * checkpoint_segments) * 16 MB`. Increasing `max_wal_size` causes a performance gain since WAL are not written very frequently to hard disks. This affects checkpoint triggering and causes a slow recovery in crash scenarios.
- `wal_buffers`: This setting is disabled by default. It is used to store WAL data that is not written to a hard disk. Increasing this value helps a busy server with several concurrent clients. The maximum value of this setting is 16 MB.
- `maintenece_work_mem`: This setting does not directly affect the performance of data insert, but it increases the performance of creating and maintaining indexes. Increasing the value of `maintenece_work_mem` increases the performance of the `INSERT` operation indirectly, especially if the target table has indexes.
- Other settings: One can disable several other settings to increase performance, for example, logging and logging collection can increase performance if one is logging data heavily. Also, autovacuum can be disabled on bulk load scenarios in order to not interrupt the loading process.
- DDL and DML statements:
  - In bulk load scenarios, there are a lot of tricks to speed up performance. For example, one can disable triggers, indexes, and foreign keys on the table that one needs to copy. Also, one can use an `UNLOGGED` table and then convert it to a logged table using `ALTER TABLE <table name> SET LOGGED;`.
  - For a heavy insert scenario, there are several common tricks. The first trick is to increase the batch size of each transaction. This is quite useful because it will decrease the delay caused by `synchronous_commit`. In addition to that, it will preserve transaction IDs, thus, less vacuum is required to prevent transaction IDs wraparound. The second trick is to use `COPY` command. The JDBC driver `CopyManager` can be used for this purpose. Finally, it is a good practice to use prepared statements. Prepared statements are faster to execute since the statements are precompiled on the PostgreSQL side.

- External tools: For bulk uploads one can use `pg_bulkload`, which is quite fast.

To sum up, for a heavy write systems it is good to write to the hard disk in batches instead of single `INSERT` SQL statements. Also, it is better to use a ;`COPY` statement instead of an `INSERT` statement. Finally, one can also parallelize statements using several sessions instead of one session. Starting from PostgreSQL 9.3, one can use `COPY` with the `FREEZE` option, which is used often for initial data loading. The `FREEZE` option violates the MVCC concept in PostgreSQL, which means the data is immediately visible to other sessions after it is loaded.

To test the effect of `fsync`, let's prepare a SQL script for `pgbench` as follows:

```
$ cat test.sql
\set aid random(1, 100000 * :scale)
\set bid random(1, 1 * :scale)
\set tid random(1, 10 * :scale)
\set delta random(-5000, 5000)
BEGIN;
UPDATE pgbench_accounts SET abalance = abalance + :delta WHERE aid = :aid;
UPDATE pgbench_branches SET bbalance = bbalance + :delta WHERE bid = :bid;
INSERT INTO pgbench_history (tid, bid, aid, delta, mtime) VALUES (:tid,
:bid, :aid, :delta, CURRENT_TIMESTAMP);
END;
```

Now let's run `pgbench` before making any changes to test the system base performance. Note that, in this test, all settings have default values:

```
$pgbench -t 1000 -c 15 -f test.sql
starting vacuum...end.
transaction type: test.sql
scaling factor: 1
query mode: simple
number of clients: 15
number of threads: 1
number of transactions per client: 1000
number of transactions actually processed: 15000/15000
latency average = 18.455 ms
tps = 812.801437 (including connections establishing)
tps = 813.032862 (excluding connections establishing)
```

To test the effect of disabling `fsync`, one can alter the system settings and restart the server as follows:

```
$ psql -U postgres << EOF
> ALTER SYSTEM RESET ALL;
> ALTER SYSTEM SET fsync to off;
> EOF
ALTER SYSTEM
ALTER SYSTEM

$/etc/init.d/postgresql restart
[ ok ] Restarting postgresql (via systemctl): postgresql.service.

$ pgbench -t 1000 -c 15 -f test.sql
starting vacuum...end.
transaction type: test.sql
scaling factor: 1
query mode: simple
number of clients: 15
number of threads: 1
number of transactions per client: 1000
number of transactions actually processed: 15000/15000
latency average = 11.976 ms
tps = 1252.552937 (including connections establishing)
tps = 1253.082492 (excluding connections establishing)
```

To test the effect of `synchronous_commit` and `commit_delay`, one can alter the settings as follows:

```
$ psql -U postgres << EOF
> ALTER SYSTEM RESET ALL;
> ALTER SYSTEM SET synchronous_commit to off;
> ALTER SYSTEM SET commit_delay to 100000;
> EOF
ALTER SYSTEM
ALTER SYSTEM
ALTER SYSTEM
$ /etc/init.d/postgresql restart
[ ok ] Restarting postgresql (via systemctl): postgresql.service.

$ pgbench -t 1000 -c 15 -f test.sql
starting vacuum...end.
transaction type: test.sql
scaling factor: 1
query mode: simple
number of clients: 15
number of threads: 1
number of transactions per client: 1000
```

```
number of transactions actually processed: 15000/15000
latency average = 12.521 ms
tps = 1197.960750 (including connections establishing)
tps = 1198.416907 (excluding connections establishing)
```

Tuning performance for read

PostgreSQL provides the means to figure out why a certain query is slow. Behind the scenes, PostgreSQL analyzes tables, collects statistics from them, and builds histograms using autovacuuming. Autovacuuming, in general, is used to recover disk space, update table statistics, and perform other maintenance tasks, such as preventing transaction ID wraparound. Table statistics allow PostgreSQL to pick up an execution plan at the least cost. The least cost is calculated by taking into account the IO and, naturally, the CPU cost. Also, PostgreSQL enables users to see the generated execution plan by providing the EXPLAIN command.

For beginners, it is extremely useful to write the same query in different ways and compare the results. For example, in some cases, the NOT IN construct can be converted to LEFT JOIN or NOT EXIST. Also, the IN construct can be rewritten using INNER JOIN as well as EXISTS. Writing the query in several ways teaches the developer when to use or avoid a certain construct and what the conditions that favor a certain construct are. In general, the NOT IN construct can sometimes cause performance issues because the planner cannot use indexes to evaluate the query.

Another important issue is to keep tracking new SQL commands and features. The PostgreSQL development community is very active, and their contributions are often targeted toward solving common issues. For example, the LATERAL JOIN construct, which was introduced in PostgreSQL 9.3, can be used to optimize certain GROUP BY and LIMIT scenarios.

Explain command and execution plan

The first step in tuning PostgreSQL queries is to understand how to read the execution plans generated by the EXPLAIN command. The EXPLAIN command shows the execution plan of a statement and how data from tables is scanned; for example, a table might be scanned using an index or sequential scan. Also, it shows how tables are joined, the join method, and the estimated number of rows.

The EXPLAIN command also has several options; the ANALYZE option causes the statement to be executed and returns the actual time and number of rows. Finally, the EXPLAIN command can give insights into a buffer's usage and caching. The synopsis for the EXPLAIN command is as follows, where the option can be one of: ANALYZE, VERBOSE, COSTS, BUFFERS, TIMING, SUMMARY, and FORMAT :

```
\h EXPLAIN
Description: show the execution plan of a statement
Syntax:
EXPLAIN [ ( option [, ...] ) ] statement
EXPLAIN [ ANALYZE ] [ VERBOSE ] statement
```

To experiment with EXPLAIN command, one can create a simple table and populate it with data, as follows:

```
postgres=# CREATE TABLE guru ( id INT PRIMARY KEY, name TEXT NOT NULL );
CREATE TABLE
postgres=# INSERT INTO guru SELECT n , md5 (random()::text) FROM
generate_series (1, 100000) AS foo(n);
INSERT 0 100000
postgres=# -- To update table statistics
postgres=# ANALYSE guru;
ANALYZE
```

To get the execution plan of selecting all the records for the table guru, one can use EXPLAIN command, as follows:

```
postgres=# EXPLAIN SELECT * FROM guru;
 QUERY PLAN
----------------------------------------------------------
 Seq Scan on guru (cost=0.00..1834.00 rows=100000 width=37)
(1 row)
```

The execution plan is only a one-node sequential scan on the guru table, as shown in the preceding code. The number of rows is estimated correctly, as we analyzed the table after insert. Autovacuum is important for keeping your database's statistics up to date.

Certainly, wrong statistics mean poor execution plans. After database bulk operations, it is good to run the ANALYZE command to update the statistics. Also, one could control the data sampling performed by ANALYZE using the following:

```
ALTER TABLE <table name> ALTER COLUMN <column name> SET STATISTICS
<integer>;
```

Increasing column statistics allows a better estimation of rows, but also makes the autovacuum process slower. The cost is an estimation of the effort required to execute the query. In the preceding example, the cost, `0.00`, is the cost to retrieve the first row, while the cost, `1834.00`, is the cost to retrieve all rows, which is calculated as follows: `(relpages * seq_page cost) + (reltuples * cpu_tuple_cost)`. The number of relation pages (`relpages`) and the number of rows in relation (`reltuples`) can be found in `pg_class`. `seq_page_cost` and `cpu_tuple_cost` contains planner related configuration settings. So, the cost `1834` is calculated as shown in the following example:

```
postgres=# SELECT relpages*current_setting('seq_page_cost')::numeric +
reltuples*current_setting('cpu_tuple_cost')::numeric as cost FROM pg_class
WHERE relname='guru';
 cost
------
 1834
(1 row)
```

For the simple case of a sequential scan, it is quite straightforward to calculate the cost. However, when a query involves predicates' evaluation, grouping, ordering, and joining, cost estimation becomes complicated. Finally, the width `37` is the average width of the tuple in bytes. This information can be found in the `pg_stats` table. To execute and get the cost in real time, one could use `EXPLAIN (ANALYZE)` or `EXPLAIN ANALYZE`. The following example returns all the rows where the ID is between `10` and `20`:

```
postgres=# EXPLAIN ANALYZE SELECT * FROM guru WHERE id >= 10 and id < 20;
                                       QUERY PLAN
-----------------------------------------------------------------------------
-----------------------------------------------
 Index Scan using guru_pkey on guru (cost=0.29..8.51 rows=11 width=37)
(actual time=0.007..0.010 rows=10 loops=1)
   Index Cond: ((id >= 10) AND (id < 20))
 Planning time: 0.132 ms
 Execution time: 0.028 ms
(4 rows)
```

In the preceding query, the planner got a very close estimation compared to the real values: it estimated 11 rows instead of 10. Also, the planner-generated execution plan now uses an index scan because we have used predicates. In the execution plan, one could also see other information, such as the number of loops and actual time. Note that the execution plan is four lines with different indentations. One should read the execution plan bottom-up and from the most to least indented. The `Index Cond: ((id >= 10) AND (id < 20))` is indented and belongs to the `Index Scan` node.

The EXPLAIN (BUFFERS) option shows the effect of caching and whether the cache is used and configured properly. To take a look at the complete effect of caching, one needs to perform cold and hot testing. Also, one can control the format of the execution plan. The following example shows the effect of using the BUFFERS and FORMAT options' cold and hot testing. To do cold testing, let's stop and start the server, as follows:

```
$ /etc/init.d/postgresql stop
$ /etc/init.d/postgresql start
```

 Often, PostgreSQL restart is not enough to clean the cache. Note that PostgreSQL also utilizes the operating system buffers. In Ubuntu, one can clean the cache with the following command: echo 3 > /proc/sys/vm/drop_caches.

Now, let's read the guru table:

```
postgres=# EXPLAIN (ANALYZE, FORMAT YAML, BUFFERS) SELECT * FROM guru;
         QUERY PLAN
--------------------------------
 - Plan: +
     Node Type: "Seq Scan" +
     Parallel Aware: false +
     Relation Name: "guru" +
     Alias: "guru" +
     Startup Cost: 0.00 +
     Total Cost: 1834.00 +
     Plan Rows: 100000 +
     Plan Width: 37 +
     Actual Startup Time: 0.016+
     Actual Total Time: 209.332+
     Actual Rows: 100000 +
     Actual Loops: 1 +
     Shared Hit Blocks: 0 +
     Shared Read Blocks: 834 +
     Shared Dirtied Blocks: 0 +
     Shared Written Blocks: 0 +
     Local Hit Blocks: 0 +
     Local Read Blocks: 0 +
     Local Dirtied Blocks: 0 +
     Local Written Blocks: 0 +
     Temp Read Blocks: 0 +
     Temp Written Blocks: 0 +
   Planning Time: 0.660 +
   Triggers: +
   Execution Time: 213.879
 (1 row)
```

To perform hot testing, the query needs to be executed again, as follows:

```
postgres=# EXPLAIN (ANALYZE, FORMAT YAML, BUFFERS) SELECT * FROM guru;
           QUERY PLAN
---------------------------------
 - Plan: +
     Node Type: "Seq Scan" +
     Parallel Aware: false +
     Relation Name: "guru" +
     Alias: "guru" +
     Startup Cost: 0.00 +
     Total Cost: 1834.00 +
     Plan Rows: 100000 +
     Plan Width: 37 +
     Actual Startup Time: 0.009+
     Actual Total Time: 10.105 +
     Actual Rows: 100000 +
     Actual Loops: 1 +
     Shared Hit Blocks: 834 +
     Shared Read Blocks: 0 +
     Shared Dirtied Blocks: 0 +
     Shared Written Blocks: 0 +
     Local Hit Blocks: 0 +
     Local Read Blocks: 0 +
     Local Dirtied Blocks: 0 +
     Local Written Blocks: 0 +
     Temp Read Blocks: 0 +
     Temp Written Blocks: 0 +
   Planning Time: 0.035 +
   Triggers: +
   Execution Time: 14.447
(1 row)
```

The first thing one can notice is the execution time difference. The second execution time is around 93% less than the first execution time. This behavior is due to reading the data from memory instead of the hard disk, as we saw in the execution plan. For more details, have a look on `Shared Hit Blocks`, which simply means the data is found in the memory.

Detecting problems in query plans

The EXPLAIN command can show why a certain query is slow, especially if the two options BUFFER and ANALYZE are used. There are some hints that enable us to decide whether the execution plan is good or not; these hints are as follows:

- **The estimated row number in comparison with the actual rows**: This is important because this parameter defines the method of the query's execution. There are two cases: the estimated number of rows may either be overestimated or underestimated. Wrong estimation affects the entire algorithm, which is used to fetch data from the hard disk, sort it, join it, and so on. In general, if the number of rows is overestimated, this affects performance, but not as much as if the number of rows is underestimated. On one hand, if one performs a nested loop join on very big tables, the execution time will increase exponentially assuming the nested loop join cost is $O(n^2)$ for simplicity. On the other hand, executing hash join on a small table will reduce the query execution speed, but the effect will not be devastating, as in the first case.

- **In-memory or in-disk sort operation**: When performing a sorting operation, such as DISTINCT, LIMIT, ORDER, GROUP BY, and so on, if there is enough memory, this operation will be performed in the RAM, otherwise the hard disk will be used.

- **Buffer cache**: It is important to check how much data is buffered and dirtied. Reading data from buffers will increase performance.

In order to show a wrong execution plan, let's confuse postgres planner by performing an operation on the column ID, as follows:

```
postgres=# EXPLAIN SELECT * FROM guru WHERE upper(id::text)::int < 20;
 QUERY PLAN
------------------------------------------------------
 Seq Scan on guru  (cost=0.00..3334.00 rows=33333 width=37)
   Filter: ((upper((id)::text))::integer < 20)
(2 rows)
```

In the preceding example, PostgreSQL planner is not able to evaluate upper(id::text)::int < 20 properly. Also, it cannot use the index scan because there is no index matching the column expression, and in any case, index will not be chosen here because of the high number of estimated rows. If this query were a subquery of another query, the error would be cascaded because it might be executed several times. We have artificially created this problem, but a wrong number in row estimation is one of the most common issues. It might be a result of wrong autovacuum configuration. In big tables, it might be a result of small target statistics.

Finally, knowledge about different algorithms, such as the nested loop join, hash join, index scan, merge join, bitmap index scan, and so on, can be useful in detecting the root cause of performance degradation. In the following example, the effect of nested loop join is examined on a big table. To check different algorithms on execution plans, let's first execute the query without disabling the planner settings, as follows:

```
postgres=# EXPLAIN ANALYZE WITH tmp AS (SELECT * FROM guru WHERE id
<10000) SELECT * FROM tmp a inner join tmp b on a.id = b.id;
                                                       QUERY PLAN
-------------------------------------------------------------------------
-----------------------------------------------------------------
 Merge Join (cost=2079.95..9468.28 rows=489258 width=72) (actual
time=8.193..26.330 rows=9999 loops=1)
   Merge Cond: (a.id = b.id)
   CTE tmp
     -> Index Scan using guru_pkey on guru (cost=0.29..371.40 rows=9892
width=37) (actual time=0.022..3.134 rows=9999 loops=1)
           Index Cond: (id < 10000)
   -> Sort (cost=854.28..879.01 rows=9892 width=36) (actual
time=6.238..8.641 rows=9999 loops=1)
         Sort Key: a.id
         Sort Method: quicksort Memory: 1166kB
         -> CTE Scan on tmp a (cost=0.00..197.84 rows=9892 width=36)
(actual time=0.024..5.179 rows=9999 loops=1)
   -> Sort (cost=854.28..879.01 rows=9892 width=36) (actual
time=1.950..2.658 rows=9999 loops=1)
         Sort Key: b.id
         Sort Method: quicksort Memory: 1166kB
         -> CTE Scan on tmp b (cost=0.00..197.84 rows=9892 width=36)
(actual time=0.001..0.960 rows=9999 loops=1)
 Planning time: 0.143 ms
 Execution time: 26.880 ms
(15 rows)
```

To test nested loop, we need to disable other join methods, mainly merge join and hash join:

```
postgres=#set enable_mergejoin to off ;
SET
postgres=#set enable_hashjoin to off ;
SET
postgres=# EXPLAIN ANALYZE WITH tmp AS (SELECT * FROM guru WHERE id <10000)
SELECT * FROM tmp a inner join tmp b on a.id = b.id;
                                                       QUERY PLAN
-------------------------------------------------------------------------
-----------------------------------------------------------------
 Nested Loop (cost=371.40..2202330.60 rows=489258 width=72) (actual
time=0.029..15389.001 rows=9999 loops=1)
   Join Filter: (a.id = b.id)
```

```
    Rows Removed by Join Filter: 99970002
    CTE tmp
      -> Index Scan using guru_pkey on guru (cost=0.29..371.40 rows=9892
width=37) (actual time=0.022..2.651 rows=9999 loops=1)
            Index Cond: (id < 10000)
    -> CTE Scan on tmp a (cost=0.00..197.84 rows=9892 width=36) (actual
time=0.024..1.445 rows=9999 loops=1)
    -> CTE Scan on tmp b (cost=0.00..197.84 rows=9892 width=36) (actual
time=0.000..0.803 rows=9999 loops=9999)
 Planning time: 0.117 ms
 Execution time: 15390.996 ms
(10 rows)
```

Notice the huge difference of execution between merge join and nested loop join. Also, as shown in the example, merge join requires a sorted list.

PostgreSQL is clever; the previous example can be written in SQL without using CTE. The previous example is written using CTE to demonstrate extreme scenarios when rows are underestimated. In the preceding example, even though the hash join and merge join are disabled, PostgreSQL used nested loop with index scan to execute the query. In this case, instead of doing two loops, it was executed in one loop, which has increased the performance dramatically compared with the CTE example.

```
EXPLAIN ANALYZE SELECT * FROM guru as a inner join guru b on a.id = b.id
WHERE a.id < 10000;
                                                          QUERY PLAN
---------------------------------------------------------------------------
---------------------------------------------------------
 Nested Loop (cost=0.58..7877.92 rows=9892 width=74) (actual
time=0.025..44.130 rows=9999 loops=1)
    -> Index Scan using guru_pkey on guru a (cost=0.29..371.40 rows=9892
width=37) (actual time=0.018..14.139 rows=9999 loops=1)
            Index Cond: (id < 10000)
    -> Index Scan using guru_pkey on guru b (cost=0.29..0.76 rows=1
width=37) (actual time=0.003..0.003 rows=1 loops=9999)
            Index Cond: (id = a.id)
 Planning time: 0.123 ms
 Execution time: 44.873 ms
(7 rows)
```

 If you have a very long and complex execution plan and it is not clear where the bottleneck is, try to disable an algorithm that has exponential effects, such as nested loop join.

Common mistakes in writing queries

There are some common mistakes and bad practices that a developer may fall into, which are as follows:

Unnecessary operations

There are different ways to introduce extra operations such as hard disk scans, sorting, and filtering. For example, some developers often use DISTINCT even if it is not required, or do not know the difference between UNION, UNION ALL, EXCEPT, EXCEPT ALL, and so on. This causes slow queries, especially if the expected number of rows is high. The following two queries are equivalent simply because the table has a primary key, but the one with DISTINCT is much slower:

```
postgres=# \timing
Timing is on.
postgres=# SELECT * FROM guru;
Time: 85,089 ms
postgres=# SELECT DISTINCT * FROM guru;
Time: 191,335 ms
```

Another common mistake is to use DISTINCT with UNION, as in the following query:

```
postgres=# SELECT * FROM guru UNION SELECT * FROM guru;
Time: 267,258 ms
postgres=# SELECT DISTINCT * FROM guru UNION SELECT DISTINCT * FROM guru;
Time: 346,014 ms
```

Unlike UNION ALL, the UNION statement eliminates all duplicates in the final result set. Due to this, there is no need to do sorting and filtering several times.

Another common mistake is to use ORDER BY in a view definition. If ORDER BY is used when selecting data from the view, it also introduces unnecessary sort operations, as in the following query:

```
postgres=# CREATE OR REPLACE VIEW guru_vw AS SELECT * FROM guru order by 1
asc;
CREATE VIEW
Time: 42,370 ms
postgres=#
postgres=# SELECT * FROM guru_vw;
Time: 132,292 ms
```

In the preceding examples, retrieving data from the view takes 132 ms, while retrieving data from the table directly takes only 85 ms.

Misplaced or missing indexes

Missing indexes on column expressions causes a full table scan. There are several cases where indexes can help to increase performance. For example, it is a good practice to index foreign keys. To test this case, let's create a table and populate it as follows:

```
CREATE TABLE success_story (id int, description text, guru_id int
references guru(id));
INSERT INTO success_story (id, description, guru_id) SELECT n,
md5(n::text), random()*99999+1 from generate_series(1,200000) as foo(n) ;
```

Now, to get a certain guru success_story, one can write a simple query that joins both guru and success_story tables, as follows:

```
postgres=# EXPLAIN ANALYZE SELECT * FROM guru inner JOIN success_story on
guru.id = success_story.guru_id WHERE guru_id = 1000;
                                                         QUERY PLAN
-------------------------------------------------------------------------
-------------------------------------------
 Nested Loop (cost=0.29..4378.34 rows=3 width=78) (actual
time=0.030..48.011 rows=1 loops=1)
   -> Index Scan using guru_pkey on guru (cost=0.29..8.31 rows=1 width=37)
(actual time=0.017..0.020 rows=1 loops=1)
         Index Cond: (id = 1000)
   -> Seq Scan on success_story (cost=0.00..4370.00 rows=3 width=41)
(actual time=0.011..47.987 rows=1 loops=1)
         Filter: (guru_id = 1000)
         Rows Removed by Filter: 199999
 Planning time: 0.114 ms
 Execution time: 48.040 ms
(8 rows)
```

Note that the success_story table was sequentially scanned. To fix this, an index can be created on the foreign key, as follows:

```
postgres=# CREATE index on success_story (guru_id);
CREATE INDEX
postgres=# EXPLAIN ANALYZE SELECT * FROM guru inner JOIN success_story on
guru.id =success_story.guru_id WHERE guru_id = 1000;
 QUERY PLAN
-------------------------------------------------------------------------
-----------   ------------------------------------------------
 Nested Loop (cost=4.74..24.46 rows=3 width=78) (actual time=0.023..0.024
```

```
rows=1 loops=1)
 -> Index Scan using guru_pkey on guru (cost=0.29..8.31 rows=1 width=37)
(actual time=0.010..0.010 rows=1 loops=1)
 Index Cond: (id = 1000)
 -> Bitmap Heap Scan on success_story (cost=4.44..16.12 rows=3 width=41)
(actual time=0.009..0.010 rows=1 loops=1)
 Recheck Cond: (guru_id = 1000)
 Heap Blocks: exact=1
 -> Bitmap Index Scan on success_story_guru_id_idx (cost=0.00..4.44 rows=3
width=0) (actual time=0.006..0.006 rows=1 loops=1)
 Index Cond: (guru_id = 1000)
 Planning time: 0.199 ms
 Execution time: 0.057 ms
```

Note the execution time difference between timings after the index has been created. The execution time was reduced from 48 ms to around .057 ms.

Text search can also benefit from indexes. In several cases, one needs to search case-insensitive data, such as search and login. For example, one could log into their account using the login name as case-insensitive. This could be achieved using lower or uppercase matching. To test this, let's create another function, as follows, as the md5 hashing only generates lowercase text:

```
CREATE OR REPLACE FUNCTION generate_random_text ( int ) RETURNS TEXT AS
$$
SELECT
string_agg(substr('0123456789abcdefghijklmnopqrstuvwxyzABCDEFGHIJKLMNOPQRST
UVWXYZ', trunc(random() * 62)::integer + 1, 1), '') FROM
generate_series(1, $1)
$$
LANGUAGE SQL;
```

To create a table with a lower and uppercase login, one can execute the following SQL code:

```
CREATE TABLE login as SELECT n, generate_random_text(8) as login_name FROM
generate_series(1, 1000) as foo(n);
CREATE INDEX ON login(login_name);
VACUUM ANALYZE login;
```

The generate_random_text() function is used to generate random text of a certain length. Let's assume that we want to check whether an entry exists in table one; we could do this as follows:

```
postgres=# EXPLAIN SELECT * FROM login WHERE login_name = 'jxaG6gjJ';
                            QUERY PLAN
--------------------------------------------------------------------------
--------
```

```
   Index Scan using login_login_name_idx on login (cost=0.28..8.29 rows=1
width=13)
   Index Cond: (login_name = 'jxaG6gjJ'::text)
(2 rows)
```

As seen in the preceding example, an index scan is used, as there is an index on `login_name`. Using functions on constant arguments also causes the index to be used if this function is not volatile, as the optimizer evaluates the function as follows:

```
postgres=# EXPLAIN SELECT * FROM login WHERE login_name =
lower('jxaG6gjJ');
                                QUERY PLAN
--------------------------------------------------------------------------
--------
   Index Scan using login_login_name_idx on login (cost=0.28..8.29 rows=1
width=13)
   Index Cond: (login_name = 'jxag6gjj'::text)
(2 rows)
```

Using functions on columns, as stated in the preceding example, causes a sequential scan, as shown in the following query:

```
postgres=# EXPLAIN SELECT * FROM login WHERE lower(login_name) =
lower('jxaG6gjJ');
 QUERY PLAN
---------------------------------------------------------
 Seq Scan on login (cost=0.00..21.00 rows=5 width=13)
 Filter: (lower(login_name) = 'jxag6gjj'::text)
(2 rows)
```

Note that, here, the number of rows returned is also five, as the optimizer cannot evaluate the predicate correctly. To solve this issue, simply add an index, as follows:

```
postgres=# CREATE INDEX ON login(lower(login_name));
CREATE INDEX
postgres=# analyze login;
ANALYZE
postgres=# EXPLAIN SELECT * FROM login WHERE lower(login_name) =
lower('jxaG6gjJ');
                                QUERY PLAN
--------------------------------------------------------------------------
---
   Index Scan using login_lower_idx on login (cost=0.28..8.29 rows=1
width=13)
   Index Cond: (lower(login_name) = 'jxag6gjj'::text)
(2 rows)
```

Also, text indexing is governed by the access pattern. In general, there are two ways to index text: the first approach is to use an index with `opclass`, which allows an anchored text search, and the second approach is to use `tsquery` and `tsvector`:

```
postgres=# CREATE INDEX on login (login_name text_pattern_ops);
CREATE INDEX
postgres=# EXPLAIN ANaLYZE SELECT * FROM login WHERE login_name like 'a%';
                                                            QUERY PLAN
-----------------------------------------------------------------------------------
----------------------------------------------------------
 Index Scan using login_login_name_idx1 on login (cost=0.28..8.30 rows=1
width=13) (actual time=0.019..0.063 rows=19 loops=1)
   Index Cond: ((login_name ~>=~ 'a'::text) AND (login_name ~<~ 'b'::text))
   Filter: (login_name ~~ 'a%'::text)
 Planning time: 0.109 ms
 Execution time: 0.083 ms
(5 rows)

Time: 0,830 ms
```

Finally, if one would like to have an anchored case insensitive search, one can combine the function `lower` and `text_pattern_ops`, as follows:

```
postgres=# CREATE INDEX login_lower_idx1 ON login (lower(login_name)
text_pattern_ops);
CREATE INDEX
postgres=# EXPLAIN ANaLYZE SELECT * FROM login WHERE lower(login_name) like
'a%';
                                                            QUERY PLAN
-----------------------------------------------------------------------------------
---------------------------------------------------
 Bitmap Heap Scan on login (cost=4.58..11.03 rows=30 width=13) (actual
time=0.037..0.060 rows=30 loops=1)
   Filter: (lower(login_name) ~~ 'a%'::text)
   Heap Blocks: exact=6
   -> Bitmap Index Scan on login_lower_idx1 (cost=0.00..4.58 rows=30
width=0) (actual time=0.025..0.025 rows=30 loops=1)
         Index Cond: ((lower(login_name) ~>=~ 'a'::text) AND
(lower(login_name) ~<~ 'b'::text))
 Planning time: 0.471 ms
 Execution time: 0.080 ms
(7 rows)
```

Using CTE when not mandatory

Common table expressions (**CTEs**) allow developers to write very complex logic. Also, a CTE can be used in several places to optimize performance. However, using a CTE may be problematic in the case of predicate push down, as PostgreSQL does not optimize beyond CTE boundaries; each CTE runs in isolation. To understand this limitation, let's have a look at the following two dummy equivalent examples and note the difference between their performance:

```
\o /dev/null
\timing
postgres=# SELECT * FROM guru WHERE id = 4;
Time: 0,678 ms
postgres=# WITH gurus as (SELECT * FROM guru) SELECT * FROM gurus WHERE id
= 4;
Time: 67,641 ms
```

Using the PL/pgSQL procedural language consideration

PL/pgSQL language caching is an amazing tool to increase performance; however, if the developer is not careful, it may lead to bad execution of their plans. For example, let's assume that we want to wrap the following query in a function:

```
SELECT * FROM guru WHERE id <= <predicate>;
```

In this example, we should not cache the execution plan, since the execution plan might differ depending on the predicate value. For example, if we use the value 1 as the predicate, the execution planner will favor an index scan. However, if we use the predicate 90,000, the planner will mostly favor the use of a sequential scan. Due to this, caching the execution of this query is wrong. However, consider that the preceding select statement is as follows:

```
SELECT * FROM guru  WHERE id = <predicate>;
```

In this case, it is better to cache it, as the execution plan is the same for all the predicates due to the index on the ID column. Also, exception handling in PL/pgSQL is quite expensive, so one should be careful when using this feature.

Cross column correlation

Cross column correlation can cause a wrong estimation of the number of rows, as PostgreSQL assumes that each column is independent of other columns. In reality, there are a lot of examples where this is not true. For example, one could find patterns where the first and last names in certain cultures are correlated. Another example is the `country` and `language` preference of clients. To understand cross column correlation, let's create a table called `client`, as follows:

```
CREATE TABLE client (
    id serial primary key,
    name text,
    country text,
    language text
);
```

To test the cross correlation statistics, the following sample data is generated as follows:

```
INSERT INTO client(name, country, language) SELECT generate_random_text(8),
'Germany', 'German' FROM generate_series(1, 10);
 INSERT INTO client(name, country, language) SELECT
generate_random_text(8), 'USA', 'English' FROM generate_series(1, 10);
 VACUUM ANALYZE client;
```

If one wants to get users where `language` is `German` and `country` is `Germany`, one will end up with a wrong estimation of rows, as both columns are correlated, as follows:

```
postgres=# EXPLAIN SELECT * FROM client WHERE country = 'Germany' and
language='German';
                             QUERY PLAN
-----------------------------------------------------------------
 Seq Scan on client (cost=0.00..1.30 rows=5 width=26)
   Filter: ((country = 'Germany'::text) AND (language = 'German'::text))
(2 rows)
```

Note that the number of estimated rows is five instead of ten, which is calculated as follows: *estimated number of rows = total number of rows * selectivity of country * selectivity of language*, thus, *the estimated number of rows = 20 * .5 * .5 = 5*. Prior to PostgreSQL 10, a simple way to correct the number of rows is to change the physical design of the table and combine both fields into one, as follows:

```
CREATE TABLE client2 (
    id serial primary key,
    name text,
    client_information jsonb
);
```

```
   INSERT INTO client2(name, client_information) SELECT
generate_random_text(8),'{"country":"Germany", "language":"German"}' FROM
generate_series(1,10);
   INSERT INTO client2(name, client_information) SELECT
generate_random_text(8),'{"country":"USA", "language":"English"}' FROM
generate_series(1, 10);
   VACUUM ANALYZE client2;
```

In the preceding example, jsonb is used to wrap the country and language; the explain plan gives the correct estimation of the number of rows, as follows:

```
postgres=# EXPLAIN SELECT * FROM client2 WHERE client_information =
'{"country":"USA","language":"English"}';
                                      QUERY PLAN
-----------------------------------------------------------------------------
----------
 Seq Scan on client2 (cost=0.00..1.25 rows=10 width=60)
    Filter: (client_information = '{"country": "USA", "language":
"English"}'::jsonb)
(2 rows)
```

In postgreSQL 10, cross column statistics have been introduced, which means one does not need to change the physical structure to overcome this issue. However, one needs to inform the planner about these dependencies. In order to extend the statistics, one can run the following statement:

```
CREATE STATISTICS stats (dependencies) ON country, language FROM client;
```

To view the newly statistic object one needs to first analyze the table and then query the pg_catalog schema, as follows:

```
postgres=# analyze client;
ANALYZE
Time: 5,007 ms
postgres=# SELECT stxname, stxkeys, stxdependencies FROM pg_statistic_ext
WHERE stxname = 'stats';
 stxname | stxkeys | stxdependencies
---------+---------+----------------------------------------
 stats   | 3 4     | {"3 => 4": 1.000000, "4 => 3": 1.000000}
(1 row)

Time: 0,671 ms
```

The column `stxkey` contains information about the column's locations in the original table, in this case, 3 and 4. `stxdependencies` defines the correlation dependencies; in our case we have 100% dependency between the `language` and `country` and visa versa. Finally, let's rerun the previous to see whether the extended statistics helped to solve the cross column statistics:

```
postgres=# EXPLAIN SELECT * FROM client WHERE country = 'Germany' and
language='German';
 QUERY PLAN
----------------------------------------------------------------------
 Seq Scan on client (cost=0.00..1.30 rows=10 width=26)
 Filter: ((country = 'Germany'::text) AND (language = 'German'::text))
(2 rows)
```

Table partitioning

Table partitioning is used to increase performance by physically arranging data in the hard disk based on a certain grouping criteria. There are two techniques for table partitioning:

- **Vertical table partitioning**: The table is divided into several tables in order to decrease the row size. This allows a faster sequential scan on divided tables, as a relation page holds more rows. To explain, let's assume that we want to store pictures for each client in the database by adding a column of the byte or blob type to the client table. Now, since we have a table that might contain a big row, the number of rows per page is reduced. To solve this, one can create another table that references the client table, as follows:

```
CREATE TABLE client_picture (
id int primary key,
client_id int references client(id),
picture bytea NOT NULL
);
```

- **Horizontal table partitioning**: This is used to decrease the whole table size by splitting rows over multiple tables; it is supported by table inheritance and the constraint exclusion. In horizontal table partitioning, the parent table is often a proxy, while the child tables are used to store actual data. Table inheritance can be used to implement horizontal table partitioning, whereas constraint exclusion is used to optimize performance by only accessing the child tables that contain the required data when performing a query.

Constraint exclusion limitations

Sometimes, constraint exclusion fails to kick in, leading to very slow queries. There are limitations on constraint exclusion, which are as follows:

- The constraint exclusion setting can be disabled
- Constraint exclusion does not work if the where expression is not written in the equality or range manner
- Constraint exclusion does not work with non-immutable functions such as CURRENT_TIMESTAMP, so if the predicate in the WHERE clause contains a function that needs to be executed at runtime, then the constraint exclusion will not work
- A heavily partitioned table might decrease performance by increasing planning time

Let's assume that we want to partition a table based on a text pattern, such as pattern LIKE 'a%'. This can be achieved by rewriting the LIKE construct using range equality, such as pattern >='a ' and pattern < 'b'. So, instead of having a check constraint on a child table using the LIKE construct, one should have it based on ranges. Also, if a user performs a SELECT statement using the LIKE construct, the constraint exclusion will not work.

Query rewriting

Writing a query in several ways enables the developer to detect some issues in coding best practices, planner parameters, and performance optimization. The example of returning the guru IDs, names, and the count of success_stories can be written as follows:

```
postgres=# \o /dev/null
postgres=# \timing
Timing is on.
postgres=# SELECT id, name, (SELECT count(*) FROM success_story where
guru_id=id) FROM guru;
Time: 144,929 ms
postgres=# WITH counts AS (SELECT count(*), guru_id FROM success_story
group by guru_id) SELECT id, name, COALESCE(count,0) FROM guru LEFT JOIN
counts on guru_id = id;
Time: 728,855 ms
postgres=# SELECT guru.id, name, COALESCE(count(*),0) FROM guru LEFT JOIN
success_story on guru_id = guru.id group by guru.id, name ;
Time: 452,659 ms
postgres=# SELECT id, name, COALESCE(count,0) FROM guru LEFT JOIN ( SELECT
count(*), guru_id FROM success_story group by guru_id )as counts on guru_id
```

```
= id;
Time: 824,164 ms
postgres=# SELECT guru.id, name, count(*) FROM guru LEFT JOIN success_story
on guru_id = guru.id group by guru.id, name ;
Time: 454,865 ms
postgres=# SELECT id, name, count FROM guru , LATERAL (SELECT count(*) FROM
success_story WHERE guru_id=id ) as foo(count);
Time: 137,902 ms
postgres=# SELECT id, name, count FROM guru LEFT JOIN LATERAL (SELECT
count(*) FROM success_story WHERE guru_id=id ) AS foo ON true;
Time: 156,294 ms
```

In the previous example, using LATERAL gave the best performance results, while CTE and joining a subquery gave the worst performance. Note that the result shown here might deviate on other machines due to hardware specifications such as hard disk specifications. LATERAL is very powerful at optimizing queries that require limiting the results, such as *give me the top ten stories for each journalist*. Also, LATERAL is very useful when joining table functions.

Summary

There are several aspects to tuning the performance of PostgreSQL. These aspects are related to hardware configuration, network settings, and PostgreSQL configuration. PostgreSQL is often shipped with a configuration that is not suitable for production. Due to this, one should at least configure the PostgreSQL buffer settings, RAM settings, number of connections, and logging. Note that several PostgreSQL settings are correlated, such as the RAM settings and the number of connections. In addition to this, one should take great care with settings that require a server restart, because these are difficult to change in the production environment. Often, PostgreSQL produces a good execution plan if the physical structure of a database is normalized and the query is written properly. However, this is not always the case. To overcome performance issues, PostgreSQL provides the EXPLAIN utility command, which can be used to generate execution plans. The EXPLAIN command has several options, such as ANALYZE and BUFFERS. Also, one should know the limitations of PostgreSQL in order to write good queries, such as cross column statistics, CTE execution boundaries, and PL/pgSQL features. In addition to these, one should know the exact difference between different SQL statements and how they are executed, such as UNION, UNION ALL, DISTINCT, and so on. Furthermore, one should learn how to rewrite the same query in different ways and compare the performance of each.

Finally, one should know the limitation of PostgreSQL. There are some limitations for CTE, constraint exclusion, cross column statistics and so on. In addition to that, one should consider the caching behavior of PL/pgSQL.

The next chapter, covers some aspects of the software testing process and how it can be applied to databases. Unit tests for databases can be written as SQL scripts or stored functions in a database.

14
Testing

Software testing is the process of analyzing program components, programs, and systems with the intention of finding errors in them, and to determine or check their technical limits and requirements.

The database is a specific system that requires special approaches for testing. This is because the behavior of database software components (views, stored procedures, or functions) may depend not only on their code, but also on the data. In many cases, functions are not immutable. This means that executing them again with the same parameters can produce different results.

That is why one should use specific techniques to test database modules. PostgreSQL provides some features that help developers and testers in doing this.

In software architecture, the database usually lays at the lowest level. User interface components display information and pass commands to backend systems. The backend systems implement the business logic and manipulate data. The data is modeled and stored in a database. This is the reason why, in many cases, changes in the database schema affect many other software components. Changes are necessary when businesses develop. New tables and fields are created, old ones are removed, and the data model is getting improved.

Developers should make sure that when changing the database structure, they do not break existing applications and they can use the new structures properly.

In this chapter, some techniques for testing database objects are discussed. They can be applied when implementing changes in the data structure of complex systems and when developing database interfaces.

The examples in this chapter can be executed in the same database, `car_portal`, but they do not depend on the objects in that database. To create the database, use the `schema.sql` script ;from the attached media, `data.sql` to fill it with sample data. All the code samples are provided in the file, `examples.sql`.

Unit testing

Unit testing is a process in software development that makes it possible to check for errors in the various components or modules of the software. In databases, those components are stored procedures, functions, triggers, and so on. A view definition, or even a code of queries that applications use, can also be an object for unit testing.

The idea behind unit testing is that for every module of a software system, like class or function, there is a set of tests that invokes that module with a certain input data and checks whether the outcome of the invocation matches the expected result. When a module being tested needs to interact with other systems, those systems can be emulated by the test framework so that the interaction can also be tested.

The set of tests should be big enough to cover as much of the source code of the tested module as possible. This can be achieved when the tests imply invocation of the tested code with all possible logical combinations of values of the input parameters. If the tested module is supposed to be able to react on invalid data, the tests should include that as well. The execution of those tests should be automated, which makes it possible to run the tests each time a new release of the tested module is developed.

All this makes it possible to change the software, and then quickly check whether the new version still satisfies the old requirements. This approach is called regression testing.

 There is a technique in software development called **test-driven development**. It implies writing tests that reflect the requirements of a software component first, and then developing code which satisfies the tests. In the end, the developer will have working code that is covered with tests and good, formally defined functional requirements for the module.

Specificity of unit testing in databases

The particularity of database unit tests is that not only the parameters of a function, but also the data, which is stored in database tables, can be both the input and the outcome of the module being tested. Moreover, the execution of one test could influence the following tests due to the changes it makes to the data, so it might be necessary to execute the tests in a specific order.

Therefore, the testing framework should be able to insert data into the database, run tests, and then analyze the new data. Furthermore, the testing framework could also be required to manage the transactions in which the tests are executed. The easiest way to do all of that is by writing the tests as SQL scripts. In many cases, it is convenient to wrap them into stored procedures (functions in case of PostgreSQL). These procedures can be put in the same database where the components being tested were created.

Testing functions can take test cases from a table iterating through the records. There could be many testing functions, and one separate function that executes them one by one and then formats the result protocol.

Let's create a simple example. Suppose there is a table in the database and a function performing an action on the data in the table:

```
car_portal=> CREATE TABLE counter_table(counter int);
CREATE TABLE
car_portal=> CREATE FUNCTION increment_counter() RETURNS void AS $$
  BEGIN
    INSERT INTO counter_table SELECT count(*) FROM counter_table;
  END;
  $$ LANGUAGE plpgsql;
CREATE FUNCTION
```

The table contains only one integer field. The function counts the number of records in the table, and inserts that number in the same table. So, subsequent calls of the function will cause insertion of the numbers 0, 1, 2, and so on into the table. Suppose we want to test this functionality. So, the test function can be as follows:

```
CREATE FUNCTION test_increment() RETURNS boolean AS $$
  DECLARE
    c int; m int;
  BEGIN
    RAISE NOTICE '1..2';
    -- Separate test scenario from testing environment
    BEGIN
    -- Test 1. Call increment function
      BEGIN
```

```
        PERFORM increment_counter();
        RAISE NOTICE 'ok 1 - Call increment function';
     EXCEPTION WHEN OTHERS THEN
        RAISE NOTICE 'not ok 1 - Call increment function';
     END;
     -- Test 2. Test results
     BEGIN
        SELECT COUNT(*), MAX(counter) INTO c, m FROM counter_table;
        IF NOT (c = 1 AND m = 0) THEN
          RAISE EXCEPTION 'Test 2: wrong values in output data';
        END IF;
        RAISE NOTICE 'ok 2 - Check first record';
     EXCEPTION WHEN OTHERS THEN
        RAISE NOTICE 'not ok 2 - Check first record';
     END;
     -- Rollback changes made by the test
     RAISE EXCEPTION 'Rollback test data';
  EXCEPTION
     WHEN raise_exception THEN RETURN true;
     WHEN OTHERS THEN RETURN false;
  END;
 END;
$$ LANGUAGE plpgsql;
```

The preceding test function works in the following way:

- The whole test scenario is executed in its own BEGIN-EXCEPTION-END block. It isolates the test from the transaction that executes the tests, and makes it possible to run another test afterward, which could use the same data structures.

- Each test in the test scenario is also executed in its own BEGIN-EXCEPTION-END block. This makes it possible to continue testing even if one of the tests fails.

- The first test runs the function, increment_counter(). The test is considered successful if the function is executed without any error. The test is considered unsuccessful if an exception of any kind occurs.

- The second test selects the data from the table and checks whether it matches the expected values. If the data is wrong, or if the select statement fails for any reason, the test fails.

- The result of testing is reported to the console by the RAISE NOTICE commands. The output format follows the **Test Anything Protocol (TAP)** specification, and can be processed by a test harness (external testing framework), like Jenkins.

- The function returns true when the execution of the tests succeeded, regardless of the results of the tests. Otherwise, it returns false.

If we run the test function, we will get the following protocol:

```
car_portal=> SELECT test_increment();
NOTICE: 1..2
NOTICE: ok 1 - Call increment function
NOTICE: ok 2 - Check first record
 test_increment
----------------
 t
(1 row)
```

The test is successful!

Suppose the requirements have been changed, and now it is necessary to add another field to the table to record the time when a value was inserted:

```
car_portal=> ALTER TABLE counter_table ADD insert_time timestamp with time
zone NOT NULL;
ALTER TABLE
```

After the change, one should run the test again to see if the function still works:

```
car_portal=> SELECT test_increment();
NOTICE: 1..2
NOTICE: not ok 1 - Call increment function
NOTICE: not ok 2 - Check first record
 test_increment
----------------
 t
(1 row)
```

The test fails. This happens because the `increment_counter()` function does not know about the new field. The function should also be changed:

```
car_portal=> CREATE OR REPLACE FUNCTION increment_counter() RETURNS void AS
$$
  BEGIN
    INSERT INTO counter_table SELECT count(*), now() FROM counter_table;
  END;
  $$ LANGUAGE plpgsql;
CREATE FUNCTION
```

Now the tests are successful again:

```
car_portal=> SELECT test_increment();
NOTICE: 1..2
NOTICE: ok 1 - Call increment function
NOTICE: ok 2 - Check first record
```

```
     test_increment
     ----------------
     t
 (1 row)
```

The preceding `test` function is not perfect. First, it does not check whether the `increment_counter()` function actually counts the records. The test will succeed even if the `increment_counter()` function just inserts the constant value of zero in the database. To fix this, the `test` function should run the test twice and check the new data.

Secondly, if the test fails, it would be good to know the exact reason for the failure. The testing function could get this information from PostgreSQL using the `GET STACKED DIAGNOSTICS` command, and show it with `RAISE NOTICE`.
The improved version of the test function code is available in the attached media in the file `examples.sql`. It is too big to put it here.

It is a very good practice to have unit tests for the database components in complicated software systems. This is because, in many cases, the database is a component that is shared by several services or modules. Any development in the database on behalf of one of those services can cause others to break. In many cases, it is not clear which service uses which object in the database and how they are used. That's why it is essential to have unit tests that emulate the usage of the database by each of the external services. And when developers work on changes to the data structure, those tests should be executed to check whether the whole system can work with the new structure.

The tests could be run in a newly created testing environment. In that case, the install script should include some code to create testing data. Alternatively, the tests could be executed in a copy of the production database. The test script could also contain some cleanup code.

Unit test frameworks

The example in the previous section has some more drawbacks. For example, if the function being tested raises warnings or notices, they will spoil the test protocol. Moreover, the testing code is not clean. The same pieces of code repeated several times, those `BEGIN-END` blocks are bulky, and the result protocol is not formatted very well. All these tasks could be automated using any of the **unit test frameworks**.

There is no unit test framework that comes out of the box with PostgreSQL, but there are several of them available from the community.

One of the most commonly used ones is pgtap (http://pgtap.org/). One can download it from GitHub (https://github.com/theory/pgtap/), compile and install it in the test database. The installation in a Linux system is quite easy and described well in the documentation. To compile and install the framework, the postgresql-server-dev-10 package needs to be installed. To install the framework in a particular database, you will need to create an extension in PostgreSQL, as follows:

```
car_portal=> CREATE EXTENSION pgtap;
CREATE EXTENSION
```

The tests are written as SQL scripts and they can be run in batches by the utility called pg_prove, which is provided with pgtap. There is also a way to write tests as stored functions using PL/pgSQL.

The pgtap framework provides the user with a set of helper functions that are used to wrap the testing code. They also write the results into a temporary table, which is used later to generate the testing protocol. For example, the ok() function reports a successful test if its argument is true, and a failed test, if not. The has_relation() function checks the database whether the specified relation exists. There are about a hundred of these functions.

The test scenario that was described in the preceding section can be implemented in the following script using pgtap:

```
-- Isolate test scenario in its own transaction
BEGIN;
-- report 2 tests will be run
SELECT plan(2);
-- Test 1. Call increment function
SELECT lives_ok('SELECT increment_counter()','Call increment function');
-- Test 2. Test results
SELECT is( (SELECT ARRAY [COUNT(*), MAX(counter)]::text FROM
counter_table), ARRAY [1, 0]::text,'Check first record');
-- Report finish
SELECT finish();
-- Rollback changes made by the test
ROLLBACK;
```

The code is much cleaner now. This script is available in the attached media in the file, pgtap.sql. This is how it looks when the file is executed in the psql console. To make the test protocol look more compact, the Tuples only mode is switched on:

```
car_portal=> \t
Tuples only is on.
car_portal=> \i pgtap.sql
BEGIN
 1..2
 ok 1 – Call increment function
 ok 2 – Check first record
ROLLBACK
```

Another unit test framework that is worth mentioning is plpgunit. The tests are written as functions in PL/pgSQL. They use the provided helper functions to perform tests, for example, assert.is_equal() checks whether two arguments are equal. The helper functions format the results of the tests and display them on the console. The managing function unit_tests.begin() runs all the testing functions, logs their output into a table, and formats the results protocol.

The advantage of plpgunit is its simplicity—it is very lightweight and easy to install, and there is only one SQL script that you need to execute to get the framework in your database.

The plpgunit framework is available in GitHub at https://github.com/mixerp/plpgunit.

Schema difference

When one works on a changes of the database schema for an application, sometimes it is necessary to understand the difference between the old and the new structure. This information can be analyzed to check whether the changes might have any undesired impact on other applications or used in documentation.

The differences can be found using conventional command line utilities.

For example, suppose one changed the structure of the car portal database.

First, let's create another database that will contain the updated schema. Assuming that the user can access the database running on localhost and is allowed to create databases and connect to any databases, the following command will create a new database using the old one as a template:

```
user@host:~$ createdb -h localhost car_portal_new -T car_portal -O
car_portal_app
```

Now there are two identical databases. Connect to the new one and deploy the changes in the schema to the new database:

```
user@host:~$ psql -h localhost car_portal_new
psql (10.0)
Type "help" for help.
car_portal_new=# ALTER TABLE car_portal_app.car ADD insert_date timestamp
with time zone DEFAULT now();
ALTER TABLE
```

Now the structure of these two databases is different. To find the difference, dump the schema of both databases into files:

```
user@host:~$ pg_dump -h localhost -s car_portal > old_db.sql
user@host:~$ pg_dump -h localhost -s car_portal_new > new_db.sql
```

The files `old_db.sql` and `new_db.sql` that would be created after executing the preceding commands are available in the attached media. It is easy to compare these files using conventional utilities. On Linux, it can be done with the command, `diff`:

```
user@host:~$ diff -U 7 old_db.sql new_db.sql
--- old_db.sql 2017-09-25 21:34:39.217018000 +0200
+++ new_db.sql 2017-09-25 21:34:46.649018000 +0200
@@ -351,15 +351,16 @@
 CREATE TABLE car (
 car_id integer NOT NULL,
 number_of_owners integer NOT NULL,
 registration_number text NOT NULL,
 manufacture_year integer NOT NULL,
 number_of_doors integer DEFAULT 5 NOT NULL,
 car_model_id integer NOT NULL,
- mileage integer
+ mileage integer,
+ insert_date timestamp with time zone DEFAULT now()
 );
```

On Windows, this can be done with the command, `fc`:

```
c:\dbdumps>fc old_db.sql new_db.sql
Comparing files old_db.sql and NEW_DB.SQL
***** old_db.sql
 car_model_id integer NOT NULL,
 mileage integer
);
***** NEW_DB.SQL
 car_model_id integer NOT NULL,
 mileage integer,
 insert_date timestamp with time zone DEFAULT now()
```

```
);
*****
```

Both make it visible that one line of the schema dump has changed and another one was added. There are a lot of more convenient ways to compare files; for example, using text editors like **Vim** or **Notepad++**.

In many cases, it is not enough to just see the difference in the schema. It could also be necessary to synchronize the schema of the two databases. There are commercial products that can do this; for example, *EMS DB Comparer* for PostgreSQL.

Database abstraction interfaces

When a big database is shared between many applications, it is sometimes hard to understand who is using what and what would happen if the database schema changes. On the other hand, when a database is big and complex, changing the data structure is a constant process: business requirements do change, new features got developed, and refactoring of the database itself for the sake of normalization is quite usual.

In that case, it makes sense to build the whole system using layered architecture. The physical data structure is located at the first layer. Applications do not access it directly.

Moving upward from the bottom, the second layer contains structures that abstract logical entities from their physical implementation. These structures play the role of data abstraction interfaces. There are several ways to implement them. They can be created in the database as functions. In that case, applications will work with the data by invoking them. Another approach is using updatable views. In that case, applications can access the logical entities with conventional SQL statements.
Additionally, this interface can be implemented outside the database as a lightweight service processing the requests of high-level systems, performing queries, and making changes to the database. Each approach has its own benefits and drawbacks, for example:

- Database functions keep the database abstraction logic in the database and are easy to test, but they hide the logical model and could be difficult to be integrated with high level applications;
- Updatable views expose the relational model (although they do not have foreign keys) but implementation of logic that goes beyond simple INSERT, UPDATE or DELETE functions can be very complex and counter-intuitive;
- Micro-services working outside of the database are more difficult to implement and test, but could provide additional functionally, like providing access to the using HTTP REST API.

At the top layer are the applications that implement business logic. They do not care about the physical structure of the data and interact with the database through the data abstraction interfaces.

This approach reduces the number of agents that access the physical data structures. It makes it easier to see how the database is used or can be used. The database documentation should contain the specification of these interfaces. So the database developer, when working on refactoring the database schema, should only make sure that the interfaces follow the specification, and until they do, the rest of the database is free to change.

The existence of these interfaces makes its easier to develop unit tests: it is clear what to test and how, as the specification is given. With test-driven development, the tests themselves will play the role of the interface specification.

Data difference

The easiest way to create a database abstraction interface is to use views to access the data. In this case, if one wants to change the table structure, it can be done without changing the code of the external applications. The only thing necessary is to update the definitions of the interface views. Moreover, if one would, for example, remove a column from a table that is used in a view, PostgreSQL will not allow this. This way, the objects in the database that are used by applications will be protected.

Nevertheless, if the database structure was changed and the view definitions were updated accordingly, it is important to check whether the new views return the same data as the old.

Sometimes it is possible to implement the new view in the same database. In this case one just needs to create a copy of the production database in the test environment, or prepare a test database containing all possible combinations of the attributes of the business entities. Then the new version of the view can be deployed with a different name. The following query can then be used to see if the new view returns the same data:

```
WITH
  n AS (SELECT * FROM new_view),
  o AS (SELECT * FROM old_view)
SELECT 'new', * FROM (SELECT * FROM n EXCEPT ALL SELECT * FROM o) a
UNION ALL
SELECT 'old', * FROM (SELECT * FROM o EXCEPT ALL SELECT * FROM n) b;
```

Here, the names, `new_view` and `old_view`, refer to the names of the respective relations. The query returns no rows if both views return the same result.

However, this works only when both views are in the same database, and the old view works as it worked before the refactoring. In case the structure of underlying tables changes, the old view cannot work as it did before and comparison is not applicable. This problem can be solved by creating a temporary table from the data returned by the old view before refactoring, and then comparing that temporary table with the new view.

This can also be done by comparing the data from different databases; the old one before refactoring and the new one. One can use external tools to do so. For example, data from both the databases can be dumped into files using `psql`, and then these files can be compared using `diff` (this will work only if the rows have the same order). There are also some commercial tools that provide this functionality.

Another approach is connecting two databases, making queries, and making the comparison inside the database. This might seem complicated, but in fact, it is the fastest and most reliable way. There are a couple of methods to connect two databases: through the extensions, `dblink` (database link) or `postgres_fdw` (foreign data wrapper).

Using the `dblink` extension may seem easier than using `postgres_fdw`, and it allows performing different queries for different objects. However, this technology is older, and uses a syntax that is not standard-compliant and has performance issues, especially when big tables or views are queried.

On the other hand, `postgres_fdw` requires creating an object in the local database for each object in the remote database that is going to be accessed, which is not that convenient. However, this makes it easy to use the remote tables together with the local tables in queries, and it is faster.

In the example in the previous section, another database was created from the original database `car_portal`, and another field was added to the table, `car_portal_app.car`.

Let's try to find out if that operation caused changes in the data. The following would need to be done:

1. Connect to the new database as a super user:

```
user@host:~$ psql -h localhost -U postgres car_portal_new
psql (10beta3)
Type "help" for help.
car_portal_new=#
```

2. Then create an extension for the foreign data wrapper. The binaries for the extension are included in the PostgreSQL server package:

```
car_portal_new=# CREATE EXTENSION postgres_fdw;
CREATE EXTENSION
```

3. Once the extension has been created, create a server object and a user mapping:

```
car_portal_new=# CREATE SERVER car_portal_original FOREIGN DATA
WRAPPER postgres_fdw
    OPTIONS (host 'localhost', dbname 'car_portal');
CREATE SERVER
car_portal_new=# CREATE USER MAPPING FOR CURRENT_USER SERVER
car_portal_original;
CREATE USER MAPPING
```

4. Create a foreign table and check whether we can query it:

```
car_portal_new=# CREATE FOREIGN TABLE car_portal_app.car_orignal
(car_id int, number_of_owners int,
    registration_number text, manufacture_year int, number_of_doors
int, car_model_id int, mileage int)
    SERVER car_portal_original OPTIONS (table_name 'car');
CREATE FOREIGN TABLE
car_portal_new=# SELECT car_id FROM car_portal_app.car_orignal
limit 1;
 car_id
--------
      1
(1 row)
```

Now the table that is in fact in a different database can be queried as if it was a normal table. It can be used in joins, filtering, grouping, everything that you would do in SQL will work.

Now the table is ready and it can be queried. To compare the data, the same query can be used as in the example we just saw for the old and new views:

```
car_portal_new=# WITH n AS (
  SELECT car_id, number_of_owners, registration_number, manufacture_year,
number_of_doors,
      car_model_id, mileage
    FROM car_portal_app.car),
o AS (SELECT * FROM car_portal_app.car_orignal)
SELECT 'new', * FROM (SELECT * FROM n EXCEPT ALL SELECT * FROM o) a
UNION ALL
SELECT 'old', * FROM (SELECT * FROM o EXCEPT ALL SELECT * FROM n) b;
 ?column? | car_id | number_of_owners | registration_number |
```

```
manufacture_year | number_of_doors |  car_model_id | mileage
----------+--------+-----------------+--------------------+--------------
----+----------------+
-------------+---------
(0 rows)
```

The result is empty. This means that the data in both tables is the same.

Performance testing

An important question regarding a database system is: how fast is it? How many transactions can it handle per second, or how much time does a particular query take to execute? The topic on the performance of a database has been covered in Chapter 13, *Optimizing Database Performance*. Here, we will only discuss the task of measuring it.

The psql meta-command \timing is used to measure the time of execution of a particular SQL command. Once timing is enabled, psql shows the execution time for each command:

```
car_portal=> \timing
Timing is on.
car_portal=# SELECT count(*) FROM car_portal_app.car;
 count
-------
 229
(1 row)
Time: 0.643 ms
```

Usually, that is enough to understand which query is faster and if you are doing it right when optimizing a query. However, one cannot rely on this timing when it comes to estimating the number of requests that the server can handle per second. This is because the time for a single query depends on many random factors: the current load of the server, the state of the cache, and so on.

PostgreSQL provides a special utility that connects to the server and runs a test script many times. It is called pgbench. By default, pgbench creates its own small database and executes a sample SQL script on it, which is quite similar to what a typical OLTP (Online transaction processing) application usually does. This is already enough to understand how powerful the database server is, and how changes to the configuration parameters affect the performance.

To get more specific results, one should prepare a test database that has a size comparable to the database in production. A test script, which contains the same or similar queries that the production system performs, should also be prepared.

For example, it is assumed that the car portal database is used by a web application. The typical usage scenario is querying the car table to get the number of records, and then querying it again to retrieve the first 20 records, which fit into a page on the screen. The following is the test script:

```
SELECT count(*) FROM car_portal_app.car;
SELECT * FROM car_portal_app.car INNER JOIN car_portal_app.car_model
USING (car_model_id) ORDER BY car_id LIMIT 20;
```

It is saved in a file called `test.sql`, available in the attached media, which will be used by pgbench.

It is necessary to initialize the sample data for pgbench (assuming that the database is running on the same machine and the current user can access the database):

```
user@host:~$ pgbench -h localhost -i car_portal
NOTICE: table "pgbench_history" does not exist, skipping
NOTICE: table "pgbench_tellers" does not exist, skipping
NOTICE: table "pgbench_accounts" does not exist, skipping
NOTICE: table "pgbench_branches" does not exist, skipping
creating tables...
100000 of 100000 tuples (100%) done (elapsed 0.17 s, remaining 0.00
s).
vacuum...
set primary keys...
done.
```

The test can now be started, as follows:

```
user@host:~$ pgbench -h localhost -f test.sql -T 60 car_portal
starting vacuum...end.
transaction type: test.sql
scaling factor: 1
query mode: simple
number of clients: 1
number of threads: 1
duration: 60 s
number of transactions actually processed: 98314
latency average = 0.610 ms
tps = 1638.564670 (including connections establishing)
tps = 1638.887817 (excluding connections establishing)
```

As you can see, the performance is about 1.6 thousand transactions per second, which is more than enough for a small car portal application. However, pgbench was running on the same machine as the database server, and they shared the same CPU. On the other hand, the network latency was minimal.

To get more realistic statistics, pgbench should be started on the machine where the application server is installed, and the number of connections in use should match the configuration of the application server. Usually, for such simple queries, the network connection and transmit times play a bigger role than database processing.

pgbench allows a user to specify the number of connections it establishes to the database server. Moreover, it provides the functionality to generate random queries to the database. So, it can be quite useful to assess database performance and tune database server configurations.

Summary

In this chapter, we covered some aspects of software testing and the way it is applicable to databases.

Unit testing techniques can be used when developing code in a database, for example, functions or triggers. Test-driven development is a very good approach in software development. Unit testing in databases has its own specificity. Unit tests for databases could be written as SQL scripts or stored functions in the database. There are several frameworks that help in implementing unit tests and processing the results of testing.

Another aspect of testing the database software is comparing data in the same database or between databases to test the results of refactoring the data model. This can be done via SQL queries, and sometimes, it requires establishing connections between databases. Connections between databases can be established via dblinks or foreign data wrapper objects.

Database schemas can be compared quite simply using command-line tools provided with PostgreSQL and operating systems. Additionally, there are more advanced software products that do this as well.

pgbench is a utility provided with PostgreSQL that can be used to assess the performance of a database system.

In the next chapter, we will continue talking about integrating PostgreSQL with other software and will discuss how to use the database in Python applications.

15
Using PostgreSQL in Python Applications

A database is a storage component of a software solution. However, it does not just store information, it also ensures consistency when the data is properly modeled in relational structures. Additionally, a database can implement more complicated logic related to consistency, which goes beyond normalization, with triggers and rules. Of course, business logic can also be fulfilled by a database with functions written in PostgreSQL in PL/pgSQL or other languages supported by the DBMS. Implementation of business logic in a database is questionable from an architecture point of view but this is out of topic here.

Nevertheless, the tasks related to interaction with users or I/O cannot be performed by the database. External applications do this. In this chapter, you will learn how to connect and interact with a database from an external application written in Python.

Python is a language that is very easy to learn and quite powerful at the same time. It has a huge support from the community and a lot of modules that extend the functionality of the standard library. It is very expressive from the point of view that humans can easily read and understand code written in Python. On the other hand, it is an interpreted language, which makes it quite slow. Python is dynamically typed. This can be convenient but also error prone.

In the chapter the following topics will be covered:

- Python DB API 2.0 - an application programming interface that is used to work with databases from Python applications
- Low level access to databases using `psycopg2` - most commonly used PostgreSQL driver for Python

- Alternative drivers for PostgreSQL
- The concept of object relational mapping and its implementation with `SQLAlchemy`

To proceed with the chapter, you need to have a basic understanding of object-oriented programming. If you want to try the examples, you will need to install Python. The examples are made with Python 3.5.

For Windows, you can download the installer package from `https://www.Python.org/`. Simply let it install the software in the default location and make sure that you also install PIP, which is the installer for additional modules. Make sure that the location where Python is installed is included in the system variable `PATH`. To enter the Python shell, type `python` in the command line. Alternatively, there is an interactive Python shell available from the Start menu called idle.

Python is available in standard repositories for many Linux distributions. Run `sudo apt-get install python3.5 python3-pip` to install Python and PIP. To enter the Python shell, type `python3` in the command line.

In the examples, we will use the same database `car_portal` as we did in the other chapters. The scripts to create the database and fill it with sample data are available in the enclosed media in the `schema.sql` and `data.sql` files. The examples will work as they are if the database server is running on `localhost` and the user `car_poral_app` is allowed to connect to the database `car_portal` without a password (using the `trust` authentication method). In other cases, you may need to change the connection parameters in the sample script files.

Python DB API 2.0

PostgreSQL is not the only relational database and of course it is not the only one you can use with Python. There is an API in Python that is designed to unify the way applications work with databases. It is called the **Python Database API**. By the time this book was written, it already had the second specification, defined in the **Python Enhancement Proposal (PEP) 249**. The specification of the Python DB API 2.0 is available at `https://www.python.org/dev/peps/pep-0249/`.

The API defines the following objects that are used when connecting to a database and interacting with it:

- connection: This implements the logic of connecting to the database server, authenticating and managing transactions. A connection is created by calling the connect() function with a number of parameters that can differ depending on the database and the driver that is used.

- cursor: This represents a cursor in the database. It is an object that is used to manage the context of execution of a SQL command. For example, it allows executing a SELECT query and fetching rows one by one or in bulks, and in some implementations sees to different positions in the result set. A cursor is created by calling the method connect() of a connection object.
- Exceptions: The API defines a hierarchy of different exceptions that may occur during the execution. For example, there is an exception class, IntergrityError, which is supposed to be raised when the database reports an integrity constraint violation. It is a subclass of DatabaseError.

Using the API makes it easy to switch between different database drivers or event databases. It also makes the logic standardized and therefore understandable and maintainable by others. However, details may be different by different database drivers.

As an example, here is a small program in Python that uses the module psycopg2, selects some data from the database, and prints it to the console (how to install psycopg2 will be explained in the next section):

```
#!/usr/bin/python3
from psycopg2 import connect

conn = connect(host="localhost", user="car_portal_app",
               dbname="car_portal")

with conn.cursor() as cur:
    cur.execute("SELECT DISTINCT make FROM car_portal_app.car_model")
    for row in cur:
        print(row[0])

conn.close()
```

The program is available in the file print_makes.py in the enclosed code bundle.

There are several Python modules for PostgreSQL. We will take a closer look at the following:

- `psycopg2`: This is one of the most commonly used; it utilizes the native PostgreSQL library `libpq` that makes it quite efficient but probably less portable
- `pg8000`: This is the pure Python driver and does not depend on `libpq`
- `asyncpg`: This is a high performance driver and uses binary protocol to talk to the database to achieve great performance, but does not implement the DB API though

Low-level database access with psycopg2

`psycopg2` is one of the most popular PostgreSQL drivers for Python. It is compliant to the Python's DB API 2.0 specification. It is mostly implemented in C and uses the library, `libpq`. It is thread safe, which means that you can share the same `connection` object between several threads. It can work both with Python 2 and Python 3.

The official web page of the library is located at `http://initd.org/psycopg/`.

The driver `psycopg2` can be installed with PIP on Linux from the command line as follows:

```
user@host:~$ sudo pip3 install psycopg2
[sudo] password for user:
Collecting psycopg2
  Downloading psycopg2-2.7.3.1-cp35-cp35m-manylinux1_x86_64.whl (2.6MB)
  100% |                                    | 2.6MB 540kB/s
Installing collected packages: psycopg2
Successfully installed psycopg2-2.7.3.1
```

Type this in Windows from the command line:

```
C:\Users\User>python -m pip install psycopg2
Collecting psycopg2
  Downloading psycopg2-2.7.3.1-cp35-cp35m-win_amd64.whl (943kB)
  100% |################################| 952kB 1.1MB/s
Installing collected packages: psycopg2
Successfully installed psycopg2-2.7.3.1
```

Let's take a closer look at the script from the previous section. We will go line by line to understand what it is happening:

```
#!/usr/bin/python3
```

This is called a **shebang** or **hashbang** line: the two characters #! followed by a path will indicate that the file is actually a script that is supposed to be interpreted by the specified interpreter. This makes it possible to make the file executable in Linux and simply run it. In Windows, this line is not used by the shell but it does not hurt to have it to make the script portable. In this case, the shebang line indicates that Python 3 is supposed to be used.

```
from psycopg2 import connect
```

Here, the module `psycopg2` is imported and the function `connect()` will be available in the current namespace. Alternatively, the syntax `import psycopg2` could be used but that would make the module itself imported to the namespace and the function would be called `psycopg.connect()`.

```
conn = connect(host="localhost", user="car_portal_app",
               dbname="car_portal")
```

The connection to the database is established in this line. The function `connect()` is returning the `connection` object and the variable `conn` refers to it.

```
with conn.cursor() as cur:
```

The method `cursor()` of the connection is used to create a cursor object. The construct `with ... as` is used to create a **context manager** in Python. This is a very convenient technique used to allocate and release resources. In our case, the cursor is created, the variable `cur` refers to it but when the execution leaves the with-block, the cursor will be automatically closed. This will happen no matter how exactly the execution leaves the block, normally or if an exception is raised:

```
cur.execute("SELECT DISTINCT make FROM car_portal_app.car_model")
```

The query `SELECT DISTINCT make FROM car_portal_app.car_model` is executed, and the cursor now represents the context of the query execution. Note that this line and the two following lines are indented. In Python, indentation is used to indicate nested lines of code. In our case, this line and the two following lines are inside the with-block created earlier. Indentation in Python is used instead of braces as in Java or C. Indentation of four spaces should be used according to the Style Guide for Python Code.

Refer to the documentation for details at https://www.python.org/dev/peps/pep-0008/.

```
for row in cur:
    print(row[0])
```

These two lines are also the part of the with-block. The first line of the two defines a for loop that will iterate over the records, returned by the cursor object. The records in the body of the loop are referred to by the variable `row`. The second line prints the first field of the record to the console. The variable `row` is of the type `tuple`, which works here as a zero-based array that contains the record's data, and the expression `row[0]` returns the value of the first field:

```
conn.close()
```

This closes the connection to the database. Note that this line is not indented, which means that the execution has left the with-block and therefore the cursor is also closed implicitly.

Now let's consider some of the aspects of usage of `psycopg2` in more detail.

Connecting to a database

Connections to databases are handled by the objects of the class `connection`. These objects represent database sessions in the application. The objects are created using the function `connect()` from the module `psycopg2`. This way of creating connections is defined by the **DB API 2.0**.

To specify the location and authenticate in the database, a connection string can be used, like this:

```
conn = connect("host=db_host user=some_user dbname=database "
               "password=$ecreT")
```

Alternatively, named parameters can be used, like this:

```
conn = connect(host="db_host", user="some_user", dbname="database",
               password="$ecreT")
```

Here, the connection would be established to the database named `database`, located at server `db_host` as user `some_user` identified by the password, `$ecreT`.

Optionally, the function `connect()` can take two parameters, which are `connection_factory` and `cursor_factory`. They can be used to specify a custom function that would create connections or cursors. This feature can be used to extend the default functionality; for example, if you want to log all the SQL queries that are executed by the application, a customized `cursor` class can be a good solution for this.

The connection object returned by the function `connect` is referred to by the variable `conn` in the preceding examples. The object is used to create cursor objects to execute queries and manage the database session. The most common methods of the class `connection` are as follows:

- `commit()`: This is used to commit the current transaction in the database. By default, `psycopg2` will open a transaction before executing any command. For this reason, there is no method to explicitly begin a transaction.
- `rollback()`: This is used to roll back the current transaction.
- `close()`: This is used to disconnect from the database and close the `connection`.
- `cancel()`: This is used to cancel a current command. This can be executed from a different thread. This method is not defined in the DB API 2.0.

There are also a number of methods used to perform two-phase commit. **Two-phase commit protocol** is an algorithm that is used when several systems should perform a commit action or a rollback all together in a coordinated way. There are more fields (some of them are read-only) and methods of the class `connection` that can be used to check the state of the connection, set and get its properties, manage the transaction isolation level, and perform other operations.

An object of the class `connection` cat be instantiated with the context manager syntax, as follows:

```
with connect(host="db_host", user="some_user", dbname="database",
             password="$ecreT") as conn:
    cur = conn.cursor()
    ...
```

After the execution left the with-block, the connection will be closed automatically, regardless of whether the program continued normally or an exception was raised.

> When a connection is established in a with-block, if the execution continues normally then the transaction will be committed before closing the connection. If an exception is raised, then the transaction will be rolled back.

Connection pooling

Establishing a connection to a database can be quite expensive. It implies the connection on the network level and handshaking, authentication, and allocating server resources to the new session. Imagine a web application that would connect to a database for each request from users, perform a query, and disconnect. It could take milliseconds, but when the number of requests is huge, in total it can take a lot of time. If these requests are processed simultaneously, it can happen that too many connections are created and the database server will be overloaded because each connection consumes resources from the server and even if the sessions do nothing, the number of them is always limited.

In web applications (and not only there), it is a common practice to create a fixed number of database connections once and reuse them for different tasks. When there are more tasks than the number of connections, they should be blocked until there is a free connection. This is called **connection pooling**. The benefits of using connection pooling are as follows:

- No time spent to connect to the database as the connections are created in advance
- The number of connections is limited, which makes it easier to manage server resources

`psycopg2` offers a connection pooling feature with a simple API. There are three different implementations:

- Simple connection pool, designed to be used in single-threaded applications
- Threaded connection pool for multi-threaded applications
- Persistent connection pool, designed to work with **Zope**, a web application server

 Unfortunately, `psycopg2` does not support blocking when trying to get a `connection` from a pool that is already exhausted, which is why one should be careful when using this `connection` pool. It also does not support the context manager syntax, which makes it not as convenient to use.

In the attached media, there is an example script called `psycopg_pool.py` that shows you how to use the `connection` pool provided by `psycopg2`. It is too big to put it here. We will return to this topic later when another library SQLAlchemy is described.

Executing SQL commands

Suppose that the connection is established and there is a variable `conn` that refers to the instance of the class `connection`. To execute a SQL command, it is necessary to first create a cursor object that will represent the context of the command. Cursors are created by calling the `connection.cursor()` method of a connection, as follows:

```
cur = conn.cursor()
```

Now the variable `cur` refers to the cursor object. Optionally, the method `cursor()` can take the following parameters:

- `name`: When specified, the cursor will represent a server-side cursor. The difference between client-side and server-side cursors is that the first would usually download the whole result set and store it in memory, and the last would ask the server to give the data in portions when the application is ready to process it.
- `cursor_factory`: This is used to create non-standard cursors.
- `scrollable`: This only works with server-side cursors. When set to `true`, the cursor will be able to scroll back when iterating over the result set.
- `withhold`: This only works with server-side cursors. When set to true, the cursor will be able to fetch data even after the transaction commit (but not after rollback).

After a cursor is created, the method `cursor.execute()` should be used to execute an SQL command. For example to select rows or to delete records, the following code can be used:

```
cur.execute("SELECT * FROM car_portal_app.car_model")

cur.execute("DELETE FROM car_portal_app.car_model WHERE car_model_id = 2")
```

To use query parameters, one should specify them in the query and pass their values as a second argument to the method `cursor.execute()`. For example, to insert a record into a table, the following code would be used:

```
new_make = "Ford"
new_model = "Mustang"
sql_command = "INSERT INTO car_portal_app.car_model (make, model) " \
    "VALUES (%s, %s)"
cur.execute(sql_command, [new_make, new_model])
```

Here, **positional notation** was used, meaning that the order of the parameter values must be the same as the order of the parameters placeholder's in the query string. Note the backslash \ at the end of the third line in the preceding example. It is used to separate long lines of code and tells the Python interpreter that the expression continues on the following line.

psycopg2 also supports named notation for specifying parameter values. The same example could look like this:

```
new_make = "Ford"
new_model = "Mustang"
sql_command = "INSERT INTO car_portal_app.car_model (make, model) " \
    "VALUES (%(make)s, %(model)s)"
cur.execute(sql_command, {"model": new_model, "make": new_make})
```

Using parameters when executing SQL commands may seem more complicated than including the values of them directly in the command text, like this:

```
new_make = "Ford"
new_model = "Mustang"
sql_command = "INSERT INTO car_poral_app.car_model (make, model) " \
    "VALUES ('" + new_make + "', '" + new_model + "')"
cur.execute(sql_command)
```

However, this is wrong! Never put data directly in to the SQL command. This can lead to a serious security issue. Imagine if the value of the variable new_model was a single quote character '. Then the SQL that is sent to the server will look like this: INSERT INTO car_portal_app.car_model (make, model) VALUES ('Ford', '''), which is obviously wrong. This command will simply not work, causing the database to raise an exception. In a web application, this could crash the server or make it possible to retrieve data that is secret. If parameters were used, then psycopg2 would take care that this character ' is properly inserted into the table as if it was a valid car model name.

This misbehavior is called **SQL injection**.

 The same cursor object can be used multiple times to execute several queries. However, cursors are not thread safe. This means the same cursor should not be used by multiple threads. Several cursors should be created in this case. The connection object is thread safe though.

There is a sample script that inserts a record into the table car_model in the psycopg2_insert_data.py file in the attached media.

Reading data from a database

When a query that returns a dataset is executed in a cursor, this data can be made available in the application. This is not only about SELECT queries, but also any data changing query that has a RETURNING clause.

Suppose there is a cursor that has executed a query as follows:

```
cur = conn.cursor()
cur.execute("SELECT make, model FROM car_portal_app.car_model")
```

The cursor object provides several ways to retrieve the data:

- Use the object as an iterator as follows:

```
for record in cur:
    print("Make: {}, model: {}".format(record[0], record[1]))
```

Here, record is a tuple and the values of the fields can be accessed using the square-bracket syntax, specifying the number of the field.

- Invoke the method cursor.fetchone() to get a record. Subsequent calls will return next records. When no more records are available, the method returns None:

```
while True:
    record = cur.fetchone()
    if record is None:
        break
    print("Make: {}, model: {}".format(record[0], record[1]))
```

- Invoke the method curosr.fetchmany() to get the next set of records. The method can take a parameter specifying the number of records to retrieve. Otherwise, the number of records can be specified in the field cursor.arraysize. When there are no more records, the method returns an empty set. Here is an example:

```
while True:
    records = cur.fetchmany()
    if len(records) == 0:
        break
    print(records)
```

After the data is retrieved and processed in the application, it is better to close the cursor. This will happen automatically if the cursor was created in a with-block. If cursors are not closed explicitly, they will eventually be removed by the garbage collector or when the database connection is closed, but anyway they will consume some system resources until then.

There is a sample script that uses all three methods in the file `psycopg_query_data.sql` in the attached media.

The COPY command

`psycopg2` is able to execute the `COPY` command to quickly retrieve big amounts of data from the database or to store data in the database. The methods `copy_to()` and `copy_from()` of the class `cursor` are used respectively to copy data to a file-like object from a database table, and from a file-like object to a database table. There is another method `cursor.copy_expert()` that provides more advanced functionality with all the flexibility that the `COPY` command provides.

The method `cursor.copy_to()` takes the following parameters:

- `file`: A file-like object, which will receive the data. It can be a file or a `StringIO` object, or any other object that supports the method `write()`.
- `table`: The name of the table to copy.
- `sep`: A column separator. By default, it is the tabulation character.
- `null`: A textual representation of NULLs.
- `columns`: A list of columns to copy from the table.

The records in the object referred to by the parameter `file` will be separated by a newline. Here is an example of applying the method `cursor.copy_to()`:

```
import io
with io.StringIO() as s:
    cur.copy_to(table='car_portal_app.car_model', file=s)
    print(s.getvalue())
```

This will print the contents of the table `car_portal_app.car_model` to the console as if the `COPY car_portal_app.car_model TO STDOUT;` command was executed in `psql`.

The method `cursor.copy_from()` takes the same parameters and, additionally, another parameter size specifying the size of the buffer used to read from the `file` object. The `file` object must support the methods, `read()` and `readline()`. Here is an example of how to write a record to the table `car_portal_app.car_model` using the `COPY` command:

```
import io
with io.StringIO('Tesla\tModel-X\n') as s:
    cur.copy_from(table='car_portal_app.car_model', file=s,
                  columns=['make', 'model'])
```

In the attached media, there is a script in the file named `psycopg2_copy_data.py` that uses these two methods to copy data to and from the database.

Asynchronous access

In the preceding examples, the method `cursor.execute()` will block the program for the time a query is executing in the database. When the query is long, the program can be blocked for a long time, which sometimes is not a desired behavior. `psycopg2` provides a way to execute queries asynchronously. Basically, it means that the program can do something else while a long query is executing.

To use this feature, the database connection should be created as an asynchronous one. This is done by passing the `async=1` argument to the function `connect()`. The process of connection itself is also asynchronous. Now the Python program should be made to wait until the connection is established. This can be done using the method `connection.poll()` and Python's function `select()`, which is a wrapper for a corresponding system call. This is quite complicated and is out of the scope of this book. Luckily, `psycopg2` provides a helper function that can be used to block the execution and wait for an asynchronous operation to finish. The function is named `psycopg2.extras.wait_select(conn)` where `conn` is a parameter used to pass the database connection object.

Here is a simplified example of how to use an asynchronous connection and perform a SELECT query:

```
from psycopg2 import connect
from psycopg2.extras import wait_select

aconn = connect(host="localhost", user="car_portal_app",
                dbname="car_portal", async=1)
wait_select(aconn)
acur = aconn.cursor()
# Supposing the following query takes a lot of time
```

```
acur.execute("SELECT DISTINCT make FROM car_portal_app.car_model")
# Do something else here
# ...
# When done with other tasks wait until the query is finished
wait_select(aconn)
for row in acur:
   print(row[0])
acur.close()
aconn.close()
```

More advanced examples of asynchronous execution are available in the attached media in the script, `print_makes_async.py`.

More information about asynchronous operations with `psycopg2` can be found in the documentation here: `http://initd.org/psycopg/docs/advanced.html#asynchronous-support`.

Alternative drivers for PostgreSQL

In this section, we will take a closer look at two other PostgreSQL libraries for Python. The first one, `pg8000`, also implements the DB API 2.0. This makes it very similar to `psycopg2`. The difference though is that it is not dependent on the library `ligpq` and is written entirely in Python. This makes the library very lightweight and applications, that would use it, easily portable.

The second one, `asyncpg`, does not implement the Python DB API. It uses a binary protocol to communicate with a PostgreSQL database and asynchronous API in the applications. This makes it possible to create very fast database applications performing great amounts of commands in a short time.

pg8000

To install the library `pg8000`, one should use `pip` in the same way as with `psycopg2`. Here is an example of how it looks in Windows:

```
c:\Users\user>python -m pip install pg8000
Collecting pg8000
 Downloading pg8000-1.11.0-py2.py3-none-any.whl
Collecting six>=1.10.0 (from pg8000)
 Downloading six-1.11.0-py2.py3-none-any.whl
Installing collected packages: six, pg8000
Successfully installed pg8000-1.11.0 six-1.11.0
```

In Linux, one should execute the command `pip3 install pg8000`. The output will be very similar.

As the library also implements DB API 2.0, it is used almost in the same way as `psycopg2`.

Here is a small program that connects to the database, and queries and prints to the console the list of car makes entered into the system:

```python
#!/usr/bin/python3

from pg8000 import connect

conn = connect(host="localhost", user="car_portal_app",
               database="car_portal")
query = "SELECT make, model FROM car_portal_app.car_model"
with conn.cursor() as cur:
    cur.execute(query)
    for record in cur:
        print("Make: {}, model: {}".format(record[0], record[1]))

conn.close()
```

The only difference from using `psycopg2` here is the name of the module that is imported in the beginning. There are some differences in functions that are not a part of DB API 2.0--for example, the `COPY` command is executed in `pg8000` by invoking the method `cursor.execute()`. Database data types are converted into Python data types slightly differently. `pg8000` does not offer an asynchronous API, and it does not have connection pools.

The main benefit of using `pg8000` over `psycopg2` is that it does not have any dependencies on PostgreSQL drivers or libraries that would need to be installed in the system. The main drawback is performance. Depending on what is being done, `pg8000` can be significantly slower.

asyncpg

Another library, `asyncpg`, does not implement Python's DB API. Instead it provides an asynchronous API that is supposed to be used with `asyncio`--a Python library used to write concurrent code. It is out of the scope of this book to learn asynchronous programming, so we will only provide and explain a couple of simplified examples.

As mentioned before, asynchronous execution implies firing a task and, while it is executing, doing something else. The `asyncio.connect()` function that is used to connect to the database is asynchronous. Functions that are used to execute queries or close the `connection` are also asynchronous.

There is a concept of callbacks in asynchronous programming. A **callback function** is a function that belongs to your application that is executed automatically when a certain event happens. Here is an example of using a callback function that reacts on messages from the database:

```
import asyncio
import asyncpg

async def main():
    conn = await asyncpg.connect(host='localhost', user='car_portal_app',
                                 database='car_portal')
    conn.add_log_listener(lambda conn, msg: print(msg))
    print("Executing a command")
    await conn.execute('''DO $$ BEGIN RAISE NOTICE 'Hello'; END; $$;''')
    print("Finished execution")
    await conn.close()

asyncio.get_event_loop().run_until_complete(main())
```

If you are not familiar with asynchronous features of Python, to understand the preceding code, you need to know the following keywords and expressions:

- `async` is used to indicate that the function defined after it is a **coroutine**, which means that it is asynchronous and should be executed in a special way.
- `await` is used to execute coroutines synchronously. Basically, when a coroutine function is called with `await` statement, it is working as a normal function and the execution will continue only when the function returns.
- `lambda` defines an inline function. In the preceding example, the expression `lambda conn, msg: print(msg)` defines a function with two parameters, `conn` and `msg`, that prints the value of `msg`. `lambda` expressions are not specific to asynchronous programming, but they are very convenient to use as simple callbacks.

The preceding script executes a piece of code in the database written in PL/pgSQL. This code is doing nothing but generating a NOTICE. This code is executed asynchronously in the database. Although the script waits for the function `conn.execute()` to finish, the callback function is triggered immediately when the NOTICE is raised. You may add some delays into the expression DO by calling the function `pg_sleep()` to see that.

In the last line of the code sample, the function `main()` is invoked. The function is defined as a coroutine, that is why it is not possible to simply call it. In the example, the expression in the last line invokes the function and waits until it finishes.

More explicit examples are available in the enclosed code bundle in the file `asyncpg_raise_notice.py`.

The benefit of using `asyncpg` over `psycopg2` is performance. The developers of `asyncpg` claim that it is about three times faster than `psycopg2`. It does not require any PostgreSQL libraries present in the system. It is asynchronous, which makes it possible to develop very efficient applications.

The drawback is that it is quite complicated to develop and debug asynchronous code. It does not comply to DB API 2.0 and for this reason, other libraries that use this database abstraction API could not use `asyncpg`. It is a relatively new software. There is not that much information or examples available yet.

Object relational mapping with SQLAlchemy

The libraries that have been described earlier are low level. A developer must understand how databases work and must know SQL to use them. On the other hand, when a database is just a storage component in the software solution and all the logic lays in high-level applications, developers of such applications should concentrate on business logic instead of implementing the interaction with a database dealing with individual queries.

In high-level applications, the business objects are represented as classes and their instances. Methods of these classes represent business methods. Tasks of saving the state of the object in the database and loading it do not belong to business methods.

There is a concept of **object relational mapping (ORM)** in software development. It means implementation of a software layer that represents records that are stored in a database table as instances of a class in a high-level application. When instances of such a class are created, the records are inserted into the table. When the instances are modified, the records are updated.

There is a library for Python named `SQLAlchemy` that implements ORM and can work with many different databases. It can also work with PostgreSQL.

SQLAlchemy consists of two major components, which are *Core* and *ORM*. *Core* is responsible for the interaction with the database and performing SQL commands. *ORM* works on top of *Core* and implements object relational mapping. Both of them are briefly described in the following sections.

To get more information about SQLAlchemy, refer to the official website: https://www.sqlalchemy.org/.

Installation of SQLAlchemy is similar to the other libraries described in this chapter. To install the library with pip, execute the following in Windows:

```
> python —m pip install sqlalchemy
```

In Linux, type the following:

```
$ sudo pip3 install sqlalchemy
```

Main components of SQLAlchemy

SQLAlchemy works on top of DB API. It can use psycopg2 to connect to PostgreSQL or any other driver that implements the API, like pg8000. There are several components that belong to the *Core* of SQLAlchemy:

- *Dialects* are used to communicate with a particular database driver. SQLAlchemy has several dialects for different databases such as Oracle, MS SQL Server, PostgreSQL, MySQL, and some others. Each of the dialects of SQLAlchemy requires the respective Python library installed.
- *Connection pooling* component is responsible for establishing connections to databases using a dialect, managing connection pools, and providing connection API to the *Engine*.
- *Engine* represents the database to other components performing SQL commands. It is the starting point for an application that is using SQLAlchemy.
- *SQL Expression Language* is an abstraction layer that translates high-level API calls to SQL that *Engine* could execute. It is another component accessible directly to the application using *SQLAlchemy*.
- *Schema* and *Types* are objects that define a logical data model. They are used by *ORM* or can be used directly with SQL Expression language to manipulate the data.

Object Relational Mapper or *ORM* stands on top and uses the *Core* components. It implements the representation of database records as instances of classes that define business entities. *ORM* also manages relationships between the classes that are implemented as foreign keys in the database, though this is not mandatory.

Connecting to a database and retrieving data with SQL Expression Language

The component *SQL Expression Language* can be used to manipulate data in the database.

To connect to a database, it is necessary to first create an `engine` object. This is done with the function `create_engine()` as follows:

```
from sqlalchemy import *

engine = create_engine(
    "postgresql+pg8000://car_portal_app@localhost/car_portal",
    echo=True)
```

Here, a connection string was used. It has a format: `dialect[+driver]://user:password@host/dbname`. The parameter `echo` is set to `True`. This commands `SQLAlchemy` to log every SQL statement that was executed for debugging purposes. In the preceding example, the driver `pg8000` is used to connect to the database. Note that the application does not connect to the database at this point. It has created a connection pool and, once `SQLAlchemy` would need to execute a command, a connection from the pool will be requested. When there is no existing connection, it will be established.

Next, the `MetaData` object needs to be created. It is an object that keeps the information about data structures the application is dealing with:

```
metadata = MetaData()
```

Now we need to define the table that we want to work with:

```
car_model = Table('car_model', metadata,
                  Column('car_model_id', Integer, primary_key=True),
                  Column('make', String),
                  Column('model', String),
                  schema='car_portal_app')
```

The metadata now knows about the data structure. However, no interaction with the database has happened so far.

It is possible to implement the logical structure defined in metadata in the database by invoking metadata.create_all(engine). It is also possible to load a physical data structure into a MetaData object, which is called **reflection**. Here, the definition of the table car is loaded into the metadata object:

```
car = Table('car', metadata, schema='car_portal_app', autoload=True,
            autoload_with=engine)
```

Now let's get data from the database. To do this, it is necessary to obtain a connection object by executing the method engine.connect(), which effectively will take a connection from the connection pool. The application has already connected to the database when it was retrieving the information about the table car. The same connection will be reused now.

```
conn = engine.connect()
```

The variable conn refers to the connection object.

An object of type Select is used to define a query. It is created using the function select(). The method connection.execute() is used to run the query as follows:

```
query = select([car_model])
result = conn.execute(query)
```

The result is an object of a class ResultProxy, which represents a cursor. It can be used as an iterator to get the records:

```
for record in result:
    print(record)
```

To insert new data, the following code can be used:

```
ins = car_model.insert()
conn.execute(ins, [
    {'make': 'Jaguar', 'model': 'XF'},
    {'make': 'Jaguar', 'model': 'XJ'}])
```

The logic is similar. At first, the object of type Insert is created. Then it is executed in the connection. The conn.execute() method takes the list of parameters for the query to be executed. SQLAlchemy is smart enough to understand that two records are inserted here and the values for the fields make and model are provided in the list of dictionaries.

No SQL was written so far. However, SQLAlchemy is executing SQL commands in the background because this is the only language that the database can understand. SQLAlchemy provides an easy way to check which SQL statement stands behind each high-level object. Simply print it! print(ins) will make this print to the console:

```
INSERT INTO car_portal_app.car_model (car_model_id, make, model) VALUES
(:car_model_id, :make, :model)
```

It is possible to filter results when querying the data using the *SQL Expression Language*. The object that represent a query provides a method where(), which is used for the filtering. There are a lot of operators and functions defined in SQLAlchemy that represent SQL operators and expressions. Here, we use the operator == to filter rows:

```
query = select([car_model]).where(car_model.c.make == "Jaguar")
```

This query will return only the Jaguar models.

These objects also have the methods order_by() and group_by() that implement the corresponding SQL clauses.

The library can do a lot more already on this level. For example, it can join tables, use subqueries, perform set operations (UNION), and even execute window functions. You can learn more about *SQL Expression Language* from the tutorial at http://docs.sqlalchemy. org/en/latest/core/tutorial.html.

A sample script performing the operations described in this section is located in the attached media in the file sqlalchemy_sql_expression_language.py.

ORM

Even though *SQL Expression Language* already provides a good level of abstraction, it still operates with a physical data model, not with business entities.

ORM makes it possible to map business objects to data structures in the database. To show this, let's create a class Car and define the mapping.

When using *ORM*, we describe the database structure and, at the same time, define the classes that represent business entities. This is done using a system named `declarative`. In `SQLAlchemy`, this system is initiated by creating a class that is then used as a base class for other classes:

```
from sqlalchemy.ext.declarative import declarative_base
Base = declarative_base()
```

The high-level class can now be defined as follows:

```
class Car(Base):
    __tablename__ = "car"
    __table_args__ = {'schema': 'car_portal_app'}
    car_id = Column(Integer, primary_key=True)
    registration_number = Column(String, nullable=False)
    def __repr__(self):
        return "Car {}: '{}'".format(self.car_id, self.registration_number)
```

Only two fields are defined here to save space. However, to emphasize that this is a business entity and not just a definition of a data structure, a custom representation method is defined in the class. It will be called when a text representation of an instance of the class is requested, for example, to print it. You can find the complete code of the class in the enclosed code bundle in the file `sqlalchemy_orm.py`.

To query the data from the database and get some instances of the defined class in the application, it is necessary to create an object of the class `Session`. This class implements a session--a dialogue with a database that is related to the current business operation the application is performing. If the application accesses several objects in the same operation, the same session is used. For example, in the car portal application, it could query cars and corresponding car models in the same session if a user is searching for a car. At the same time, another user could create a user account. This will be done in a different session. In many cases, one session is bound to one transaction in the database.

The session is created as follows--first create a class `Session` that is bound to the object `engine` that was create before, and then instantiate an object of that class:

```
from sqlalchemy.orm import sessionmaker
Session = sessionmaker(bind=engine)
session = Session()
```

The object `session` is used to query the data. It is done in a way similar to when using the *SQL Expression Language* and in fact, the same operators and methods are used when building a query. Let us create a query to retrieve the first five cars with the smallest ID:

```
query = session.query(Car).order_by(Car.car_id).limit(5)
```

When this query is used to retrieve data, it actually returns instances of the class `Car`:

```
for car in query.all():
    print(car)
```

Note that when the objects are printed, the custom text representation is used, which was defined in the class. This is the output on console:

```
Car 1: 'MUWH4675'
Car 2: 'VSVW4565'
Car 3: 'BKUN9615'
...
```

Let's update one of the cars. To get the first object of the class `Car` that the `query` returns, use the method, `query.first()`:

```
car = query.first()
```

To change its number plate, simply change the value of the field:

```
car.registration_number = 'BOND007'
```

The attribute of that instance is now changed. *ORM* knows that this instance is mapped to the database row with `car_id = 1` and it will perform an UPDATE in the database.

Finally, to commit the transaction and close the `session`, the following methods need to be invoked:

```
session.commit()
session.close()
```

Relational databases are all about relations and relationships. *ORM* takes care about relationships too. The table `car` has a field `car_model_id`, which points to a record in the table `car_model`. Logically, it means that the class `Car` has the attribute `car_model`. The physical implementation (namely another table) does not matter for the business logic.

Please note, that in the following examples the class `Car` will be redefined. SQLAlchemy does not provide an easy way to redefine classes that were mapped to database tables. That means, if you used to type the code in Python console, you should close it and start again, import the module `sqlalchemy`, initialize the `engine` and create the classes `Base` and `Session` as follows:

```
from sqlalchemy import *
from sqlalchemy.ext.declarative import declarative_base
from sqlalchemy.orm import sessionmaker
```

```
engine = create_engine(
    "postgresql+pg8000://car_portal_app@localhost/car_portal",
    echo=True)
Base = declarative_base()
Session = sessionmaker(bind=engine)
```

To implement this relationship, let us create another class that will represent car models, `Car_model`. It should be defined <u>before</u> the class `Car` as follows:

```
class Car_model(Base):
    __tablename__ = "car_model"
    __table_args__ = {'schema': 'car_portal_app'}
    car_model_id = Column(Integer, primary_key=True)
    make = Column(String)
    model = Column(String)
```

Change the class `Car`: add the two attributes and redefine the method, `__repr__` as follows:

```
from sqlalchemy.orm import relationship

class Car(Base):
    __tablename__ = "car"
    __table_args__ = {'schema': 'car_portal_app'}
    car_id = Column(Integer, primary_key=True)
    registration_number = Column(String, nullable=False)
    car_model_id = Column(Integer, ForeignKey(Car_model.car_model_id))
    car_model = relationship(Car_model)
    def __repr__(self):
        return "Car {}: {} {}, '{}'".format(
            self.car_id, self.car_model.make, self.car_model.model,
            self.registration_number)
```

Now perform the same query as before as follows:

```
session = Session()
query = session.query(Car).order_by(Car.car_id).limit(5)
for car in query.all():
    print(car)
```

The following will be printed to the console:

```
Car 1: Peugeot 308, 'BOND007'
Car 2: Opel Corsa, 'VSVW4565'
Car 3: Citroen C3, 'BKUN9615'
...
```

ORM can also be used to create new objects and save them in the database and delete them. To create a new car model, the following code is used:

```
new_car_model = Car_model(make="Jaguar", model="XE")
session = Session()
session.add(new_car_model)
session.commit()
session.close()
```

This is to delete it:

```
session = Session()
old_car_model = session.query(Car_model).filter(
    and_(Car_model.make == "Jaguar", Car_model.model == "XE")).one()
session.delete(old_car_model)
session.commit()
session.close()
```

SQLAlchemy provides you with a very powerful and flexible API to work with entities that are mapped to database tables. Relationships can be set up in a way that would, for example, when a car model is deleted, delete also all the cars of that model, namely cascade delete. The class Car_model could have an attribute cars that would represent a list of instances of Car of that model. It is possible to make SQLAlchemy join the table car_model with the table car when the entity Car is queried to make it work faster.

The sample script that shows how to manipulate data using SQLAlchemy ORM API is available in the enclosed media in the file sqlalchemy_orm.py.

Summary

Databases are often used as a storage component of a complex software solution. Even if they could implement complex logic in triggers and functions, there is still a need for external applications to implement user interface. It is quite common to separate storage logic from business logic. In this case, the business logic is also performed in external applications.

In this chapter, you learned how to connect to a PostgreSQL database from applications written in Python. There are several libraries for Python that provide different programming interfaces for developers. Some of them implement the standard Python DB API and some do not. There are implementations of ORM (Object Relational Mapping) for Python that work well with PostgreSQL.

The following low level libraries were described in this
chapter: psycopg2, pg8000 and asyncpg. They make it possible to connect to a database
from a Python application and execute SQL commands to retrieve or modify data.

Another library, SQLAlchemy, was described in the last section of the chapter. SQLAlchemy
provides object relational mapping functionality that eases the implementation of business
logic by mapping business entities to database tables. This makes it possible for a developer
to concentrate on the application logic instead of low-level database interaction. Although
developers must know what is happening in the systems they work with and be aware of
how databases work, using ORM frameworks removes the necessity of writing SQL code.

From the last chapter of the book you will know how to use multiple PostgreSQL servers
together to achieve greater performance or high availability, or both. This will make the
software solution scalable and able to grow with the growth of the business using it.

16
Scalability

This final chapter of the book will be dedicated to the problem of **scalability**. This term means the ability of a software system to grow with the growth of the business using it. PostgreSQL does provide some features that help building a scalable solution but, strictly speaking, PostgreSQL itself is not scalable. It can effectively utilize the resources of a single machine:

- It uses multiple CPU cores to perform a single query faster with parallel query
- When configured properly, it can use all available memory for caching
- The size of the database is not limited by PostgreSQL; supporting multiple tablespaces, it can use several hard disks and with partitioning, it can do this quickly and transparently to the users

However, when it comes to spreading a database solution to multiple machines, it can be quite problematic because a standard PostgreSQL server can only run on a single machine. That's why in this chapter, we will talk not only about PostgreSQL itself, but rather about where to go next.

Particularly, the following topics will be covered:

- The problem of scalability and the CAP theorem
- Data replication in PostgreSQL, including physical replication and logical replication
- Different scaling scenarios and their implementation in PostgreSQL

This topic is very large and itself deserves a dedicated book. That's why we will not describe too much about the practical recipes, but rather discuss the concepts so that you can get an understanding of possible options and then learn particular topics yourself.

We can recommend other books offered by Packt Publishing on this topic:

- PostgreSQL Replication - Second Edition by Hans-Jürgen Schönig, explaining very well how PostgreSQL replication features work internally and providing a lot of practical examples of how to use them.
- PostgreSQL High Availability Cookbook - Second Edition by Shaun M. Thomas, providing comprehensive hand-on recipes of how to build highly available database solutions based on PostgreSQL using its replication capabilities.

The examples for the chapter require setting up multiple database instances. That's why for this chapter, we are using Docker compositions to set up and implement sample scenarios. If you are not familiar with Docker, refer to the documentation at `https://docs.docker. com/get-started/`. To run the examples, you will need to install `docker engine` and `docker-compose`.

The examples are also based on the `car_portal` database that we have used in the whole book.

The problem of scalability and the CAP theorem

The requirement for a system to be scalable means that a system that supports a business now should also be able to support the same business with the same quality of service when it grows. A database can store 1 GB of data and effectively process 100 queries per second. What if the business grows 100 times? Will it be able to support 10,000 queries per second processing 100 GB of data? Maybe not now and in not the same installation. However, a scalable solution should be ready to be expanded to be able to handle the load as soon as it is needed.

Usually, scalability comes together with the distributed architecture of a system. If the database was able to utilize the power of multiple computers, then in order to scale it, one would need to add more computers to the cluster. There are solutions that do this. In fact, many NoSQL databases (even if they implement SQL) are distributed systems. One of the most spectacular examples of a scalable solution is **Cassandra**--a distributed NoSQL database. There are clusters of tens of thousands of nodes, operating petabytes of data and performing hundreds of millions of operations per day. This could never be possible for a single server.

On the other hand, these systems are less flexible in functionality. Simply speaking, Cassandra provides a key-value storage and does not provide consistency in the sense of ACID principles. PostgreSQL, in contrast, is a relational database management system that supports big concurrent isolated transactions and integrity constraints.

There is a theorem in computer science that was formulated by Eric Brewer in 2000, called the **CAP theorem**, stating that a distributed data storage system can support only two of the three features:

- **Consistency** (defined differently from the ACID principles): Any read operation always returns the most current state of the data, that is, after the last write operation, regardless of which node was queried
- **Availability**: Any request to the system is always successful (but the result may not be consistent)
- **Partition tolerance**: A system can survive even if some parts of it are not available or if a cluster is separated

The theorem is named for the first letters of these features: CAP. It says that all three features are not possible at the same time. Having in mind a distributed system, one may expect that it should tolerate the unavailability of some nodes. To achieve consistency, the system has to be able to coordinate all reads and writes, even if they happen on different nodes. To guarantee availability, the system needs to have copies of the same data on different nodes and to keep them in sync. In this definition, these two features cannot be achieved at the same time when some nodes are not available.

Cassandra provides availability and partition tolerance, so it is **cAP**:

- **Not consistent**: It is possible that a read operation performed on one node does not see the data written on another node, until the data is replicated to all the nodes that are supposed to have it. This will not block the read operation.
- **Available**: Read and write operations are always successful.
- **Partition tolerant**: If a node breaks, it does not break the whole database. When the broken node is returned to the cluster, it receives the missing changes in the data automatically.

One can increase the consistency level when working with Cassandra to make it absolutely consistent, but in this case, it will not be partition tolerant.

The relational databases that comply to the ACID principles are consistent and available. PostgreSQL is **CAp**:

- **Consistent**: Once a sessions commits a transaction, all other sessions immediately can see the results. Intermediate states of the data are not visible.
- **Available**: When the database is running, all the queries will succeed if they are correct.
- **Not partition tolerant**: If one makes part of the data not available, the database will stop working.

For example, for banking operations, consistency is required. If money is transferred from one account to another, we expect that either both accounts' balances are updated or none. If, for some reason, the application that performs the transfer crashes after it has updated one of the accounts, the whole transaction will be canceled and the data will return to the previous consistent state. Availability of the data is also important. Even if the transaction is committed, what if the hard disk fails and the whole database is lost? Therefore, all the operations have to be replicated into a backup storage and the transaction can only be considered successful when it is consistent and it is also durable. The money transfer in a bank can take some time because consistency is extremely important and the performance has lower priority.

If the online banking system is not available for a while because they need to restore a database from a backup, the customers can tolerate the inconvenience because they do not want to lose their money.

On the other hand, if someone likes a picture on Instagram, the system tracks this action in the context of the picture and also in the context of the user who likes. If any of the two operations fails, the data will be not consistent, but that is not critical. This does not mean that the data Instagram operates is less valuable. The requirements are different. There are millions of users and billions of pictures and nobody wants to wait when using the service. If likes are not displayed correctly, it does not matter too much, but if the whole system is not available for some time to be recovered to a consistent state after a failure, the users may decide to leave.

This means different solutions for different business requirements, but unfortunately there is a natural limitation making it not possible to achieve everything at once.

Data replication in PostgreSQL

In scenarios when it is required to achieve better performance, it is quite common to set up more servers that would handle additional load and copy the same data there from a master server. In scenarios when high availability is required, this is also a typical solution to continuously copy the data to a standby server so that it could take over in case the master server crashes.

Transaction log

Before explaining how to set up data replication, let's quickly look at how PostgreSQL handles changes in data at the lower level.

When PostgreSQL processes a command that changes the data in the database, it writes the new data on disk to make it persistent. There are two locations on disk where the data is written:

- The data files located on Linux by default
  at `/var/lib/postgresql/10/main/base`. Here, the data is stored: tables, indexes, temporary tables, and other objects. The size of this directory is only limited by the size of the disk.
- The transaction log located by default at
  `/var/lib/postgresql/10/main/pg_wal`. Here, the log of most recent changes into the data files is stored. Its size is limited in the configuration and by default is around 1 GB.

The same data is always written into both locations. This may seem redundant, but there is a reason for this:

Imagine there is a transaction inserting a record with a text value test into a big table, and it so happens that the server crashes in the middle of the transaction. The letters *te* are written and the rest was not written to disk. When the database is started again, it would not be able to tell if the record is corrupted, because it would not know if it is the word test or only the letters *te* were supposed to be in the field. OK, this can be solved using check sums. How would the database find the corrupted record? It would be very expensive to validate the check sums for the whole database after every unexpected restart.

The solution for this is that before writing data into the data files, PostgreSQL always writes it into the transaction log. The **transaction log** (also called the **write-ahead log**) is a list of changes made by PostgreSQL to a data file. The transaction log appears as a set of 16 MB files (called **WAL-files**) located in the subdirectory `pg_wal` under the PostgreSQL database path. Each file contains a lot of records that basically tell which data file should be changed in which way. Only when the transaction log is saved on disk the database write the data to the data files. When the transaction log is full, PostgreSQL deletes the oldest segment of it to reuse disk space. The transaction log is relatively small, and the server is able to go through it after an unexpected shutdown.

Now, after a system failure, the following will happen after restart:

- If the system crashed during the writing of the transaction log, PostgreSQL will identify that the log record is incomplete because the check sum will not match. It would discard this log record and perform a rollback of transactions that were writing the data into that record.
- If the system crashed during writing to the data files but the transaction log is not corrupted, PostgreSQL will go through the transaction log, validate that the content is written into the data files, and correct the data files when necessary. There is no need to scan all the data files because it knows from the transaction log which part of which data file was supposed to be changed and how.

The process of replaying the transaction log is called recovery, and this is what the database is always doing after unexpected restarts. If one had the full transaction log from the time the database server was initialized until the current time, then it would be possible to recover the state of the database to any point in time in the past. To provide this functionality, PostgreSQL can be configured to archive the transaction log somewhere instead of deleting old WAL files. This archive can be then used to perform so called **point-in-time recovery** of the database on another machine.

Physical replication

The transaction log entries can be taken from one database server--the master server--and applied to the data files on another server--the standby server. In this case the standby server will then have the exact replica of the database of the master server. The process of transferring transaction log entries and applying them on another server is called **physical replication**. It is called physical because the transaction log works on low level and the database replica on the standby server will be exact byte copy of the master database.

Physical replication works for the entire database cluster for all the databases. When a new database is created, this is reflected in the transaction log, and therefore replicated to the standby server.

Log shipping replication

One of the ways to set up physical replication is to constantly ship new WAL files from the master server to the standby and apply them there to have the synchronized copy of the database. This scenario is called **log shipping**.

To set up log shipping, the following actions should be taken:

- On the master server:
    - Make sure that the WAL files have enough information for replication: In the `postgresql.conf` file, set the configuration parameter `wal_level` to `replica` or `logical`.
    - Enable archiving of the WAL files by setting the configuration parameter `archive_mode` to `on`.
    - Make PostgreSQL archive the WAL files to a safe location specified using the configuration parameter, `archive_command`. PostgreSQL will apply this OS command to every WAL file that needs to be archived. This command can, for example, compress the file and copy it to a network drive. If the command is empty but archiving of WAL files is enabled, then those files will be accumulated in the folder, `pg_wal`.
- On the standby server:
    - Restore the base backup taken from the master server. The easiest way to do it is to use the tool, `pg_basebackup`. The command, executed on the standby machine, may look like this:

```
postgres@standby:~$ pg_pasebackup -D /var/lib/postgresql/10/main -h
master -U postgres
```

Here is a detailed description of the command: https://www.postgresql.org/docs/10/static/app-pgbasebackup.html.

- Create a `recovery.conf` file in the data directory. This file is used to configure how the server should perform the recovery and if it should work as a standby server. To set up the server as a standby server, at least the following two lines should be included in the file:

```
standby_mode = on
restore_command = 'cp /wal_archive_location/%f %p'
```

The value of the `restore_command` parameter will depend on the location of the WAL archive. It is an OS command that would copy a WAL file from the WAL archive location to the location of the transaction log in the data directory. More about `recovery.conf` can be found at https://www.postgresql.org/docs/10/static/recovery-config.html.

When all this is set up and both servers are running, the master server will copy all the WAL files to the archive location and the standby server will take them from there and replay over its base backup. This process will continue until there is the line `standby_mode = on` in the file `recovery.conf`.

If the master server crashes and it is necessary to switch to the standby server, it should be promoted. This means that it should stop the recovery and allow read-write transactions. To do this, simply remove the `recovery.conf` file and restart the server. After this, the standby server becomes the new master. It would make total sense to make the old master a standby after it is back in service to keep the cluster redundant. In that case, the preceding steps should be repeated, with the servers switching roles. Never start the master server as a master if the standby was promoted. It could cause differences in the replicas and eventual data loss!

The benefits of replication implemented via log shipping are as follows:

- It is relatively easy to set up.
- There is no need to connect the standby server and the master server.
- The master does not know that there is a standby and it does not depend on it.
- The number of standby servers can be more than one. In fact, a standby can be used as a master for other standby servers. This would be called cascading replication.

On the other hand, there are also some problems:

- It is necessary to provide a network location for the WAL archive, which both master and standby can access. This implies involvement of a 3rd entity. It is possible though to archive the WAL files directly to the standby server. Then the setup would not be symmetrical and in case of failure of the master and promotion of the standby, setup of the new standby will be a bit more complex.
- The standby can replay a WAL file only after it is archived. This happens only when the file is complete, meaning it reached the size of 16 MB. That means the latest transactions performed on the master may not be reflected on the standby and if the transactions on the master are small and do not happen very often, it may be that the backup database is far behind after the master database. In the case of master failure, some data will be lost.

Streaming replication

There is another physical replication scenario that can work on top of log shipping or without log shipping at all. It is **streaming replication**. Streaming replications implies a connection between the standby and the master servers and the master would send all the transaction log entries directly to the standby. By doing this the standby will have all the recent changes without waiting for the WAL files to be archived.

To set up streaming replication, in addition to the steps mentioned previously the following should be done on the master:

- A database role for replication should be created in the database, for example, like this:

```
postgres=# CREATE USER streamer REPLICATION;
CREATE USER
```

- Connections for this user should be allowed in the file pg_hba.conf to the virtual database called replication, for example, like this:

```
host    replication    streamer    172.16.0.2/32    md5
```

And the following actions should be taken on the standby server:

- Add the parameter primary_conninfo to the file recovery.conf that would set up the connection from the standby to the master, for example, as follows:

```
primary_conninfo = 'host=172.16.0.1 port=5432 user=streamer
password=secret'
```

This is already enough. If the WAL archive was enabled and configured, then the log shipping scenario will be performed first until all the WAL files from the archive are applied to the backup database. When there are no more files, the standby server will connect to the master server and start receiving new WAL entries directly from the master. If that connection breaks or if the standby is restarted, the process will start again.

It is possible to set up streaming replication without the WAL archive at all. The master server by default stores last 64 WAL files in the folder `pg_wal`. It can send them to the standby when necessary. The size of each file is 16 MB. That means, as long as the amount of changes in the data files is less then 1 GB, the streaming replication is able to replay these changes in the backup database without using the WAL archive.

Additionally, PostgreSQL provides a way to make the master server aware of which WAL files were processed by the standby and which were not. In case the standby is slow (or simply disconnected), the master would not delete the files that are not yet processed even if the number of them is more than 64. This is done by creating a replication slot on the master. Then the standby will use the replication slot and the master will keep track of which of the WAL files were processed for this replication slot.

To use this feature, make the following on the master:

- Create the replication slot on the master by executing the function `pg_create_physical_replication_slot()` in the database:

```
postgres=# SELECT * FROM
pg_create_physical_replication_slot('slot1');
 slot_name | lsn
-----------+-----
 slot1     |
(1 row)
```

- Make sure the configuration parameter `max_replication_slots` in the file `postgresql.conf` is big enough

And make the following on the standby server:

- Add the parameter `primary_slot_name` to the file `recovery.conf`:

```
primary_slot_name = 'slot1'
```

After this, the master will not delete the WAL files that are not received by the standby even if the standby is not connected. When the standby connects again, it will receive all the missing WAL entries and the master will delete the old files then.

The benefits of streaming replication over log shipping are as follows:

- The lag between the backup and the master is smaller because the WAL entries are sent immediately after the transactions are finished on the master, without waiting for the WAL files to be archived
- It is possible to set up the replication without WAL archiving at all, therefore no need to set up a network storage or another common location for the master and the standby

Synchronous replication

Streaming replication is asynchronous by default. This means that if a user commits a transaction on the master, it gets the confirmation of the commit immediately, and the replication will happen only afterward. This means that it is still possible that a transaction that was finished on the master is not replicated to the standby in case the master crashes right after commit and the WAL records were not sent yet.

When high availability is a requirement in a sense that no data loss is acceptable, streaming replication can be set to synchronous mode.

To enable it on the master, in the file `postgresql.conf`, the configuration parameter `synchronous_standby_names` should be set to the name identifying the standby server, for example, `synchronous_standby_names = 'standby1'`.

Then on the slave, the same name should be used in the connection string in the `recovery.conf` file, as follows:

```
primary_conninfo = 'host=172.16.0.1 port=5432 user=streamer password=secret
application_name=standby1'
```

After this is done, the master server will wait for the standby confirming that it has received and processed every WAL record before confirming the commit request. This will make commits slightly slower of course. In case the standby server is disconnected, all the transactions on the master will be blocked. It will not fail though, it will only wait until the is standby connected again. The read only queries will work normally.

The benefit of the synchronous replication is that it is guaranteed that if a transaction is finished and the commit command returned, the data is replicated to the standby server. The drawback is the performance overhead and the dependency of the master on the standby.

There is a Docker composition in the attached media that implements a streaming replication set up. To try it on Linux, change directory to `streaming_replication` and bring up the composition executing the command `docker-compose up` as follows:

```
user@host:~/learning_postgresql/scalability/streaming_replication$ docker-
compose up
Creating network "streamingreplication_default" with the default driver
Creating streamingreplication_master_1
Creating streamingreplication_standby_1
Attaching to streamingreplication_master_1, streamingreplication_standby_1
...
```

Now there are two database instances running in two Docker containers named `master` and `standby`. Synchronous replication is already enabled. The database on master is empty. The log output from both servers will be printed in that terminal window. Open another terminal window, change directory to `streaming_replication`, connect to the container `master`, start psql console, and create the database `car_portal`:

```
user@host:~/learning_postgresql/scalability/streaming_replication$ docker-
compose exec master bash
root@master:/# psql -h localhost -U postgres
psql (10.0)
SSL connection (protocol: TLSv1.2, cipher: ECDHE-RSA-AES256-GCM-SHA384,
bits: 256, compression: off)
Type "help" for help.
postgres=# \i schema.sql
...
car_portal=> \i data.sql
...
```

Now the database is created on the master and it is already replicated to the standby. Let's check. Exit the shell session in the container `master`, connect to the container `standby`, start psql, and run some queries:

```
user@host:~/learning_postgresql/scalability/streaming_replication$ docker-
compose exec standby bash
root@standby:/# psql -h localhost -U car_portal_app car_portal
psql (10.0)
SSL connection (protocol: TLSv1.2, cipher: ECDHE-RSA-AES256-GCM-SHA384,
bits: 256, compression: off)
Type "help" for help.
car_portal=> SELECT count(*) FROM car;
 count
-------
```

```
 229
(1 row)
car_portal=> UPDATE car set car_id = 0;
ERROR: cannot execute UPDATE in a read-only transaction
```

The data is replicated but it is read only; the server that is running in recovery mode does not allow any changes.

More on this topic can be found in the PostgreSQL documentation at `https://www.postgresql.org/docs/current/static/high-availability.html`.

Logical replication

Physical data replication has a small disadvantage: it requires identical configuration of the servers that are in sync. Simply speaking, the data has to be placed at the same locations on the filesystem. Another thing is that every change in the data files will be replicated, even if that does not change the data itself. For example, this happens when the `VACUUM` command is executed on the master that removes dead tuples from tables, or the `CLUSTER` command that is rearranging rows. Even if an index is created on a table, it is not the `CREATE INDEX` command that is sent to the standby, but the contents of the data file with the index data. This can create excessive load on the network and it can become a bottleneck for a system under heavy load.

Logical replication, which does not send the results of SQL commands but the commands themselves, is an alternative to physical replication. In this case, the amount of data sent over a network can be much smaller and the servers do not need to be identical. Even more, the data structure on the servers does not need to be the same.

For example, if one would execute an `INSERT INTO table_a (a, b) VALUES (1, 2)` command on the master and this command is replicated to the standby server, then it is not a problem when the table has more columns on the standby than `a` and `b`. The SQL is correct, therefore it can be executed; the extra columns will get their default values.

PostgreSQL supports logical replication. The way it works makes it possible for the same server to receive some data from one server and send data to another server. That's why when talking about logical replication, there is no master and standby, there is the **publisher**--the server that sends the data, and the **subscriber**--the one that receives it. The same server can be both publisher and subscriber for different tables or sets of tables, and a subscriber can receive data from multiple publishers.

Logical replication works on the level of individual tables or sets of tables. It is also possible to set it up for all the tables in a database, and this will be automatically enabled for any new tables. However, logical replication does not affect other schema objects like sequences, indexes, or views.

To set up logical replication, the following actions should be performed on the publisher side:

- Create a database role for replication or enable REPLICATION for the existing user:

  ```
  postgres=# ALTER USER car_portal_app REPLICATION;
  ALTER USER
  ```

- Allow this user to connect to the virtual database replication in the file pg_hba.conf:

  ```
  host      replication      car_portal_app      172.16.0.2/32      md5
  ```

- Set the configuration parameter wal_level to logical in postgresql.conf. This is necessary to make PostgreSQL write enough information for logical replication into WAL files.
- Make sure that the value of the configuration parameter max_replication_slots is equal or more than the number of subscribers that are supposed to connect to this publisher server.
- Set the configuration parameter max_wal_senders to be not less than max_replication_slots.
- Create a publication object. A publication is a named set of tables. When it is created, the server will track changes to the data in these tables to send them to any subscriber that would use the publication. The SQL command CREATE PUBLICATION is used for it; here is an example that would create a publication for all the tables in the database car_portal:

  ```
  car_portal=> CREATE PUBLICATION car_portal FOR ALL TABLES;
  CREATE PUBLICATION
  ```

On the subscriber side, a subscription has to be created. Subscription is a special object that stands for a connection to an existing publication on the publisher server. The CREATE SUBSCRIPTION command is used for this, as shown in the following example:

```
car_portal=# CREATE SUBSCRIPTION car_portal CONNECTION 'dbname=car_portal
host=publisher user=car_portal_app' PUBLICATION car_portal;
CREATE SUBSCRIPTION
```

The tables to replicate are defined in the publication. The tables should be created in advance on the subscriber side. In the preceding example, the subscription `car_portal` connects to a publication `car_portal`, which publishes all the tables in the database. Therefore, the same tables should also exist on the subscriber side.

Once the subscription is created, the replication will start automatically. At first, by default, PostgreSQL will replicate the whole table and after that, it will replicate the changes asynchronously, after they happen on the publisher side. If any of the servers are restarted, the connection will be re-established automatically. If the subscriber is offline for some time, the publisher will remember all the pending changes and they will be sent to the subscriber once it is connected again. This functionality is implemented using replication slots, in the similar way as with streaming replication.

Logical replication can be treated as if the publisher would send all the data-changing SQL commands, which are performed on the published tables to the subscriber. The subscriber would then apply the commands in its database to the same tables. This happens at the level of SQL, not at the low level of the physical replication. As mentioned before, that allows the subscriber to have different data structure: as long as the SQL commands can be executed, it will work.

Logical replication does not affect sequences. It does not apply any DDL commands and it does not apply the command TRUNCATE. It respects primary keys, UNIQUE and CHECK constraints on the target tables, but it ignores FOREIGN KEY constraints.

Logical replication can be set up to be synchronous in the same way as streaming replication. To do it, on the publisher set the subscriber name in the configuration parameter `synchronous_standby_names` in `postgresql.conf`, and on the subscriber specify this name in the connection string when executing the command CREATE SUBSCRIPTION.

Logical replication has the following benefits over physical replication:

- It is simple to set up
- It can be very flexible:
    - It does not require identical database schema on the two servers and it does not require identical set up of the servers in general
    - The same server can work as subscriber and a publisher at the same time
    - The same table can be used in multiple subscriptions, so it would collect the data from several servers
    - A publication can be configured to replicate only certain type of operations (INSERT and DELETE, but not UPDATE, for example)

   • The target table on the subscriber is accessible to write
 • Logical replication can be used with different major versions of PostgreSQL (so far it is supported only by PostgreSQL 10 though)
 • It does not require any third-party software or hardware and works out of the box in PostgreSQL
 • The changes in data on the physical level (like VACUUM or CLUSTER) are not replicated

On the other hand, flexibility brings complexity. When implementing logical replication, the following should be kept in mind:

 • Logical replication does not respect foreign keys, so it can bring the target database into an inconsistent state.
 • When the schema changes on the publisher side, the replication can suddenly break if the schema on the subscriber is not compatible.
 • Logical replication only replicates changes from publisher to subscriber. If somebody changes the data directly on the subscriber, the replication will not bring the tables back in sync.
 • Only tables are replicated; other schema objects are not. This can be an issue when auto incremented fields based on sequences are used in the databases.

There is a sample Docker composition in the attached media that implements a logical replication scenario. To try it, change directory to logical_replication and run docker-compose up. This will bring up two instances of PostgreSQL: publisher and subscriber, create the database car_portal on the publisher, and create a publication. The subscriber also has the database but it is empty yet. Now in another terminal, start a bash shell on the subscriber, open psql, and run the following commands:

```
user@host:~/learning_postgresql/scalability/logical_replication$ docker-
compose exec subscriber bash
root@subscriber:/# psql -h localhost -U postgres car_portal
psql (10.0)
SSL connection (protocol: TLSv1.2, cipher: ECDHE-RSA-AES256-GCM-SHA384,
bits: 256, compression: off)
Type "help" for help.
car_portal=# CREATE SUBSCRIPTION car_portal CONNECTION 'dbname=car_portal
host=publisher user=car_portal_app' PUBLICATION car_portal;
psql:subscriber.sql:2: NOTICE: created replication slot "car_portal" on
publisher
CREATE SUBSCRIPTION
```

At this moment, there will be a lot of output in the first terminal window telling you that all the tables in the database `car_portal` were replicated to the subscriber. Now let's query the data on the subscriber:

```
car_portal=# select count(*) from car_portal_app.car;
 count
-------
 229
(1 row)
```

Replication works. Now you may open a session in the container `publisher`, start `psql`, and insert some data into the publisher's database. Then check how it is replicated to the subscriber.

There is another example in the directory `logical_replication_multi_master` that shows how the same table can get changes from two different publishers.

More about logical replication can be found in the PostgreSQL documentation at `https://www.postgresql.org/docs/current/static/logical-replication.html`.

Using replication to scale PostgreSQL

Replication can be used in many scaling scenarios. Its primary purpose of course is to create and maintain a backup database for the case of system failure. This is especially true for physical replication. However, replication can also be used to improve the performance of a solution based on PostgreSQL. Sometimes third-party tools can be used to implement complex scaling scenarios.

Scaling for heavy querying

Suppose there is a system that is supposed to handle a lot of read requests. For example, that could be an application that implements HTTP API endpoint supporting the auto-completion functionality on a web site. Each time a user enters a character in a web form, the system searches in the database for objects whose name starts with the string the user has entered. The number of queries can be very big because of the large number of the users and also because several requests are processed for every user session. To handle big numbers of requests, the database should be able to utilize multiple CPU cores. In case the number of requests is really big, the number of cores required can be bigger than a single machine could have.

The same applies to a system that is supposed to handle multiple heavy queries at the same time. There does not need to be a lot of queries, but when the queries themselves are big, using as many CPUs as possible would make a performance benefit. Especially when parallel query execution is used.

In such scenarios, when one database cannot handle the load, it is possible to set up multiple databases, set up replication from one master database to all of them, and make the application query different databases for different requests. The application itself can be smart and query a different database each time, but that would require special implementation of the data access component of the service. Such architecture could look as follows:

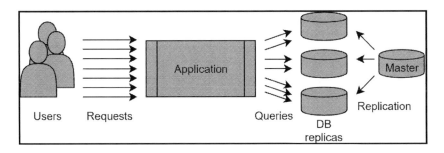

Application querying multiple database replicas

Another option is to use a tool called **Pgpool-II** that can work as a load balancer in front of several PostgreSQL databases. The tool exposes an SQL interface and applications can connect there as if it was a real PostgreSQL server. Then the tool would redirect the queries to databases that are running the least number of queries, in other words perform load balancing:

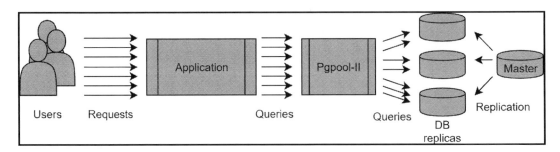

Using Pgpool-II to balance load between database servers

More information about Pgpool-II can be found at http://www.pgpool.net.

Yet another option is to scale the application together with the databases so that one instance of the application will connect to one instance of the database. In that case, the users of the application should connect to one of the many instances. This can be achieved with HTTP load balancing, as follows:

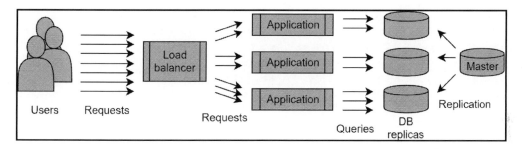

Data sharding

When the problem is not the number of concurrent queries, but the size of the database and the speed of a single query, a different approach can be implemented. The data can be separated into several servers, which will be queried in parallel, and then the result of the queries will be consolidated outside of those databases. This is called data **sharding**.

PostgreSQL provides a way to implement sharding based on table partitioning when partitions are located on different servers and the master server uses them as foreign tables. We mentioned already the topics of partitioning in Chapter 08, *OLAP and Data Warehousing*, and foreign tables in Chapter 14, *Testing*. When performing a query on a parent table defined on the master server, depending on the WHERE clause and the definitions of the partitions, PostgreSQL can recognize which partitions contain the data that is requested and would query only these partitions. Depending on the query, sometimes joins and aggregation could be performed on the remote servers. Unfortunately, PostgreSQL cannot query different partitions in parallel. The work on this is being done and maybe in upcoming future releases this feature will be introduced. Currently, having all this it is still possible to build a solution when applications would connect to a single database that would physically redirect their queries to different databases depending on the data that is being queried. If different user sessions query different data and partitioning was implemented taking that into the account, there will be performance benefit.

It is possible to build sharding algorithms into the applications that use PostgreSQL. In short, applications would be supposed to know which data is located in which database, write it only there and read it only from there. This would add a lot of complexity to the applications.

Another option is to use one of the PostgreSQL-based sharding solutions available on the market or open source solutions. They have their own pros and cons, but the common thing is that they are based on previous releases of PostgreSQL and do not use the most recent features (sometimes providing their own features instead).

One of the most popular sharding solutions is **Postgres-XL** (https://www.postgres-xl.org/), which implements a shared-nothing architecture using multiple servers running PostgreSQL. The system has several components:

- Multiple **data nodes**: Store the data
- Single **global transaction monitor** (GTM): Manages the cluster, providing global transaction consistency
- Multiple **coordinator nodes**: Support user connections, build query execution plans, and interact with the GTM and the data nodes

Postgres-XL implements the same API as PostgreSQL, therefore the applications do not need to treat the server anyhow in a special way. It is ACID-compliant, meaning that it supports transactions and integrity constraints. The COPY command is also supported.

The main benefits of using Postgres-XL are as follows:

- It can scale for the reading by adding more data nodes.
- It can scale for the writing by adding more coordinator nodes.
- The current release of Postgres-XL (at the moment of writing this) is based on PostgreSQL 9.5, which is relatively new. The alpha release of Postgres-XL based on PostgreSQL 10 is already available.

The main downside of Postgres-XL is that it does not provide any high-availability features out of the box. When more servers are added to a cluster, the probability of failure of any of them increases. That's why one should take care with backups or implement replication of the data nodes themselves.

Postgres-XL is open source, but commercial support is available.

Another solution that is worth mentioning is **Greenplum** (http://greenplum.org/). It is positioned as an implementation of a massive parallel processing database specifically designed for data warehouses. It has the following components:

- **Master node**: Manages user connections, builds query execution plans, manages transactions
- **Data nodes**: Store the data and perform queries

Greenplum also implements PostgreSQL API and applications can connect to a Greenplum database without any changes. It supports transactions, but support for integrity constraints is limited. The COPY command is supported.

The main benefits of Greenplum are as follows:

- It can scale for the reading by adding more data nodes.
- It supports column-oriented table organization that can be useful for data warehousing solutions.
- Data compression is supported.
- High availability features are supported out of the box. It is possible (and recommended) to add a secondary master that would take over in case of primary master crashes. It is also possible to add mirrors to the data nodes to prevent data loss.

The drawbacks are as follows:

- It does not scale for writing. Everything goes through the single master node and adding more data nodes does not make writing faster.
- It uses PostgreSQL 8.4 in its core. Greenplum has a lot of improvements and new features added to the base PostgreSQL code, but it is still based on a very old release.
- Greenplum does not support foreign keys and support for unique constraints is limited.

There are commercial and open source editions of Greenplum.

Scaling for big number of connections

Yet another use case related to scalability is when the number of database connections is huge. We have already mentioned connection pooling in the Chapter 15, *Using PosgreSQL in Python Applications*, and discussed the necessity and benefits of it. However, when a single database is used in an environment with a lot of micro services and each of them has its own connection pool, even if they do not perform too many queries it is possible that hundreds or even thousands connections are opened in the database. Each connection consumes server resources and only the requirement to handle huge number of connections can already be a problem without even performing any queries.

If the applications would not use connection pooling and would open connections only when they need to query the database and close them immediately, another problem could happen. Establishing a database connection takes time. Not too much, but when the number of operations is huge, the total overhead will be significant.

There is a tool named **PgBouncer** (https://PgBouncer.github.io/) that implements connection pool functionality. It can accept connections from many applications as if it was a PostgreSQL server and then open a limited number of connections towards the database. It would reuse the same database connections for multiple applications' connections. The process of establishing a connection from an application to PgBouncer is much faster then connecting to a real database because PgBouncer does not need to initialize a database backend process for the session.

The way PgBouncer works can be represented in a diagram, as follows:

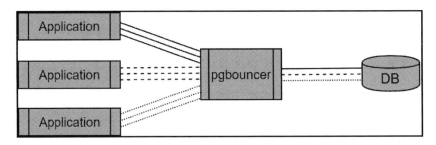

PgBouncer working as a connection pool

PgBouncer establishes several connections to the database. When an application connects to PgBouncer and starts a transaction, PgBouncer would assign an existing database connection to that application, forward all SQL commands to the database, and deliver the results back. When the transaction is finished, PgBouncer will dissociate the connections, but not close it. If another application starts a transaction, the same database connection could be used.

Pgbouncer can also assign a database connection to an application for every single SQL statement. That can be useful when applications perform only read queries and the number of them is big. Another option is to assign a database connection to the whole lifetime of the application's connection. This can be used to reduce the connection overhead, but not to reduce the number of connections.

Summary

In the chapter, we discussed the problem of building scalable solutions based on PostgreSQL utilizing resources of several servers. There is a natural limitation for such systems--basically, there is always a compromise between performance, reliability, and consistency. It is possible to improve one aspect but others will suffer.

PostgreSQL providers several ways to implement replication that would maintain a copy of the data from a database on another server or servers. This can be used as a backup or a standby solution that would take over in case the main server crashes. Replication can also be used to improve, performance of a software system by making it possible to distribute load on several database servers.

In some cases, the functionality of replication provided by PostgreSQL can be not enough. There are third-party solutions that work around a PostgreSQL providing extra features, such as PgBouncer working as a connection pool or Pgpool-II, which can work as a load balancer. There are also more complex solutions that are based on the code of PostgreSQL, which store different parts of data on different nodes and query them simultaneously. They implement a multi-server distributed database solution that can operate very big amounts of data and handle huge load. We mentioned Posgres-XL and Greenplum, but there are more that are commercial and open source.

Index

Printed in Great Britain
by Amazon